THE COALITION (
AND SOCIA
Restructuring the

Hugh Bochel and Martin Powell

First published in Great Britain in 2016 by

Policy Press
University of Bristol
1-9 Old Park Hill
Bristol
BS2 8BB
UK
t: +44 (0)117 954 5940
pp-info@bristol.ac.uk
www.policypress.co.uk

North America office:
Policy Press
c/o The University of Chicago Press
1427 East 60th Street
Chicago, IL 60637, USA
t: +1 773 702 7700
f: +1 773-702-9756
sales@press.uchicago.edu
www.press.uchicago.edu

British Library Cataloguing in Publication Data
A catalogue record for this book is available from the British Library

Library of Congress Cataloging-in-Publication Data
A catalog record for this book has been requested

ISBN 978 1 44732 456 0 hardcover
ISBN 978 1 44732 457 7 paperback
ISBN 978-1-4473-2460-7 ePub
ISBN 978-1-4473-2461-4 Mobi

The right of Hugh Bochel and Martin Powell to be identified as editors of this work has been asserted by them in accordance with the Copyright, Designs and Patents Act 1988.

The statements and opinions contained within this publication are solely those of the editors and contributors and not of the University of Bristol or Policy Press. The University of Bristol and Policy Press disclaim responsibility for any injury to persons or property resulting from any material published in this publication.

Policy Press works to counter discrimination on grounds of gender, race, disability, age and sexuality.

Cover design by Lyn Davies
Front cover image: Getty
Printed and bound in Great Britain by CMP, Poole
Policy Press uses environmentally responsible print partners

Contents

Notes on contributors

Rob Baggott is Professor of Public Policy and Director of the Health Policy Research unit at De Montfort University. He has published extensively on health policy and his publications include *Understanding health policy* (The Policy Press, 2007), *Health and health care in Britain* (Palgrave Macmillan, 2004), *Public health: policy and politics* (2nd edition) (Palgrave Macmillan, 2010) and *Partnerships for public health and wellbeing* (Palgrave Macmillan, 2013).

Patrick L.J. Bailey is a part-time tutor in the Department of Education, Practice and Society at the University College London Institute of Education. His research interests and publications fit broadly within the sociology of education and policy sociology, with a current focus on: the governing of education and education policy; contemporary and historical discourses of the 'good teacher'; the neoliberalisation of the education state; and developing innovative approaches to policy conceptualisation and analysis. He was awarded a PhD in Sociology in 2015.

Stephen J. Ball is Distinguished Service Professor of Sociology of Education at the University College London Institute of Education. He was elected Fellow of the British Academy in 2006, and is also Fellow of the Academy of Social Sciences. He is co-founder and Managing Editor of the *Journal of Education Policy*. His main areas of interest are in sociologically informed education policy analysis and the relationships between education, education policy and social class. Recent books include *How schools do policy* (with Meg Maguire and Annette Braun) (Routledge, 2012), *Global education inc.* (Routledge, 2012), *Networks, new governance and education* (with Carolina Junemann) (The Policy Press, 2012) and *Foucault, power and education* (Routledge, 2013).

Derek Birrell is Professor of Social Policy at Ulster University. He has published widely on devolution and social policy, including *The impact of devolution on social policy* (The Policy Press, 2009), *Comparing devolved governance* (Palgrave Macmillan, 2012) and *Multi-level governance and Northern Ireland* (with Cathy Gormley Heenan) (Palgrave Macmillan, 2015).

Catherine Bochel is a Reader in Policy Studies at the University of Lincoln. She has published widely on the policy process, participation and petitions systems.

Hugh Bochel is Professor of Public Policy at the University of Lincoln. He has published widely on public and social policy, including *Welfare policy under New Labour: views from Westminster* (with Andrew Defty) (The Policy Press, 2007), *Watching the watchers: Parliament and the intelligence services* (with Andrew Defty and Jane Kirkpatrick) (Palgrave Macmillan, 2014) and the edited collection *The Conservative Party and social policy* (The Policy Press, 2011).

Harriet Churchill is a Lecturer in Social Work in the Department of Sociological Studies, University of Sheffield. Her social policy and social services research interests are in family policy, family support, parenting education, children's services reform and youth policies. Recent publications and current research examine policy and practice in intensive, multi-agency family support services and family intervention programmes.

Anne Daguerre is an Associate Professor in the Business School at Middlesex University. She has particular interests in welfare reform and the labour market, and has published widely, including *Active labour market policies and welfare reform: Europe and the US in comparative perspective* (Palgrave, 2007).

Andrew Defty is a Reader in Politics at the University of Lincoln. He has published widely on Parliament, public opinion and the politics of welfare including, *Welfare policy under New Labour: views from inside Westminster* (with Hugh Bochel) (The Policy Press, 2007) and *Watching the watchers: Parliament and the intelligence services* (with Hugh Bochel and Jane Kirkpatrick) (Palgrave Macmillan, 2014).

Rosalind Edwards is Professor of Sociology and Social Sciences Director of Research at the University of Southampton. She is a co-director of the Economic and Social Research Council National Centre for Research Methods. She has published widely in the field of family lives and family policies, including a recent co-edited book on *Understanding families over time* (Palgrave, 2014), as well as on methodology, including *What is qualitative interviewing?* (with Janet Holland) (Bloomsbury, 2013).

Nick Ellison is Professor of Social Policy and Head of Department at the University of York. He has published on UK and comparative social policy, the impact of globalisation on welfare states, and contemporary theories of citizenship and social exclusion. Recent articles in *Information, Communication and Society* and *Local Government Studies* have examined the role of social media in local forms of citizenship and engagement.

David Etherington is Principal Researcher in the Business School, Middlesex University. He has research interests in comparative welfare and active labour market policy, employment and skills policy, and social inclusion. He has published widely in these areas, including *New welfare spaces: labour market policies in the UK and Denmark* (VDM Verlag Dr Müeller, 2008).

Val Gillies is a Research Professor in the Department of Sociology at Goldsmiths College, University of London. She has researched and published in the area of family, social class and marginalised children and young people. Her latest book is *Pushed to the edge: inclusion and behaviour management in schools* (The Policy Press, 2016).

Jon Glasby is Professor of Health and Social Care, and Head of the School of Social Policy, at the University of Birmingham. A qualified social worker by background, he is currently a Non-Executive Director of a National Health Service Foundation Trust and is involved in a national programme of research, teaching and policy advice around future social care and health services.

Ann Marie Gray is a Senior Lecturer in Social Policy at Ulster University. She has published on devolution and social policy, the governance of social policy, and adult social care policy, including *Transforming adult social care* (with Derek Birrell) (The Policy Press, 2013) and articles on social security and devolution, and health services and devolution.

Stephen McKay, Distinguished Professor of Social Research at the University of Lincoln, conducts research on socio-economic inequalities. Recent work includes *Wealth and the wealthy* (with Karen Rowlingson) (The Policy Press, 2011) and articles on patterns of family formation and disability. He is a contributor to past edited collections about the social security policies of New Labour and the Conservatives.

Martin Powell is Professor of Health and Social Policy at the Health Services Management Centre, University of Birmingham. He is the editor of a trilogy of texts exploring the social policy of the Labour governments of 1997–2010: *New Labour, new welfare state?* (The Policy Press, 1999), *Evaluating New Labour's welfare reforms* (The Policy Press, 2002) and *Modernising the welfare state: the Blair legacy* (The Policy Press, 2008).

Karen Rowlingson is Professor of Social Policy at the University of Birmingham, as well as Deputy Director of the Centre on Household Assets and Savings Management (CHASM). Karen's research interests lie in the field of social security, inequality and personal finance.

Kirstein Rummery is Professor of Social Policy at the University of Stirling, where she is the co-director of the Centre for Gender and Feminist Studies and a senior fellow of the Centre on Constitutional Change. She has published widely on gender, disability and social policy. Her latest book, *What works in improving gender equality* (with Craig McAngus), is due to be published by Policy Press in 2016.

Peter Somerville is Professor of Social Policy at the University of Lincoln. He has published widely on housing policy, homelessness, community development and democratic governance. His latest book, *Understanding community* (2nd edition), is due to be published by Policy Press in 2016.

Peter Squires is Professor of Criminology and Public Policy at the University of Brighton. Much of his recent work has focused upon firearms control, criminalisation and policing, and he is interested in politics, ideology and criminal justice. His most recent book is *Gun crime in global contexts* (Routledge, 2014). In 2015, he was elected President of the British Society for Criminology for three years.

ONE

The transformation of the welfare state? The Conservative–Liberal Democrat coalition government and social policy

Hugh Bochel and Martin Powell

Introduction

This chapter considers the coalition government, and the relationship between the two coalition parties and their policies. It identifies the key themes underpinning developments in social policy, and highlights some of the implications of those developments for the Conservative government elected in 2015.

It addresses the following issues:

- to what extent was the coalition government similar to and different from Conservative governments of 1979 to 1997;
- how significantly and in what ways did the policies and approaches of the coalition government differ from those of the Labour governments of 1997 to 2010;
- in what ways did the Liberal Democrats influence the coalition government's social policies;
- what underlying themes can be identified in the coalition government's social policies; and
- what were the implications of the 2010–15 coalition government for social policy.

It begins by providing a broad review of the coalition government's approach to social policy. It traces the development of the views and approaches that were reflected in policy and rhetoric in the years from 2010 to 2015, within both Conservative and Liberal Democrat parties and the government as a whole, and the extent to which each party was successful in pushing its own agenda and, where appropriate, mitigating that of the other. Finally, it draws upon a framework reflecting a number of political dimensions against which to analyse the coalition government's policies and rhetoric.

Towards coalition

During the period between 2005 and 2010, each of the major political parties experienced changes of leadership and, to some extent, policies. In addition, the 'external shock' of the financial crisis from 2008 produced further new challenges for the parties. This section therefore considers the developments within the Conservative and Liberal Democrat parties that helped lead to the creation of a coalition government in May 2010.

The Conservatives' path

Following the 1997 general election defeat, the Conservative Party struggled to find its way back to electoral credibility and to government. This was arguably for a number of reasons. First, there was the legacy of Thatcherism, in particular, both the image of the Conservative Party among much of the electorate as the 'nasty party' (as recognised by Theresa May in her speech to the party conference in 2002) and, in contrast, the continuing popularity of Thatcherite policies among party members. In addition, the Conservatives' reputation for economic competence had been badly damaged by Black Wednesday in 1992, when the government was forced to withdraw sterling from the Exchange Rate Mechanism. Indeed, while it has been argued that 'strong leadership' and 'governing competence' were characteristics often attributed to the Conservatives in the past (eg Bulpitt, 1985; Crewe, 1988), for the period from 1992 to 2005, it would have been hard to recognise them in the parliamentary party.

Second, there were the challenges that the emergence of New Labour had posed for the Conservatives. Taken together with the Conservatives' attachment to Thatcherism, the move of Labour to the political centre and its apparent control of the political agenda made it difficult for the Conservatives to develop alternative policies and a distinct identity that appealed to the electorate beyond the party's core voters.

Third, these tensions were reflected in a period of changing leadership and vacillating policy development, with William Hague, Iain Duncan Smith and Michael Howard successively appearing to embrace more socially inclusive ideas early in their leaderships but then shifting back to the Right. All three also failed to increase the Conservatives' popularity.

In December 2005, David Cameron defeated David Davis for the leadership of the Conservative Party in what some saw at the time as a victory for a 'moderniser' over a Thatcherite traditionalist, particularly given Cameron's emphasis on more socially liberal policies and creating a party that would be more socially representative in its membership and within Parliament. Between 2005 and 2010, Cameron appeared to seek to reposition the Conservatives, not just in relation to arguments over social justice and combating poverty, but in stating that economic stability would take precedence over tax cuts and in emphasising the importance of environmental issues. He was aided in his endeavours by right-of-centre think tanks – not only those that had been influential in the Thatcher period, such as the Institute of Economic Affairs, but also those that had been created more recently, such as Policy Exchange and the Centre for Social Justice – and a number of Conservative thinkers, such as Jesse Norman and David Willetts. These helped not only by providing critiques of Labour's approach, but also in bringing new ideas into and supporting Cameron's modernisation of the Conservative Party (Pautz, 2013).

Some therefore saw the emergence of a form of 'compassionate', 'modern' or 'progressive' Conservatism (eg Dorey, 2007; Bochel, 2011; Page, 2011), with something of a return to One Nation thinking, although with a greater emphasis on non-state action and the importance of neighbourhoods and communities in responding to social problems. However, at the same time, Cameron also continued to highlight long-standing Conservative issues, such as crime and support for traditional families. In addition, there was relatively little in terms of major policy commitments by the party's leadership during this period.

By the middle of Labour's third term in government, it had clearly lost its grip on the political agenda, and the media was increasingly focusing on the travails of the government. The financial crisis, the recession and the Labour government's decision to borrow substantially to stabilise the banks, maintain public expenditure and stimulate the economy meant that the Conservatives were able to dismiss their earlier promise to match Labour's public expenditure plans and instead fight the 2010 general election by emphasising the need to significantly reduce the UK's deficit over a five-year period.

Given the lack of firm policy and the very mixed rhetoric that was emerging from the Conservative Party – with claims about socially liberal ideas and the need to tackle social injustice and the lack of social mobility in the UK but, at the same time, arguments about British society being 'broken' and the need for public expenditure cuts – it is perhaps unsurprising that commentators came to different judgements about the extent to which the party under Cameron was drawing on its Thatcherite past, reverting to more of a One Nation position, reflecting an approach more similar to that of New Labour or developing in a complicated and dynamic fashion (eg Bochel, 2011; King, 2011).

In the event, the Conservatives fought the 2010 general election on a platform that emphasised a need to substantially reduce the UK's public deficit over the course of the next Parliament. They undertook to do this more rapidly than proposed by Labour or the Liberal Democrats, and to do so primarily through reductions in public expenditure, which would inevitably have major implications for much social policy, rather than through tax increases. Yet, at the same time, the manifesto undertook to protect spending on health and foreign aid, and to link increases in the basic state pension to inflation in the higher of either earnings or prices. It also emphasised the need to tackle Britain's 'broken' society but argued that rather than the state, it was necessary to develop a 'Big Society', with charities, social enterprises and voluntary and community groups playing a much greater role in tackling social problems. Other significant social policy manifesto pledges included tax and benefits reforms to help families and pensioners, support for Sure Start, increased patient choice in the National Health Service (NHS), and the expansion of academy schools (Conservative Party, 2010).

The Liberal Democrats' 'Orange book' road

While, prior to 2010, commentators had paid considerable attention to the problems faced by the Labour Party and the development of the Conservative Party under David Cameron, much less attention had been focused on the Liberal Democrats, even though the opinion polls highlighted the potential for a hung Parliament.

Yet, the Liberal Democrats had arguably also gone through significant change, particularly at the more senior level of the parliamentary party. That this went largely unnoticed was perhaps, in part, down to their 'third party' status and, in part, due to some of the party's eye-catching election promises, including to abolish tuition fees for higher education in England and to introduce a 'mansion tax' on high-value homes (Liberal Democrats, 2010).

However, it was arguably apparent that after a series of leaders drawn from the social-democratic wing of the party (including Charles Kennedy, Menzies Campbell and Paddy Ashdown), the election of Nick Clegg in 2007 marked a resurgence of the more economically liberal side of the party. Indeed, even earlier, the publication of *The orange book: Reclaiming liberalism* (Marshall and Laws, 2004) had seen a number of senior Liberal Democrats, including some who would play a key role in the coalition government, such as Vince Cable, Nick Clegg, Ed Davey, Chris Huhne and Steve Webb, bringing forward their ideas for policy development, many of which drew strongly on economically liberal beliefs.

In the opening chapter of *The orange book*, David Laws rated the Liberal Democrats quite highly for their positions on personal, political and social liberalism (although he did identify a number of weaknesses, including an unwillingness to use economically liberal means for socially liberal ends), but poorly for economic liberalism. Indeed, the bulk of the contributions to *The orange book* can be seen as emphasising the role of markets (including privatisation) and individual choice, while increasing tax thresholds, rather than raising benefits, was portrayed as the best response to poverty. *The orange book* therefore reflected a significant change in orientation, at least in part of the Liberal Democrat Party (although, at the same time, highlighting internal divisions), and arguably both foreshadowed and made easier a post-election centre-right alignment, rather than the realignment of the centre-left that previous Liberal Democrat leaders had aspired to.

In some respects, rather like the Conservatives, the Liberal Democrats therefore fought the 2010 general election on the basis of a somewhat unusual policy mix, including over £15 billion of reductions in government spending each year but also £5 billion of spending to go on initiatives such as raising the threshold for income tax to £10,000 per year and spending £2.5 billion per year on a 'pupil premium' for disadvantaged children in schools. Their manifesto also included pledges to make it easier for people to access their personal pension funds, to ban politicians from involvement in the day-to-day running of schools, to remove tuition fees for higher education and to allow councils to borrow against their assets in order to build housing.

Interpreting the coalition government, 2010–15

While the Conservatives had held opinion poll leads over Labour for much of 2008 and 2009, in the months before the 2010 general election, the gap had narrowed somewhat, and by the start of the campaign, it was far from certain whether the Conservatives would be able to win a majority in the House of Commons. The televised debates between party leaders during the campaign appeared to make the outcome even less certain, with an apparent surge in support for the Liberal Democrats after Nick Clegg appeared on equal terms with Gordon Brown and David Cameron and was seen by some as having 'won' the first debate. The final election result was therefore not entirely unexpected, with the Conservatives winning 36% of the vote and 307 seats (19 short of a majority) to Labour's 29% and 258 seats and the Liberal Democrats' 23% and 57 seats, with other parties receiving 12% and 28 seats. However, the final make-up of the new government nevertheless came as a surprise to many as, after four days of negotiations, the Liberal Democrats joined the Conservatives in a coalition, with David Cameron as Prime Minister and Nick Clegg as Deputy Prime Minister.

While the form of the new government may have been largely unanticipated, the Conservatives, in particular, may have been prepared for it to some extent. Bale (2011) argues, for example, that senior Conservatives had recognised, perhaps even before the 2010 general election, some of the changes that the Liberal Democrats had been undergoing, and that the Liberal Democrats' leadership, in particular, were not irredeemably left of centre, although they may not have realised the extent to which they had accepted the Conservatives' economic analysis, and that this made the creation of the coalition considerably easier. In addition, given the make-up of the House of Commons, even if the Liberal Democrats had sought to side with Labour, the two parties together would have remained significantly short of a majority, so that the only other likely outcome might have been a minority Conservative government. Indeed, on some key areas, although by no means all, the policies of the three main parties were not that dissimilar, for example: all prioritised cutting the deficit primarily through reductions in public expenditure, although at different speeds and with somewhat different balances of tax increases; all favoured greater use of the market within the NHS; and all supported some degree of academisation and freeing of schools from local authority control.

The cabinet and the Programme for government

At the time, and since, there have been a number of attempts by the media and academics to assess the formation of the coalition and the influence of the Conservatives and the Liberal Democrats on the policies and direction of the government (eg BBC, 2010; *The Guardian*, 2010; Debus, 2011; Quinn et al, 2011; Hayton, 2014). Here, we seek to focus primarily on policies, in particular, social policy.

The new cabinet contained 17 Conservatives and five Liberal Democrats, a pattern maintained throughout the coalition government despite a number of resignations and relatively minor reshuffles.

However, where social policy (and, indeed, public expenditure in general) was concerned, the Conservatives clearly held most of the major posts. In addition to George Osborne as Chancellor, the Conservatives took the posts of Secretary of State for Health, Education, Work and Pensions, and Communities and Local Government. The Liberal Democrats had Nick Clegg as Deputy Prime Minister and David Laws, shortly to be succeeded by Danny Alexander, as Chief Secretary to the Treasury. The 'Quad' of David Cameron, George Osborne, Nick Clegg and Danny Alexander was the main forum used for resolving difficult issues (Hazell and Yong, 2012).

The agreement between the two parties, set out in the *Programme for government* (Cabinet Office, 2010), provided for tax cuts of around £10 billion. However, with the promised protection for the NHS and international development, and increases in the state pension in line with the higher of wage inflation, price inflation or 2.5%, reductions in public expenditure for other areas would have to be substantially greater than had cuts been made across all areas broadly equally (see Chapter Two).

In terms of assessing the influence of the two partners on the coalition's programme, clearly much depends on the starting point. Bochel (2011) noted media and other estimates that around 40% of the actions outlined in the *Programme for government* had been included in the Liberal Democrats' manifesto or those of both government parties (see also Hazell and Young, 2012), although others suggested that the Liberal Democrats had been even more successful in having their measures adopted (eg Quinn et al, 2011). In that sense, it would appear relatively easy for the Liberal Democrats to claim that despite their much smaller numbers in the House of Commons, they were able to exercise considerable influence over the new government's policies, including, for example, the commitment to raising the threshold for income tax. The Conservatives made some significant concessions, such as the proposal to raise the threshold for inheritance tax to £1 million and the acceptance of a referendum on a switch to the Alternative Vote electoral system.

Equally, however, some of the Liberal Democrats' ideas were very similar to those of the Conservatives, while several of their key policies were excluded from the coalition agreement, including (and perhaps most notably and damagingly for the party) the promise to remove higher education tuition fees and the idea of a 'mansion tax' on properties worth more than £2 million. In addition, the acceptance of the Conservatives' emphasis on and plans for reductions in public expenditure, together with their control of the big spending departments, noted earlier, meant that across large swathes of social policy, the Conservatives' approach was dominant. Indeed, given the shift within the Liberal Democrats in the preceding decade, and the relative sidelining of the social-democratic wing of the party, the emergence of a strongly economically liberal approach is perhaps less surprising than it might once have been. This coincidence of views was reflected in the *Programme for government*, in phrases such as 'We share a conviction that the days of big government are over' (Cabinet Office, 2010, p 7) and 'We have found that a combination of our parties' best ideas and attitudes has produced a programme for government that is more radical and comprehensive than our individual manifestos' (Cabinet Office, 2010, p 8), as well as the clear statement in the tailpiece that 'The deficit reduction programme takes precedence over any of the other measures in this agreement' (Cabinet Office, 2010, p 35).

Locating the coalition

Prior to the 1997 general election, the creation of the label of 'New Labour' was seen by some as an important feature of Labour once again becoming electable, and arguments about a distinctive approach, portrayed as the 'Third Way', were an important element of that for politicians such as Tony Blair and Peter Mandelson. In the same way, on becoming leader of the Conservative Party, David Cameron expended considerable time and energy in seeking to 'detoxify' the party and to portray it as different from its Thatcherite period. This section draws upon Powell's (1999) discussion of New Labour and the Third Way to examine changes to the provision of welfare under the coalition by setting them against the framework of alternative political approaches, including the New Right and the Third Way. Table 1.1 suggests that, in most respects, the coalition government can be seen as having significant similarities with the New Right. The scale and impact of 'austerity' and public expenditure cuts was also such that, in some respects, they dominate any reflection on this period. Nevertheless, while there are inevitably considerable overlaps between the different dimensions, the following discussion considers some of the key features of the position of the coalition government within each dimension.

Table 1.1: Dimensions of political approaches

Dimension	Old Left	Third Way	One Nation	New Right	Coalition
Approach	Leveller	Investor	Investor	Deregulator	Deregulator
Citizenship	Rights	Rights and responsibilities	Rights and responsibilities	Responsibilities	Responsibilities
Outcome	Equality	Inclusion	Inclusion/some inequality	Inequality	Inequality
Mixed economy of welfare	State	State/private; civil society	State/private	Private	Private
Mode	Command and control	Cooperation/ partnership	Command and control/cooperation	Competition	Competition
Expenditure	High	Pragmatic	Pragmatic	Low	Low
Benefits	High	Low/medium	Low/medium	Low	Low
Services	High	Medium	Medium	Low	Low/medium
Accountability	Central state/upwards	Central state/ upwards and market/ downwards	Central state/ upwards and market/ downwards	Market/downwards	Market/downwards and civil society
Politics	Left	Left/post-ideological	Right/pragmatic	Right	Right

Source: Adapted from Powell (1999, p 14, Table 1.1).

Approach

Across the social policy arena, the policies of the coalition government appear to have been significantly closer to the 'deregulatory' approach of the New Right than to the 'Investor' approach of the Third Way, or even arguably that of One Nation Conservatism, certainly as it is often typified from the 1950s to the 1970s. There was clearly some shared discourse with elements of the Third Way, such as in relation to transforming the welfare state from a safety net in times of trouble to a springboard for economic opportunity, the emphasis on 'welfare' offering a hand up rather than a hand-out, the centrality of paid work as the route out of poverty and the emphasis on individual agency and choice. Both Labour and coalition governments remained committed to the National Minimum Wage, and also to the provision of high-quality affordable childcare. However, while both New Labour and coalition governments sought to 'make work pay', and to use a mix of carrots and sticks, for the coalition, reducing benefits and raising the income tax threshold were important tools, in contrast to the widespread use of tax credits under Labour, while the development and gradual introduction of Universal Credit was intended not only to reduce the complexity of the system, but also to increase conditionality. In general, therefore, the coalition favoured stronger measures than did Labour, which could, indeed, be argued to be in line with a significant proportion of public opinion (Deeming, 2014). Perhaps to some extent as a result of the coalition's measures, one of the interesting features of the economy from 2010 to 2015 was the relative success in creating jobs despite the major impact of job losses in much of the public sector; yet, at the same time, wage inflation remained very low, in part because of an increase in part-time and temporary employment.

The deregulatory approach was also obvious across other areas of social policy, such as: in education, with the coalition's determination to remove or reduce the powers of local authorities through a major increase in the number of academies and the creation of 'free schools'; in local government, with major spending cuts being accompanied by an emphasis on 'localism'; in health care, with the changes introduced by the Health and Social Care Act 2012, including further opening up the NHS in England to private and not-for-profit providers; and in the relaxation of controls on how individuals use their pension investments.

Citizenship

Where citizenship was concerned, as with New Labour and the Third Way, the coalition government placed considerable stress on responsibilities. It argued that the state is no longer the answer, that state provision has been ineffective and damaging, and that responsibility should therefore shift to individuals and families, and to communities and civil society. Perhaps the most obvious example of this was around the obligation to look for work, as the coalition took up and expanded Labour's rhetoric of conditionality (particularly in relation to searching for a job), increased the level of active enforcement and changed the balance of carrots and sticks for different groups, although the use of medical tests for Employment and Support Allowance was widely seen as severely flawed and led to the private company, Atos, withdrawing from the contract before it was due to end. Yet, while some elements of conditionality were seen as problematic, and there remains considerable support for the benefits system among the public, there was also evidence that opinion on benefits claimants has hardened (eg Baumberg, 2014; Deeming, 2014) and that significant proportions of the British public believed that sanctions should be tougher (see, eg, Oakley and Saunders, 2011). Other examples of the responsibilisation of citizens and families could be seen with the introduction of the benefit cap, which set a limit on the amount of benefit that people in a household could get, and the 'bedroom tax' (the removal of the 'spare room subsidy'), which had a significant impact on many groups, including poorer and disabled people. Critics of the government noted, however, that perceptions of the degree of responsibility appeared to be very different for poor and unemployed people than for bankers and senior public sector leaders, who appeared to be rewarded for failure as well as for success.

As part of the response to these reforms, there was the development of charitable and social initiatives, including food banks and clothing banks; yet, at the same time, funding for charities and community groups was being reduced by both central and local government, while the Transparency of Lobbying, Non-party Campaigning and Trade Union Administration Act 2014 threatened to make it harder for some charities to campaign.

There were, however, other and very different issues associated with other aspects of citizenship that faced the coalition government during its term in office. One, which was hard to ignore, particularly during 2014, was a fundamental issue over citizenship of the UK in the shape of the referendum on independence for Scotland, where there was clearly strong support for a more social-democratic form of social policy among many of those in favour of separation. The final weeks of the campaign were fraught, with a significant narrowing of the gap between those favouring Scotland remaining in the UK and those who sought independence. While the 'Better Together' campaign was ultimately successful, winning by 55% to 45%, the unionist parties pledged to devolve significantly more powers to Scotland. Foreshadowing elements of the 2015 general election campaign, that served not only to raise questions about what shape social policy in Scotland might take in the future, but also to highlight that not all parts of the UK were seeking to move in the direction taken by the coalition government (see also Chapter Fifteen), and that there were already significantly differing priorities and approaches under devolution, even if the ongoing impact of public expenditure cuts would be felt in each of the devolved areas.

The other significant political and policy challenge faced by the coalition government related to citizenship was immigration. Despite Cameron's undertaking in 2010, reiterated in 2011, to bring net immigration down to the tens of thousands, it remained stubbornly high, with annual net immigration being over 230,000 in the year to March 2014 and reaching 330,000 in the following 12 months. While politicians from all of the three main parties found it difficult to respond to the apparent concerns of voters over immigration, including from within the European Union (EU), for the Conservative part of the coalition there was a particular problem, made worse by the more general anti-EU sentiment of many on the political Right. This was, in part, because of the increasingly hard line taken by many of the party's own Eurosceptics, who were keen to use issues such as immigration to push Cameron, and, indeed, the country, towards a referendum on EU membership and the UK's potential exit. It was also, in part, as a result of the rise of the United Kingdom Independence Party (UKIP), who seemed able to reach disillusioned voters in a way that the Conservatives were not, as demonstrated by its strong performance in the 2014 European elections, when it topped the poll with 27% of the vote, and later that year with the resignation of the Conservative MPs for Clacton and Rochester and Strood and their successful return to Parliament at by-elections under the UKIP banner. Towards the end of the coalition government, politicians from all parties were seeking to prevent EU migrants from claiming some benefits for some considerable time after arriving in the UK.

Outcome

Like much of New Labour, the coalition government appeared to be 'relaxed' about the richer getting richer, despite David Cameron's early statements arguing that 'we are all in this together' (Cameron, 2009) and 'It is fair that those with broader shoulders should bear a greater load' (Cameron, 2010). Given the policy paths of reductions in benefits and increased marketisation, it was perhaps unsurprising that many suggested that under the coalition government, the gap between rich and poor widened further, following a slight closing under Labour (eg Belfield et al, 2014). Similarly, both New Labour and the coalition appeared to preside over decreasing levels of social mobility, despite expressing concerns over such developments, and a report by the former Labour cabinet minister Alan Milburn in 2009 (Panel on Fair Access to the Professions, 2009) and a progress report in 2012 (Independent Reviewer on Social Mobility and Child Poverty, 2012) showed that professions such as medicine and law had become increasingly closed to all but the most affluent families, and had become more, rather than less, exclusive over time. Yet, the coalition government sought to present Labour's approach to tackling child poverty and improving social mobility as expensive and wasteful, with a view of social justice underpinned by the view that:

> far from seeking to maximise the position of those at the bottom, the moral imperative is to reduce state hand-outs to the poorest in society, lest they become trapped in a state of welfare dependency that erodes personal and social responsibility and destroys individual agency and moral autonomy. (Bamfield, 2012, p 832)

Bamfield suggests that this seeks to redefine the problem of poverty by attributing its causes to personal and social failings rather than to labour market conditions or broader demographic change, and to move away from the relative measurement of poverty, reflecting the dominance of both discourse and policy around social integration and the existence of a moral underclass, rather than about equality and redistribution (Levitas, 1998).

Mixed economy

Despite the apparently less critical stance towards the public sector that they had taken in opposition, in government, the Conservatives, together with the Liberal Democrats, showed a marked preference for the private and not-for-profit sectors, including provision by social enterprises and voluntary organisations. This was even seen in the NHS, which, while 'protected' from expenditure cuts, was subject to extensive reorganisation and increased provision by the private sector following the introduction of Any Qualified Provider in 2013. Even former Labour ministers, who had themselves been responsible for increasing the role of the private sector in the NHS in England, criticised the government for privatising the NHS. Early in the government's term, talk about the strengths of a mutual approach (the John Lewis model) were reflected in a small number of public sector groupings becoming mutual organisations, but the model did not spread widely, and by early 2015, there were only 101 'public service mutuals' delivering public services (Cabinet Office, 2015). Indeed, the direction implied by massive cuts in public expenditure and the 'localism' and 'Big Society' narratives was clearly towards a much smaller state, with no real clarity over what, if anything, would replace it. Where they did appear to recognise the shortcomings of markets, the coalition rejected Labour's use of the central state and argued for a much greater role for local and community organisations, social enterprises, and the voluntary sector, although there was little evidence to suggest that there was any significant expansion of provision from such quarters (eg NCVO [National Council for Voluntary Organisations] figures show that income for voluntary organisations from government fell from £15 billion in 2010/11 to £13.7 billion in 2011/12, with social services and employment and training being the areas most affected (NCVO, 2015)).

Mode

At the same time, there was a clear alignment with past Liberal Democrat ideas, and the views of some Conservatives, about decisions being made at the local level and with notions of active citizenship, or through the necessity of replacing disappearing public sector provision. In the early part of the coalition government, there was some attempt to build upon the pre-election ideas of 'localism' and the 'Big Society' (see also Chapter Three). However, the Big Society idea, which Cameron and the Conservatives had found so difficult to sell to voters at the 2010 general election, remained problematic at best, and as the Parliament progressed, it became less and less visible. A similar picture was largely the case for localism, and despite the Localism Act 2011 and initiatives such as the introduction of Police and Crime

Commissioners (who were then elected on derisory turnouts), there was little real evidence of any resurgence of power at the local level (Lowndes and Pratchett, 2012), and by the end of the government, many in local government, including some Conservatives, were calling for a much greater devolution of power and financial control (eg Communities and Local Government Committee, 2014; Local Government Association, 2014).

Indeed, the attempts to push the 'Big Society', and perhaps also 'localism', might be seen as the counterpart to Thatcherite economics, rolling back the state in the social sphere (eg Dorey et al, 2011). Dorey et al also argue that while Cameron's rhetoric suggested that active citizens and social enterprises would step in to fill the gaps in provision left by the retreating state, not least as a result of the large-scale cuts in public expenditure, 'ministers were not quite so idealistic.... Rather they assumed that profit-seeking companies would take over many of the state's activities' (Dorey et al, 2011, p 4). Certainly, in areas ranging from probation through social care to health care, where provision was left to the market, it appeared to be the case that for-profit providers dominated in most instances, and even within the NHS, many contracts were going to the private sector, albeit apparently at a lower value than those won by NHS providers and the voluntary sector (*Financial Times*, 2014).

There was a significant departure from the early New Labour 'Third Way' stress placed on collaboration (or partnerships or networks) (Powell, 1999; Glendinning et al, 2002) as the coalition continued the emphasis of Conservative governments from the 1980s, and later New Labour governments (notably, some time after about 2000), on choice and competition in delivering social policies, and, in particular, the importance of individual choice in health and social care and education. However, the need for 'joined-up government' and 'integration' was still recognised, although efforts made to secure this remained problematic, as shown by, for example, the National Audit Office's (2014) critical report on the 'Better Care Fund' in health and social care.

Expenditure

Arguably, and unsurprisingly given the extent of change, the dominant theme in relation to social policy under the coalition was reductions in public expenditure, although this was also accompanied by important changes in the balance of spending across policy areas. In this respect, there were clear reflections of the approach of the Thatcher governments. While Margaret Thatcher's government's first public expenditure White Paper famously opened with the statement that 'Public expenditure is at the heart of Britain's current economic difficulties' (HM Treasury, 1979, p 1), the coalition government's spending review stated equally forthrightly (HM Treasury, 2010, p 5):

> The Coalition Government inherited one of the most challenging fiscal positions in the world. Last year, Britain's deficit was the largest in its peacetime history – the state borrowed one pound for every four it spent. The UK currently spends £43 billion on debt interest, which is more than it spends on schools in England.

However, the coalition's strategy for attempting to reduce the deficit was designed almost entirely on the basis of the reduction of public spending and the public debt, and was effectively dependent upon private household debt increasing over the period of the government. Indeed, the coalition government was considerably more successful than the Thatcher governments in reducing public expenditure, in part due to major cuts to spending on social security benefits, and in part due to the imposition of cuts across many other areas of state activity. This emphasis on reducing public expenditure in the name of cutting the deficit clearly had major, if differing, implications for many areas of social policy, as is clearly apparent throughout this book. However, it is perhaps worth highlighting briefly here the extent to which particular areas were treated differently. For example, spending on health increased from £116 billion in 2009/10 to £129 billion in 2013/14, on education from £88 billion to £90 billion, and on social protection from £223 billion to £250 billion, but spending on housing fell from £16 billion to £11 billion (HM Treasury, 2014, p 70, Table 5.2). Within housing, the big cuts were in housing development, with a drop from almost £11 billion to under £7 billion per year. For social protection, spending on pensions rose markedly, from £84 billion in 2009/10 to £104 billion in 2013/14, while spending on families and children, in the form of family benefits, income support and tax credits, fell from £22 billion to £16 billion. As is made clear throughout this book, reductions and increases in spending were not spread evenly across policy domains, and instead reflected the coalition government's preferences and priorities. Despite the avowed interest in localism, the 2010 Spending Review outlined disproportionately high reductions for local government, with the Department for Communities and Local Government seeing its budget fall by half over a four-year period.

While the level of public expenditure has long been a point of political argument, and particularly so from the 1970s, Taylor-Gooby (2012) argued that the coalition government's approach was largely ideological, and summarises its programme as being: cuts in public expenditure of an exceptional scale, speed, composition and distributional impact; and a restructuring of the role of government in social provision so far-reaching as to be systemic, rather than programmatic (Pierson, 1994). On top of the reductions in public expenditure, he noted the extent of reform of non-pension cash benefits, the reorganisations of the NHS and of higher education, and the substitution of private for-profit and not-for-profit agencies for state services in social housing, social welfare and aspects of health, education and welfare to work, with new opportunities for the private sector to enter, including in the higher education, NHS and social care internal markets, training and activation programmes for unemployed people, and potentially free schools and academies. He suggested that the reforms shifted responsibility for provision away from the government, and they weakened and divided groups of benefit claimers and service users so that future pressures for state spending might weaken. Indeed, while much of the initial rhetoric from the coalition, and particularly from the Conservatives, focused on the need for cuts in spending to reduce the deficit, towards the end of the Parliament, the argument appeared to have shifted significantly, with the Chancellor, George Osborne, announcing plans for a further reduction in public expenditure of £25 billion, including £12 billion from the welfare budget, in the event of the Conservative Party winning the 2015 general election (Osborne, 2014; Conservative Party, 2015). Despite their acquiescence in the reductions in public expenditure from 2010, many Liberal Democrats appeared unwilling to countenance further cuts of such a scale, with, for example, the Deputy Prime Minister, Nick Clegg, accusing Osborne of placing the burden of cuts on those with the 'narrowest shoulders' (Channel 4 News, 2010) and Vince Cable saying that they would 'destroy public services in the way that we know them' (BBC, 2014).

Benefits

As is clear from much of the preceding discussion, and, indeed, elsewhere in this book (see particularly Chapters Two and Eight), one of the main targets for expenditure cuts under the coalition government was benefits. While Labour arguably took a harder line than some of their predecessors on benefits, and made much greater use of active labour market policies, the coalition government took this considerably further, including through reforms such as the introduction of the benefits cap and the ending of the spare room subsidy (also known as the 'bedroom tax'). Labour, of course, had pledged in 1999 to end child poverty within 20 years, and although even before the financial crisis, it was unlikely to be close to its target, it did achieve significant reductions in the prevalence of child poverty. While Labour had used tax credits to target support at groups such as families with children and poorer pensioners, the coalition government reduced the use of tax credits and significantly restricted the payment of child benefit, despite remaining notionally committed to ending child poverty.

However, it is possible to identify some areas where the coalition government's policies were somewhat different from those of the Thatcher governments and from those that might be expected of a New Right-influenced approach. One of the most obvious examples of this was the state pension, where the government introduced a 'triple lock' of an annual increase in line with the highest of wage growth, inflation or 2.5%, together with the introduction of a single-tier pension (see Chapters Eight and Fourteen).

Services

Indeed, pensions were not the only area of provision that was subject to less significant cuts by the coalition. In terms of services, spending on the NHS was, to some extent, protected or even marginally increased in real terms. There were different possible interpretations of this, including that the coalition parties had a genuine and deep-seated commitment to the NHS and to the well-being of older people, who would in most respects fall into the category of 'the deserving', and both parties had, prior to the 2010 general election, made much of their support for the NHS and for pensioners. On the other hand, it could be argued that the NHS was an issue on which Labour has always been strong, and that demonstrating support for it was a way of neutralising, or at least reducing, the potential electoral benefit to Labour of its association with the NHS.

Similarly, the greater propensity of older people to vote than younger people is well known, so that a government seen to be supporting them, including through the state pension, might expect to reap some rewards at the ballot box. The coalition government's perhaps uncharacteristic support for public expenditure in these areas might therefore be seen as having at least some degree of pragmatic political underpinning. Of course, maintaining expenditure in some areas (education also did not suffer as substantially) had the inevitable consequence that the cuts in other areas, notably, benefits and local government, were much greater than if they had been made more equally across all areas of provision.

Accountability

Given the coalition government's emphasis on the role of markets and choice, and the increasing responsibilisation of individuals and families, it is perhaps not surprising that for much social policy, the direction of accountability was seen as running through the market downwards towards users of services. However, there was also the localist tendency, which ran through large areas of the coalition's approach, albeit perhaps mainly in rhetorical terms, and an emphasis on the failure of the state to resolve problems, again suggesting the need for a greater role for neighbourhoods, communities, voluntary groups and social enterprises in providing services for and being accountable to their local areas. As noted elsewhere (see, eg, Chapter Three), there was, at best, limited evidence of any real progress in these respects.

Politics

In political terms, the coalition government frequently sought to present different faces to the electorate, but while there had been considerable debate about whether there had been the emergence of a form of compassionate or civic conservatism before the 2010 general election, and the creation of the coalition had surprised many given the Liberal Democrats' claims to a left-of-centre position, it became clear early in the life of the government that there was a clear preference for an approach more closely related to that of the New Right, and, indeed, in some ways, it was even more committed to the reduction of the size and role of the state than the Thatcher governments. Both parties did, from time to time, seek to make different arguments to the electorate, for example, with regard to the introduction of the pupil premium in schools, and Business Secretary Vince Cable's periodic criticisms of his coalition partners, but significant areas of the Liberal Democrats' ideas in the *Programme for government* had been focused on constitutional reform (which itself was largely unsuccessful).

However, one area in which there was perhaps a more compassionate approach in social policy terms was with regard to social issues. Taking a rather different stance from his predecessors, and reflecting the socially liberal views of his coalition partners, Cameron and a substantial proportion of Conservative parliamentarians had come to accept the idea of gay marriage and the existence of a diversity of family types, although, at the same time, he and the Conservative Party sought to reiterate the benefits of having two parents raising a child within a long-term stable relationship. At the 2010 general election, the party had promised to reform the tax and benefits system to recognise marriage and civil partnerships, and while they failed to make such changes, the coalition did pass the Marriage (Same Sex Couples) Act 2013, despite the opposition of a substantial part of the parliamentary Conservative Party.

Conclusions

It is now possible to provide some provisional answers to our main questions. In Chapter Sixteen, we will return to these, drawing on the perspectives of the contributors. However, for the moment, given the dominance of a discourse that focused on the need to make massive cuts in public expenditure, and that blamed Labour for the deficit, together with the agreed emphasis on a deregulatory approach, the responsibilisation of individuals and communities, and the desirability of the use of markets and consumer choice that initially united the Conservatives and Liberal Democrats in the coalition government, it appears unsurprising that in many respects the government exhibited a range of characteristics, policies and rhetoric that were often very similar to those of the New Right-influenced Thatcher governments.

However, it is also possible to identify areas where the coalition government was also influenced by some New Labour ideas and policies, many of which were aligned with the consumer and market-oriented influence, such as the centrality of work and conditionality for benefits, academisation, and a greater role for the private sector in the NHS; however, there were other areas, such as maintaining spending on the NHS and on pensions, where, whether for politically pragmatic or other reasons, the coalition appeared to be unwilling to adopt such a strong approach.

Given the shift in the orientation of the leadership of the Liberal Democrats prior to the 2010 general election, and the similarities of the two parties' manifesto promises in many, although by no means all, areas, it is clear that the coalition and the agreement on the *Programme for government* was much less problematic for both parties than it might have been five years earlier. Indeed, in some areas, their policies were broadly similar, although there were differences of emphasis. Crines (2013) has argued that while the coalition partners were aligned in their emphasis on individualism, the need for market reform and the need for austerity, the Liberal Democrats retained some aspiration for egalitarian objectives in terms of outcomes, which would include the provision of benefits and services. At the same time, the Conservatives' greater commitment to marketisation and morality in social policy was highlighted in their positions on the citizenship, mixed economy of welfare, mode and politics dimensions of Table 1.1. In coming together to form a government, each party had to make some concessions, although, in both cases, their leaders might not have been entirely unhappy with them. However, the overarching influence of public expenditure cuts, and the fact that the Conservatives held the positions of Chancellor and Secretaries of State of the big spending departments, meant that in many respects it was their interpretations that had the greatest influence on social policy.

While the chapters that follow provide more detailed coverage across a range of key issues and policy areas, as noted earlier, the dominance of the austerity narrative and the large-scale cuts in public expenditure were clearly going to have significant implications for both the scale and scope of social provision. These were further reinforced by the broad political consensus around largely neoliberal approaches, and the Liberal Democrats' shift to more economically liberal positions, which meant that their differences with the Conservatives were perhaps less than might have been the case a decade earlier, so that long-standing themes such as choice, marketisation and responsibilisation were likely to be maintained and developed, together with some degree of localism and perhaps a greater acceptance of economic inequality than had been the case under Labour.

In many respects, therefore, the period of the coalition was likely to reflect a significant degree of continuity with previous Conservative and Labour governments, so that broad trends in social policy were likely to be continued, although the new government's enthusiasm for public expenditure cuts and the replacement of state provision with that by the not-for-profit and particularly by the private sectors was arguably even greater than had been the case during the Thatcher era. However, particularly given the apparent lack of enthusiasm for Cameron's Big Society, a key question was likely to be over what, if anything, would replace the diminished role for the state in many areas of social provision.

References

Bale, T. (2011) 'I *don't* agree with Nick: retrodicting the Conservative–Liberal Democrat coalition', *The Political Quarterly*, 82(2): 244–50.

Bamfield, L. (2012) 'Child poverty and social mobility: taking the measure of the coalition's "new approach"', *The Political Quarterly*, 83(4): 830–7.

Baumberg, B. (2014) 'Benefits and the cost of loving', in A. Park, J. Curtice and C. Bryson (eds) *British social attitudes: the 31st report*, London: NatCen Social Research, pp 95–122.

BBC (British Broadcasting Corporation) (2010) 'Policy-by-policy: the coalition government's plans', 21 May. Available at: http://news.bbc.co.uk/1/hi/uk_politics/8693832.stm (accessed 20 January 2015).

BBC (2014) 'Cable: Tories would destroy public services', 14 December. Available at: http://www.bbc.co.uk/news/uk-politics-30468974 (accessed 20 January 2015).

Belfield, C., Cribb, J., Hood, A. and Joyce, R. (2014) *Living standards, poverty and inequality in the UK: 2014*, London: Institute for Fiscal Studies.

Bochel, H. (2011) 'Conservative approaches to social policy since 1997', in H. Bochel (ed) *The Conservative Party and social policy*, Bristol: The Policy Press.

Bulpitt, J. (1985) 'The discipline of the new democracy: Mrs Thatcher's domestic statecraft', *Political Studies*, 34(1): 19–39.

Cabinet Office (2010) *The coalition: our programme for government*, London: Cabinet Office.

Cabinet Office (2015) 'Mutuals Information Service'. Available at: https://www.gov.uk/government/groups/mutuals-information-service (accessed 21 January 2015).

Cameron, D. (2009) Speech to the Conservative Party Conference, 8 October.

Cameron, D. (2010) Speech to the Conservative Party Conference, 6 October.

Channel 4 News (2010) 'Nick Clegg: Osborne's cuts to welfare a "monumental mistake"', 6 January. Available at: http://www.channel4.com/news/george-osborne-budget-economy-2014-hard-truths-video (accessed 20 January 2015).

Communities and Local Government Committee (2014) *Devolution in England: the case for local government*, London: The Stationery Office.

Conservative Party (2010) *Invitation to join the government of Britain: the Conservative manifesto 2010*, London: Conservative Party.

Conservative Party (2015) *The Conservative Party manifesto 2015*, London: Conservative Party.

Crewe, I. (1988) 'Has the electorate become Thatcherite?', in R. Skidelsky (ed) *Thatcherism*, Oxford: Basil Blackwell, pp 25–49.

Crines, A. (2013) 'The rhetoric of the coalition: governing in the national interest', *Representation*, 49(2): 207–18.

Debus, M. (2011) 'Portfolio allocation and policy compromises: how and why the Conservatives and the Liberal Democrats formed a coalition government', *The Political Quarterly*, 82(2): 293–304.

Deeming, C. (2014) 'Foundations of the workfare state – reflections on the political transformation of the welfare state in Britain', *Social Policy and Administration*, Early View version. Available at: http://onlinelibrary.wiley.com/doi/10.1111/spol.12096/full (accessed 20 January 2015).

Dorey, P. (2007) 'A new direction or another false dawn? David Cameron and the crisis of British Conservatism', *British Politics*, 2(2): 137–66.

Dorey, P., Garnett, M. and Denham, A. (2011) *From crisis to coalition: the Conservative Party, 1997–2010*, Basingstoke: Palgrave Macmillan.

Financial Times (2014) 'Third of NHS contracts go to private sector', 10 December. Available at: http://www.ft.com/cms/s/0/ed6594ca-7fc4-11e4-acf3-00144feabdc0.html#axzz3PRsfYq8X (accessed 21 January 2015).

Glendinning, C., Powell, M. and Rummery, K. (eds) (2002) *Partnerships, New Labour and the governance of welfare*, Bristol: The Policy Press.

Hayton, R. (2014) 'Conservative Party statecraft and the politics of coalition', *Parliamentary Affairs*, 67(1): 6–24.

Hazell, R. and Yong, B. (2012) *Politics of coalition: how the Conservative–Liberal Democrat government works*, Oxford: Hart.

HM Treasury (1979) *The government's expenditure plans, 1980–81*, London: HMSO.

HM Treasury (2010) *Spending review 2010*, London: The Stationery Office.

HM Treasury (2014) *Public expenditure statistical analyses 2014*, London: HMSO.

Independent Reviewer on Social Mobility and Child Poverty (2012) *Fair access to professional careers: a progress report by the Independent Reviewer on Social Mobility and Child Poverty*, London: Cabinet Office.

King, P. (2011) *The new politics: liberal conservatism or the same old Tories?*, Bristol: The Policy Press.

Levitas, R. (1998) *The inclusive society: social exclusion and New Labour*, Basingstoke: Macmillan.

Liberal Democrats (2010) *Liberal Democrat manifesto 2010*, London: Liberal Democrats.

Local Government Association (2014) 'United Kingdom council leaders united on devolution', LGA press release, 5 November. Available at: http://www.local.gov.uk/media-releases/-/journal_content/56/10180/6693211/NEWS (accessed 21 January 2015).

Lowndes, V. and Pratchett, L. (2012) 'Local governance under the coalition government: austerity, localism and the "Big Society"', *Local Government Studies*, 38(1): 21–40.

Marshall, P. and Laws, D. (eds) (2004) *The orange book: reclaiming liberalism*, London: Profile Books.

National Audit Office (2014) *Planning for the Better Care Fund*, London: National Audit Office.

NCVO (National Council for Voluntary Organisations) (2015) 'What is the sector's most important source of income?'. Available at: http://data.ncvo.org.uk/a/almanac14/what-is-the-sectors-most-important-source-of-income/ (accessed 21 January 2015).

Oakley, M. and Saunders, P. (2011) *No rights without responsibility: rebalancing the welfare state*, London: Policy Exchange.

Osborne, G. (2014) 'New Year economy speech by the Chancellor of the Exchequer', 6 January. Available at: https://www.gov.uk/government/speeches/new-year-economy-speech-by-the-chancellor-of-the-exchequer (accessed 20 January 2015).

Page, R. (2011) 'The Conservative Party and the welfare state since 1945', in H. Bochel (ed) *The Conservative Party and social policy*, Bristol: The Policy Press, pp 23–39.

Panel on Fair Access to the Professions (2009) *Unleashing aspiration: the final report of the Panel on Fair Access to the Professions*, London: Cabinet Office.

Pautz, H. (2013) 'The think tanks behind Cameronism', *British Journal of Politics and International Relations*, 15(3): 362–77.

Pierson, P. (1994) *Dismantling the welfare state*, Cambridge: Cambridge University Press.

Powell, M. (1999) 'Introduction', in M. Powell (ed) *New Labour, new welfare state*, Bristol: The Policy Press, pp 1–27.

Quinn, T., Bara, J. and Bartle, J. (2011) 'The UK coalition agreement of 2010: who won?', *Journal of Elections, Public Opinion and Parties*, 21(2): 295–312.

Taylor-Gooby, P. (2012) 'Root and branch restructuring to achieve major cuts: the social policy programme of the 2010 UK coalition government', *Social Policy & Administration*, 46(1): 61–82.

The Guardian (2010) 'Conservative–Liberal Democrat coalition agreement', 15 May. Available at: http://www.theguardian.com/politics/interactive/2010/may/15/coalition-conservative-liberal-democrat-agreement (accessed 20 January 2015).

TWO

The coalition government, public spending and social policy

Nick Ellison

Introduction

This chapter sets out the key features of the Conservative–Liberal Democrat coalition government's approach to public spending between 2010 and 2015. If the overall argument outlined here about the nature and direction of public spending cuts is unsurprising, in view of the publicity accorded to them by the government and the enthusiasm with which they were embraced (certainly in Conservative circles), it is important to understand the coalition's approach to public spending both at a general level and in detail. Starting with a brief analysis of the economic and political context in which the new government assumed power in May 2010, the chapter will examine general trends in public spending over the period before focusing on key elements of social security spending. Two issues are of significance. First, it is important to take account of how the idea of 'austerity' was used by the coalition to justify a particular approach to public spending, an interpretation of the 'deficit' and the policies required to reduce it. Second, it is equally important to recognise how, within the overall frame of austerity and the assault on public spending, *social* spending was less 'cut' than comprehensively rebalanced. The general argument set out here is that public spending has been 'disaggregated', and that the process of disaggregation has had a profound impact on the shape and nature of welfare in the UK – a view that chimes with the summary of the coalition's position set out in Table 1.1 in Chapter One. Taken together, the analysis of these twin dimensions of austerity and disaggregation opens onto the wider issue of the sustainability of the UK's welfare system as an institution capable of protecting those sections of the population that are most in need. This matter will be considered in the concluding section of the chapter.

A 'coalition' government?

In the wake of the 2008/09 financial crisis, it is clear that the major political parties engaged in a reassessment of their approach to economic policy, each adopting more (the Conservatives and the Liberal Democrats) or less (Labour) draconian policies towards public spending. This reassessment was carried out in the context of an economic storm created by the banking crisis, which saw general government spending rise as a proportion of gross domestic product (GDP) from 42.9% in 2007/08 to 49.7% in 2009/10 (OECD, 2015a). The rise is not in itself surprising. A combination of increased spending on benefits as a result of rising unemployment, demand-friendly fiscal policies such as the cut in the rate of value added tax (VAT) from 17.5% to 15% and falling tax revenues as the economy contracted inevitably left a hole in the public finances that had to be filled by increased borrowing. This situation was compounded by Labour's decisions both to increase capital spending in 2008/09 as a temporary stimulus to mitigate the economic and social impact of the downturn, and to bail out key banks[1] in the wake of the banking crisis, however necessary these measures may have been.

Whether or not Labour effectively rescued the UK economy through this economic strategy will remain the subject of debate for some time to come. What is not in doubt is the Conservative Party's reaction to the rapid rise in public spending – a reaction that was wholly endorsed by the coalition government when it came to office in May 2010. Although the phrase 'coalition government' will be used throughout this chapter, it is clear that where public spending is concerned, responsibility for the development and pursuit of the government's economic and financial strategy lay primarily with the Conservative Party and, within that, specifically with the Chancellor of the Exchequer, George Osborne. There is, of course, much disagreement about the necessity or otherwise of adopting an approach to the public finances that focused on deficit reduction through public spending constraints, with some tax rises, while simultaneously looking towards 'rebalancing' the economy in favour of private enterprise and export-led growth (Taylor-Gooby, 2012; Berry and Hay, 2014; Gamble, 2015). This, however, was the strategy promoted by Osborne as the financial crisis deepened. Despite pre-crisis Conservative commitments to Labour's spending plans, by the time of the 2010 general election, Osborne was committed to a new economic model that had public sector austerity at its heart. As his February 2010 Maïs Lecture made clear, Osborne's (2010, p 1) ambition was to 'move away from an economic model that was based on unsustainable private and public debt'. The lecture signalled his intention not simply to reduce, but to remove, the deficit in the course of a single Parliament.

For their part, the Liberal Democrats had stated in their election manifesto that 'public spending has reached unsustainable levels and needs to be brought under control to protect the country's economic future' (Liberal Democratics, 2010, p 14). In keeping with ideas set out in *The orange book* (Marshall and Laws, 2004), the party placed rather more stress on tax changes than did the Conservatives – and specifically on increases in the personal allowance – but there were sufficient hints about public spending constraints (including a promise to cap public sector pay rises at £400 per year) to suggest a willingness to go further in some areas, particularly if pensions could be protected and made more flexible. Certainly, by the time that David Cameron and Nick Clegg signed the *Programme for government*, there was clear agreement between the two parties that 'deficit reduction … is the most urgent issue facing Britain' and, further, that 'the main burden of deficit reduction [would be] borne by reduced spending rather than increased taxes' (Cabinet Office, 2010, p 15). This message was communicated unequivocally in the 2010 Budget. Table 2.1, taken

Table 2.1: Total consolidation plans over the forecast period

	£ billion					
	2010/11	2011/12	2012/13	2013/14	2014/15	2015/16
Discretionary policy announced at Budget	8.1	15	24	32	40	
Spending	5.2	9	17	24	32	
Tax	2.8	6	7	9	8	
Spending share of consolidation (%)	65	59	71	74	80	
Policy inherited by the government	0.8	26	42	57	73	
Spending	0.0	14	25	39	52	
Tax	0.8	11	17	18	21	
Spending share of consolidation (%)	0	56	60	68	71	
Total discretionary consolidation	8.9	41	66	90	113	128
Spending	5.2	23	42	63	83	99
Tax	3.6	18	24	27	29	29
Spending share of consolidation (%)	59	57	64	70	74	77

Source: HM Treasury (2010a).

from the Treasury's summary of spending plans (HM Treasury, 2010a, p 15), shows how the coalition planned to make deeper inroads into public spending than Labour had undertaken to do before the 2010 general election – and also shows that public spending, as opposed to increased taxation, would take the greater strain. In general terms, by 2014/15, the coalition committed to taking £32 billion out of public spending over and above the reduction that Labour had planned, with a view to achieving a *spending* reduction of £99 billion (77% of the total) by 2015/16 and an overall reduction of £128 billion.

Although the coalition partners disagreed fundamentally over certain areas of policy – and increasingly so as time went on (Hayton, 2014) – over the course of the Parliament, there was little, if any, significant disagreement about this stated approach to public spending and deficit reduction. Whether the coalition's fixation on the deficit was borne of a genuine belief that the country's economic position could only be secured by a single-minded assault on the public sector and public spending, or whether it was essentially a political strategy designed to lay responsibility for upcoming austerity at Labour's door, is open to debate. However, it is worth noting that once past the 2009/10 peak associated with the bank bailouts, the deficit was not dramatically large by historical UK standards; nor, for that matter, was it unusually large when compared with other developed economies (see Figure 2.1 and Table 2.2). In fact, as Jowett and Hardie (2014) make clear, the UK has run a Public Sector Current Budget Deficit for the majority of years since 1974, and has also seen net borrowing rise to high percentages of GDP in 1975/76 and 1993/94, as well as 2009–11. It is also important to recognise that although public spending plainly increased under New Labour from 2001/02 onwards, spending levels only once noticeably breached the European Union's (EU's) Stability and Growth Pact Deficit Reference Value,[2] in 2004/05. Just prior to the financial crisis in 2007, 'the UK's current budget deficit and public sector net debt were both lower than when Labour came to power' (Lupton et al, 2015, p 9).

There is some evidence, then, to suggest that in the wake of the financial crash, politics rather than economics played a significant part in Osborne's calculations in the run-up to, and aftermath of, the 2010 general election. Certainly, once the new coalition government had agreed to 'heap all the blame for the financial crash and ensuing recession onto Labour's mismanagement of the public finances and wider economy', and with the Liberal Democrats now 'prisoners of the austerity narrative' (Gamble, 2015, p 47), the subsequent pursuit of austerity was politically 'risk-free' to an unusual extent. With the public prepared for spending cuts, and a scapegoat in the form of an apparently tongue-tied Labour Party ready to hand, the Chancellor was in a strong position to announce reductions in public spending that matched the goals set out in his Maïs Lecture. In the event, and

Figure 2.1: General government net borrowing ('deficit')

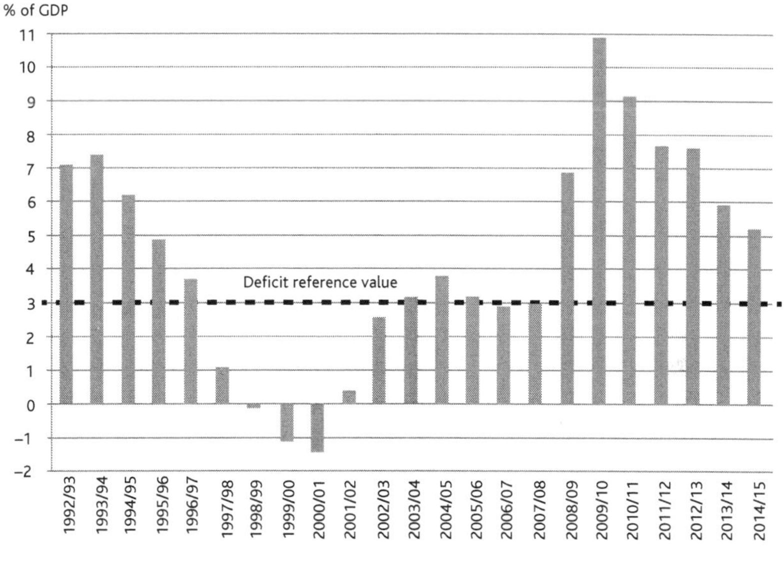

% of GDP

Deficit reference value

Source: Office for National Statistics (2015).

Table 2.2: General government debt as a percentage of GDP – selected countries (ranked according to 2010 levels)

	2007	**2010**	2013
Australia	34.1	**46.9**	58.6
Denmark	34.6	**53.8**	57.3
Spain	41.7	**66.4**	102.0
Germany	64.0	**83.8**	81.5
UK	50.1	**87.1**	111.6
France	75.6	**96.8**	110.5
Canada	84.3	**103.8**	105.7
USA	75.7	**115.3**	122.6
Italy	110.6	**124.8**	143.0
Greece	112.8	**128.3**	179.2
Japan	180.0	**210.6**	239.3

Note: Countries selected to represent different regime types (Esping-Andersen, 1990).
Source: OECD (2015b).

for reasons that will be discussed later, Osborne reduced the deficit to £88.2 billion (5.1% of GDP) by the end of the coalition's period, which, ironically, was more in line with the stated ambitions of Alistair Darling, the outgoing Labour Chancellor, in 2010.

Patterns of public spending, 2010–15

What is 'public spending'? Without getting too mired in detail, the most frequently accepted general definition of this term is 'total managed expenditure' (TME). Since 1998, this overall category has been divided into Departmental Expenditure Limits (DELs) and Annually Managed Expenditure (AME). Both DEL and AME are subdivided into 'resource' and 'capital' spending, with the bulk of expenditure in the majority of government departments being devoted to the former (exceptions are the Departments for Communities and Local Government [DCLG], Energy and Climate Change, and Transport). Capital spending should not be neglected, however. It accounts both for infrastructural investments at central and local levels and for the depreciation of those investments over time. Not surprisingly, this element of spending is vulnerable to cuts when pressures on public spending mount – mainly for two reasons. First, the immediate political costs of economies in this area, whether these be the disposal of public assets like nationalised industries or the cancelling of infrastructural projects such as spending on transport, tend to be lower than those associated with tax rises or cuts in current social expenditure. Second, cuts in capital spending can make a fairly rapid contribution to the state of the public finances. This is particularly true where the public sector owns significant amounts of assets – and it was chiefly for this reason that capital investment declined so markedly in the UK between the mid-1970s and mid-1990s, local authority capital spending fell, and the nationalised industries were sold off. These changes saw capital expenditure decline from 9% of national income in 1966 to under 2% in 2000 (Keynes and Tetlow, 2014, p 55). During New Labour's period in office, in an effort to 'reverse falling standards in the quality of public service assets' (HM Treasury, 2004, p 46), governments gradually increased local and central government capital spending from 0.7% of GDP (1999/2000) to 2.2% (2007/08). The onset of the financial crisis saw a significant temporary rise in capital spending – this, in turn, being followed by equally significant retrenchment between 2010 and 2013. The coalition government cut spending by 3% of national income (HM Treasury, 2010b) in its first three years in office, since which time the total capital budget (DEL and AME) has stabilised at around an annual figure of £62 billion, with new investment allocated to departments such as Transport and Business, Innovation and Skills (BIS) in the later years of the government (HM Treasury, 2014).

Capital spending apart, 'resource' spending accounts for the bulk of activity in the public finances. As the title suggests, resource DEL, which accounts for over half of TME, refers to expenditure that is considered to be 'controllable', for example, spending on health, defence or education, where it is deemed feasible to set spending targets. DEL is monitored and managed through periodic spending reviews, and over the period of the coalition government, strict DELs were imposed on the majority of government departments – although, as discussed later, exceptions were made in the cases of health, aspects of school spending and overseas aid. Resource AME, is concerned with areas of spending that are more vulnerable to fluctuations in demand, such as social security benefits, which can be affected by factors relating to the economic cycle, like employment levels, as well as other phenomena, such as the demographic changes associated with rising numbers of older people. Clearly AME is more difficult to control, although the coalition took steps to rein it in by bringing key areas, including major elements of social security expenditure, under the auspices of the spending reviews (HM Treasury, 2010b, p 5). The best example of the attempt to control AME is the coalition's imposition of both a 'benefit cap' and a 'welfare cap' in 2014. The former set a maximum benefit limit of £500 per week for couples and those with children, and £350 per week for single adults (certain benefits like Disability Living Allowance [DLA] are excluded from the cap), while the latter imposed a limit on total welfare spending (see also Chapter Eight). If the cap is breached, the government is required either to reduce spending on certain benefits, seek permission from Parliament to increase spending, or justify the breach according to the Charter for Budget Responsibility.[3]

For all the heated debate about the deficit and austerity, TME declined only by approximately 2.3% in real terms between 2010/11 and 2014/15 (HM Treasury, 2014, p 61). Expressed as a proportion of national income, TME appears to have fallen more noticeably – by 4% – because the economy began to grow from 2012 while spending in many areas was held back (IFS, 2015a). Many observers (see, eg, Hood and Phillips, 2015; Lupton et al, 2015) recognise, however, that it is less the overall level of spending reductions and more the *pattern* of reductions and increases that defines the coalition's attitude to the public finances. In this sense, the overall approach to public spending during the coalition years is best understood as one of

'systematic disaggregation', meaning that spending was maintained
or even enhanced in certain areas and reduced in others – in some
cases, significantly. As an underlying feature of public spending policy,
disaggregation involved developing a rationale to identify economies
both *among* and *within* different government departments, clear
examples of the latter being the Department for Work and Pensions
(DWP) and BIS (see later). At its broadest, the most significant result
of this approach has been the dramatic remodelling of the UK's public
sector. For example, the decision to protect the National Health
Service (NHS), Overseas Development and Schools budgets from the
worst of the spending cuts stands in marked contrast to the imposition
of drastic economies elsewhere – and particularly in sections of the
DWP, DCLG, BIS, Environment, Food and Rural Affairs, Justice, and
Culture, Media and Sport. Figure 2.2 provides an indication of how
different departments fared during the coalition years.

Figure 2.2: Distribution of spending cuts across government departments

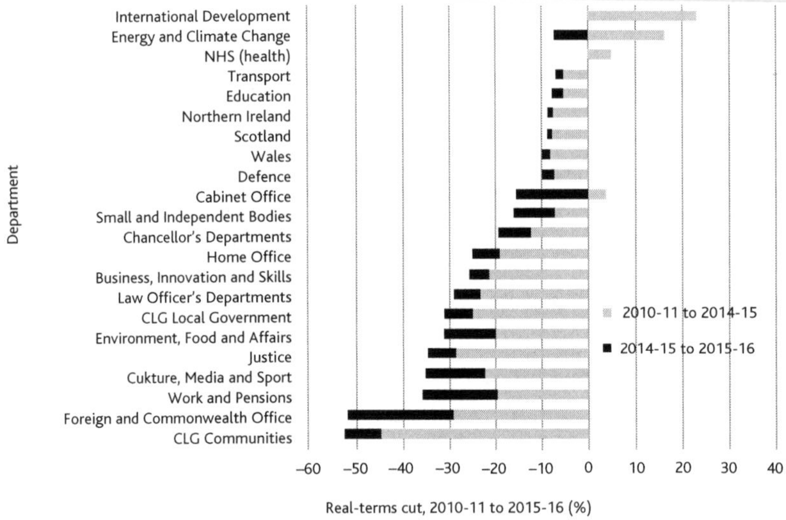

Source: Keynes and Tetlow (2014, p 52).

'Controlled' spending

Chief among the departments in the front line of cost-cutting was the
DCLG, where efforts to set DELs combined with the coalition's stated
intention of exercising greater control over local government (AME)
spending. Although the 2010 Spending Review attempted to advance
an ostensibly attractive coalition principle about the need to localise

power and funding, and to remove 'ringfencing around resources to local authorities', it was also made clear that this apparent increase in budgetary freedom would need to be accompanied by 'tough choices on how services are delivered within reduced allocations' (HM Treasury, 2010b, p 8). At departmental level, depending on how the figures are calculated, by 2015/16, the DCLG had experienced a cash cut that amounted to roughly 28% of its 2010 budget. According to Hastings et al (2012, p 14), this figure could be nearer 40% in real terms. As for local authorities, an estimated £3.7 billion of council tax revenue was 'lost' as a result of the government's decision to exercise greater direct control over council spending by restricting council tax rises to 2% before penalties were incurred (LGA, 2014). The fate of the DCLG is clearly of great significance for social policy because of the control that the department has over local authority spending and, through that, the ability to influence how key public services are delivered. Owing to the severe reductions built into the DCLG's DELs, local authorities saw their grants from central government significantly reduced while simultaneously being prevented from making compensatory council tax rises. Further, local councils also experienced average cuts of 30% in their capital spending over the period. Bearing in mind the theme of disaggregation, as Hastings et al (2012, 2015) argue, due to the ways in which central government grants were distributed, the weight of the grant reductions fell disproportionately on those authorities, such as Liverpool, that contain the most deprived sections of the population, while better-off councils, such as Surrey, were less severely affected.

A number of studies have discussed the impact of these cuts, with some commentators pointing out that those groups who tend to be most affected by local authority retrenchment typically include young people, disabled people, minority ethnic populations and those with low skills and few educational qualifications (Lowndes and McCaughie, 2013). Although Lowndes and McCaughie (2013), Shaw (2012) and others have commented on the resilience shown by local government during the coalition period, with the development of new forms of collaboration and partnership working, and a tendency to reduce 'backroom' activities, such as planning, as opposed to core services, it is nonetheless the case that children's services, including Sure Start Centres, and housing suffered – and particularly so in more deprived areas (Hastings et al, 2012; Toynbee and Walker, 2015; see also, eg, Chapters Seven and Twelve). A particularly good example of the pressure exerted on public spending in local government concerns the area of social care (see Chapter Ten). Here, in order to keep overall spending roughly at 2010 levels, savings of £3.53 billion were achieved between 2010 and 2014 at a time of rising demand on care services as a result of increasing demographic pressures (LGA, 2014, p 11). These pressures are significant. According to Age UK (2015), the number of people over the age of 65 increased by 4.1% between 2012 and 2014, while the number of those aged 85 and over is growing proportionately faster. In this context, it is not surprising that the Care Quality Commission commented critically on the social cost of these savings, pointing to rising levels of service user abuse, cuts in the time that carers can spend with service users and reductions in the numbers and pay of care staff (Boffey, 2015).

Outside the DCLG, other departments also experienced significant spending reductions. For example, the Home Office and the Ministry of Justice cut spending on public order and safety in real terms and as a share of national income by 5.6% and 8.1%, respectively, between 2009/10 and 2015/16 (Keynes and Tetlow, 2014, p 32). In addition, the Ministry of Justice reduced the legal aid budget by £700 million over this period – a decision that deprived roughly 650,000 people of legal representation (Hynes, 2015). Elsewhere, BIS experienced overall reductions of 30.7% between 2010/11 and 2015/16 (Crawford et al, 2013), largely as a result of the fundamental reorganisation of university funding. The total loss of Higher Education Council for England funding in arts and humanities subjects and its reduction in the sciences were replaced by annual tuition fees derived from student loans, the result of this being a significant increase in university income – but an increase that made English higher education among the most expensive in the world. Arguments about the effects of this move abound – the most heated aspect being the question of whether fees, and therefore the prospect of future debt, could be having a negative impact on the willingness of students from low-income families to apply for university places. Whatever the finer points of the fee increase may be, there can be no doubt that the universities fared considerably better under the coalition than did colleges of further education. Here, reductions in the BIS 19+ further education budget amounted to 35% overall between 2009/10 and 2015/16, including a 50% reduction in capital spending and a 50% reduction in the non-apprentice adult skills budget. The introduction of 24+ loans did little to offset the impact of these cuts (Association of Colleges, 2014).

As noted earlier, certain departments – or parts of departments – were protected from the full force of public spending cuts. Of relevance here are the Department of Health and the Department for Education, which, at 2009/10 prices, were responsible for 17% and 10% of TME respectively. Health, which had enjoyed annualised average real increases of 5.9% between 1996/97 and 2007/08, and 3% between 2007/08 and 2010/11, continued to enjoy increases, though at a considerably more modest 0.9%, between 2010/11 and 2013/14 (Keynes and Tetlow, 2014, p 12) – not a rate that allowed spending to keep up with rising GDP. In consequence, it is more accurate to say that 'protection' for health spending amounted to a real-terms freeze and a fall in terms of health spending as a proportion of GDP. World Bank figures, which show UK health expenditure falling from 9.4% to 9.1% of GDP between 2010 and 2014, confirm this picture (World Bank, 2015).

School spending, which had risen sharply under New Labour, showed a modest fall of less than 1% during the coalition period, although this figure masks two issues in particular. First, the government restricted spending increases to the 5–16 age group, meaning that other groups fared less well. For example, spending on early years education was cut by 11% and on the Sure Start programme by 32% over the period (Lupton et al, 2015), while spending on 16–18 education also suffered from extensive cuts, which fell disproportionately on sixth form and further education colleges as opposed to school sixth forms (Association of Colleges, 2014). Second, shifts also occurred *within* the 5–16 schools budget as a result of the introduction of the Pupil Premium. This broadly progressive initiative saw extra money allocated to children in receipt of free school meals, looked-after children and children whose parents were in the armed forces, the result being that schools in deprived areas saw funding increases while those in affluent areas either experienced falls in funding (secondary schools) or less generous increases (primary schools) (Jarrett et al, 2015; Sutton Trust and Educational Endowment Foundation, 2015; see also Chapter Six).

Coalition government spending on social security

Although other chapters in this volume look at the fortunes of key social policy areas under the coalition government in greater detail, it is important to consider the various elements of social security spending in some depth because of the overall significance that this area plays in the public finances. Social security expenditure, which stood at a total of £214 billion in 2014/15, is responsible for over 23% of TME, with spending being divided among a range of areas (see Figure 2.3). In common with its overall spending record, the government's social security expenditure did not fall as much as could have been expected given the febrile environment of 'austerity' and the sustained efforts to blame its predecessor for the financial crisis. According to Hood and

Phillips (2015, p 1), the forecast level of benefit spending for 2014/15 'is virtually unchanged in real terms since 2010/11'. Nevertheless, it needs to be appreciated that overall spending on benefits will have been reduced by £16.7 billion between 2010/11 and 2015/16 (IFS, 2015a, p 2) – the amount that would have been spent on social security had no changes been imposed in 2009/10. These headline figures only provide a rough indication of what has happened in the area of social security over the past five years – and they mask a complex picture that, once taken into account, not only defines the government's approach to social policy, but also highlights the essentially political nature of its public spending agenda.

Figure 2.3: Social security spending in the UK, 2014/15

Note: 'Welfare Cap' denotes those areas subject to government-imposed cash limits.

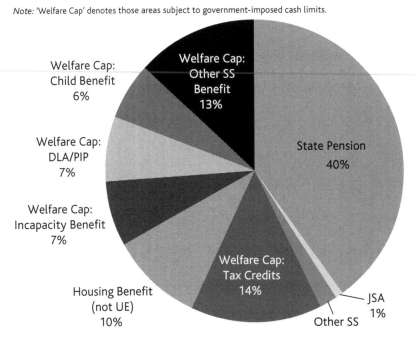

JSA (Jobseeker's Allowance), SS (social security), UE (unemployed), DLA (Disability Living Allowance), PIP (Personal Independence Payments)
Source: Calculated from OBR (2015a).

Despite widespread scepticism about New Labour's approach to welfare spending – most obviously its concern to move people into paid employment by tightening and widening eligibility rules (Dwyer and Ellison, 2009) – 'welfare spending has risen in cash, real and real spending per capita terms' over the past 30 years (OBR, 2015a, p 23). According to the Office for Budget Responsibility (OBR), this overall increase did not outstrip, but kept pace with, economic growth, with the result that 'the proportion of national income devoted to welfare spending has not shown a significant upward or downward trend over time' (OBR, 2015a, p 23). Over the period of the coalition government, this broad pattern held true, with social security slightly increasing in relation to GDP by 1.3%. In view of the coalition's undoubted stress on the importance of reducing the deficit and the consequent need for austerity in the public finances, it is perhaps surprising that social security spending increased at all. One possible explanation for the increase could be that it was caused by the higher levels of unemployment that occurred in the wake of the financial crisis, which necessitated a corresponding rise in Jobseeker's Allowance (JSA) and linked benefits, such as Housing Benefit (HB). In fact, from 2011, unemployment rates decreased from a short-lived high of just over 8% (a lower rate than those recorded in the recessions of the 1980s and early 1990s, when they topped 10%) to just over 6% by 2014 (OECD, 2015c). These comparatively low figures, which relate to what is, after all, a small component of social security spending, mean that JSA did not contribute to the overall spending increase (see OBR, 2015a, p 26). Rather, as many commentators (Hills, 2015; Hood and Phillips, 2015; Lupton et al, 2015; OBR, 2015a) have acknowledged, the principal reasons for the rise in social security spending were, first, the decision to increase the real-terms value of the state pension between 2010/11 and 2015/16 and, second, the 2.8% rise in the numbers of people of pensionable age over this period. To compensate for the increase in pensions spending, extensive economies were made elsewhere in the social security budget, as discussed later. The consequence of these changes has been a disaggregation of social security expenditure that is chiefly characterised by a shift away from support for those of working age towards those who have retired and left the labour market.

Turning to pensions first, the coalition's *Programme for government* stated that 'people need dignity and respect in old age, and that they should be provided with the support they need' (Cabinet Office, 2010, p 26). The evidence indicates that the government's pension policy broadly conformed to this objective. In his 2010 Budget, Osborne restored the earnings link for the basic state pension, originally removed by the Conservatives in 1980. The new system commenced in April 2011 and was, indeed, made potentially more generous by the 'triple lock' arrangement, whereby the value of the state pension was uprated annually in line with earnings, prices (Consumer Prices Index [CPI]) or 2.5%, whichever is the greatest. Reductions in pension credit and winter fuel allowances helped to balance the costs of the pension increase, although the overall effect of spending in this area over the period of the coalition government was an increase of £7 billion.

The generosity displayed by the coalition over the state pension was not extended to those areas of social security that relate to working-age benefits, all of which experienced reductions (see Chapter Eight). Figure 2.4 provides an overview of spending on the range of benefits dispensed by the DWP and Her Majesty's Revenue and Customs (HMRC), the latter being responsible for administering tax credits. As the chart makes clear, the state pension has risen consistently over time. However, spending aimed at those of working age, including tax credits and child benefits, which rose during New Labour's period of office, stabilised over the coalition period and is set to fall as a proportion of future social security expenditure. There is a need for caution here because, on one reading, even as spending on certain benefits was restrained, it nevertheless increased in real terms, largely due to factors beyond the government's immediate control. HB provides a good example of an area that the coalition wanted to control more tightly but was unable to cut significantly. Efforts to control the HB budget mainly took the form of a straightforward cash reduction for particular groups of claimants, including the vast majority of those who rented from private landlords. This was achieved by cutting Housing Allowance rates from April 2011 and therefore reducing the amount of rent covered by HB. Additional measures included the abolition of Housing Allowance rates for five-bedroom properties, and the imposition of national caps on these rates, which are now set according to movements in CPI. The latter change removed the link between local rent levels and the amount of HB paid to claimants, with the result that tenants in more expensive areas, such as London and many parts of the South East, immediately experienced a loss of income. Perhaps more notoriously, an Under-Occupancy Charge – better known as the 'bedroom tax' – of 14% for one extra bedroom and 25% for two was levied on tenants in social housing who were judged to have space that they did not 'need'.

These measures clearly caused difficulties for those in both the private and social housing sectors. Private renters, particularly those living in London, faced with the lowered Housing Allowance rates, saw the amounts of HB they could claim fall dramatically, while tenants in social housing were forced to find extra resources to pay the bedroom tax, or move to less spacious accommodation. In public spending terms, only modest savings amounting to roughly £350 million were achieved by the bedroom tax in 2013/14 – and this figure does not take account of the cost of supporting affected households, including evictions

Figure 2.4: DWP/HMRC social security spending 1991/92 to 2019/20, real terms (2015/16 prices)

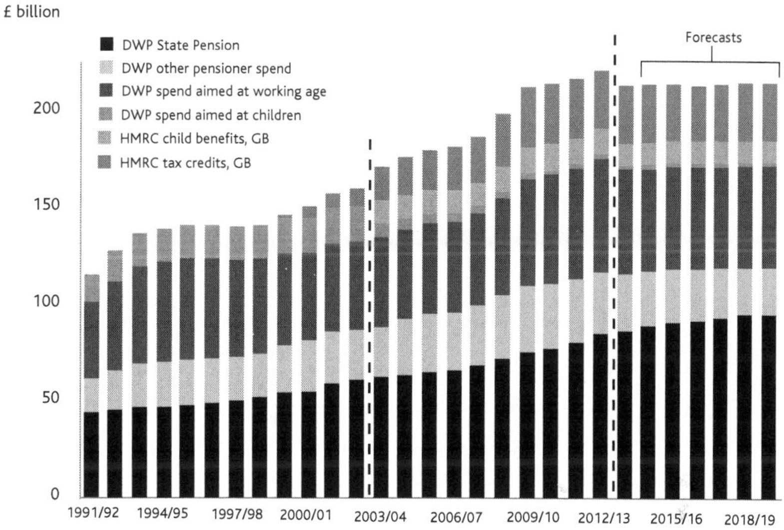
£ billion
DWP State Pension
DWP other pensioner spend
DWP spend aimed at working age
DWP spend aimed at children
HMRC child benefits, GB
HMRC tax credits, GB
Forecasts
200
150
100
50
0
1991/92
1994/95
1997/98
2000/01
2003/04
2006/07
2009/10
2012/13
2015/16
2018/19

Source: House of Commons Library (2015).

(Butler, 2014). Annual savings of roughly £500 million by 2015/16 are expected from the changes made to Housing Allowance rates and other reforms in the private rented sector, with savings continuing to increase as private rents rise (Hood and Phillips, 2015, p 17). These relatively modest economies were complemented by a £500 million fall in the amount of HB passported to JSA as unemployment declined, but this overall picture is offset by a number of countervailing factors. The OBR (2015a, pp 28–29) notes errors in its earlier Welfare Trends Reports that underestimated HB spending, and attributes these to three main factors associated with a 54% rise in the 'Housing Benefit only' caseload: the share of the population living in rented accommodation had risen, probably as a result of high and rising house prices in parts of England; earnings growth was weak during the coalition's period of office, which meant that some people who were in work but on low wages were eligible for HB; and, despite the cuts in, and indexation of, Housing Allowance rates, private rents continued to rise more quickly than anticipated, which clearly had an impact on HB payment levels.

This pattern of attempting to make savings by reforming aspects of the benefits system but seeing these efforts thwarted by factors beyond the immediate control of policymakers is evident in other areas of social security spending. For instance, the coalition made concerted efforts to reduce the size of disability benefits by tightening eligibility criteria. On coming to office, the government decided to implement New Labour's intended policy of migrating claimants off Incapacity Benefit into Employment and Support Allowance (ESA) and, further, attempted to reduce the rising numbers claiming DLA by replacing this benefit with more rigorously assessed Personal Independence Payments (PIPs). In both cases, a good deal of individual anxiety and hardship was created by policies that have, to date, not delivered significant savings. The transition to ESA not only progressed more slowly than anticipated, but was also complicated by highly controversial work capability assessments, the decisions of which were contested by 40% of claimants – with some success (Patrick, 2015a). Meanwhile, delays in the move to PIPs meant that predicted savings were not realised, at least in the short term. According to the OBR (2015a, p 27), higher caseloads were responsible for higher spending of £1.1 billion on ESA and DLA/PIPs than had been anticipated for 2014/15. It is likely, of course, that the complexities and delays associated with benefit migration contributed to the increased caseloads.

Given the relatively small value of these spending cuts, and the fact that spending on the state pension increased so rapidly between 2010 and 2015, where did the majority of reductions in the social security budget come from? A key factor here is the government's decision to index the majority of benefits, including the state pension, and tax credits to the CPI rather than the Retail Price Index (RPI). It is generally acknowledged that the RPI tends to provide higher estimates of inflation than the CPI, and this assumption broadly held true during the coalition's time in office. Both the Institute for Fiscal Studies (IFS) (Hood and Phillips, 2015) and the OBR (2015a) estimate that approximately £4 billion was saved by the move to CPI indexation, with just under a further £2 billion being saved by the decision to cap rises in working-age benefits and the value of tax credits to 1% for three years from 2013/14. Other headline changes involved reforms to tax credits themselves, which saw fewer adults eligible for support, a reduction of the income level at which child tax credit could be claimed, a cut in eligible childcare costs from 80% to 70% and significant reductions (from £25,000 in 2010 to £5,000 from April 2013) in income disregards. Hood and Phillips (2015, pp 8–9) estimate the overall saving from these measures to be just over £5 billion over the period, or £1.9 billion per year by 2015/16 relative to the position in 2009/10. A further significant saving came in the form of various cuts and adjustments to child benefit. The most eye-catching reform was the progressive removal of the benefit from families that had one individual earner with a taxable income of more than £50,000 – the entire benefit being removed for those with taxable earnings of £60,000 or more (see also Chapter Twelve). The policy came into effect in early 2013, and was accompanied by a freeze in the value of child benefit for 2013/14, with a further two years of increases of only 1%. Taken together, the saving from these adjustments amounted to a 0.1% fall in the cost of child benefit as a percentage of GDP, or roughly £3.5 billion.

These reforms, together with other more minor adjustments, produced the £16.7 billion total 'takeaway' in social security spending referred to by the IFS (2015b, p 2; see also earlier). It is important, however, that these changes are considered in the context of others that also affected income levels. For example, once tax changes such as increases in the personal allowance and Council Tax reductions are taken into account, the *overall* impact of the social security reforms in terms of the public finances was neutral. As Hills (2015, p 39) observes, although working-age benefits and tax credits were cut in real terms over the period:

> people paid less net Council Tax (as cuts of what was Council Tax Benefit were more than offset by Council Tax itself falling in value in real terms), and some gained from reduced Income Tax liabilities (with the increased personal allowance) and from state pensions rising faster than CPI-inflation.

To demonstrate neutrality so far as the public finances are concerned is, however, not the same thing as 'neutrality' in terms of the impact of spending cuts on different population groups. As Hills (2015, p 39) also points out, the distributional effects of the coalition's benefit and tax changes were, and continue to be, substantial. The fact that those in the poorest 20th percentile 'lost nearly 3 per cent of their incomes (before allowing for indirect taxes) and the next five-twentieths approaching 2 per cent' while those in the top half of the distribution – excluding the top 20th – were net gainers (largely as a result of increases in the personal allowance), says much about the nature of the coalition's approach to public spending, and demonstrates clearly that different groups were, indeed, treated differently (see also Chapter Fourteen).

The reasons for this differentiation are not hard to discern and have much to do with the coalition government's attempt to reset the moral contours of state and society. From the outset, the coalition, and specifically the Chancellor, mounted an intense and persistent campaign to convince the public that welfare spending was both too high and counterproductive because it created dependency. As Osborne (2010) made clear in his 2010 Budget statement, the policy response would be to 'increase the incentives to work, and reduce the incentives to stay out of work'. This general strategic approach was subsequently honed into a sharper assault on those who were not in paid work. Osborne, for example, in his speech to the Conservative Party conference in 2012, distinguished explicitly between 'strivers' and 'shirkers' in his comment about 'the shift-worker leaving home in the dark hours of the early morning, who looks up at the closed blinds of their [sic] next door neighbour sleeping off a life on benefits' (Osborne, 2012). David Cameron echoed these sentiments, stating in his New Year message for 2013 (Cameron, 2012) that the government wanted to 'get behind everyone who wants to work hard and get on in life' and those 'who work hard and aspire for a better life for their families'. For the Liberal Democrats, Nick Clegg referred frequently to 'alarm clock Britain' as a means of demonstrating support for low- and middle-income earners – the implication being that the low incomes and living standards of those in receipt of benefits are somehow of less concern, presumably because of their absence from the paid labour market.

Welfare and public spending in the UK

This resort to a politics of division, redolent of the former Poor Law distinctions between the deserving and undeserving, poses fundamental questions about the future of the UK welfare state. Until recently, it has been possible to depict the changes that have been made to the UK's welfare system over the past 30 years as a gradual process of 'reshaping' or 'recalibration' rather than outright retrenchment (see Pierson, 1994, 2001). This view can be contested, to be sure (Taylor-Gooby, 2013; Farnsworth and Irving, 2015) – certainly in terms of the impact of various 'reforms' on individuals' lives (Garthwaite, 2013; Patrick, 2015b) – but it is nevertheless possible to argue that the institutional structures and functions of welfare systems in the developed economies have broadly persisted despite increasingly restrictive eligibility rules and cuts in replacement rates (Pierson, 2001). In some quarters, there is even optimism that where institutional change has occurred, it has taken the form of a positive response to significant changes in the nature of social risks (Bonoli and Natali, 2012; Hemerijck, 2013). Certainly, fickle labour markets, underemployment, the absence of appropriate services for families and children as gender roles shift, the need to invest in social care, and the increasingly complex problems posed by ageing societies demand imaginative solutions that arguably require new forms of social investment to complement traditional institutional responses to the 'old' risks associated with poverty and inequality originally targeted by post-war collectivist welfare states.

Whether, in fact, 'social investment' is quite the panacea that its supporters hope is not entirely clear, not least because so much depends on the political, or 'regime', context in which new welfare responses are developed and implemented. It is not possible to consider this issue in detail here. Suffice it to say that there is a danger that the 'social investment state' of the kind Hemerjick discusses amounts in reality to little more than a softer version of neoliberalism – at least in certain contexts. This, after all, is the charge commonly levelled at New Labour, whose preoccupation with labour market activation, in-work benefits and education and family policies has been regarded as an example of the social investment approach (Bonoli and Natali, 2012). New Labour, however, is long gone and of more immediate importance is the question of whether the coalition's attitude to public and social spending (and that of the current Conservative government) has ignored *both* a social investment and a more straightforward 'social protection' approach to welfare in favour of a broad assault on the very idea of welfare itself.

There is clearly reason for concern. As this chapter has demonstrated, not only have many government departments responsible for delivering core components of social policy had their budgets severely cut, but both out-of-work and in-work benefits have also been reduced in various ways. This downward pressure has caused hardship for the most deprived and marginal sections of the UK population, including children and disabled people, and those of working age who are both in and out of paid employment. 'Austerity' and 'deficit reduction' have been the ideological tools, deployed as policy rationales, to effect far-reaching 'disaggregating' changes in spending patterns – and, of course, the austerity programme is destined to continue until at least 2019/20. With a real, if slender, parliamentary majority, Osborne's renewed focus on the deficit means that it remains the guiding principle of his 'responsible' economic policy. In his July 2015 Budget Speech, Osborne claimed that the achievement of a predicted £10 billion budget surplus by 2019/20 would signal that the UK would 'finally [be] doing the responsible thing and raising more money than it spends' (HM Treasury, 2015a, p 4). The policies designed to meet this questionable objective are draconian. They include £37 billion of 'consolidation measures' (HM Treasury, 2015b, p 19), with policies designed to achieve £17 billion of this total, including a further £12 billion of welfare cuts, having been announced in the July 2015

Budget (IFS, 2015b). To achieve the latter, the current freeze on tax credits and the Housing Allowance rate is to be extended to 2020, and further reductions in the earnings levels required to qualify for tax credits and Universal Credit (when the latter is finally fully introduced) are also planned. These measures will be accompanied by the removal of tax credit increments for those who have more than two children, the lowering of the benefits cap from £26,000 to £23,000 for those living in London and £20,000 for others, and the removal of HB for 18 to 21 year olds. In Johnson's (2015, p 2) view, 'the changes overall are regressive – taking much more from poorer households than richer ones'. Meanwhile, according to the IFS (Emmerson, 2015), cuts to unprotected departments will need to average 15.3% between 2015/16 and 2018/19 if the overall £37 billion target is to be met. If these reductions are achieved, TME is predicted to fall from its current 40.7% of GDP to approximately 36.3% (OBR, 2015b, p 108) – the lowest level for generations.

Looking at the coalition's public spending record and the proposed spending strategy of the current Conservative government, it is hard to detect any commitment to a programme of social investment, let alone to more traditional forms of social protection for those experiencing the sharp end of austerity. In closing, it is worth contrasting the current approach to public and social spending with the expansive integrationist strategy that would be required to support a 'welfare society' grounded not in a politics of deficit reduction, but in a universal ethic of care. Here, spending would be used to create a coherent, integrated set of institutions that, as Williams (2001, p 489) has written, would bring together 'strategies for childcare, for the care and support of older people and disabled people, for income support, for family policies and family law, for employment and education policy, for anti-poverty and antidiscrimination measures, and for the environment'. Such an approach would grant as much space to the 'social' as to the 'economic' and, in addition to a developed growth strategy (Hay, 2013), would require a tax structure designed to ensure that private corporations and the better-off sections of society contributed appropriately to a fair distribution of wealth and income (see, eg, Wilkinson and Pickett, 2009; Piketty, 2014). We are, indeed, a long way from this.

Notes

[1]   All figures in this chapter are exclusive of government spending on the banks. According to the National Audit Office (NAO), the actual *cash* cost of the bank bailouts in 2008/09 was £132 billion, but a further £1 trillion was pledged in the form of guarantees. These figures have reduced over time, and, indeed, the NAO regards the

overall cash transfer as an 'investment' from which returns to the taxpayer are expected over the long term. The cost of interest payments on government borrowing to support the banks is hard to estimate. An annual figure of between £4 billion and £5 billion has been produced by the NAO, but this reduces to roughly £1.5 billion once bank payments to government in the form of fees and charges on the loans are taken into account.

[2] The deficit reference value is part of the EU's Stability and Growth Pact and refers to the point above which (3% of GDP) a member state's deficit is deemed to be excessive and in need of correction through the Excessive Deficit Procedure.

[3] The Charter, originally produced in 2011, sets out the terms of operation of the welfare cap. The Department for Work and Pensions has to account to Parliament for unapproved breaches of the agreed spending limit within 28 sitting days of the breach (Rhodes, 2015, pp 7–8).

References

Age UK (2015) 'Later life in the United Kingdom'. Available at: http://www.ageuk.org.uk/Documents/EN-GB/Factsheets/Later_Life_UK_factsheet.pdf?dtrk=true (accessed 28 August 2015).

Association of Colleges (2014) *College funding and finance*, London: Association of Colleges.

Berry, C. and Hay, C. (2014) 'The Great British "rebalancing act": the construction and implementation of an economic imperative', *British Journal of Politics and International Relations*, Early View version. Available at: http://onlinelibrary.wiley.com/doi/10.1111/1467-856X.12063/full (accessed 15 September 2015).

Boffey, D. (2015) 'Cash-starved, demoralised and sometime cruel: how England's social care system fails the most frail among us', *The Observer*, 9 August, pp 8–9.

Bonoli, G. and Natali, D. (2012) 'The politics of the "new" welfare states: analysing reforms in Western Europe', in G. Bonoli and D. Natali (eds) *The politics of the new welfare state*, Oxford: Oxford University Press, pp 3–17.

Butler, P. (2014) 'The Bedroom Tax has failed on every count', *The Guardian*, 28 March.

Cabinet Office (2010) *The coalition: our programme for government*, London: The Stationery Office.

Cameron, D. (2012) 'New Year message', *The Daily Telegraph*, 31 December.

Crawford, C., Crawford, R. and Winchao, J. (2013) *The outlook for higher education spending by the Department of Business, Education and Skills*, London: Institute of Fiscal Studies.

Dwyer, P. and Ellison, N. (2009) 'Work and welfare: the rights and responsibilities of unemployment in the UK', in M. Giugni and P. Statham (eds) *The politics of unemployment in Europe: policy issues and collective action*, Aldershot: Ashgate, pp 53–66.

Emmerson, C. (2015) 'Public service spending: more cuts to come', *Observations*, 16 June, London: IFS.

Esping-Andersen, G. (1990) *The three worlds of welfare capitalism*, Cambridge: Polity Press.

Farnsworth, K. and Irving, Z. (2015) 'Austerity: more than the sum of it parts', in K. Farnsworth and Z. Irving (eds) *Social policy in times of austerity: global economic crisis and the new politics of welfare*, Bristol: The Policy Press.

Gamble, A. (2015) 'Austerity as statecraft', *Parliamentary Affairs*, 68(1): 42–57.

Garthwaite, K. (2013) 'Fear of the brown envelope: exploring welfare reform with long-term sickness benefits recipients', *Social Policy and Administration*, 49(2): 199–212.

Hastings, A., Bailey, N., Gannon, M., Besemer, K. and Bramley, G. (2012) *Serving deprived communities in recession*, York: Joseph Rowntree Foundation.

Hastings, A., Bailey, N., Gannon, M., Besemer, K. and Bramley, G. (2015) 'Coping with the cuts: the management of the worst financial settlement in living memory', *Local Government Studies*, 41(4): 601–21.

Hay, C. (2013) 'Treating the symptom not the condition: crisis definition, crisis reduction and the search for a new British growth model', *British Journal of Politics and International Relations*, 15(1): 23–37.

Hayton, R. (2014) 'Conservative Party statecraft and the politics of coalition', *Parliamentary Affairs*, 67(1): 6–24.

Hemerjick, A. (2013) *Changing welfare states?*, Oxford: Oxford University Press.

Hills, J. (2015) *The coalition's record on cash transfers, poverty and inequality 2010–2015*, CASE Working Paper 11, London: CASE/LSE.

HM Treasury (2004) 'A stronger, more productive economy', Spending review. Available at: http://webarchive.nationalarchives. gov.uk/20071204130111/http:/hm-treasury.gov.uk/media/B/6/ sr2004_ch4.pdf (accessed 15 August 2015).

HM Treasury (2010a) 'Budget report'. Available at: http://webarchive. nationalarchives.gov.uk/20130129110402/http:/www.hm-treasury. gov.uk/d/junebudget_complete.pdf (accessed 15 July 2015).

HM Treasury (2010b) *Spending review 2010*, London: The Stationery Office.

HM Treasury (2014) *Public expenditure statistical analyses 2014*, Cm 8902, London: HMSO.

HM Treasury (2015a) *Chancellor George Osborne's Summer Budget 2015 speech*. Available at: http://www.gov.uk/government/people/george-osborne (accessed 6 December 2015).

HM Treasury (2015b) *Budget Report*, London: The Stationery Office.

Hood, A. and Phillips, D. (2015) *Benefit spending and reforms: the coalition government's record*, IFS Briefing Note BN160/Election 2015 Briefing Note 3, London: IFS/Nuffield Foundation.

House of Commons Library (2015) 'Social security expenditure: social indicators summary'. Available at: http://researchbriefings.parliament. uk/ResearchBriefing/Summary/SN02656#fullreport (accessed 27 August 2015).

Hynes, S. (2015) 'The choice is yours', *New Law Journal*, 16 April. Available at: http://www.newlawjournal.co.uk/nlj/content/choice-yours (accessed 15 July 2015).

IFS (Institute for Fiscal Studies) (2015a) *This government has delivered substantial spending cuts*, Election Brief, London: IFS.

IFS (2015b) *Underlying pressures mean that benefit has not fallen, despite significant cuts in generosity*. Available at: http://election2015.ifs.org. uk/benefits (accessed 6 December 2015),

Jarrett, T., Long, R. and Foster, D. (2015) *School funding; the Pupil Premium*, Briefing Paper, The House of Commons Library, London: House of Commons.

Johnson, P. (2015) 'Opening remarks', IFS Summer Post-Budget Briefing. Available at: http://www.ifs.org.uk/uploads/publications/ budgets/Budgets%202015/Summer/opening_remarks.pdf (accessed 27 August 2015).

Jowett, A. and Hardie, M. (2014) *Longer-term trends – public sector finance*, London: Office for National Statistics.

Keynes, S. and Tetlow, G. (2014) *Survey of public spending in the UK*, London: IFS.

LGA (Local Government Association) (2014) *Adult social care funding: state of the nation report*, London: Local Government Association/ Association of Directors of Social Services.

Liberal Democrats (2010) *Liberal Democrat manifesto*, London: Liberal Democratic Party.

Lowndes, V. and McCaughie, K. (2013) 'Weathering the perfect storm? Austerity and institutional resilience in local government', *Policy and Politics*, 41(4): 533–49.

Lupton, R. with Burchardt, T., Fitzgerald, A., Hills, J., McKnight, A., Obolenskaya, P., Stewart, K., Thomson, S., Tunstall, R. and Vizard, P. (2015) *The coalition's social policy record: policy, spending and outcomes 2010–2015*, CASE Research Report 4, January, London: CASE/LSE.

Marshall, P. and Laws, D. (2004) *The orange book: reclaiming liberalism*, London: Profile Books.

OBR (Office for Budget Responsibility) (2015a) *Welfare trends report*, London: The Stationery Office.

OBR (2015b) *Economic and fiscal outlook for 2015*, London: The Stationery Office.

OECD (Organisation for Economic Co-operation and Development) (2015a) 'Government at a glance'. Available at: http://www.oecd. org/gov/govataglance.htm (accessed 28 July 2015).

OECD (2015b) 'Country statistical profiles'. Available at: https://stats. oecd.org/Index.aspx?DataSetCode=CSP2012 (accessed 6 July 2015).

OECD (2015c) 'OECD statistics'. Available at: http://stats.oecd.org/ Index.aspx?DatasetCode=STLABOUR# (accessed 6 July 2015).

Office for National Statistics (2015) 'Government net borrowing and gross debt'. Available at: http://www.ons.gov.uk/ons/rel/psa/maast-supplementary-data-tables/q1-2015/stb---june-2015.html#tab-Summary-of-general-government-net-borrowing-and-gross-debt (accessed 6 July 2015).

Osborne, G. (2010) 'A new economic model', Maïs Lecture, 10 February. Available at: http://www.totalpolitics.com/print/ speeches/35193/george-osborne-mais-lecture-a-new-economic-model.thtml (accessed 6 July 2015).

Osborne, G. (2012) Speech to Conservative Party conference, 8 October. Available at: www.newstatesman.com (accessed 6 August 2015).

Patrick, R. (2015a) 'Working on welfare: findings from a qualitative longitudinal study into the lived experiences of welfare reform', *Journal of Social Policy*, 43(4): 705–25.

Patrick, R. (2015b) 'Irresponsible citizens? The lived experiences of welfare reform', unpublished PhD thesis, School of Sociology and Social Policy, University of Leeds.

Pierson, P. (1994) *Dismantling the welfare state? Reagan, Thatcher and the politics of retrenchment*, Cambridge: Cambridge University Press.

Pierson, P. (2001) 'Coping with permanent austerity: welfare state restructuring in affluent democracies', in P. Pierson (ed) *The new politics of the welfare state*, Oxford: Oxford University Press, pp 410–56.

Piketty, T. (2014) *Capital in the twenty-first century*, Boston, MA: Harvard University Press.

Rhodes, C. (2015) *The welfare cap*, Briefing Paper 06852 27th November, London: House of Commons Library.

Shaw, K. (2012) 'The rise of the resilient local authority?', *Local Government Studies*, 38(3): 281–300.

Sutton Trust and Educational Endowment Foundation (2015) *The Pupil Premium: the next steps*, London: Sutton Trust.

Taylor-Gooby, P. (2012) 'Root and branch restructuring to achieve major cuts: the social policy programme of the 2010 UK coalition government', *Social Policy and Administration*, 46(1): 61–82.

Taylor-Gooby, P. (2013) *The dual crisis of the welfare state*, Basingstoke: Palgrave.

Toynbee, P. and Walker, D. (2015) *Cameron's coup: how the Tories took Britain to the brink*, London: Guardian Books/Faber and Faber.

Wilkinson, R. and Pickett, K. (2009) *The spirit level*, London: Allen Lane.

Williams, F. (2001) 'In and beyond New Labour: towards a new political ethics of care', *Critical Social Policy*, 21(4): 467–93.

World Bank (2015) 'Health expenditure'. Available at: http://data.worldbank.org/indicator/SH.XPD.TOTL.ZS (accessed 22 August 2015).

THREE

The changing governance of social policy

Catherine Bochel

Introduction

In recent decades, we have become more aware that the ways in which policies are formulated, implemented and evaluated can, in many respects, be as important as the policies themselves, and this has been particularly evident in social policies, particularly from the 1980s onwards. Under successive governments, we have seen considerable continuities in the ways in which social policies have been made and implemented, with, for example, broad preferences for markets and competition as ways of delivering services, together with a shift in responsibility from the state towards individuals and families, and, perhaps to a more limited extent, communities. However, there have also been some differences in emphasis, perhaps most obviously in Labour's greater willingness to increase public expenditure on public services from 1997 until the financial crisis of 2008, and in the introduction of devolved legislatures for Northern Ireland, Wales and Scotland under the Labour government, which, to some extent, ran counter to the centralising tendency of much of the period since 1979, and which, in turn, allowed for a potentially greater diversity of approaches across the UK, as discussed in Chapter Fifteen.

Prior to the 2010 general election, both the Conservatives and Liberal Democrats had developed a variety of proposals that might have been expected to impact upon the ways in which social policy is made and delivered. For the Conservatives, those included changes to the ways in which legislation passes through the House of Commons (such as a Public Reading Stage for bills), some devolution of power to local authorities (although, at the same time, proposing to allow local residents to veto high council tax rises), reducing the number and power of quasi-autonomous non-governmental organisations (quangos), replacing the Human Rights Act with a Bill of Rights, and emphasising a significant role for voluntary and community groups, rather than the state, in the provision of social policy. Among the Liberal Democrats' proposals were support for mutuals, cooperatives and social enterprises, a ban on politicians being involved in the day-to-day running of schools, and changing the electoral system. The *Programme for government* negotiated by the two parties included a number of proposals drawn from the manifestos of the two parties (Cabinet Office, 2010). This chapter considers the governance of social policy under the Conservative–Liberal Democrat coalition government, including the implications of its broader political and public service reforms, and, more recently, the initial weeks of the Conservative government elected in May 2015.

Why the governance and mechanisms of policymaking and implementation matter

From the 1990s, there has been a growing awareness of the importance of the processes of formulation, implementation and evaluation in the development and management of policies. Prior to this period, 'government' and 'governance' tended to be seen as synonymous, so that Finer (1970, pp 3–4) defined government as 'The activity or process of governing' or 'governance' and 'The manner, method or system by which a particular society is governed'. More recently, there has been a greater emphasis on the differences between the two terms, with Rhodes (1997, p 15, emphasis in original), for example, noting that 'The term "governance" refers to a change in the meaning of government, referring to a *new* process of governing', so that 'Governance' therefore 'tries to make sense of the changing nature of the state' (Richards and Smith, 2002, p 14), recognising that we no longer live (if, indeed, we ever did) in a society where everything is controlled by a government at the centre. Instead, there are many different actors, organisations and centres of power at local, regional, national, transnational and global levels, all linking a less coherent and more fragmented process of policy- and decision-making.

The notion of governance is clearly complex. Rhodes (1997, p 15), for example, notes that 'There are many uses of governance', and suggests that 'It has too many meanings to be useful'. Yet, much has been and continues to be written on 'governance', and it is not the intention to explore these debates further here. For present purposes, Stoker's (1998, p 18, cited in Newman, 2001, p 12) observation that 'Governance recognises the capacity to get things done which does not rest on the power of government to command or use its authority. It sees government as able to use new tools and techniques to steer and guide' is perhaps appropriate (see also Pierre and Peters, 2000; Newman, 2001; Richards and Smith, 2002).

The discussion in this chapter reflects a number of the dimensions of political approaches identified in Table 1.1 in Chapter One of this book, perhaps most significantly those associated with citizenship, the mixed economy of welfare, mode and accountability, although it also draws upon several of the other dimensions. The chapter also considers the tools, or 'instruments', that governments have sought to use to achieve their ends. Most policy goals could, at least in theory, probably be accomplished using different instruments, but the choice of instruments may tell us something about the preferences of governments and their preferences for particular means in seeking to achieve their policy ends. There have been many attempts to produce categories, or taxonomies, of policy instruments, but that produced by Christopher Hood (1983), known as 'NATO', has been influential. Hood argued that all policy tools derive from one of four broad categories of governing resource, so that governments address problems through: the use of the information that they possess as key policy actors ('Nodality' – being at the centre of a network); legal powers ('Authority' – the power to demand, forbid, guarantee or adjudicate); financial resources ('Treasure'); or the formal organisations available to them ('Organisation'). So, governments might make certain information available (or not), may choose to finance different things, could use their coercive powers to force other actors to undertake particular activities or might simply undertake activities themselves. While direct provision by governments, funded through taxation, was arguably fairly widely used in social policy from 1945 to 1979, the period since then has seen governments using other instruments in their attempts to achieve their social policy goals. Much early work on policy instruments was heavily influenced by economists, and therefore tended to focus on *substantive* instruments – tools that more or less directly affect the type, quantity or price of goods or services. Later on, more attention came to be paid to *procedural* instruments – those that might affect other parts of the policy process, rather than simply social or economic behaviour. While there are alternative classifications (eg Salamon and Elliott, 2002; Howlett, 2011), Hood's remains valuable, not least for its relative simplicity and its widespread adoption by other authors. Another relatively simple categorisation might be to view governance through the '"structures" by which social policy is governed, and ... "styles" of governance' (Bochel and Bochel, 1998, p 58), with styles, from that perspective, being essentially the broad approaches taken by governments, for example, 'managerialism' and 'the new institutional economics', while structures are the specific policy delivery mechanisms, which might include markets, privatisation, standards and performance measures, the centralisation of power, devolution, and mechanisms to give consumers more say in service provision. These different categorisations are useful for the purposes of this chapter because they enable the governance of social policy to be viewed and interpreted through a variety of lenses.

Governance under the Conservatives, 1979–97

Between 1979 and 1997, the Conservatives introduced a wide range of changes to the ways in which policy was made and implemented, reinforcing the perception of a shift from government to governance. Many of these directly impacted upon social policy. These structures included the use of internal markets in the National Health Service (NHS) and education, privatisation, the use of performance measures and standards, the increased use of arm's-length government (including quangos and Next Steps Agencies), the reform and residualisation of local government, and the introduction of a range of mechanisms designed to give consumers a greater say in the operation and delivery of services (see, eg, Bochel and Bochel, 2004).

In addition, the general style of governance changed under the Conservatives. Until 1988, their approach arguably reflected an emphasis on 'managerialism', based on a belief that private sector performance tools could benefit the public sector in order to make central and local government more efficient and effective. From 1988, there was a shift towards approaches based on 'the new institutional economics', with 'incentive structures' being introduced into public service provision and 'Greater competition through contracting out and quasi-markets; and consumer choice' being central to this (Rhodes, 1997, pp 48–49). These changes were underpinned by New Right beliefs that bureaucracies lacked central control and were self-interested, inefficient and wasteful of public resources (Niskanen, 1971, 1973). The Conservatives therefore took a top-down approach in an attempt to address the perceived problems of bureaucracy through the transfer of performance measures and initiatives seen as successful in the private sector to the public sector, and an emphasis on efficiency, effectiveness and economy. This led to the reduction and removal of functions from local authorities, including through legislation such as the Education Reform Act 1988, the Housing Act 1988 and the Local Government Act 1988. Attempts to extend consumer influence over services were also reflected in the introduction of new methods of redress and the introduction of charters for citizens. However, the use of macro-governance structures such as quangos, non-departmental government bodies and Next Steps Agencies to undertake a range of non-essential functions previously undertaken by central and local government reflected tensions around power and control, which continue to the present day, with the devolution of power and control over non-essential functions such as policy implementation and service delivery, while control over core functions such as policy formulation is retained, described by Rhodes (1997) as indicative of the shift from government to governance.

Governance under Labour, 1997–2010

When Labour came to power in 1997, they continued the approach of previous Conservative governments in a range of areas, including: stressing the role of local authorities as enablers rather than providers of services; the utilisation of a range of providers from the public, voluntary and private sectors; and the use of mechanisms of audit and inspection to try to improve quality and standards in services. However, at the same time, they demonstrated a new and more radical approach in some areas. In particular, following referendums in the autumn of 1997, the Scottish Parliament and the Welsh Assembly came into being on 1 July 1999, while the Northern Ireland Assembly came into existence on 2 December 1999. While there were already significant differences in social policies between the constituent elements of the UK, the creation of these bodies arguably served to raise awareness of these, as well as enabling the possibility of a greater diversity of approaches, particularly as political control of the UK's various legislative bodies changes. The Human Rights Act 1998 incorporated the European Convention of Human Rights (ECHR) into law, giving individuals who believed that their human rights had been infringed the opportunity to pursue their case in the domestic courts, a cheaper and less time-consuming process than having to appeal to the European Court of Human Rights, which was the process before the Act was passed. In addition, Labour sought to 'modernise' local government in England through encouraging, and later requiring, councils to adopt new decision-making structures, mirroring those in Westminster in order to try to improve the transparency and accountability of local government (DETR, 1998).

As with the Conservatives, alongside structural change, Labour sought to bring new approaches to policymaking and implementation, including through encouraging 'joined-up government' and 'evidence-based' policymaking. In general, particularly from 1997 to 2005, these changes were associated with a more 'rational' approach to policymaking, with its focus on coordination and cooperation (Bochel and Duncan, 2007). This was also reflected by a somewhat more open and consultative approach, including attempts to engage with pressure groups and the public, and through the use of reviews, commissions and inquiries. However, like the Conservatives, Labour retained a fondness for top-down approaches and for central control, including through the widespread use of performance measures, league tables and mechanisms of audit and inspection. Like the Conservatives, they also sought to encourage consumer choice in public services, but while few people would disagree with being given more choice, its presentation as a straightforward uncontested concept is far from the reality in public services (Clarke and Newman, 2006).

A preference for a broadly rational approach to policymaking was arguably also visible in other parts of Labour's approach, including through the introduction of the Comprehensive Spending Reviews and Public Service Agreements. Comprehensive Spending Reviews set out public spending plans, usually for a period of three years rather than on the annual basis that had previously been the norm. Linked to this, Labour established Public Service Agreements for government departments, setting out targets for each and how these would be measured (Cabinet Office Strategic Policy Making Team, 1999).

It is clearly possible to identify common themes and approaches by Conservative and Labour governments from 1979 to 2010, particularly those associated with the use of managerialism, markets and consumer choice in attempts to improve the quality of provision, and a general preference for top-down policymaking by the centre, with a continued residualisation of the role of local government in social policy. Perhaps the greatest differences were in Labour's greater willingness to use public expenditure to develop social provision, even if, like the Conservatives, they remained keen to use market-like mechanisms and user choice, and in the creation of the devolved legislatures, as discussed further in Chapter Fifteen.

The governance of social policy under the coalition government, 2010–15

The Conservative–Liberal Democrat coalition government, led by David Cameron as Prime Minister, with Nick Clegg as Deputy Prime Minister, was formed following the general election of May 2010. The parties set out their initial plans in the *Programme for government* as part of the coalition agreement (Cabinet Office, 2010). Although a hung Parliament was not unexpected, there was a lack of recent precedents for a coalition government, and neither party was likely to be able to govern in the way they might have if there were a majority government. An inner cabinet comprising David Cameron, George Osborne, Nick Clegg and Danny Alexander, known as the Quad, was set up in order to facilitate the working of the coalition in practice, and was also intended to underline a commitment by both parties to making the coalition work.

This section analyses a number of elements of social policy governance as they developed under the coalition. While some of these, such as initiatives around the 'Big Society', were largely focused around social issues and policy responses, others were part of much wider attempts to reform and reshape the public sector.

Although to some extent overshadowed by debates over levels of public expenditure and their implications (as emphasised throughout this book), reform of the public sector did receive considerable attention under the coalition government, as highlighted by a speech in 2014 by Francis Maude, Minister for the Cabinet Office, in which he identified five key components of the reforms: open government, using transparency and open data; tight centralised control over activities that cross government, such as procurement and management information, including reducing the size of the civil service and consequent reductions in the need for buildings and such like; loose control over operations, including breaking up the public sector monopoly over service provision; digital developments, providing services online by default, and using open standards and open source software; and innovation, with public servants developing commercial and leadership skills and having the freedom to take risks and to try new ideas (Maude, 2014). These reforms clearly draw on ideas associated with 'nodality', 'authority' and 'organisation'.

However, while those may have been key means behind the coalition government's reforms, the two parties' views of the role of the state meant that, as with the Thatcher governments, there was significant emphasis placed on rolling back the state, including some aspects of what they perceived as intrusion into people's lives, with reforms of the public sector as a key dimension of this.

Austerity and public expenditure

As noted throughout this book, the dominance of the austerity narrative for the bulk of the period of the coalition government, with an emphasis almost entirely on lowering the deficit by reducing public expenditure rather than through increasing taxes, was clearly important in terms of policymaking and implementation. This was the case for a number of reasons: it set the tone for much policymaking, with the emphasis on restricted budgets (and how the government would use its 'treasure'); decisions to protect some policy areas (notably, the NHS and state pension, and also international aid) inevitably meant that others, such as housing, tax credits and income support, would be harder hit, and that cuts would not fall evenly across government departments; and the similarities between the parties over key policy areas, such as reducing the deficit, increasing the marketisation of the NHS, promoting academies and giving schools greater freedom from local authority control, served to facilitate a neoliberal approach to many aspects of social policy (Taylor-Gooby, 2012), reflecting the preferences and priorities of many in the coalition government and its similarities with New Right ideas, as highlighted in Table 1.1.

The decision of the government to deal with the consequences of the economic downturn primarily through cuts in public expenditure, and the determination to reduce the deficit through rapid and deep cuts in spending, made it unlikely that some of the pre-election ambitions of the two parties, such as ending child poverty, would figure significantly in the goals of the coalition government. There were also other casualties, so that, for example, the Liberal Democrats abandoned their commitment to abolish higher education tuition fees, while the Conservatives' plan to raise the threshold for inheritance tax to £1 million was withdrawn. However, that did not stop some key members of the government, such as David Cameron, Nick Clegg, Iain Duncan Smith and George Osborne, continuing to use language referring to compassion, fairness and social justice in relation to the government's social policy aims.

Commissioning and efficiency savings

Commissioning was central to much of the coalition's reform agenda, at least partly underpinned by an idea that it would make the public sector more efficient and would increase productivity, including through the greater use of payment by results (eg KPMG, 2010).

Perhaps in part in an attempt to allay anxieties that commissioning and payment by results would lead to privatisation and the dominance of private sector organisations, but also reflecting manifesto commitments from both parties (and linking 'treasure' and 'organisation' forms of policy instruments), in 2011, the government created a Mutuals Taskforce, led by Professor Julian LeGrand of the London School of

Economics (LSE), which was intended to support the development of mutuals and cooperatives. An early assessment by the All Party Group on Employee Ownership (2011) suggested that those organisations that had made the transition to become public service mutuals were very satisfied, but that the idea behind them was not well understood within government, and that there was a need for safeguards to ensure that they were not demutualised before they were able to demonstrate the value of the approach. According to what is now the Mutuals Information Service (2015), there are currently over 100 public service mutuals operating across England, the great majority of which are providing health care, social care or children's services. However, in many service areas, not only has provision by mutuals been limited, but other third sector organisations have also found that larger private providers have dominated.

Even in the NHS, following Andrew Lansley's reorganisation (see Chapter Five), Timmins (2014) has argued that commissioning has not worked as intended, so that, for example:

> Some clinical commissioning groups are succumbing to advice to put services out to tender when they do not really want to, while some organisations that want to resist change are citing the potential loss of competition as a reason to block changes that others believe are to patients' advantage.

Alongside commissioning, there were a series of other managerialist-type approaches used by the coalition to try to improve efficiency and reduce public expenditure, many of which, as with the reforms of the Thatcher period, clearly drew on a belief that the private sector is a model of good practice that the public sector should mirror. As discussed in greater detail in Chapter Six, in education, for example, the role and powers of local government appear to be being eroded, with new providers being given the opportunity to enter the education sector, while a number of local councils, such as Barnet and Suffolk, put forward radical proposals to outsource all but a handful of services.

However, while widening the diversity of provision across the public sector may increase choice for the consumer, at the same time, it can create problems in terms of the fragmentation of services: economies of scale are less likely because of the wide variety of providers, and there are often problems with implementation because of the different agendas of the implementing agencies, inadequate resources and because no single body has overall control over these agencies. This can also lead to problems with accountability since, often, no one is sure who is accountable to whom and for what (Clarke et al, 2007).

Localism and the Big Society?

'Localism' was a topic that the coalition government placed considerable emphasis on, particularly in its early years; yet, it was never a particularly clear or consistent concept, with a wide range of policies being labelled 'localist'. It has also been characterised as giving responsibility for responding to problems to local authorities and communities without allowing them the resources to do so, resulting in a further rolling back of the state (Featherstone et al, 2012; Clarke and Cochrane, 2013; Maclennan and Sullivan, 2013).

The most obvious sign of the coalition's approach in this area came with the Localism Act 2011, which set out a range of measures to shift power away from central government, through the granting of supposed freedoms and flexibilities for local government, and powers for individuals and communities. Some of the initiatives intended to 'empower' communities were embodied in new 'community rights'. For example, a 'community right to bid' required local authorities to keep a list of assets of community value, which have been nominated by the local community, such as libraries, community centres and swimming pools, and provides time for community groups to raise money to bid for such an asset when it comes up for sale. If a community group expresses an interest in bidding, then a moratorium is applied, beginning from when the asset is put up for sale (House of Commons Library, 2015). It is, however, only a community right to bid, and not to buy, so that there is no certainty that any bid by a local community will be successful.

On similar lines, a 'community right to challenge' gave voluntary and community groups, parish councils, and council employees new powers to challenge and bid for running local authority services. The Act also introduced a 'community right to build', which came into force in 2012 and was intended to allow local communities to take forward their own plans for development without the need for a conventional planning application, providing they meet minimum criteria and can demonstrate local support through a referendum, which, in theory, gives neighbourhoods more control over planning in their area.

There is not a great deal of information available on the use of these schemes, with the most useful source being the House of Commons Department for Communities and Local Government (DCLG) Committee report from February 2015, which noted that for the community right to bid, 11 assets had been bought by community groups and 122 had triggered the moratorium period. In addition, 1,800 had been listed, of which 500 were pubs (House of Commons Library, 2015). However, DCLG evidence to the Committee stated that only nine assets had been bought. The 'community right to challenge' is backed by the Social Investment Business, the largest social investor in the UK, which administers a fund of £10 million in grants. As of December 2014, the DCLG Committee reported that there had been 50 expressions of interest (House of Commons Library, 2015). Finally, despite being supported by funding of £20 million, by July 2014, only eight applications to fund community right to build orders had been made, and by December 2014, referendums had taken place on three where voters were in favour. Under the coalition government, therefore, these aspects of 'localism' can perhaps be described, at best, as a very lukewarm success.

A key concern of the Conservative manifesto, and, indeed, much of their talk in the run-up to the May 2010 general election, was about the need to mend Britain's broken society and how a change 'from big government to Big Society' (Conservative Party, 2010, p vii) could help achieve this. The Liberal Democrat manifesto talked of putting 'power back where it belongs: into the hands of the people. We want to see a fair and open political system, with power devolved to all the nations, communities, neighbourhoods and peoples of Britain' (Liberal Democrats, 2010, p 87). Both party manifestos emphasised localism and devolving power, including the idea of mutual providers, as discussed earlier. However, much of this was arguably a continuation of a broader theme, a shift away from state provision and the development of a more market-like consumerist approach, together with attempts to encourage citizen participation and involvement in decision-making and the shaping of services, which, as noted earlier, had been apparent under both previous Labour and Conservative governments, each of which stressed, at various times, the importance of consumer choice, citizen involvement and responsive services, with the Conservatives, in particular, favouring greater use of market mechanisms.

While there was less talk of the Big Society by the coalition after the election, particularly once a series of attempts to relaunch the idea by David Cameron failed to make any significant impact upon public opinion, in terms of the realities of governance, there nevertheless continued to be a shift away from government providing and delivering services towards an increasingly diverse range of providers. However, while the government continued to talk about the role for social enterprises, and community and local groups, who were encouraged to take over local services such as libraries and parks, in many areas, such as employment services and work with offenders, the bulk of such provision came from the private sector, including large service companies such as SERCO and Atos (eg CSEI, no date; Damm, 2012; TUC 2013). For the coalition, this approach served a number of purposes: it enabled the state to take a reduced role in service provision; it worked to contract the size and scope of the welfare state, including through greater marketisation; and it removed powers from local authorities. However, as with previous governments, shifting control of services away from the state and the fragmentation of systems of provision meant a consequent need for more regulation, through the use of ranking systems, inspections, targets, business plans, performance data and, potentially, the increasing encouragement of Open Government Data (OGD), elements of which are discussed later. As the relationships between central government and the increasing diversity of providers became even more complex, this created further challenges in being able to have a clear overview of what is happening, while continuing to raise issues around accountability and the importance of regulation – the creation of Regional Schools Commissioners to oversee academies with the residualisation of local authorities in terms of education being one example of a fairly ad hoc approach to dealing with such challenges.

As with its Labour and Conservative predecessors, the coalition government sought to encourage the growth of volunteering, which was clearly in line with its vision of a smaller state and a more active civil society. However, the range of new initiatives was limited, with the most prominent being the creation of a National Citizen Service programme for 16 and 17 year olds in England. This was piloted in 2011, by 2013, there were 30,000 young people taking part, and by 2014, 100,000 individuals had been involved. A Prime Minister's Points of Light award, developed in partnership with the Points of Light programme in the US, and the Big Society Awards recognise outstanding individuals, groups and organisations who are making a difference in their communities. The Society Network Foundation charity established A Big Society Network in 2010 to support and promote initiatives in this area, including the Big Society Awards. It was funded by public sector and National Lottery grants. However, in 2014, it was put into administration.

In terms of the provision of other resources to support 'Big Society' developments, the coalition announced a Big Society Bank in 2011. By 2012, the bank had been renamed Big Society Capital (a 'social investment bank'), funded by £400 million from dormant bank accounts, enabled by the Labour government's Dormant Bank Accounts Act, and £200 million from large high street banks. The bank cannot directly invest in social enterprises, but does so through intermediaries, such as fund managers and specialist banks, who then lend funding to organisations. One initiative, social impact bonds (Sibs), were seen as a way of unlocking private investment for services that the government would not have funded, such as to help children who are otherwise likely to go into care stay safely at home. With the pressure on public expenditure, these did appear to have the potential to release additional funding, and there have been a number of relatively positive early evaluations, but while Sibs have continued to be used, they have perhaps not taken off in the way that their supporters might have wished, with only 31 Sibs established by 2015 (Big Society Capital, 2015).

Attempts to 'nudge'

Moving on to a very different approach, early in its period of office, the coalition government showed considerable interest in ideas of 'nudging' citizens to behave in what they perceived as more desirable ways, with governments' perceived ability to provide information and influence networks (nodality, in Hood's terms) perhaps helping explain some of the appeal, together with a view that such changing behaviour might be cheaper than governments providing services to deal with subsequent problems. Although such ideas have been around for some time, and, indeed, were explored by the Labour government (eg Halpern et al, 2004), they were popularised in Thaler and Sunstein's (2008) *Nudge: improving decisions about health, wealth and happiness*, which suggested that it is often possible to influence what people do through reminders and cues, rather than compulsion or control. Critics, however, have argued that nudging may be insufficient to change behaviour (eg House of Lords Science and Technology Select Committee, 2011; British Medical Association, 2012), or that a combination of interventions may be necessary.

George Osborne (2008) and Andrew Lansley were among the enthusiasts for such an approach, with Lansley suggesting that people would be nudged into making healthier choices around food, exercise, smoking and alcohol (eg *The Telegraph*, 2010), although he was criticised for attempting to use voluntary rather than regulatory agreements with big business to tackle obesity and alcohol abuse by nudging customers into making healthier choices (House of Commons Health Committee, 2011).

A Behavioural Insight Team was established in the Cabinet Office only two months after the 2010 general election, which was intended to act as a champion for such ideas and to work across many areas of government (Hickman, 2011), and, indeed, a number of changes followed (eg Cabinet Office, 2011), which were claimed to have saved £300 million by 2012 (Cabinet Office, 2012). However, there appears to have been no further move to mainstream such ideas and activities within government, and from 2014, the Behavioural Insight Team became a free-standing company, part-owned by the government, its employees and Nesta (formerly the National Endowment for Science Technology and the Arts).

Evidence-based policy and the use of government data

While the coalition government continued to pay lip service to the use of evidence in policy, its critics suggested that this idea was even more fraught than it had been under Labour. Developments such as the creation of the Office for Budget Responsibility and the Educational Endowment Foundation may have been seen as encouraging developments by some (Rutter, 2012), but others were more sceptical, perhaps reflecting the views expressed by the Liberal Democrat MP Norman Baker, who resigned as a Home Office minister in 2014, saying that there was little evidence for rational evidence-based policy in the Home Office (see also, eg, Partos, no date; Exley and Ball, 2011; Bamfield, 2012; Williams, 2015).

In March 2013, the government announced the establishment of a number of 'what works' centres to guide decision-making on £200 billion of public spending in areas such as crime, ageing, early intervention and local economic growth (Cabinet Office, 2013). These centres, supported by organisations such as the ESRC (Economic and Social Research Council), Nesta and the Big Lottery Fund, were intended to provide high-quality evidence for decision-makers. However, by the time of the 2015 general election, it was arguably too early to assess their influence, and it may be that the view of the Institute for Government in 2014 remains the most appropriate assessment of their role and success so far:

> Together, these centres have made considerable progress in pulling together available evidence on effective interventions and sharing it with frontline practitioners. Some have also helped fill gaps in our knowledge by commissioning trials. But they will need far greater support

from Whitehall if they're to fulfil their ultimate objective of informing decision-making on £200 billion of public spending. (Gold, 2014)

Building on the previous Labour government's focus on evidence-based policy and the trend for OGD, the coalition government appeared to be determined to release, and make better use of, much of the data collected by governments. The argument was that local authorities, government departments and other public bodies should make available non-personal data for all, free of charge. Under the coalition, David Cameron published commitments to release data in the health sphere on prescribing by GP practices and complaints against NHS hospitals, among other things. There have perhaps been two main strands to this: the first is primarily at the level of making information available to individuals, and chimes with ideas such as choice, efficiency, accountability, political and civic engagement, and trust in government bodies, as well as with the potential to improve policy outcomes through consumer (or perhaps citizen) pressures; the second is more closely linked with ideas of evidence-based policy and improving productivity in public services through providing organisations (private, public or not-for-profit) with information that would enable them to develop new services and ideas, or to improve existing provision. However, there may also be a further motive underlying the OGD agenda, since, as Bates (2014) has argued:

> [by] making the core of the agenda a focus on the transparency of public spending data, the government were also able to use OGD to help bolster a broader public discourse that framed public spending as wasteful and unaccountable, and thus pave the way for the implementation of a policy of long term austerity.

Quangos and 'arm's-length' government

Previous Labour and Conservative governments had both been committed to reducing the number of 'arm's-length' bodies, but both also made significant use of them (drawing on elements of 'authority' and 'nodality', as well as 'organisation', so that while from 1979 to 1997, there was a reduction in the number of non-departmental public bodies (NDPBs), the levels of public expenditure going through them soared, and from 1997 to 2009, there was a further reduction in the number of such bodies but expenditure continued to increase significantly (see Flinders et al, 2014). The coalition government came to office promising to reduce 'the number and cost of quangos' (Cabinet Office, 2010). It therefore undertook a review suggesting that NDPBs would only be retained where:

1. they undertook a precise technical operation;
2. there was a need for impartial decisions to be made about the distribution of public monies; or
3. there was a need for facts to be transparently determined, independent of political interference. (Flinders et al, 2014, p 69)

Views of the extent of change achieved vary. For example, initially, 901 bodies were reviewed and, as a result, 192 were to be axed or merged, 380 were to be kept, while the remainder would stay under consideration (see: http://www.number10.gov.uk/news/public-body-review-published/). In addition, the government's arguments over the purposes of the reforms altered somewhat, from a position that had emphasised both savings and transparency, to one where transparency was given as the main justification, although the National Audit Office (2012) had reservations over whether the promised level of savings would be achieved. However, Flinders et al note that while the number of NDPBs fell only slightly between 2009 and 2012 (from 192 to 185), the level of spending fell markedly, from £46.5 billion to £31.2 billion. Even where NDPBs have been abolished, Flinders et al argue that, in many instances, their functions have been transferred to other forms of arm's-length bodies. Indeed, the continued importance of NDPBs in social policy is apparent from the continued role of those such as Ofsted and Ofqual, the Pensions Advisory Service and Pensions Regulator, the National Institute for Health and Care Excellence, Monitor, and the Care Quality Commission in the fields of education, pensions and health and social care.

In addition, the coalition's changes have resulted in changes to the governance of public bodies, with the centre, and, in particular, the Cabinet Office, having much greater knowledge and much tighter control over NDPBs, to the extent that some have questioned the viability of the 'arm's-length' relationship. It is also apparent that the coalition government's focus had 'been on one species of arm's-length body (the NDPB) while other equally important species (e.g. public corporations, executive agencies, special health authorities, non-ministerial departments, etc.) have received far less attention' (Flinders et al, 2014). The coalition government also stopped providing the level of information on NDPBs that had been given by the Major, Blair and Brown governments.

Devolution and the union

Although devolution is covered in more depth in Chapter Fifteen, it forms an important element of the governance of social policy. It is therefore perhaps worth noting that the 2010 Conservative manifesto supported the changes 'proposed by the Calman Commission for clarifying the devolution settlement' and 'will not stand in the way of a referendum on further legislative powers requested by the Welsh Assembly' (Conservative Party, 2010, p 83). The coalition government accepted the report of the Calman Commission (2009) for a further transfer of financial powers to the Scottish Parliament and legislated for that in the Scotland Act 2012. Similarly, in Wales, the Silk Commission's recommendations on fiscal powers were legislated for in the Wales Act 2014, including making provision for the devolution of taxation powers to the National Assembly, and for the setting by the Assembly of a rate of income tax.

Perhaps most notably, in September 2014, a referendum on Scottish Independence was held, with the result seeing 55% voting to remain part of the union, following a promise by the three main UK political parties of further devolution of power to Scotland. As it transpired, the implementation of that promise would fall to the Conservative government elected in May 2015, although its manifesto promised to 'honour in full our commitments to Scotland to devolve extensive new powers' (Conservative Party, 2015, p 69), and to 'provide the Scottish Parliament with one of the most extensive packages of tax and spending powers of any devolved legislature in the world' (Conservative Party, 2015, p 70).

Devolution to England's regions

Along with questions over the oversight of 'England-only' legislation, the existence of the devolved legislatures had also prompted demands for some form of devolution within England, and while the previous Labour government's proposals had fallen by the wayside, in June 2014, the Chancellor, George Osborne, made a speech in Manchester in which he argued:

> The cities of the north are individually strong, but collectively not strong enough. The whole is less than the

sum of its parts. So the powerhouse of London dominates more and more. And that's not healthy for our economy. It's not good for our country. We need a Northern Powerhouse too.… Able to provide jobs and opportunities and security to the many, many people who live here, and for whom this is all about. (Osborne, 2014)

He announced plans to create an elected mayor for Greater Manchester, 28 years after Margaret Thatcher's Conservative government had abolished Greater Manchester Council. The new position, to come into being in 2017, was to run across the 10 councils in the region, which were responsible for £5 billion of public expenditure in 2014, with suggestions that a further £2 billion would follow. The new mayor will have substantial powers over transport, housing and planning (including a housing investment fund of up to £300 million), and will also oversee social care and police budgets. In addition, in early 2015, it was announced that there would be the devolution of £6 billion allocated for health and social care to the region's 10 councils and health groups, with full powers being devolved in 2016. However, some have criticised the latter initiative as it will involve no powers to determine levels of funding, and with major challenges in both health and social care, this was seen as problematic.

It is, of course, too early to assess the likely positive or negative impacts of such developments. From the government's perspective, they allow it to claim to be devolving power, including some elements of expenditure, together with a consequent ability to respond to local needs and priorities, as well as enhancing accountability through the creation of directly elected mayors. On the other hand, while the new arrangements may allow for control over spending, they have no influence over the total levels of spending and may end up simply having to make decisions over where to reduce expenditure, and perhaps taking the blame for decisions that are made by central government.

Parliament

While the Fixed Term Parliaments Act 2011, the referendum on the Alternative Vote system for general elections the same year and the Conservatives' proposals to reduce the number of MPs were the subject of considerable attention early in the life of the coalition government, it was some of the coalition's ideas for changes to the way that Parliament operates that could arguably have had more immediate significance for the making and scrutiny of social policy, although, ultimately, their impact was much less than it might have been. For example, while a new Backbench Business Committee was created, in theory, giving the House of Commons more control over its own timetable, in practice, the Committee's powers were quite limited, including in relation to the number of debates it could schedule. In addition, while both parties had developed proposals for reform of the House of Lords prior to the 2010 general election, there was no progress on these, and, indeed, the number of peers continued to increase as the coalition parties built up their numbers in the Upper House.

There was also some emphasis on enabling the public to get more involved, such as through the introduction of an e-petition system in July 2011. However, while there were thousands of petitions and millions of signatures, including on a variety of social policy topics, such as health, education, benefits and immigration, these remained largely peripheral to the work of both government and Parliament.

Following a proposal in the 2010 Conservative manifesto to introduce a new Public Reading Stage for bills in order to give the public an opportunity to comment on proposed legislation online, the coalition did pilot a public reading for a number of government bills, including the Children and Families Bill 2012–13. However, given that many interest groups are already involved in the scrutiny of legislation through links with MPs, and that the media frequently raise issues of concern, it might be questionable whether this new stage in the legislative process will add any significant value, and, indeed, it has yet to be rolled out further.

Conclusions

Given the apparent broad agreement between the two coalition parties on many issues related to policymaking and implementation, and on the desirability for a reduction in the size of the public sector, it is perhaps unsurprising that there were relatively few areas of conflict between them on these topics. Where there were differences, they were largely related to long-standing party commitments, such as that of the Liberal Democrats to electoral reform, or where there were perceived to be fairly direct electoral or political benefits or risks, largely in relation to electoral and parliamentary reform, and these perhaps explain the lack of progress in those areas.

Away from Parliament, the developments outlined in this chapter highlight, from a policy instruments perspective, particular changes under the coalition in the government's use of 'treasure' and 'organisation' together, with the emphasis on reducing the deficit through cuts in public expenditure rather than increasing taxes, and attempts to encourage the provision of services by new providers though the creation and use of markets, social enterprises and community organisations, supported to varying degrees by payments, grants and loans, in place of the direct provision of services funded through taxation. However, one consequence of this was that the government was forced to use elements of its 'authority' in a different way, in that there were pressures on it to respond to the consequent fragmentation of delivery and concerns about quality through the establishment of standards and new regulatory bodies. In addition, the coalition government also sought to change the use of information-based (nodality) instruments, as in the use of 'behavioural insights' and the release of government data, in ways that it believed would help fulfil its wider objectives. These also clearly reflect the political positioning of the coalition government, as identified in Table 1.1, and its emphases on deregulation, the shifting of responsibilities to individuals and civil society, and its preference for the market and competition. Other areas of activity, such as devolution, can be seen as reflecting different changes in the use of authority, nodality and treasure.

Drawing on the 'dimensions of political approaches' set out in Chapter One, it is possible to identify a number of dimensions similar to both parties at this time. Perhaps most evident is the focus on the 'citizenship' dimension, with a shift from the state providing services to responsibility being shifted to individuals, families, communities and civil society, together with the preference for competition and private and other non-state provision in the 'mode' and 'mixed economy of welfare' dimensions, while accountability is transmitted through both market-type and informational mechanisms to individuals and civil society.

The 2015 Conservative government

The May 2015 general election gave the Conservatives their first working majority since 1992, leaving them free to implement the promises set out in their manifesto. Whereas during 2010–2015, they had been constrained by being in coalition with the Liberal Democrats, this was no longer the case, although, paradoxically, it did mean that David Cameron was more reliant on his backbench MPs than he had been previously.

Public spending, devolution and Europe were some of the main issues highlighted in the Queen's Speech of May 2015, which had the potential to impact on social policy in the 2015–20 Parliament.

In the first few months of the Parliament, the government underlined their commitment to reducing the deficit and bringing public finances 'under control' through plans to implement a further £30 billion of cuts, including £12 billion to welfare expenditure. In the Budget, George Osborne announced a significant increase in the minimum wage by 2020, designed to offset some of the welfare cuts. However, with a freeze on tax credits and working-age benefits for four years, limiting the child element of tax credits for new claimants to two children, alongside changes to Housing Benefit, the impact of the cuts was likely to be felt mainly by the poor.

The devolution of powers to Scotland and Wales, legislation to give effect to the Stormont House Agreement in Northern Ireland, and at the regional level, the announcement of a Cities and Local Government Devolution Bill, designed to enable cities and combined authorities that agree to an elected mayor to receive more powers over strategic planning, transport, health, social care and skills training and to help bring about a 'northern powerhouse', were all a feature of the Queen's speech. However, at the time of writing, there was uncertainty over the extent to which the devolution of powers would actually take place. Furthermore, investment in the rail infrastructure intended to drive the 'northern powerhouse' was either shelved or put on hold in June 2015, bringing into question the government's commitment to the wider project. Similarly, in 2015, the Conservatives promised to introduce legislation to provide an in/out referendum on membership of the European Union before the end of 2017. They also said that they would renegotiate the UK's relationship with the European Union and pursue reform of the European Union for the benefit of all member states. However, again, there was a significant lack of clarity over what such reform might entail, including its relevance for social policy.

References

All Party Group on Employee Ownership (2011) *Sharing ownership: the role of employee ownership in public service delivery*, London: All Party Group on Employee Ownership.

Bamfield, L. (2012) 'Child poverty and social mobility: taking the measure of the coalition's "new approach"', *Political Quarterly*, 83(4): 830–7.

Bates, J. (2014) 'The progressive ideals behind Open Government Data are being used to further interests of the neoliberal state'. Available at: http://blogs.lse.ac.uk/impactofsocialsciences/2014/10/02/open-government-data-and-the-neoliberal-state/ (accessed 7 July 2015).

Big Society Capital (2015) 'We're planning to call for a new outcome finance fund'. Available at: http://www.bigsocietycapital.com/blog/were-planning-call-new-outcome-finance-fund (accessed 26 August 2015).

Bochel, C. and Bochel, H. (1998) 'The governance of social policy', in E. Brunsdon, H. Dean and R. Woods (eds) *Social policy review 10*, London: Social Policy Association, pp 57–74.

Bochel, C. and Bochel, H. (2004) *The UK social policy process*, Basingstoke: Palgrave.

Bochel, H. and Duncan, S. (2007) *Policy-making in theory and practice*, Bristol: The Policy Press.

British Medical Association (2012) *Behaviour change, public health and the role of the state – BMA position statement*, London: British Medical Association.

Cabinet Office (2010) *The coalition: our programme for government*, London: Cabinet Office.

Cabinet Office (2011) *Applying behavioural insights to reduce fraud, error and debt*, London: Cabinet Office.

Cabinet Office (2012) 'Government's nudge unit goes global', press release, 20 September. Available at: https://www.gov.uk/government/news/governments-nudge-unit-goes-global (accessed 29 June 2015).

Cabinet Office (2013) *What works: evidence centres for social policy*, London: Cabinet Office.

Cabinet Office Strategic Policy Making Team (1999) *Professional policy making for the twenty first century*, London: Cabinet Office.

Calman Commission (2009) *Serving Scotland better: Scotland and the United Kingdom in the 21st century*, Edinburgh: Commission on Scottish Devolution.

Clarke, J. and Newman, N. (2006) 'The people's choice? Citizens, consumers and public services', paper for International Workshop 'Citizenship and Consumption: Agency, Norms, Mediations and Spaces', Kings College Cambridge, 30 March to 1 April.

Clarke, J., Newman, J., Smith, N., Vidler, E. and Westmarland, L. (2007) *Creating citizen-consumers: changing publics & changing public services*, London: Sage.

Clarke, N. and Cochrane, A. (2013) 'Geographies and politics of localism: the localism of the United Kingdom's coalition government', *Political Geography*, 34: 10–23.

Conservative Party (2010) *The Conservative manifesto 2010: invitation to join the government of Britain*, London: Conservative Party.

Conservative Party (2015) *The Conservative Party manifesto 2015: strong leadership, a clear economic plan, a brighter, more secure future*, London: Conservative Party.

CSEI (Centre for Social and Economic Inclusion) (no date) 'Policy guides: work programme'. Available at: http://cesi.org.uk/keypolicy/work-programme (accessed 2 July 2015).

Damm, C. (2012) *The third sector delivering employment services: an evidence review*, Working Paper 70, Birmingham: Third Sector Research Centre, University of Birmingham.

DETR (Department of the Environment, Transport and the Regions) (1998) *Modern local government: in touch with the people*, London: The Stationery Office.

Exley, S. and Ball, S. (2011) 'Something old, something new: understanding Conservative education policy', in H. Bochel (ed) *The Conservative Party and social policy*, Bristol: The Policy Press, pp 97–117.

Featherstone, D., Ince, A., Mackinnon, D., Strauss, K. and Cumbers, A. (2012) 'Progressive localism and the construction of political alternatives', *Transactions of the Institute of British Geographers*, 37(2): 177–182.

Finer, S.E. (1970) *Comparative government*, London: Allen Lane.

Flinders, M., Dommett, K. and Tonkiss, K. (2014) 'Bonfires and barbecues: coalition governance and the politics of quango reform', *Contemporary British History*, 28(1): 56–80.

Gold, J. (2014) 'What works centres: can they deliver', Institute for Government. Available at: http://www.instituteforgovernment.org.uk/blog/9633/what-works-centres-can-they-deliver/ (accessed 2 July 2015).

Halpern, D., Bates, C., Mulgan, G., Aldridge, S., Beales, G. and Heathfield, A. (2004) *Personal responsibility and changing behaviour: the state of knowledge and its implications for public policy*, London: Cabinet Office.

Hickman, M. (2011) 'Nudge, nudge, wink wink … how the government wants to change the way we think', *The Independent*, 3 January. Available at: http://www.independent.co.uk/news/uk/politics/nudge-nudge-wink-wink-how-the-government-wants-to-change-the-way-we-think-2174655.html (accessed 11 September 2015).

Hood, C. (1983) *The tools of government*, London: Macmillan.

House of Commons Health Committee (2011) *Public health, twelfth report of session 2010–12*, London: The Stationery Office.

House of Commons Library (2015) *Assets of community value*, SN/PC/06366, London: House of Commons.

House of Lords Science and Technology Select Committee (2011) *Behaviour change*, Second Report of Session 2010–12, London: The Stationery Office.

Howlett, M. (2011) *Designing public policies: principles and instruments*, London: Routledge.

KPMG (2010) *Payment for success – how to shift power from Whitehall to public service customers*, London: KPMG.

Liberal Democrats (2010) *Liberal Democrat manifesto 2010*, London: Liberal Democratic Party.

Maclennan, D. and Sullivan, A. (2013) 'Localism, devolution and housing policies', *Housing Studies*, 28(4): 599–615.

Maude, F. (2014) 'Future of government services: 5 public service reform principles', speech in Dubai, 10 February. Available at: https://www.gov.uk/government/speeches/future-of-government-services-5-public-service-reform-principles (accessed 2 July 2015).

Mutuals Information Service (2015) 'Mutuals Information Service'. Available at: https://www.gov.uk/government/groups/mutuals-information-service (assessed 11 September 2015).

National Audit Office (2012) *Reorganising central government bodies*, London: The Stationery Office.

Newman, J. (2001) *Modernising governance: New Labour, policy and society*, London: Sage.

Niskanen, W. (1971) *Bureaucracy and representative government*, Chicago, IL: Aldine-Atherton.

Niskanen, W. (1973) *Bureaucracy: servant or master?*, London: Institute of Economic Affairs.

Osborne, G. (2008) 'Nudge, nudge, win, win', *The Guardian*, 14 July. Available at: http://www.theguardian.com/commentisfree/2008/jul/14/conservatives.economy (accessed 11 September 2015).

Osborne, G. (2014) 'Chancellor: "We need a Northern Powerhouse"', speech at the Museum of Science and Industry, Manchester, 23 June. Available at: https://www.gov.uk/government/speeches/chancellor-we-need-a-northern-powerhouse (accessed 29 June 2015).

Partos, R. (no date) 'No immigrants, no evidence? The making of Conservative Party immigration policy'. Available at: http://www.psa.ac.uk/insight-plus/no-immigrants-no-evidence-making-conservative-party-immigration-policy (accessed 3 July 2015).

Pierre, J. and Peters, B.G. (2000) *Governance, politics and the state*, Basingstoke: Macmillan.

Rhodes, R. (1997) *Understanding governance: policy networks, governance, reflexivity and accountability*, Buckingham: Open University Press.

Richards, D. and Smith, M.J. (2002) *Governance and public policy in the UK*, Oxford: Oxford University Press.

Rutter, J. (2012) *Evidence and evaluation in policy making: a problem of supply or demand?*, London: Institute for Government.

Salamon, L. and Elliott, O. (2002) *The tools of government: a guide to the new governance*, Oxford: Oxford University Press.

Stoker, G. (1998) 'Governance as theory: 5 propositions', *International Social Science Journal*, 155: 17–28.

Taylor-Gooby, P. (2012) 'Root and branch restructuring to achieve major cuts: the social policy programme of the 2010 UK coalition government', *Social Policy & Administration*, 46(1): 61–82.

Thaler, R.H. and Sunstein, C.R. (2008) *Nudge: improving decisions about health, wealth and happiness*, New York, NY: Penguin.

The Telegraph (2010) 'A healthy nudge', 1 December. Available at: http://www.telegraph.co.uk/comment/telegraph-view/8172546/A-healthy-nudge.html (accessed 11 September 2015).

Timmins, N. (2014) 'Happy returns for the health reforms?'. Available at: http://www.instituteforgovernment.org.uk/blog/7526/happy-returns-for-the-health-reforms/ (accessed 30 June 2015).

TUC (Trades Union Congress) (2013) *Justice for sale – the privatisation of offender management services*, London: TUC.

Williams, Z. (2015) 'The strange new world of evidence-free government', *The Guardian*, 8 February. Available at: http://www.theguardian.com/commentisfree/2015/feb/08/government-ministers-cost-cutting-pr (accessed 3 July 2015).

FOUR

The coalition, social policy and public opinion

Andrew Defty

Introduction

The 2015 general election is likely to be the election that opinion pollsters prefer to forget. The unexpected election of a majority Conservative government represented the most significant failure of UK opinion polling since the 1992 general election. Whether the failure of many of the polls to predict a Conservative majority is attributed to sampling error, shy Tories or some other reason may, or may not, be revealed by the British Polling Council inquiry, which was announced shortly after the election. However, a broader assessment of public attitudes towards central parts of government policy on public spending and welfare does perhaps suggest that the political climate was conducive to a Conservative victory in 2015, and perhaps more so than in 2010.

Several studies have highlighted a hardening of public attitudes towards the poor in recent years, and towards the unemployed in particular. This began under the previous Labour government and continued under the coalition (Taylor-Gooby, 2013; Baumberg, 2014; Hills, 2015). This chapter will examine public attitudes towards social policies, focusing in particular on those adopted by the Conservative– Liberal Democrat coalition and Conservative governments elected since 2010. It argues that while there is considerable evidence for a hardening of public attitudes towards benefits recipients, the public remain committed to state provision in a range of areas, and that evidence of public support for benefit cuts should be seen in the context of other areas of public concern, such as inequality. The chapter draws on British Social Attitudes data to examine long-term trends in attitudes towards public expenditure and the role of state in welfare provision. The annual British Social Attitudes survey has tracked changes in public support for state-funded provision in a wide range of areas since 1983, and is widely regarding as having high methodological standards. The chapter also deploys public opinion polling data from a range of polling organisations, most notably, Ipsos MORI and YouGov, to examine the public's response to more recent changes. While such polls may perhaps be less accurate than has previously been assumed, they remain the best data we have on public attitudes towards recent developments, and also provide more frequent snapshots that allow for more detailed tracking of trends than annual surveys such as British Social Attitudes. Nevertheless, wherever possible, conclusions have not been based on the results of single polls or the findings of any one polling organisation.

Switching off the thermostat: attitudes towards tax and spending

The Conservatives fought the 2010 general election on the need to cut the deficit by reining in public spending. Following the election, a programme of deep and swift public spending cuts was introduced under the coalition government. Although this involved significant cuts across most government departments, spending in some areas was protected while others were subject to less stringent cuts. Overseas aid, for example, was ring-fenced and defence spending was not subject to the same level of cuts as other government departments. In relation to social policy, spending on mass welfare services such as health, education and state pensions was protected while significant cuts were made to spending on social housing and welfare benefits. There were also significant cuts to local government budgets, which had an impact on the provision of services such as housing and social care, and had the added advantage for the government of shifting responsibility for the imposition of cuts onto local authorities (see also Chapter Two). The Conservative government elected in 2015 remained committed to a deficit reduction strategy based on public spending cuts. Plans for a further £12 billion cut in welfare spending were heavily trailed in the run-up to the 2015 general election, and were announced in the new government's first Budget in July 2015.

There is some evidence of public support for retrenchment in public spending prior to and since the election of the coalition government in 2010. Data from British Social Attitudes indicate that support for increased spending on health, education and social benefits has been falling since 2003 (see Figure 4.1). Although support for cuts to tax and spending has consistently remained at a low level since the survey began in 1983, in recent years, there has been an increase in support for keeping tax and spending at the same level. Since 2008, more people have supported this than have supported tax-funded increases in provision, and throughout the period of the coalition government, more than half of respondents have been in favour of maintaining public spending at current levels.

Figure 4.1: Attitudes towards tax and spend, 1983–2014

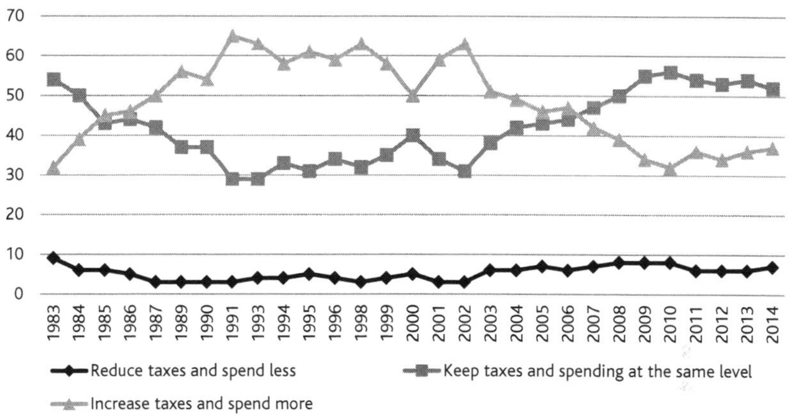

Source: Taylor-Gooby (2015).

Fluctuations in public support for taxation and public spending have been explained by reference to a 'thermostatic' effect. According to this argument, most prominently advocated by John Curtice (2010a), support for spending is linked to public perceptions about whether spending is increasing or in decline. During times of austerity as public spending declines, support for increased provision goes up. As public spending increases and is perceived to meet need, support for more spending begins to decline. The data in Figure 4.1 appear to support this thesis. During the 1980s and 1990s, as successive Conservative governments sought to cut public spending, the proportion of people supporting an increase in public spending even if this meant an increase in taxation began to rise steeply and remained at over 50% through the 1980s and 1990s. Following several years of increased spending under Labour, albeit with little increase in direct taxation, support for tax-funded increases in provision began to fall. According to Curtice (2010b), the thermostatic effect created a climate that made the election of a Conservative government in 2010 more likely. However, what is striking about recent surveys is that despite significant cuts in public spending, higher levels of unemployment and rising poverty, there is little evidence of a shift in public opinion back towards increased spending. In short, the thermostat does not, at present, appear to be working.

Indeed, other data suggest increased public acceptance of the programme of cuts imposed by the coalition government. On a regular basis, usually around twice a month, throughout most of the last Parliament, YouGov asked a series of questions about the nature, depth and speed of the government's cuts to public spending (YouGov, 2015a). The results can be seen in Figures 4.2 and 4.3. In February 2011, when it first polled on this question, 51% thought the government was cutting too deeply, while only 25% thought that the level of cuts was about right. By the time of the 2015 general election, the proportion who felt that the government was cutting too deeply had fallen to 39%, while the proportion who thought that the level of cuts was about right had risen to 36%. Although there was a small increase in support for deeper cuts during the Parliament, rising to 16% in April 2013, the proportion of those in favour of deeper cuts was the same at the end of the Parliament as in 2011.

Figure 4.2: Is the way in which the government is cutting spending too deep, too shallow or about right?

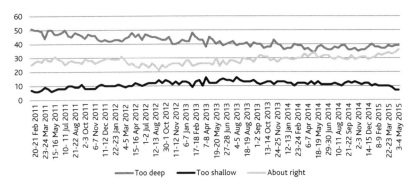

Source: YouGov (2015a).

Similarly, when asked about the speed of cuts (see Figure 4.3), in February 2011, a large proportion (58%) of those polled felt that the government was cutting spending too quickly compared to 27% who thought that the speed of cuts was about right, while only 5% felt that the government was cutting spending too slowly. Although there was some increase in support for cutting spending more quickly during the Parliament, by the time of the general election in May 2015, this had fallen back to 7%. In the same period, the proportion of those who felt that the pace of cuts was too quick and those who felt that it was about right had narrowed to four points, with a drop in those opposed to the speed of cuts from 58% to 40%, while those who felt that the pace of cuts was about right increased from 26% to 36%.

Figure 4.3: Is the government cutting spending too quickly?

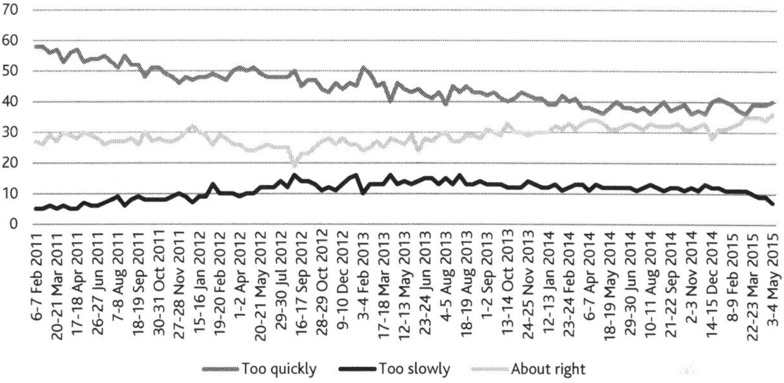

Source: YouGov (2015a).

These data suggest that while the public remain divided about the speed and depth of cuts, they have also, to some extent, grown acclimatised to austerity, which may help to explain support for the Conservatives in the 2015 general election. However, while the trend appears to suggest growing acceptance of the need for cuts during the 2010 Parliament, it is far from clear that the public are prepared to accept the need for further significant cuts of the kind announced since the 2015 general election. The YouGov data suggest that while there is growing support for keeping spending at current levels, support for further and deeper cuts, which was never strong, appears to have peaked around the middle of the last Parliament and seems to be in decline. Public concern about further cuts is reflected in other polls. In December 2014, Ipsos MORI (2014b) reported that 57% of the public felt that an incoming Conservative government would 'cut spending too much', compared to 26% who believed they would get the balance right. In pre-Budget polling in June 2015, ComRes (2015) found that 57% were opposed to a further cut of £12 billion from welfare spending and only 37% supported it, while YouGov (2015b) found that 40% agreed that a further cut in welfare spending was the right thing to do, while 42% thought that it would be wrong.

The Conservative government may also find it more difficult to justify, or at least avoid the blame for, further cuts. Under the coalition, the government went to considerable lengths to lay the blame for cuts on the previous Labour government. In this, they were helped in no small part by Labour's departing Chief Secretary to the Treasury, Liam Byrne, whose note declaring that there was 'no money left' was brandished by David Cameron throughout the 2015 election campaign (Byrne, 2015). Five years after Labour left office, it remains the case that a large proportion of the public continue to blame Labour for the cuts. However, the longer the period of austerity, the less likely it seems that the public will continue to accept that Labour are primarily to blame. Throughout the last Parliament, regular YouGov polling asked whether the coalition or the previous Labour government were most to blame for the current spending cuts (YouGov, 2015c). In June 2010, 48% of those polled blamed Labour, while 17% thought that the coalition was most to blame. By May 2015, the proportion who blamed Labour had fallen to 38%, while 32% now blamed the coalition. In similar polling, Ipsos MORI offered a wider range of possible culprits, including local councils, the banks and the state of the global economy. In March 2011, the largest proportion, 31% blamed the previous Labour government, 29% blamed the banks and 18% blamed the global economy, while only 10% thought that the coalition government was to blame. When the poll was repeated in 2013, 26% continued to think that Labour was to blame but 21% now blamed the coalition, the proportion blaming the banks had fallen to 23%, while slightly more (21%) blamed the global economy (Ipsos MORI, 2013a).

If the government hoped that cuts to local government budgets would mean that local authorities would share the blame for cuts, this appears to have been, at best, only partly successful. In monthly polling between 2011 and April 2015, YouGov asked whether central government was mainly responsible for cuts to local services 'because it is cutting sharply the money it gives to the council where I live', or whether the local council was mainly responsible 'because it could achieve most of the savings it needs by cutting costs, without cutting services'. More than 40% of those polled consistently blamed central government, while between 24% and 34% blamed local authorities (YouGov, 2015c). In the final poll on this question before the 2015 general election, 40% blamed central government, while only 26% blamed local councils. In Ipsos MORI polls, people were less likely to blame local councils for the level of cuts to public services than any other factor, with only 4% and 5% blaming local councils. This was still the case when those polled were asked directly who was most to blame for the level of cuts to *local* services, with only 13% blaming local councils, compared to 30% who blamed the coalition government and 25% who blamed the previous Labour government (Ipsos MORI, 2013b).

Public priorities and the hardening of attitudes towards benefits recipients

One possible explanation for the growing public acceptance of spending cuts may be that they have been directed primarily at services that are not used by the majority of the population. By largely protecting spending on the National Health Service (NHS), schools and state pensions, the coalition government loaded the burden of cuts onto services directed at a minority of the population, in particular, the poor and unemployed. To some extent, this reflects public priorities. British Social Attitudes has consistently shown high levels of public support for mass public services, most notably, health and education, while support for spending on social security benefits has been in, seemingly terminal, decline. Health and education have consistently topped the list of public priorities for further spending since British Social Attitudes began in 1983, with the most recent survey indicating that 60% would like to see more spending on education and that 75% would like to see extra spending on the NHS. In contrast, support for extra spending on social security benefits halved from 12% in 1983 to 6% in 2001, and has not been above that level since. There has, however, been a notable drop in support for extra spending in other areas; the police and prisons, for example, were viewed as a priority for extra spending by 15% in 2011, but only 8% in 2014, while the proportion of those who felt that the government should invest more in supporting industry also fell from a high point of 15% in 2012 to 8% in 2014 (British Social Attitudes Information Service, no date).

Looking, in particular, at spending on welfare benefits, the public appears to make a clear distinction between groups that are considered more and less deserving of support, with unemployed people and single parents consistently attracting less support than other groups such as retired people, disabled people and carers, and those who work on a low income. However, as Table 4.1 shows, over the long term, the proportion of those who would like to see more spending on benefits for different groups of people has fallen for all groups. While unemployed people and single parents remain the only groups for whom a minority would like to see additional spending, the largest drop in support has been for disabled people who cannot work, with significant falls also for parents who work on low incomes and retired people. In most cases, the most significant drop in support was between 2008 and 2011. To what extent this is a response to the onset of the financial crisis in 2008, a response to Labour policies or the rhetoric relating to the cost of welfare provision on the part of the incoming coalition government is, of course, not clear, although it is notable that there has been little change between 2011 and 2013. However, as Baumberg (2014) observes, it is important to note that these data indicate strong support for more spending for most groups, and when compared with those who would like to see less spending, only for two groups – single parents and unemployed people – would more than 10% of the public like to see less spending, and only in the case of unemployed people does the proportion who would like to see less spending (49%) exceed that which would like to see more spending.

Table 4.1: Support for more spending on ...

	1998	2002	2004	2006	2008	2011	2013
... unemployed people	22	21	15	16	14	15	15
... disabled people who cannot work	72	69	63	62	61	53	54
... parents who work on very low incomes	68	69	62	66	67	58	59
... single parents	34	39	35	38	37	29	31
... retired people	71	73	73	72	72	57	48
... people who care for those who are sick and disabled	82	82	81	82	83	74	73

Source: Hall (2012) and Baumberg (2014).

Perhaps a more significant indicator of a hardening of public attitudes to benefits recipients is shown by the response to a pair of questions that have been asked on a regular basis since British Social Attitudes began in 1983: whether benefits for unemployed people are too low and cause hardship, or whether they are too high and discourage work (see Figure 4.4). The proportion of those who thought that welfare benefits were too low and caused hardship fell from 46% in 1983 to 27% by 2014, while the proportion who thought that benefits were too high and discouraged work has increased from 35% to 52% in the same period. The steepest change in attitudes, however, appears to have been under the Labour governments from 1997 to 2010, and there is evidence of a slight softening of attitudes in recent years: 52% think that benefits are too high compared to a peak of 62% in 2011, while 27% think that benefits are too low compared to a low of 19% in the same year. Responses to other British Social Attitudes questions indicate a similar, and in some cases more marked, decline in support for benefits recipients. For example, the proportion of respondents who agreed that most unemployed people in their local area could find a job if they really wanted one rose from 39% in 1996 to 54% in 2010 and to 59% by 2014, while since 1998, more than three quarters of respondents have consistently supported the view that large numbers of people falsely claim benefit.

Figure 4.4: Perceptions of benefit levels, 1983–2014

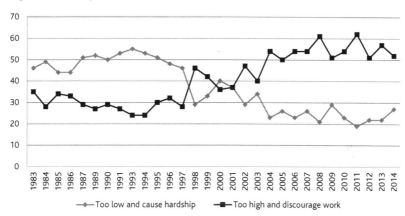

Source: Taylor-Gooby (2015).

There is now a wealth of polling data which support the conclusion that there has been a hardening of public attitudes towards benefits recipients. In two large polls on attitudes to welfare reform during the last Parliament, 72% of the public agreed that the government should do more to cut the benefits bill (Ipsos MORI, 2011a), while 74% agreed that the government pays out too much in benefits and welfare levels overall should be reduced (YouGov, 2012c). Moreover, the growing acceptance of the need to rein in spending appears to have prompted the public to make clear distinctions between deserving and less-deserving groups, and to place a greater emphasis on stricter eligibility criteria for access to benefits. Ipsos MORI (2011a) found strong support for stricter tests for people claiming incapacity benefit (84%), for jobseekers losing some of their benefits if they turn down work that they are capable of (78%) and even for compelling those who receive Housing Benefit because they live in expensive areas to move (57%). However, when asked to prioritise groups who should be subject to benefit cuts, while the public express clear and fairly consistent preferences for deserving and less-deserving groups, those considered less deserving comprise only a small proportion of those in receipt of benefits. For example, Ipsos MORI (2011a) found strong support for cutting benefits for immigrants (35%), those receiving more than £400 in Housing Benefit (27%) and the long-term unemployed (25%), but very little for any other group, such as people on incapacity benefits (4%) and lone parents (2%). Similarly, in a YouGov poll following the announcement of proposals to freeze benefits in 2014, only in relation to benefits for the unemployed did a majority (56%) of those polled agree that benefits should not be frozen, while there was considerable support for exempting a range of other benefits from a freeze, most notably, the state retirement pension (76%) and disability benefits (68%). There is also evidence of more support for in-work benefits than support for those who are unemployed, with 47% agreeing that tax credits should be exempt from a freeze compared to 39% who thought they should not (YouGov, 2014).

One group that has attracted particular attention are those in receipt of benefits because they are unable to work due to a disability. The coalition government introduced significant changes to disability benefits, including the replacement of Disability Living Allowance and stricter eligibility criteria. There is evidence for public support for this policy, which perhaps reflects distinctions in popular discourse between 'genuine' disabilities and those conditions perceived to be related to lifestyle, such as obesity, and also the historical legacy of unemployed people being moved onto incapacity benefits to mask rising unemployment. In 2011, Ipsos MORI found that 80% in total agreed with the need for stricter tests for people claiming incapacity benefit, with 60% strongly agreeing. Similarly, in a poll conducted for Mencap, only 39% agreed that all or most of those claiming incapacity benefit had genuine disabilities. However, while there is clearly some public support for greater conditionality for access to incapacity benefits, public support for this is not unequivocal, and there is some concern about the impact of cuts on those who are genuinely disabled. Cuts to incapacity benefit are not seen as a priority, with only 4% claiming that incapacity benefit should be the highest priority for benefit cuts (Ipsos MORI, 2011a). Moreover, when asked to think about the impact of cuts, 49% agreed that the cuts might make those receiving disability benefits more open to abuse from some members of the public, compared to 21% who did not (Ipsos MORI, 2011b).

While the public clearly think that different groups are more or less deserving of support, there is broad acceptance that there should be a limit or cap on the total amount of money that families should be able to receive in welfare benefits. The so-called 'benefits cap' was proposed shortly after the 2010 election and introduced in April 2013.

It was designed to ensure that no family would receive more in out-of-work benefits than the average earnings of British families, which at the time was £26,000 a year. A number of polls indicate high levels of public support for the policy, with around three quarters of the public consistently supporting the cap (YouGov, 2012a, 2014, 2015d; Ipsos Mori, 2013c). These include polling on attitudes towards the benefits cap commissioned by the Department for Work and Pensions (DWP), albeit after the cap was introduced, which revealed that 73% supported the principle of a benefits cap, and a similar proportion (70%) supported it at a level of £26,000 per annum, although those polled were evenly divided on whether this would be unfair to those living in areas with high housing costs (DWP, 2013; Ipsos MORI, 2013c). The DWP survey also showed that 67% believed that it would encourage those claiming benefits to find work, although when YouGov asked the same question in January 2015, only 29% thought that it probably had encouraged people to find work, compared to 58% who thought that it probably had not (YouGov, 2015d). Nevertheless, it is also apparent that a significant proportion of the public would support more stringent limits. A YouGov poll from 2012 found that 36% of those polled agreed that benefits for out-of-work families should be capped at less than £20,000 a year, while in 2015, 61% said that they would support a reduction in the cap to £23,000 (YouGov, 2012b, 2015d), and Ipsos MORI (2011a) found that 62% would support a benefits cap for people who have 'too many children'.

Will someone turn the thermostat on?

There is a wealth of data which suggest that a significant proportion of the public accept the need for cuts to public spending, and that at least some of those in receipt of benefits are viewed as less deserving of current levels of support. However, public support for the coalition government's approach to deficit reduction was not unqualified, and the Conservatives may face considerable challenges in seeking to persuade the public that further and deeper cuts are necessary, particularly if these are directed at groups that the public consider to be more deserving of support. Moreover, looking more broadly at the Conservative Party's approach to social policy, it is also far from clear that the public support the idea of a fundamental restructuring of the state and the replacement of current state provision in a wide range of areas, including schools and hospitals, with the private, voluntary and third sectors, or by individuals and their families.

The welfare cuts introduced by the coalition and Conservative governments have frequently been justified on the grounds of 'fairness' (see also Chapter One). As noted in a number of other chapters, to some extent, this has involved reframing poverty as attributable to personal failings, rather than wider labour market conditions or demographic change. At the 2010 Conservative Party conference, the Prime Minister stated that 'fairness means giving people what they deserve – and what people deserve depends on how they behave' (Cameron, 2010); he returned to this theme in 2012 by promising to end the 'something for nothing' culture (Cameron, 2012), while the promise of further benefit cuts in the run-up to the 2015 general election was described as 'a basic issue of fairness' (Cameron, 2015). The hardening of attitudes towards benefits recipients suggests that the public has, to some extent, been prepared to accept such explanations. However, polling data also indicate that while the public accepts the need for spending cuts, they are not entirely convinced that the burden is being equitably distributed. YouGov polling on whether the government has cut spending in a way that is fair to all sections of society indicates that for a short period after the 2010 general election, more people thought that the government was cutting spending in a fair way, but the proportion who thought that the cuts were unfair began to rise from mid-2010 (see Figure 4.5). Although there has been a slight narrowing of the gap between those who think that the cuts are fair or unfair, more than half of those polled on this question since November 2010 have thought that the cuts have been unfair, while less than one in three believe that the cuts have been instituted fairly (YouGov, 2015a).

Figure 4.5: Do you think the government is cutting spending in a way that is fair or unfair?

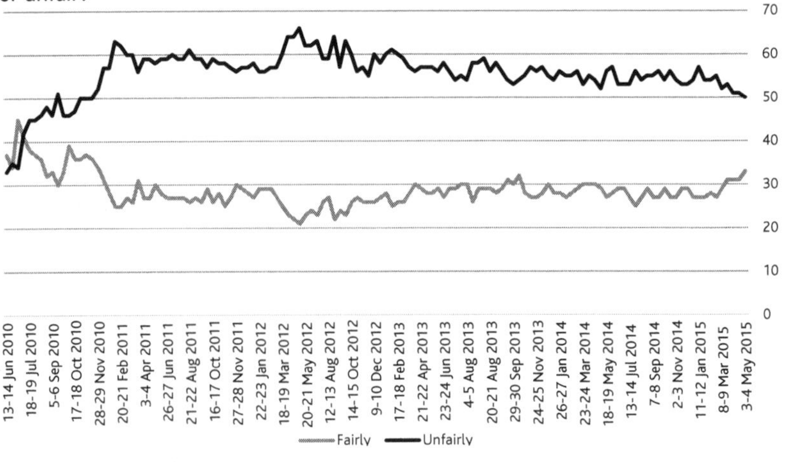

Source: YouGov (2015a).

Concern about growing inequality is also reflected in Ipsos MORI's monthly issues index, which tracks public perceptions of the most important issues facing Britain. The proportion of those who mentioned poverty/inequality as one of the most important issues facing the country rose during the last Parliament from 6% in May 2010 to a peak of 18% in July 2014, the highest percentage ever, dropping only slightly to 17% by the time of the general election (Ipsos MORI, 2010, 2014a, 2015). Concern about inequality is also reflected in long-term data from British Social Attitudes, in which more than three quarters of respondents have consistently replied that the gap between those with high and low incomes in the UK is too large, a figure that increased from 77.5% in 2010 to 84.4% in 2012, before dropping back to 81.5% in 2013. Similarly, as Hills (2015) has shown, after a period of decline, public support for government policies designed to redistribute wealth has grown since the onset of the financial crisis in 2008, and is now at a level comparable with the mid-1990s.

Moreover, when asked to express priorities for public spending, individuals are often asked to choose between different areas of welfare spending. When such questions are placed in the context of wider public spending priorities or possible tax-raising opportunities, there is considerable public support for cuts to other areas of government spending, and for policies directed at the more wealthy members of society. In a poll conducted shortly before the 2015 general election, 69% of those polled said that the richest and wealthiest in society should pay more tax than at present, 31% of whom said that they should pay 'a much larger amount', compared to 3% who said that they should pay less tax (YouGov, 2015e). Such policies often attract higher levels of support than those directed at people who are less well off. In a series of polls in the run-up to the Chancellor's Autumn Statement in 2010, while 43% supported freezing welfare benefits for two or three years and 32% supported freezing tax credits, 61% supported reducing the tax relief that higher-rate taxpayers get on pensions contributions, 82% supported a permanent levy on bank profits and 74% supported withdrawing child benefit from higher-rate taxpayers (YouGov, 2010a, 2010b). Indeed, withdrawing child benefit from higher-rate taxpayers has consistently attracted levels of public support (around 70%) comparable with those for the benefits cap. Similarly, opposition to spending on overseas aid frequently exceeds demands for cuts to welfare spending, while other areas that many believe could be subject to cuts include the BBC budget and final salary pensions, including for Members of Parliament (YouGov, 2010a). Polling in the run-up to the 2015 general election indicated strong support for a new tax on houses worth more than £2 million (64%, compared to 23% opposed) and for raising the top rate of income tax to 50% (64%, compared to 23% against) (YouGov, 2015e).

There is also a tendency to assume that because the public have concerns about the level of public spending, they no longer believe that the state should seek to meet need in a wide range of areas. However, there is little evidence of broad public support for a smaller state or for shifting responsibility for provision to other actors in the private, voluntary or third sectors. The rolling back, or replacement, of state provision was central to the Conservative vision of a 'Big Society', which featured prominently in the 2010 general election campaign. The 'Big Society' idea, however, failed to gain traction in the public mind, and despite several relaunches under the coalition, there is little evidence that the public understood, supported or had the capacity to meet the government's aspirations for a wide range of services to be shifted out of the public sphere (Defty, 2014). The media, and to some extent the coalition government, seemed to lose interest in promoting debate over the 'Big Society' and it is therefore perhaps not surprising that there was almost no change in public understanding or appetite for the Big Society between 2011 and 2015 (Defty, 2014; YouGov, 2015f).

Indeed, long-running surveys such as British Social Attitudes suggest that the public remain committed to the idea of state provision in a wide range of sectors. When asked whether responsibility for supporting people in ill health, retirement and unemployment is mainly the responsibility of the government, employers or individuals and their families, over a number of years, a consistently high proportion (between 56% and 86%) believe the primary responsibility lies with the state (Park et al, 2010; Defty, 2011). In 2012 and 2013, British Social Attitudes asked whether a number of services currently provided by the state – NHS hospitals, schools and personal care for older people – should be provided by private companies or by charities or other not-for-profit organisations (see Table 4.2). While there was more support for services to be provided by the charitable and not-for-profit sector than for private provision, only in the case of personal care for the elderly did the proportion supporting this exceed those opposed. In all other cases, a larger, and in some cases much larger, proportion were opposed to shifting responsibility for these services either to the private or to the not-for-profit sectors.

Another possible source of opposition to Conservative spending plans and policies lies in the devolved areas of the UK. As noted in the introduction, the adoption of significantly different priorities and approaches in the devolved areas has raised questions about what shape

Table 4.2: Support for private/charitable sector provision of services currently provided by the state

	NHS hospitals		Schools		Personal care for the elderly	
	Private companies	Charities or not-for-profit	Private companies	Charities or not-for-profit	Private companies	Charities or not-for-profit
Total support	20.9	37.1	19.5	38.4	33.5	50.1
Total oppose	65.5	41.4	62.4	52.8	42.5	24.5

Source: British Social Attitudes Information Service (no date).

social policy might take across the UK. Survey and polling data are less prevalent for the constituent parts of the UK, and disaggregating data from national polls can lead to conclusions based on very small samples. Nevertheless, there is some, albeit rather limited, evidence of differences in attitudes in some of the devolved areas. The occasional Scottish Social Attitudes survey indicates that people in Scotland are somewhat more concerned than people in England about income inequality, and more willing to support tax and spend and redistribution. However, support is only slightly higher than in the rest of the UK, and support for tax and spend, in particular, has fallen as heavily in Scotland as it has in the rest of the UK (Curtice and Ormston, 2011). Similarly, attitudes towards benefits recipients have hardened in Scotland as much as they have across the UK, and possibly more severely. For example, the proportion of Scots who agreed that benefits are too high and discourage work rose from 43% in 2010 to 52% in 2013, compared to a rise from 54% to 57% in the UK as a whole (Curtice, 2013). Polling data are scant, but a 2010 YouGov poll indicated that in Wales, too, there was slightly more concern about public spending cuts than in the UK as a whole, with 56% believing that the government was cutting spending too quickly, compared to 44% in the UK as a whole, while 57% thought that spending cuts were being introduced in a way that is unfair, compared to 47% across the UK (YouGov, 2010a, 2010c).

Conclusions

Long-running surveys such as British Social Attitudes, along with more recent polling data, provide strong evidence for a decline in public support for increased public spending and a hardening of attitudes towards benefits recipients. Since 2010, this has coincided with government policies designed to rein in spending in order to reduce the deficit, coupled with an ideological commitment to reducing the size of the state and combating a perceived dependency culture created by the welfare state. To some extent, opinion poll data reveal strong public support for the approach of the coalition and Conservative governments, with a distinction in the mind of the public between deserving and undeserving groups. There is evidence of considerable support for policies such as the benefits cap, and for stricter eligibility criteria, particularly for out-of-work benefits, and there is even evidence that the public would support more stringent measures to limit benefits for those groups that are viewed as less deserving, some of which were announced by the incoming Conservative government, such as a reduction in the benefits cap and cuts to benefits for families with more than two children.

However, it is not clear that public opinion has shifted entirely in line with government policy since 2010, or that there is widespread support for further cuts. The most significant shifts in public attitudes took place under the previous Labour government, and there is some evidence of a levelling off, or bottoming out, of attitudes since 2010. While there is little public support for an increase in expenditure and provision, there is also little evidence of support for further and deeper cuts, and an increasing proportion of the public think that government should seek to maintain spending at current levels. A further problem for the Conservatives could result from the fact that the public is prepared to make a distinction between deserving and undeserving groups. Thus far, this has largely benefitted the government as cuts have focused primarily on those groups that the public consider to be less deserving, while mass services have been protected. However, the public has a strong commitment to state provision in a wide range of areas and a limited perception of which groups are less deserving. There are limited savings left to be made by cutting support for groups that enjoy less public support, such as unemployed people, and it is likely that further cuts will fall on those groups that are viewed as more deserving, such as the working poor, or on those services that are used by the majority of the population, such as the NHS. An early indication of this came with the announcement in the 2015 Budget of a freeze on working-age benefits and a steep cut in tax credits. The Conservative government may find it considerably more difficult to generate public support for a deficit reduction strategy based on cutting support for groups such as these, particularly if a large proportion of the public continue to believe that alternative savings are possible by ensuring that responsibility for shouldering the burden of cuts is more fairly distributed.

References

Baumberg, B. (2014) 'Benefits and the cost of living: pressures on the cost of living and attitudes to benefit claiming', British Social Attitudes 31. Available at: http://www.bsa.natcen.ac.uk/latest-report/british-social-attitudes-31/benefits/introduction.aspx (accessed 30 June 2015).

British Social Attitudes Information Service (no date) 'Homepage'. Available at: http://www.britsocat.com/ (accessed 30 June 2015).

Byrne, L. (2015) '"I'm afraid there is no money left" the letter I will regret forever', *The Guardian*. Available at: http://www.theguardian.com/commentisfree/2015/may/09/liam-byrne-apology-letter-there-is-no-money-labour-general-election (accessed 30 June 2015).

Cameron, D. (2010) 'Together in the national interest', Speech to the Conservative Party Conference, 6 October 2010. Available at: http://www.webarchive.org.uk/wayback/archive/20101207231631/http://www.conservatives.com/News/Speeches/2010/10/David_Cameron_Together_in_the_National_Interest.aspx (accessed 30 June 2015).

Cameron, D. (2012) 'Welfare speech', 25 June. Available at: https://www.gov.uk/government/speeches/welfare-speech (accessed 30 June 2015).

Cameron, D. (2015) '26,000 benefit cap is "basic issue of fairness"'. Available at: http://www.telegraph.co.uk/news/politics/david-cameron/9033246/David-Cameron-26000-benefit-cap-is-basic-issue-of-fairness.html (accessed 23 January 2015).

ComRes (2015) 'ComRes/*Daily Mail* pre-Budget poll'. Available at: http://comres.co.uk/polls/comres-daily-mail-pre-budget-poll/ (accessed 30 June 2015).

Curtice, J. (2010a) 'Thermostat or weathervane? Public reactions to spending and redistribution under New Labour', in A. Park, J. Curtice, K. Thomson, M. Philips, E. Clery and S. Butt (eds) *British social attitudes: the 26th report*, London: Sage, pp 19–38.

Curtice, J. (2010b) 'Debate: election 2010: a new mood on tax and spend?', *Policy & Politics*, 38(2): 325–9.

Curtice, J. (2013) *Scottish social attitudes: is it really all just about economics? Issues of nationhood and welfare*, Edinburgh: ScotCen. Available at: http://www.scotcen.org.uk/media/265694/ssa_is-it-really-all-just-about-economics.pdf (accessed 30 June 2015).

Curtice, J. and Ormston, R. (2011) 'On the road to divergence? Trends in public opinion in Scotland and England', in A. Park, E. Clery, J. Curtice, M. Phillips and D. Utting (eds) *British social attitudes: the 28th report*, London: Sage.

Defty, A. (2011) 'The Conservatives, social policy and public opinion', in H. Bochel (ed) *The Conservative Party and social policy*, Bristol: The Policy Press, pp 61–76.

Defty, A. (2014) 'Can you tell what it is yet? Public attitudes towards the "Big Society"', *Social Policy and Society*, 13(1): 13–24.

DWP (Department for Work and Pensions) (2013) 'Public perceptions of the benefits cap and pre-implementation impacts'. Available at: https://www.gov.uk/government/publications/public-perceptions-of-the-benefit-cap-and-pre-implementation-impacts (accessed 30 June 2015).

Hall, S. (2012) *21st century welfare: seventy years since the Beveridge Report*, London: Ipsos MORI.

Hills, J. (2015) *Good times bad times: the welfare myth of them and us*, Bristol: The Policy Press.

Ipsos MORI (2010) 'May 2010 issues index'. Available at: https://www.ipsos-mori.com/researchpublications/researcharchive/2612/May-2010-Issues-Index.aspx (accessed 30 June 2015).

Ipsos MORI (2011a) 'Future state of welfare'. Available at: https://www.ipsos-mori.com/researchpublications/researcharchive/2876/Future-State-of-Welfare.aspx (accessed 30 June 2015).

Ipsos MORI (2011b) 'Attitudes to disability'. Available at: https://www.ipsos-mori.com/researchpublications/researcharchive/2774/Attitudes-to-disability.aspx (accessed 30 June 2015).

Ipsos MORI (2013a) 'Blame for cuts to public services poll'. Available at: https://www.ipsos-mori.com/researchpublications/researcharchive/3114/Blame-for-cuts-to-public-services-poll.aspx (accessed 30 June 2015).

Ipsos MORI (2013b) 'Public concerned about cuts to council services, but councils aren't necessarily to blame'. Available at: https://www.ipsos-mori.com/researchpublications/researcharchive/3123/Public-concerned-about-cuts-to-council-services-but-councils-arent-necessarily-to-blame.aspx (accessed 30 June 2015).

Ipsos MORI (2013c) 'Benefit cap popular with the public, but what impact is it having pre-implementation'. Available at: https://www.ipsos-mori.com/researchpublications/researcharchive/3194/Benefit-Cap-popular-with-public-but-what-impact-is-it-having-preimplementation.aspx (accessed 30 June 2015).

Ipsos MORI (2014a) 'The Economist Ipsos MORI July 2014 issues index'. Available at: https://www.ipsos-mori.com/researchpublications/researcharchive/3424/The-EconomistIpsos-MORI-Issues-Index-July-2014.aspx (accessed 30 June 2015).

Ipsos MORI (2014b) 'Political monitor December 2014'. Available at: https://www.ipsos-mori.com/researchpublications/researcharchive/3494/Economic-Optimism-falls-to-its-lowest-level-since-July-2013.aspx (accessed 20 June 2015).

Ipsos MORI (2015) 'The Economist Ipsos MORI May 2015 issues index'. Available at: https://www.ipsos-mori.com/researchpublications/researcharchive/3577/EconomistIpsos-MORI-May-2015-Issues-Index.aspx (accessed 30 June 2015).

Park, A., Curtice, J., Thomson, K., Phillips, M., Clery, E. and Butt, S. (eds) (2010) British social attitudes: the 26th report, London: Sage.

Taylor-Gooby, P. (2013) The double crisis of the welfare state and what we can do about it, Basingstoke: Palgrave.

YouGov (2010a) 'YouGov/The Sun survey results'. Available at: https://d25d2506sfb94s.cloudfront.net/today_uk_import/YG-Archives-Pol-Sun-resultsSpendingCuts-211010.pdf (accessed 30 June 2015).

YouGov (2010b) 'YouGov/Sunday Times survey results'. Available at: https://d25d2506sfb94s.cloudfront.net/today_uk_import/YG-Archives-Pol-ST-results-110610.pdf (accessed 30 June 2015).

YouGov (2010c) 'YouGov survey results'. Available at: http://d25d2506sfb94s.cloudfront.net/today_uk_import/YG-Archives-Pol-YouGov-WelshCuts-291010.pdf (accessed 30 June 2015).

YouGov (2012a) 'Lords' amended welfare cap'. Available at: https://yougov.co.uk/news/2012/01/26/lords-amended-welfare-cap/ (accessed 30 June 2015).

YouGov (2012b) 'Benefits cap proposal'. Available at: https://yougov.co.uk/news/2012/01/21/benefits-cap-proposal/ (accessed 30 June 2015).

YouGov (2012c) 'Are we experiencing compassion fatigue in the wake of welfare reform'. Available at: https://yougov.co.uk/news/2012/03/20/are-we-experiencing-compassion-fatigue-wake-welfar/ (accessed 30 June 2015).

YouGov (2013) 'YouGov/Sunday Times survey results'. Available at: http://d25d2506sfb94s.cloudfront.net/cumulus_uploads/document/5tdopkoktm/YG-Archive-Pol-Sunday-Times-results-04-060113.pdf (accessed 30 June 2015).

YouGov (2014) 'Cut out of work benefits, but not tax credits'. Available at: https://yougov.co.uk/news/2014/10/01/freeze-unemployment-benefit-not-tax-credit/ (accessed 30 June 2015).

YouGov (2015a) 'Political tracker: government cuts 2010–2015'. Available at: https://d25d2506sfb94s.cloudfront.net/cumulus_uploads/document/umkary60am/YG-Archives-Pol-Trackers-Government%20Cuts-040515.pdf (accessed 30 June 2015).

YouGov (2015b) 'Public split on Cameron's welfare cuts'. Available at: https://yougov.co.uk/news/2015/06/27/public-split-camerons-welfare-cuts/ (accessed 30 June 2015).

YouGov (2015c) 'Political tracker: economic performance 2010–2015'. Available at: https://d25d2506sfb94s.cloudfront.net/cumulus_uploads/document/b48brxdoyq/YG-Archives-Pol-Trackers-Economic-Performance-090515.pdf (accessed 30 June 2015).

YouGov (2015d) 'YouGov survey results'. Available at: https://d25d2506sfb94s.cloudfront.net/cumulus_uploads/document/jidve53qxs/InternalResults_150128_benefits_Website.pdf (accessed 30 June 2015).

YouGov (2015e) 'YouGov/*Sunday Times* survey results'. Available at: https://d25d2506sfb94s.cloudfront.net/cumulus_uploads/document/oqslggwc4a/YG-Archive-Pol-Sunday-Times-results-110415.pdf (accessed 30 June 2015).

YouGov (2015f) 'YouGov/*Times Red Box* survey results'. Available at: https://d25d2506sfb94s.cloudfront.net/cumulus_uploads/document/d3a0eiims8/TimesRedBoxResults_150412_big_society_W.pdf (accessed 30 June 2015).

FIVE

Health policy and the coalition government

Rob Baggott

Introduction

Health and the National Health Service (NHS) is a politically sensitive policy area for governments. Health policy has a high media and political profile, and is often an issue of party-political contention. The NHS is a key public service and an indicator of the competence of governments. The health budget represents a large and increasing proportion of public spending, for which central government is held responsible. In addition, health policy entails a host of challenging problems, which cannot be ignored: the rising demand for health services; shortcomings in the quality and safety of services; inefficiencies in the use of resources; problems in accessing services in a timely fashion; inadequate coordination of services (especially between health care and social care); and significant public health challenges, such as rising levels of obesity and widening health inequalities.

Although all recent governments have faced these problems, the Conservative–Liberal Democrat coalition government's task was made even more difficult by the adverse economic climate and its own budgetary policies. It was also exacerbated by the relatively generous increases in NHS funding under New Labour (which had already begun to plan for much greater efficiency savings before it left office). The coalition protected the NHS budget to some extent, but this was insufficient to meet rising demands for health care arising from demographic trends (such as the ageing population) and the costs of new technology. Meanwhile, austerity policies and budget cuts elsewhere, notably, in local authority social care and other services (such as housing), placed greater demands on the NHS. In addition, the new government embarked on what, for most observers, was an unexpected root-and-branch reorganisation of the NHS, which was both expensive and a major distraction from efforts to address the key health policy issues mentioned earlier.

This chapter begins by outlining the major themes of coalition policy, how they related to the policies of the two governing parties and how they continued or departed from the policies of the previous Labour government. It then briefly examines the coalition government's record on health and the NHS. Next, the major factors shaping policy in this period are explored. Finally, the chapter examines how policies may develop following the 2015 general election, and formation of the first Conservative majority government for almost 20 years.

Before embarking on the analysis, however, it must be made clear that the focus of this chapter is on England. Most UK health policy functions are now devolved to the governments of Scotland, Wales and Northern Ireland (see Chapter Fifteen). There are some exceptions, with some functions exercised by the Westminster government or by UK-wide public bodies on its behalf, including the regulation of the health professions, medicines and genetics. Moreover, funding decisions on the English NHS have implications for the resources available for the health services of Scotland, Wales and Northern Ireland as a result of the Barnett formula, which determines funding levels for the devolved nations. Although policy and organisational differences between the countries of the UK existed before devolution, health policy and NHS organisation has since diverged further. It is impossible to cover all of the variations here, but the main ones are as follows. There are differences in charges. For example, in all UK countries except England, all patients are entitled to free prescriptions. Furthermore, in Scotland only, free personal care is provided for everyone aged 65 and over at home and in residential care. In Scotland and Wales, all local services are organised by unified health boards, and there is no institutional division between commissioners and providers. Northern Ireland does have separate commissioning and provider bodies, but service provision is not constituted as a competitive market, as in England. Outside England, there are no foundation trusts and little competition from independent health-care providers. There are also many other institutional differences, with separate NHS bodies and regulators for each part of the UK. It is impossible to cover all policy and institutional differences across the four jurisdictions in this chapter, and the reader is referred to other sources for further analysis (Bevan et al, 2014; Baggott, 2015, ch 10).

Key themes of coalition policy

Reorganisation

Before the 2010 election, the Conservatives had criticised Labour's NHS reorganisations. Although apparently set against any further large-scale reorganisations, they were committed to reducing NHS bureaucracy, which implied at least some rationalisation of existing bodies. In addition, the Conservatives had developed several policies, notably, a strengthening of GP commissioning, which implied a large reduction of powers of the existing local commissioning bodies, Primary Care Trusts (PCTs). The Liberal Democrat manifesto also expressed a desire to reduce bureaucracy, but went further, containing commitments to replace PCTs with directly elected local health boards and to abolish strategic health authorities. The coalition agreement appeared to rule out reorganisation, however, with a commitment to 'stop the top-down reorganisations that have got in the way of patient care' (Cabinet Office, 2010, p 24). This was taken at face value by most observers. However, as Timmins (2012) documented, the NHS commitments in the coalition agreement were criticised for being something of a fudge. Undaunted, Secretary of State for Health Andrew Lansley pressed ahead with plans to reorganise the NHS in England, with little oversight from the coalition's senior figures.

The coalition's reform programme was subsequently described by the then chief executive of the NHS, Sir David Nicholson, as so big 'you could probably see it from space' (cited by Greer et al, 2014, p 3). The key changes were proposed in the White Paper *Equity and excellence: liberating the NHS* (Department of Health, 2010), only two months after the coalition agreement was published. Legislation was brought forward, which after a tortuous passage through Parliament, became the Health and Social Care Act 2012.

The Act abolished PCTs and the strategic health authorities. New bodies were created. A national commissioning board, later renamed NHS England, was established to oversee the planning and commissioning of health care, and to commission some services directly (primary care, specialised hospital services and some public health services). Local clinical commissioning groups (CCGs) were set up to commission secondary care services (eg most hospital, mental health, urgent and emergency care, and community health services). The new legislation also provided for health and wellbeing boards, new statutory bodies at local level, to plan for health improvement and join-up health, social care and related support services (Humphries et al, 2012; Humphries and Galea, 2013). It set up a new system of patient and public involvement, Healthwatch (Baggott, 2013; Gilburt et al, 2015). The Act also established the machinery for a new NHS market, promoting choice and competition, and encouraging independent sector providers to supply NHS services (Davis et al, 2015). Furthermore, the legislation transferred key responsibilities for public health to local government (see Baggott, 2013; Tudor Jones, 2013).

Funding and efficiency

The coalition agreed to fund the NHS with small, but real-term, increases. This worked out at 0.8% per annum over the 2010–15 Parliament. Although one of the few Whitehall budgets to be protected, NHS resources declined significantly relative to needs (the growing elderly population and levels of chronic illness) and costs (in particular, the rising costs of technology). It was estimated that an annual increase of 1.2–1.5% real growth in the NHS budget would be needed just to keep pace with demographic factors (Vizard and Obelenskaya, 2015). The funding settlement for health under the coalition compared unfavourably with the growth rate under New Labour (5.7% per annum) and the post-war average (4% per annum) On top of this was the cost of reorganisation and the ongoing costs of running the NHS market (such as commissioning and tendering costs). An official estimate of the one-off cost of reform was as much as £1.7 billion (National Audit Office, 2013). Others put this figure much higher. For example, Paton (2014) estimated the start-up costs of reorganisation at £3 billion and recurrent running costs at £4.5 billion a year.

The coalition continued to seek efficiency and productivity improvements. It inherited the so-called Nicholson Challenge, established under the previous government (and named after the NHS chief executive who continued in post under the coalition). This aimed to secure £15–20 billion savings in NHS budgets by 2015. This implied improvements in productivity, reinforced by the continuation of improvement and efficiency schemes set up by New Labour, such as Commissioning for Quality and Innovation (CQUIN) and Quality Innovation Productivity and Prevention (QIPP). In addition, there was a strong focus on reducing management costs, which the coalition aimed to reduce by 45%. The coalition also used pay freezes and caps on pay rises to curb the NHS pay bill. The number of NHS staff actually rose during the coalition years and productivity improved. However, these pay policies were criticised by trade unions and professional groups as unfair and unsustainable. They were associated with other problems, such as staff retention and poor morale. Meanwhile, problems of retention and poor workforce planning were linked to inefficiencies in staffing, in particular, the reliance on agency staff, which represented a significant excess cost to NHS budgets.

Commissioning, competition and choice

Like New Labour, the coalition's policies placed great faith on commissioning as a means of setting priorities, planning and allocating resources (see also Chapter Three). As noted earlier, NHS England was given overall responsibility for the commissioning system, as well as commissioning some services directly. It is responsible for national strategic planning and guidance and has a leadership role on issues such as quality and safety. NHS England oversees local commissioning, supports and monitors CCGs, and allocates resources to them. CCGs plan and commission hospital and other secondary health services for local people. They are aided by commissioning support units, which provide a range of services, including support for strategic development, financial analysis and contracts management. It is expected that CCGs' commissioning role will expand in future to cover more services. At the time of writing, some have been given powers to co-commission primary care services (along with NHS England).

New Labour supported greater competition in the provision of NHS services, both between NHS organisations and from the independent sector. A payment system was established to pay providers for the amount of activity undertaken ('Payment by Results'). The coalition placed even greater emphasis on competition. Monitor, the foundation trust regulator, was given the task of overseeing the NHS 'market' and tackling anti-competitive behaviour. The Competition and Markets Authority also has a role in some decisions (and controversially opposed some NHS mergers on competition grounds). To stimulate competition further, requirements were placed on commissioners to ensure that services were put out to tender unless there was an overwhelming reason not to do so. In practice, CCGs, fearing the wrath of regulators or legal action from potential bidders, often erred on the side of caution and opened services to tender (Welikala and West, 2015).

The coalition's plans were an extension of the previous government's policies to strengthen independent provision. For example, New Labour promoted independent sector treatment centres and created other opportunities for non-NHS bodies to run a range of NHS services, including primary and community health services. The coalition used rules introduced by New Labour to extend independent sector provision further. One of the most controversial decisions was to allow the private operator, Circle, to run an NHS hospital (Hinchingbrooke Hospital in Huntingdon, Cambridgeshire). This deal collapsed less than three years into the contract, triggered by a higher than expected deficit and an adverse report from the health and care regulator, the Care Quality Commission (CQC). Meanwhile, public–private partnerships initiated by New Labour, involving the construction of new hospitals and primary care facilities, also continued under the coalition. However, some minor changes were made in the light of the huge profits made by businesses involved in these schemes (especially hospital Private Finance Initiative [PFI] schemes) in order to give taxpayers some protection from excessive running costs, high interest payments and profiteering (though there is scepticism about what this new approach will actually achieve [eg Hellowell, 2015]).

The coalition also sought to make NHS providers more competitive, intending that all NHS trusts must become foundation trusts (previously an aspiration of New Labour, which established foundation trusts in order to give NHS providers more autonomy over finance and management), and by giving these organisations more freedom to generate private income. However, by the end of the 2010–15 Parliament, 90 remained as NHS trusts (alongside 150 foundation trusts and 16 social enterprises). Notably, New Labour and the coalition shared a desire to encourage social enterprises in health and other areas of welfare. These organisations apply business models and strategies to social and environmental problems and reinvest all or most of their profits in the pursuit of these objectives (Ridley-Duff and Bull, 2015).

New Labour had backed greater choice for patients in health care. The coalition government initially placed even greater emphasis on choice. NHS England and CCGs were given duties to enable patients to make choices with regards to health services. Statutory powers were created to protect and promote the right to make choices. Specific pledges were made to extend choices to include the choice of a named consultant, GPs and specific service providers. The coalition also endorsed plans initiated by New Labour to extend personal budgets to health care. However, over the lifetime of the government, the patient choice agenda appeared to lose ground to other priorities, such as the reorganisation of the NHS, timely access to services and issues of quality and safety. Indeed, in 2014, the Secretary of State for Health, Jeremy Hunt (who had taken over from Lansley in a cabinet reshuffle of 2012), declared that patient choice was not the key to improving performance in the NHS (West, 2014).

Accountability and performance

New Labour was renowned for its strong central grip on the NHS through targets and performance management, an approach known as 'targets and terror' (Bevan and Hood, 2006). However, it did acknowledge that the NHS needed more autonomy to deliver improvements, as reflected in reforms such as foundation trusts. The coalition government sought to legislate to limit the responsibilities of the Secretary of State for Health and strengthen the autonomy of the NHS. This was strongly opposed as the legislation proceeded through Parliament, amid fears that accountability for a comprehensive NHS would be seriously diluted. Some concessions were made, for example, the clarification of accountability of ministers to Parliament. Nonetheless, critics believed that the 2012 Act now meant that ministers no longer had an explicit duty to provide health services (Pollock and Price, 2013).

The argument advanced for strengthening NHS autonomy was to reduce political interference and enable more efficient management of the NHS. Ministers and the Department of Health would be responsible for setting overall objectives and the budget for the NHS – in a document called the Mandate. NHS England would then be responsible for implementing the Mandate, and other NHS bodies (such as CCGs) would be expected to act in accordance with it. However, in practice, the coalition continued to intervene in the NHS, and the Department of Health maintained a strong focus on operational matters (Greer et al, 2014). Furthermore, the Secretary of State for Health continued to take NHS organisations to task when targets were missed (Ham et al, 2015). The coalition pledged to abolish targets that got in the way of achieving better clinical outcomes. It introduced new outcomes frameworks (for public health, health care and social care) as a basis for measuring overall performance nationally and as a means of benchmarking the performance of local organisations. These set out a range of indicators linked to key policy objectives (eg preventing premature death) and specific areas of improvement (eg reducing cancer mortality rates in people under 75). It was envisaged that by measuring outcomes (rather than processes, such as waiting times for diagnosis and treatment), performance management would focus on improving health and care, rather than meeting bureaucratic targets. However, inpatient, outpatient and Accident and Emergency (A&E) waiting time targets remained, though with some modifications.

As noted earlier, the coalition also reformed the system of patient and public involvement, an important aspect of health service accountability. A national body, Healthwatch England, was established to support new local healthwatch organisations and raise issues of national significance. Local healthwatch replaced local involvement networks, established by the Labour Government. They had similar powers but were given additional roles, such as providing information about health and care services and, in some local areas, assistance with complaints. In addition, local healthwatch organisations were formally represented on local health and wellbeing boards, discussed further later. Despite their important and wide-ranging role, local healthwatch bodies were not generously funded. Their funding (channelled via local authorities) was not ring-fenced and many received less than their target allocations.

Quality and safety

Initially, the main focus of coalition health policy was establishing the new NHS market and ensuring the safe passage of the Health and Social Care Act. The quality, safety and effectiveness of services were covered by the Act (with explicit duties imposed on ministers and NHS bodies). This built on the work of the previous government, and, in particular, the Labour minister and surgeon Lord Darzi (Department of Health, 2008). The Act also strengthened the role of the National Institute for Health and Care Excellence (NICE) (the cost-effectiveness advisory body established by New Labour) in the setting of health and care quality standards. In addition, NICE was reconstituted as a non-departmental public body, with greater independence from government.

However, it was not until the report of the public inquiry (established by the coalition) into service failures at Mid Staffordshire Foundation Trust that a stronger policy focus on quality and safety emerged. The final report of the Mid Staffordshire NHS Foundation Trust Inquiry (Mid Staffordshire Inquiry, 2013) (the Francis Report) not only found evidence of poor-quality care and neglect, and a culture focused on financial and management issues rather than patients' needs, but was also highly critical of health-care regulation. The regulatory system failed and there was too much emphasis on self-reporting and compliance with bureaucratic procedures, and insufficient attention to the experience of patients. The Francis Report found that regulatory, scrutiny and commissioning bodies did not communicate with each other and failed to take timely action.

The Francis Report made 290 recommendations, including: a statutory duty of candour for NHS organisations and staff (to ensure that they are open and honest with patients when things go wrong); a ban on gagging clauses in staff contracts; changes to nurse training; regulation to ensure compassionate care; legal penalties for those providing misleading information to regulators; better leadership training; a process for disbarring leaders and managers who fail to achieve standards of conduct; clear fundamental standards of care with criminal liability for breaches causing serious harm or death; metrics on service quality and patient safety; more sharing of information among those who monitor services; and more powers for the CQC, strengthening its capacity to undertake inspections.

The government accepted most of the recommendations. One of the main areas of disagreement was that it did not extend the statutory duty of candour to individual staff. It also refused to create a single health regulator (effectively, combining Monitor and CQC), as recommended by Francis. Another area of contention was the government's refusal to introduce statutory regulation of health-care assistants. Nonetheless, significant changes were made in the light of the Inquiry's recommendations. Additional steps were taken following a recommendation from a further review of patient safety (National Advisory Group on the Safety of Patients in England, 2013), which led to a new offence of wilful neglect and ill-treatment.

Substantial changes were made to health and social care regulators. CQC and Monitor were placed under an obligation to work together to minimise bureaucracy, communicate and share information, and to create an integrated system of licensing and registration. Quality of care is now acknowledged as a trigger for intervention by trust regulators (Monitor for foundation trusts, and the NHS Trust Development Authority for other NHS trusts) and CQC now plays a greater role in this process. In addition, CQC was given greater statutory independence from government and greater powers to intervene. It is now expected that inspectors will be specialists in the area they are reviewing, and there is greater clinical input into the inspection process. Procedures have been overhauled, with more reliance on site visits and evidence about quality and safety, and less on self-reporting and 'tick-box' assurance processes. The coalition also renewed interest in Ofsted-style rating systems, aggregate measures of quality that echoed the 'star ratings' approach of New Labour (Nuffield Trust, 2013).

The renewed focus on quality and safety led to interventions in other health-care providers. It was widely acknowledged that Mid Staffordshire was not an isolated 'bad apple', and that similar problems of quality and safety arose elsewhere. In February 2013, the Prime Minister asked the NHS Medical Director, Sir Bruce Keogh, to review the quality of care and treatment provided by hospitals that had relatively high mortality rates. Fourteen hospital trusts were investigated and Keogh's report (Keogh, 2013) led to 11 being placed in special measures. The focus on patient safety and service quality was maintained by other inquiries and reports, for example, the investigation into maternity services at Morecambe Bay NHS Foundation Trust (Morecambe Bay Inquiry Investigation, 2015). In addition, there were other specific concerns about the abuse of vulnerable patients in hospitals and other care settings, raised, for example, by reports on the Winterbourne View case (Department of Health, 2012) and the activities of Jimmy Savile (see, eg, Department of Health, 2015).

Integration and social care

The coalition government's emphasis on NHS reorganisation meant that measures to improve collaboration between health and social care providers (and related services such as housing) took a back seat (see also Chapter Ten). At the local level, there was a reliance on existing mechanisms established under New Labour (such as pooled and delegated budgets). The coalition actually dismantled some of the collaborative machinery established by Labour to improve the interface between health and social care, and other relevant services (eg abolishing local area agreements). However, the Health and Social Care Act did establish health and wellbeing boards in an effort to join up these services. Health and wellbeing boards were established in each local authority with social services responsibilities (ie the 'upper-tier' authorities: county councils, unitary authorities and London boroughs). Health and wellbeing boards must include representatives from councils (local elected representatives and chief officers, including the director of public health [DPH]), CCGs, local healthwatch and NHS England.

Health and wellbeing boards seek to encourage bodies that provide health and social care services to work closely together and in an integrated manner to improve the health and wellbeing of the local population. They advise on, assist with and support the use of existing legal powers to pool and delegate budgets. Health and wellbeing boards have a brief to promote closer working between the health and social care system and health-related services such as housing. They are also expected to reduce health inequalities. Their key functions are to lead the process of assessing local needs (in the form of joint strategic needs assessments [JSNAs], introduced as a statutory duty of PCTs and local authorities in 2007) and strategic plans (joint health and wellbeing strategies [JHWSs], introduced as a statutory requirement by the coalition).

Health and wellbeing boards acquired additional responsibility for new budgets to promote integrated working between health and social care bodies. Initially, additional funds (around £2 billion a year) were allocated to social care, half of this from the NHS budget. Subsequently, this funding was increased to £3.8 billion per annum from 2015/16, with the additional funds being taken from CCGs. This pooled budget – renamed the Better Care Fund – was ring-fenced and placed under the aegis of health and wellbeing boards.

While the coalition's commitment to integrated care and joint working was broadly welcomed, there was much criticism of the impact of austerity budgets on social care funding (see Chapter Ten). The National Audit Office (2014) discovered an 8% cut in adult social care spending by local authorities between 2010/11 and 2012/13. Local authorities increasingly rationed care to those with the highest level of need. Concerns were expressed that insufficient resources could jeopardise efforts to establish integrated care services (Health Committee, 2012, 2014). Services that could reduce the burden on hospitals by preventing admissions or expediting discharge were under-resourced (NHS Benchmarking Network, 2013). These criticisms led to calls for an overall financial settlement for health and social care that reflected the level of need (Commission on the Future of Health and Social Care in England, 2014).

A further move, coming towards the very end of the coalition's period in office, proposed devolving health and social care budgets to large cities and regions. This built on previous efforts to delegate and integrate other budgets (eg relating to economic regeneration, employment and skills, transport and infrastructure). In 2015, the government agreed to devolve combined health and social care budgets to Greater Manchester. Similar agreements with other areas (for example, Cornwall) have been drawn up under the Conservative government. The implications of combined budgets are potentially huge, but much will depend on the implementation of the schemes, in particular, how much freedom these areas will actually have to pursue distinctive policies and allocate resources, their relationship with national regulators, and specific arrangements for accountability (Hudson, 2015).

Public health

The coalition government brought radical changes to public health. A new body, Public Health England, was created to undertake national functions, monitor health trends, provide expert advice and support, and oversee the local public health system. A new duty was placed on 'upper-tier' local authorities (those with social service responsibilities) to improve public health. Statutory responsibilities for commissioning most local public health services were transferred to these authorities. The transfer of functions was accompanied by the relocation of public health teams from PCTs to local authorities (which represented a partial reversal of the 1974 NHS reorganisation). In addition, a ring-fenced grant was established for local authority-commissioned public health functions and services (worth around £2.7 billion a year).

The new health and wellbeing boards were charged with leading on local public health priorities, through JSNAs and JHWSs. Both JSNAs and JHWSs are joint statutory responsibilities of CCGs and local authorities. CCGs must involve health and wellbeing boards in the preparation and revision of their commissioning plans. CCGs, NHS England and local authorities also have a legal obligation to have regard to the JSNAs and the JHWSs of each area for which they commission services.

There was much cross-party support for the return of public health responsibilities to local government (Health Committee, 2011a; Communities and Local Government Committee, 2013). It was argued that local authorities would take a holistic approach to health across different departments and promote better collaboration between them. It was believed that these additional duties and powers could extend the 'place-shaping' role of local authorities and ensure that health issues would feature more on council agendas. In addition, by placing key health responsibilities in elected local authorities, accountability for health services could be strengthened.

However, this transfer of functions was seen by some as dislocating good relationships where they currently existed. It was believed that the transfer of public health functions would cause further fragmentation (especially where NHS bodies retained some commissioning functions – eg sexual health services). There were particular concerns about the effects of the reforms on collaboration between councils in two-tier council areas (where health-related functions such as environmental health and housing lay with lower-tier district councils). Added to this were doubts about the capacity of local government to take on new public health roles, especially in the context of austerity and the relatively small amount of ring-fenced funding allocated. Some believed that councils might re-designate projects as 'public health', enabling them to divert resources to them (Iacobucci, 2014). Furthermore, it was suspected that directors of public health (DPHs) would not have sufficient influence within the council and could be prevented from speaking out on key public health issues, especially where their employer had a conflict of interest. The government responded by giving DPHs 'chief officer status' and introducing regulations and guidance about the appointment, employment conditions and dismissal of DPHs and other public health staff.

The coalition also adopted national policies on public health. New duties were imposed on the Secretary of State for Health, NHS England and CCGs to reduce health inequalities. Local authorities were also expected to play their part in this. Universal free school meals for infants were introduced. An increase of 4,200 health visitors was announced in order to strengthen workforce capacity in improving the health and wellbeing of young children and families. To address lifestyle illnesses, the coalition backed a new social responsibility scheme, which comprised a series of 'responsibility deals', whereby businesses and other organisations would voluntarily sign up to pledges to improve health (such as making more widely available food products low in saturated fat, sugar and salt). This built on an earlier initiative by New Labour. The coalition also continued Labour's Change4Life programme, aimed at improving diet, increasing physical activity and reducing alcohol misuse. This was part of a broader initiative by government to 'nudge' people to adopt socially responsible behaviours through incentives and changes to social norms (Thaler and Sunstein, 2009).

The coalition was, however, considerably weaker than Labour in taking on vested interests that harm health. It curbed the powers of the Food Standards Agency by removing its role in healthy nutrition policy. It also weakened the existing policy of reducing salt in food (a factor in heart disease and stroke) through food industry targets. Although initially backing a minimum alcohol price to discourage excessive alcohol consumption and related problems, the government later dropped the measure in the face of industry pressure, which contrasts with the greater persistence with minimum pricing shown by the Scottish government (see Chapter Fifteen). With regard to tobacco, the government initially rejected a proposal to adopt plain packaging as a means of discouraging smoking. However, it subsequently endorsed the plan and also agreed to ban smoking in vehicles where children are passengers.

NHS five year forward view

In 2014, the *NHS five year forward view* (NHS England et al, 2014) was published by NHS England and five other national agencies (Health Education England, Monitor, CQC, the NHS Trust Development Authority, and Public Health England). By this time, NHS England was headed by Simon Stevens, a former health advisor to the Blair government, who had also worked in both the NHS and the private health sector. Stevens was regarded as being very influential in the shaping of key health policies in the Blair era. He therefore provided a strong element of continuity between the New Labour and coalition periods. The *Five year forward view* set out a future vision for health and social care services in England. It called for action on several fronts, including: a radical upgrade in prevention and public health; greater control for patients over their care; more engagement with communities and citizens in decisions about the future of health and social care; efforts to break down the division between family doctors and hospitals, physical and mental health, and health and social care; the development of new models of care with a focus on establishing integrated care; a new deal for GPs and primary care, with greater investment in these services; CCGs to acquire more control of the NHS budget; better collaboration between regulators; and an information revolution to support performance improvement, self-management of health, paperless health records and online systems (eg for prescriptions and appointments).

This was a largely uncontroversial document, and significantly made no mention of markets, competition or privatisation. It did, however, make reference to the growing gap between resources and health needs, and the future sustainability of the NHS. It recommended that action on three fronts – demand, efficiency and additional funding – would be needed to close this gap. The *Five year forward view* was generally well received across the political spectrum, signalling much consensus on some key issues facing the health and social care system as the 2015 general election approached.

The coalition government's record on health

According to a comprehensive analysis by researchers from the King's Fund (Appleby et al, 2015a, 2015b), NHS performance held up well on several indicators in the first three years of the coalition and then began to slip. This appears to have been due to two key factors: the implementation of the government's reforms, which destabilised the

NHS; and the accumulation of small real-term increases in funding, much lower than in the previous decade.

Overall public satisfaction with the NHS fell between 2010 and 2011 (from 70% to 58%), but rose to 65% in 2014. Improved patient experience was indicated by a dramatic fall in the number of patients in mixed-sex hospital accommodation. There was also a steep decline in major healthcare infections. C. difficile and MRSA infections more than halved between 2010 and 2014, although other major infections (such as E coli) did not fall significantly. The total number of full-time equivalent NHS staff increased by approximately 2% between 2010 and 2014 (from 1,056,652 to 1,077, 268). The coalition fell marginally short of its commitment to increase the number of health visitors. The number of managers, in contrast, fell by almost 15% between May 2010 and December 2014. There were indications of some improvements in efficiency. Analysis of the available cost and output data found that NHS productivity rose for the first three successive years of the coalition (by 3.21%, 2.13% and 0.36%, respectively) (Bojke et al, 2015). However, there was scepticism that these gains could be maintained. For example, it was doubtful that pay restraint, which had helped reduce costs, could be sustained indefinitely.

Financially, the NHS was in serious difficulty, with 40% of NHS trusts and 51% of foundation trusts reporting a deficit for the financial year 2014/15. The combined net deficit for the provider sector was £822 million. The specialised services budget, held by NHS England was also overspent. However, CCGs as a whole had a surplus of £151 million. Meanwhile, NHS England (2013) forecasted a deficit of £30 billion for the NHS in England by 2020/21.

The financial state of the NHS impacted on waiting time indicators. Performance against the main targets deteriorated from the winter of 2012/13 onwards (Appleby et al, 2015b). The target that 90% of inpatients must not wait longer than 18 weeks for first treatment following a GP referral was missed for most of 2014. By May 2015, 11.8% of patients waited longer than this. The outpatient target (that 95% of outpatients should wait no longer than 18 weeks for a first appointment) was missed for a time during 2014 and in early 2015. However, this target was met in May 2015 (when 4.4% waited longer). The 'incomplete pathway' target (that 92% of patients on waiting lists should not wait more than 18 weeks) was met from 2012 onwards (although the percentage waiting longer did rise and stood at 6.5% in May 2015). It should be noted that in 2014, the Department of Health authorised a 'managed breach' of the 18-week targets, which, along with additional resources, was aimed at reducing the backlog of untreated patients.

The coalition struggled to meet other targets (Appleby et al, 2015b). The percentage of patients waiting more than four hours in A&E rose from less than 2% to over 8% between April 2010 and April 2015 (Appleby et al, 2015b). Previously, the coalition had lowered the A&E target from 98% to 95% of patients to be seen within four hours. The target of 99% of patients receiving diagnostic tests within six weeks was frequently breached during the coalition's tenure, and was still not being met in February 2015 (when 1.5% did not receive results within this time limit). One of the key cancer targets (that 85% of urgent referrals from GPs should begin treatment within 62 days) was missed from 2014 onwards. By April 2015, only 82.3% of patients were treated within this period.

After a period of stability, there was an increase in delayed transfers of patients from hospital care from 2013 onwards, which meant that hospitals could not discharge patients in a timely fashion, adding to costs and causing problems of access (Appleby et al, 2015b). Also, mental health services continued to face problems of access and quality, despite the government's commitment to improve mental health and its acknowledgement of parity with physical health (see also File on 4, 2015).

Due to time lags in data, it is not surprising that public health outcomes showed little change (Public Health England, 2015). While there were some improvements, for example, smoking, alcohol-related hospital admissions in young people and teenage pregnancies continued to reduce, health inequalities and obesity did not significantly improve, and some problems (eg suicides in men) deteriorated.

What factors influenced policy?

New Labour's legacy

In the 2000s, Labour prioritised the NHS budget and allocated resources generously. Other parties pledged to match these commitments. The financial cutbacks that followed the banking crisis led all parties to reconsider their positions on NHS funding. At the 2010 general election, the Conservatives were the only one of the three main parties to pledge a real-terms increase in NHS resources.

New Labour laid the foundations for the coalition to extend the independent provision of NHS-funded services and to strengthen the commercial ethos of the NHS. As mentioned earlier, a raft of measures were introduced in the 2000s, and the coalition built on them. Labour did oppose the changes laid out in the Health and Social Care Act. However, these efforts were undermined by the fact that when in government, they had pursued market-style policies and backed an expansion of the independent sector. There was an increase in PCT spending on non-NHS providers, by 62% between 2006/07 and 2011/12 (Arora et al, 2013). This cannot be attributed to the Health and Social Care Act. Labour had already extended the role of the independent sector and the coalition used existing regulations to expose the NHS to further competition. Nonetheless, the 2012 Act strengthened competition from the independent sector, as noted earlier. After the competition clauses came into effect in April 2013, over half (56%) of new contracts were awarded to the independent sector – although this represented less than half of contracts by value (File on 4, 2014). It should be noted however, that the independent sector's incursion into the NHS has been uneven, with some areas of service provision offering more profitability than others (Davis et al, 2015).

Despite the coalition's proclamation of a more decentralised and autonomous NHS, there were continuities with New Labour's top-down approach. Although the Health and Social Care Act was meant to herald a non-interventionist approach and signal the end of political interference, ministers continued to intervene in the NHS. Despite proclaiming the end of top-down process targets, the coalition retained most of them, thereby acknowledging their importance in managing NHS performance. After the Act was passed, central government continued to intervene. A key factor was the Francis Report and revelations of poor-quality services. The Keogh review was initiated by David Cameron. Hospitals were put in special measures, supervised directly under a process established by the Department of Health. In addition, the Department of Health intervened on a range of matters, including controversial hospital reconfigurations. As the 2015 election approached, the imperative (as with previous governments) was to reduce waiting times. Extra resources were invested, alongside the managed breach of waiting targets mentioned earlier, to paint a more positive picture of the condition of the NHS than otherwise would have been possible.

Other examples of policy continuity between New Labour and the coalition include the aim to convert all NHS trusts to foundation trusts. In addition, the quality improvement agenda set out by New Labour, and, in particular, the Darzi initiatives begun under the Brown government, were continued. Similarly, the Nicholson Challenge emerged towards the end of the New Labour era. There were also continuities in public health policy, notably, Change4life and the pursuit of voluntary approaches to strengthen corporate responsibility in public health.

Conservative policy

As the leading partner in the coalition, the Conservatives' policies were crucial to the future trajectory of health policy. As Table 5.1 shows, the majority of the coalition agreement commitments on health were drawn from the Conservative manifesto (although many were shared or based on a compromise with the Liberal Democrats). The influence of the Liberal Democrats is considered further in the next section. Concentrating on the Conservatives for the moment, it can clearly be argued that the health policies of the 2010–15 period reflected key elements of the Conservative policies outlined in the period before the 2010 election. These included: the commitment on NHS funding; a greater role for the independent sector in providing NHS services; powers for GPs over budgets and commissioning; and greater autonomy for NHS organisations.

Table 5.1: Coalition government health commitments

Manifesto source	NHS	Social Care	Public Health	Total
Conservative	9	1	9	19
Liberal Democrat	5	2	2	9
Both	6	2	7	15
Compromise	4	0	2	6
Neither	4	0	1	5
Total	**28**	**5**	**21**	**54**

Sources: Conservative Party (2010a), Liberal Democrats (2010) and HM Government (2010).

The Conservative Party's health policy underwent significant changes during its period in opposition between 1997 and 2010, and especially after the appointment of David Cameron as leader in 2005. Under his leadership, the NHS was installed as the key priority. There was a marked shift away from encouraging the private funding of health care. During the 1980s and 1990s, these policies had extended tax relief to people with private health insurance. These were reversed by Labour. In opposition, the Conservatives had adopted the Patient Passport scheme, which aimed to subsidise the cost of operations for private patients. However, this was dropped following David Cameron's appointment as leader. Cameron sought to bring Conservative policies closer to Labour. The aim was to reassure the electorate on an issue where the Conservatives tended to lose out to Labour.

As a new leader of a party that had lost three consecutive general elections, Cameron had considerable freedom to shift policy. Despite his elite background, he was able to portray himself as a more open and inclusive leader, prepared to change the party (Dorey, 2007; Lee and Beech, 2009). In the health arena, both he and his shadow health minister, Andrew Lansley (who subsequently became the Secretary of State for Health), worked hard to convince the public and those working in the NHS that their commitment to the NHS was genuine. Their emphasis was on consensus-based, organic change. The Conservatives published a range of policy papers setting out in some detail their intentions should they secure office (Conservative Party, 2007a, 2007b, 2008, 2009, 2010b). These reassurances were reinforced by public awareness of Cameron's personal experience. His son, Ivan, was born with a rare and severely disabling medical condition that required round-the-clock care and treatment. Tragically, in February 2009, Ivan died at six years of age. Cameron placed on record his gratitude to the NHS, calling it 'one of the greatest achievements of the 20th century' (Elliott, 2009).

Although, to some extent, Cameron was able to reassure the public about Conservative plans for the NHS, doubts remained about whether the party had genuinely changed. According to one survey prior to the 2010 election, two thirds of Conservative MPs supported a policy of giving tax relief on private medical insurance (Sky News, 2009). Elements within the party remained opposed to the NHS and wanted radical reform. In 2009, the comments of Conservative MEP Daniel Hannan caused a furore when he described the NHS as a '60 year old mistake' that he 'wouldn't wish on anybody' (Summers and Glendenning, 2009). Although rebuked by Cameron and portrayed as a maverick, it was suspected that Hannan was not alone and that some senior Conservatives sympathised with his perspective (Helm and Syal, 2009).

The Conservatives' approach after the general election of 2010 can be seen as a shift back to the Right. Lansley's charm offensive abruptly ended once he became Secretary of State. The coalition government initially allowed him the freedom to develop a legislative framework, which eventually became the Health and Social Care Act 2012. Central oversight of his plans (by Number 10, the Cabinet Office and the Treasury) was weak (Timmins, 2012). The result was a much more radical reorganisation than most expected (although Timmins claims that most insiders were well aware of the likelihood of radical reorganisation). At the very least, the details of the changes proposed went further than previous public announcements, making a nonsense of the commitment in the coalition agreement not to undertake a top-down reorganisation. It was also at odds with Conservative criticism of 'pointless reorganisations' (although a moratorium on reorganisation was not in the Conservative manifesto or draft manifesto [Timmins, 2012]).

The NHS reforms, which were seen a primarily a Conservative policy, reflected badly on the party and Cameron himself. It undermined the hard work undertaken to reassure the electorate in the previous five years. The overwhelming criticism of Lansley's plans led to a sense of crisis within the coalition (see Timmins, 2012). The legislation was 'paused' to enable further consultation. Liberal Democrat disquiet was important, as will become clear later, but there was also considerable hostility to the reforms among Conservatives. A 'Number 10 insider' allegedly suggested that Lansley be 'taken out and shot' (Sylvester, 2012). The reforms were criticised by Tim Montgomerie, editor of Conservative Home (a Conservative blog), for handing an electoral advantage to Labour. He claimed that three coalition ministers had contacted him expressing concern (BBC News, 2012). Montgomerie called for the reforms to be scrapped and Lansley to be replaced. Two years later, senior Conservatives reportedly admitted that the NHS reorganisation was the coalition's biggest mistake (*The Independent*, 2014).

Liberal Democrat policy

The Liberal Democrats exerted much influence on health policy, although with regard to the NHS reforms, they were initially compliant. Timmins (2012) reports that Nick Clegg, the Liberal Democrat leader and Deputy Prime Minister, approved the legislative plans 'with a warm letter'. The party's position changed for two main reasons. First, rising discontent within the ranks of Liberal Democrat MPs and Peers, coupled with concerns within the wider party, placed pressure on their leaders to press for changes to the legislation. Second, with their popularity very low, as a result of concessions made when joining the coalition (notably, the U-turn on student fees), the Liberal Democrats needed to back a cause that would improve their public standing. In addition, the defeat of the proposal to introduce the alternative vote (AV) system for Westminster elections in the May 2011 referendum may have had an impact. The loss of one of the few fruits of coalition left the Liberal Democrats with little to show for their 'sacrifice'. They needed an issue with which to demonstrate that they could exert influence and were not merely propping up a Conservative government.

Dissension in Liberal Democrat ranks combined with opposition from Labour, and with protests from NHS staff. Along with growing public concern and adverse media coverage, this prompted the government to announce a two-month pause in the legislative process to further consult on the bill. The NHS Future Forum was established as a vehicle for this. It was headed by a doctor and its membership included clinicians, managers, service users, local authority social service representatives and voluntary organisations. The Forum and its subgroups produced a range of recommendations to amend the bill (NHS Future Forum, 2011). As a result, the bill was extensively amended: 375 substantive changes were made (Timmins, 2012). These concessions led to substantial clarifications and restrictions on the initial proposals, for example: the Secretary of State for Health's responsibilities for the NHS were clarified; the governance and membership of CCGs were altered, and their duties clarified; health and wellbeing boards were given a stronger role in the development of commissioning plans; clauses on competition were amended to allow for greater service integration; and provisions on patient and public involvement were strengthened.

Liberal Democrat influence continued after the Health and Social Care Act. One of the key areas was social care. Both Liberal Democrat health ministers that served during the coalition had responsibility for social care (see also Chapter Ten). Both emphasised the importance of social care and closer working between health and social services and played a key part in the development of initiatives that involved the transfer of NHS resources into joint-working arrangements in health and social care, culminating in the Better Care Fund.

Other forces

Although coalition politics played a key part in the changes to the NHS Bill, they would not have occurred without external pressure. This took the form of media and parliamentary pressure. Opponents of the legislation were well organised. Professional groups and trade unions mobilised effectively and raised issues concerning the legislation, both directly with the government and publicly (Timmins, 2012). They also lobbied Parliament. The Labour Party and backbench Liberal Democrats acted as key contact points. The cross-party Health

Committee (2011a, 2011b) raised questions about the reforms and how they would achieve the key objective of improving the efficiency and quality of services. The House of Lords played a very important part in the tabling and discussion of amendments. In particular, the Lords Constitution Committee had an important influence on the Bill's ministerial responsibility clauses. The less partisan chamber has often been a useful target for concerns regarding legislation, but on this occasion, the door was even more open than usual. Pressure from the Lords ensured that the government kept to its promises to implement key Future Forum recommendations.

Governments have long feared the media coverage of health issues, especially when individual cases of ill-treatment or neglect are highlighted. Professional groups, trade unions and other campaigning organisations were successful in getting the media to cover their concerns, especially with regard to the potential for privatisation. In addition to the traditional media, there was much activity on social media. A significant role was played by the Web-based campaign group 38 Degrees, which highlighted what it saw as key flaws in the Bill, notably, with regard to the potential for privatisation and the proposals to limit the Secretary of State's responsibility for the NHS. Timmins (2012) noted the important role of social media (email, Facebook and Twitter) in raising issues and orchestrating opposition to the Health and Social Care Bill (see also King et al, 2013).

Following the passage of the Health and Social Care Act, the politics of health became less stormy, although punctuated by squalls on the implementation of specific regulations (such as the competition regulation of 2013, which appeared to renege on some of the commitments made during the passage of the Act and which had to be withdrawn and reintroduced). The focus shifted to important but less controversial issues, such as service integration and quality and safety (which everyone could agree was important). Importantly for the coalition government, this enabled it to portray itself as a force for good, seeking to improve the health service rather than being accused of trying to destroy it.

Conclusions

In terms of the dimensions of political approaches (see Table 1.1), the coalition's emphasis on competition, markets, independent sector provision and patient choice signalled a clear affinity with the New Right. Similarly, the very low growth in the health budget, coupled with the focus on financial efficiency and cost savings, suggested proximity to the New Right approach. Nonetheless, the commitment to a publicly funded health-care system remained, and compared with other budgets, public expenditure on health was, to some extent, protected. Moreover, the coalition was forced to trim the radical edge of its reforms in order to get the legislation through Parliament. By the end of its term of office, attention had moved on to issues such as care quality and integration, which entailed a more collaborative and pragmatic approach. In addition, the coalition did acknowledge public health issues, including health inequalities, although, as noted earlier, its policies in these areas were relatively weak.

There is currently much consensus on the future direction of health policy, reflected in the generally positive response to the *Five year forward view*. Nonetheless, much controversy remains, especially on the role of the independent sector (and, in particular, 'for-profit' companies) in service provision. It remains to be seen whether or not the Conservative government, formed in 2015 after a surprise but slender general election victory, will chance its arm and push for a more radical New Right-influenced approach. This could involve a stronger push for privatisation, the restriction of free NHS services and new or increased charges. However, at the time of writing, there was no sign of this. Indeed, conciliatory noises were being made, even to the point of acknowledging the policies of defeated opponents (eg Labour's emphasis on health and care integration, and the Liberal Democrats' championing of mental health). In addition, the Conservative government promised an additional £8 billion of public money (after adjustments for inflation) by 2020/21, along with efficiency savings to meet the £30 billion funding gap. However, it also announced a large cut in public health budgets and a new 1% pay increase cap for NHS staff. Changes to regulation were announced (the creation of a new regulatory body, NHS Improvement, to merge the provider regulation roles of Monitor and the NHS Trust Development Authority and to host a new independent patient safety regulator). The Conservative government also placed great emphasis on making NHS services more widely available seven days a week.

Although, at the time of writing, the level of controversy around health was lower than in the recent past, there is plenty of scope for future turmoil. Already, NHS staff have expressed anger and concern about continued pay restraint and the possibility of enforced flexible hours contracts. Questions have been raised about the ability of the NHS to make efficiency gains on such a massive scale. There is also a strong suspicion that a Conservative government will reinvigorate the drive towards privatisation and the increased use of markets. In addition, the cuts to public health budgets have been strongly criticised. If past experience is any guide, a crisis will emerge at some stage, and the NHS will take its usual place in the crucible of party-political conflict.

References

Appleby, J., Baird, B., Thompson, J. and Jabbal, J. (2015a) *The NHS under the coalition government: part two NHS performance*, London: King's Fund.

Appleby, J., Thompson, J. and Jabbal, J. (2015b) *King's Fund quarterly monitoring review*, July, London: King's Fund.

Arora, S., Charlesworth, A., Kelly, E. and Stoye, G. (2013) *Public payment and private provision*, London: Nuffield Trust/Institute for Fiscal Studies.

Baggott, R. (2013) *Partnerships for public health and wellbeing*, Basingstoke: Palgrave.

Baggott, R. (2015) *Understanding health policy* (2nd edn), Bristol: The Policy Press.

BBC News (2012) 'Tory blogger Tim Montgomerie questions coalition NHS plan', 10 February. Available at: http://www.bbc.co.uk/news/uk-politics-16984848 (accessed 12 July 2015).

Bevan, G. and Hood, C. (2006) 'Have targets improved performance in the English NHS?', *British Medical Journal*, 332: 419–22.

Bevan, G., Karinikolos, M., Exley, J., Nolte, E., Connolly, S. and Mays, N. (2014) *The four health systems of the United Kingdom: How do they compare?*, London: Health Foundation/Nuffield Trust.

Bojke, C., Castelle, A., Grasic, K. and Street, A. (2015) *Productivity of the English NHS 2012/13 update*, Centre for Health Economics, University of York Research Paper 110, York: University of York.

Cabinet Office (2010) *The coalition: our programme for government*, London: Cabinet Office.

Commission on the Future of Health and Social Care in England (2014) *A new settlement for health and social care – final report*, London: King's Fund.

Communities and Local Government Committee (2013) *The role of local authorities in health issues*, London: The Stationery Office.

Conservative Party (2007a) *NHS autonomy and accountability: proposals for legislation*, London: Conservative Party.

Conservative Party (2007b) *The patient will see you now doctor*, London: Conservative Party.

Conservative Party (2008) *Delivering some of the best health in Europe: outcomes not targets*, London: Conservative Party.

Conservative Party (2009) *Renewal plan for a better NHS: plan for change*, London: Conservative Party.

Conservative Party (2010a) *Invitation to join the government of Britain: the Conservative manifesto 2010*, London: The Conservative Party.

Conservative Party (2010b) *A healthier nation*, Policy Green Paper 12, London: Conservative Party.

Davis, J., Lister, J. and Wrigley, D. (2015) *NHS for sale: myths, lies and deception*, London: Merlin.

Department of Health (2008) *High quality healthcare for all*, London: The Stationery Office.

Department of Health (2010) *Equity and excellence: liberating the NHS*, London: The Stationery Office.

Department of Health (2012) *Transforming care: a national response to Winterbourne View hospital – Final Report*, London: Department of Health.

Department of Health (2015) 'NHS and Department of Health investigations into Jimmy Savile'. Available at: www.gov.uk/government/collections/nhs-and-department-of-health-investigations-into-jimmy-savile (accessed 5 September 2015).

Dorey, P. (2007) 'A new direction or another false dawn: David Cameron and the crisis of British Conservatism', *British Politics*, 2(2): 259–69.

Elliot, F. (2009) 'Short, hard life of Ivan Cameron whose suffering could change Britain', *The Times*, 26 February. Available at: www.timesoline.co.uk (accessed 17 September 2010).

File on 4 (2014) 'NHS: testing the market', BBC Radio Four, broadcast on 19 October.

File on 4 (2015) 'Minding the gap: mental healthcare', BBC Radio Four, broadcast on 19 May.

Gilburt, H., Dunn, P. and Foot, C. (2015) *Local healthwatch: progress and promise*, London: King's Fund.

Greer, S., Jarman, H. and Azorsky, A. (2014) *A reorganisation you can see from space: the architecture of power in the new NHS*, London: Centre for Health and the Public Interest.

Ham, C., Baird, B., Gregory, S., Jabbal, J. and Alderwick, H. (2015) *The NHS under the coalition government: part one NHS reform*, London: King's Fund.

Health Committee (2011a) *Public health*, London: The Stationery Office.

Health Committee (2011b) *Commissioning*, London: The Stationery Office.

Health Committee (2012) *Social care*, London: The Stationery Office.

Health Committee (2014) *Public expenditure on health and social care*, London: The Stationery Office.

Hellowell, M. (2015) *The return of PFI - will the NHS pay a higher price for new hospitals?* London: Centre for Health and the Public Interest. Available at: http://chpi.org.uk/wp-content/uploads/2015/02/CHPI-PFI-Return-Nov14-2.pdf (accessed 12 July 2015).

Helm, T. and Syal, R. (2009) 'Key Tory MPs backed calls to dismantle NHS', *The Observer*, 16 August. Available at: www.guardian.co.uk (accessed 16 September 2010).

HM Government (2010) *The coalition: our programme for government*, London: Cabinet Office.

Hudson, B. (2015) 'Devo Manc: five early lessons for the NHS', *The Guardian*, 24 March.

Humphries, R. and Galea, A. (2013) *Health and wellbeing boards: one year on*, London: King's Fund.

Humphries, R., Galea, A., Sonola, L. and Mundle, C. (2012) *Health and Wellbeing Boards: systems leaders or talking shops?*, London: King's Fund.

Iacobucci, G. (2014) 'Raiding the public health budget', *British Medical Journal*, 348: 2274.

Keogh, B. (2013) *Report into the quality of care and treatment provided by 14 hospital trusts in England overview report*, London: Department of Health.

King, D., Ramirez-Cano, D., Greaves, F., Vlaev, I., Beales, S. and Darzi, A. (2013) 'Twitter and the health reforms in the English National Health Service', *Health Policy*, 110: 291–7.

Lee, S. and Beech, M. (eds) (2009) *The Conservatives under David Cameron: built to last?*, Basingstoke: Palgrave Macmillan.

Liberal Democrats (2010) *Manifesto 2010*, London: Liberal Democrats.

Mid Staffordshire Inquiry (2013) *The Mid Staffordshire NHS Foundation Trust public inquiry – final report* (Francis Report), London: The Stationery Office.

Morecambe Bay Inquiry Investigation (2015) *Report* (Kirkup Report), London: The Stationery Office.

National Advisory Group on the Safety of Patients in England (2013) *A promise to learn: a commitment to act: improving the safety of patients in England* (Berwick Review), London: Department of Health.

National Audit Office (2013) *NHS reorganisation: making the transition to the reformed health system*, London: The Stationery Office.

National Audit Office (2014) *Adult social care in England: overview*, London: The Stationery Office.

NHS Benchmarking Network (2013) 'Report'. Available at: http://www.nhsbenchmarking.nhs.uk/CubeCore/.uploads/icsurvey/NAIC%202013/NAICNationalReport2013.pdf (accessed 1 July 2015).

NHS England (2013) *The NHS belongs to the people: a call to action*, London: NHS England.

NHS England, Health Education England, Monitor, Care Quality Commission, NHS Trust Development Authority and Public Health England (2014) *NHS five year forward view*, London: NHS England.

NHS Future Forum (2011) *Summary report on proposed changes to the NHS*, London: Department of Health.

Nuffield Trust (2013) *Rating providers for quality: a policy worth pursuing?*, London: Nuffield Trust.

Paton, C. (2014) *At what cost? Paying the price for the market in the NHS*, London: Centre for Health in the Public Interest.

Pollock, A. and Price, D. (2013) *Duty to care: in defence of universal health care*, London: Centre for Labour and Social Studies.

Public Health England (2015) *Public health outcomes framework: indicators at a glance* February, London: Public Health England.

Ridley-Duff, R. and Bull, M. (2015) *Understanding social enterprise: theory and practice*, 2nd edn, London: Sage.

Sky News (2009) 'Tory Party of NHS claims in tatters again', 23 August. Available at: www.skynews.com (accessed 16 September 2010).

Sylvester, R. (2012) 'Is Lansley the exception to the no-sacking policy?', *The Times*, 7 February.

Summers, D. and Glendenning, L. (2009) 'Cameron rebukes Tory MEP who rubbished NHS in America', *The Guardian*, 14 August. Available at: www.guardian.co.uk (accessed 16 June 2010).

Thaler, R. and Sunstein, C. (2009) *Nudge: improving decisions about health, wealth and happiness*, London: Penguin.

The Independent (2014) 'Government's reorganisation of the NHS was its biggest mistake say senior Tories', 13 October. Available at: independent.co.uk (accessed 12 June 2015).

Timmins, N. (2012) *Never again: the story of the Health and Social Care Act 2012: a study in coalition government and policy making*, London: King's Fund & Institute for Government.

Tudor Jones, G. (2013) *Assessing the transition to a more localist health system: the first step towards a marriage between the NHS and local government?*, London: Localis.

Vizard, P. and Obolenskaya, P. (2015) *The coalition's record on health: policy, spending and outcomes 2010–15*, Social Policy in a Cold Climate: Summary Working Paper 16, London: CASE/LSE.

Welikala, J. and West, D. (2015) 'Third of CCGs consider limiting access amid cash squeeze', *Health Service Journal*, 24 April, pp 4–5.

West, D. (2014) 'Patient choice is not key to improving performance says Hunt', *Health Service Journal*, 26 November. Available at: www.hsj.co.uk/news/acute-care/exclusive-patient-choice-is-not-key-to-improving-performance-says-hunt/5077051.article (accessed 12 July 2015).

SIX

The coalition government, the general election and the policy ratchet in education: a reflection on the 'ghosts' of policy past, present and yet to come

Patrick L.J. Bailey and Stephen J. Ball

Introduction

This chapter offers a general overview of the Conservative–Liberal Democrat coalition government's education policy (2010–15) and attends to some specific features and trends. It has not been possible to comment directly on early years, further and higher education as our emphasis here is on the compulsory sector. However, the main trends and emphases with coalition policy were played out in those other sectors in specific ways.[1] We also point to some of the relationships between coalition education policy and that of the Conservative government elected in May 2015 and offer some initial thoughts on the first 100 days of the new government.

One of the key things that we emphasise is *continuity* and *change*, that is, how coalition policy both built upon the policies of New Labour and also shifted the rhetorical and discursive problem-space of policy along some different lines. Related to this, we also address some of the continuing tensions within education policy that, while long and fraught, in the current context, can in part be traced back to the 'landmark' Conservative education reforms in the 1980s, and the Education Reform Act 1988 in particular.

One way of thinking about continuities and changes is through the notion of the 'policy ratchet' (Ball, 2008). This refers to the small and incremental moves whereby certain modes of policy thinking and practice become naturalised and necessary, the ways in which policy is colonised and informed by logical rationalities in which certain discursive and practical possibilities are opened up, embedded and intensified, with the consequence that what may have once seemed impossible or simply unthinkable becomes sensible, obvious and inevitable. This colonisation of thought is not simply epistemological; it is also a material process whereby certain voices and educational purposes are attributed value and legitimacy over and against others, and includes the posing and enactment of particular policy solutions for tackling social problems. These social problems are themselves mediated discursively, and a general election is one 'event' where 'policy windows' (Kingdon, 1995) are opened for new ideas and new trajectories, but also for further *ratcheting*. Indeed, the ratcheting of policy is perhaps never more apparent than around the time of a general election, although what was significant this time around was that education was *not* a key battleground for political positioning and point-scoring, and *not* a key arena over which the election was fought.

One important caveat that must be borne in mind at the outset is the wider context within which education policy is embedded and that it is subject to. On the one hand, there are the exigencies and opportunities of globalisation, the public discourse around which is both 'descriptive' and 'normative' (Furlong, 2013; Rizvi and Lingard, 2010). As we will demonstrate, the coalition was quick to position its educational policies and reform agenda within the context of a competitive and inevitable global order, including the role of education towards this end (see later), although, in some ways, this has proved to be more rhetorical than practical (Furlong, 2013). On the other hand, but relatedly, coalition policy and rhetoric also needs to be understood in relation to the economic context, and especially the public spending cuts that followed the financial crisis – the new 'age of austerity'. Although spending in the compulsory sector has maintained recent historic levels to a large extent, money has been 'saved' and/or 'rerouted' from other areas of educational planning and spending, and from other areas of welfare provision – although many schools have seen a drop in their budgets and, on recent projections, this is only set to become more pronounced:

> School costs could rise by 16% between 2014–15 and 2019–20. The Conservatives propose the smallest increase in spending of the major parties: a 7% nominal increase from 2016–20 – a cash-terms freeze per pupil. This would be for 4–16 year-olds only. Labour, meanwhile, proposes a 7.7% nominal increase by keeping the budget rising in line with inflation – and for all 3–19 year-olds. The Liberal Democrats have been keen to talk schools, in part because

they are proposing a rise in line with prices and pupils – a 15% rise – for the full age range. This is, they say, a "red line" for them to join any coalition. There will be big regional differences in the likely effects of this: different areas of England are funded at quite different levels. But the big picture is that the two main parties are proposing plans which imply the next five years may be harder to manage than the past five. (Cook, 2015)

The question of where and how money was spent (and 'saved') in education is thus a crucial one, and we will have something to say about this later on. Following on from this, then, are the implications of the economic context for the specific directions and forms of policy and rhetoric under the coalition, especially the ways in which the responsibility for social well-being and social mobility was allocated through a skilful but dubious re-territorialisation of the debate around equality and social justice.

It is also worth briefly pointing out that we view coalition education policy as very much dominated by the Conservatives, although this is not to say that the Liberal Democrats had no influence. Not only did the Liberal Democrats specifically claim responsibility for the Pupil Premium (see later), but they also blocked some of the Conservatives' 2010 manifesto pledges, including the introduction of reading tests for six year olds and the proposed organisation of the primary curriculum more rigidly around subjects like maths, science and history. On the other hand, while the Liberal Democrats pledged in their manifesto to replace the National Curriculum with a 'minimum curriculum entitlement', and to reduce class sizes, both of these key policies were left out of the coalition agreement (for a full breakdown of the Liberal Democrat and Conservative pledges that did and did not form part of the coalition agreement, see Lupton and Thomson, 2015, pp 55–60). These differences in policy notwithstanding, the two parties formed an agreement underpinned by the following approach to education:

The Government believes that we need to reform our school system to tackle educational inequality, which has widened in recent years, and to give greater powers to parents and pupils to choose a good school. We want to ensure high standards of discipline in the classroom, robust standards and the highest quality teaching. We also believe that the state should help parents, community groups and others come together to improve the education system by starting new schools. (Cabinet Office, 2010, p 28)

It should also be said that neither party developed an extensive education policy agenda in their election manifestos.

Coalition education policy

Coalition education policy was characterised by both continuity and change from New Labour. However, this framing device is a little misleading in that the continuities were in some respects also characterised by change, and the changes were in some ways characterised by continuity. This rather counterintuitive argument will make more sense following a brief discussion of the key philosophical influences on coalition policy, and by providing some historical context.

Philosophy and historical context

Two dominant philosophical seams or rationalities underpinned coalition policy. On the one hand, there was the continuing neoliberal emphasis on the minimal state and a belief in the sanctity, efficiency and effectiveness of the market – to which both partners of the coalition were wedded and in agreement. In this sense, the coalition was 'guided by a [New Right] vision of the weak state. Thus, what is private is necessarily good and what is public is necessarily bad' (Apple, 2000, p 59). The marketisation and privatisation of education was ratcheted up by the coalition with the further mobilisation of new actors and agencies in the policy process – begun by New Labour – and there was a continuing move to open up service delivery to new providers and to offer some schools greater freedom and autonomy in order that they may innovate, diversify and 'drive up standards', and offer greater choice to parents and students as consumers. However, Furlong (2013) makes the point that this continuity has also taken a somewhat different form under the coalition, which he suggests has articulated a different 'version' of neoliberalism to New Labour. He suggests that, '[l]ike New Labour, neoliberalism is central to government thinking. It is the market that will deliver greater equality, global competitiveness, and more traditional (neoconservative) forms of teaching and learning' (Furlong, 2013, p 42) – the latter clearly reflecting a version of 'one nation' conservativism. However, he also notes that:

now, rather than being the means whereby government can impose its will in a centralized way, neoliberalism is understood in more traditional terms. It is being presented as the key to localism, with an aim to abolish centralised bureaucracies and allow a wide variety of agencies to deliver state services. (Furlong, 2013, p 42)

The coalition also continued to invoke the exigencies and opportunities of globalisation, positioning education, schools and teachers as vital to ensuring economic competiveness in the 'global race'. The White Paper *The Importance of Teaching* (Department of Education, 2010), published shortly after the 2010 general election, opens:

So much of the education debate in this country is backward looking: have standards fallen? Have exams got easier? These debates will continue, but what really matters is how we are doing compared with our international competitors. That is what will define our economic growth and our country's future. The truth is, at the moment we are standing still while others race past. (Department of Education, 2010, p 3)

On the other hand, coalition policy was characterised by neo-conservatism, evident in the continued central command and control over knowledge and values, and the ongoing mistrust and surveillance of the teacher. In this way, the coalition government was 'guided by a vision of the strong state. This is especially true surrounding issues of knowledge, values, and the body' (Apple, 2000, p 67). Schools and teachers continued to be told what and how to teach through a prescriptive and narrow curriculum, and there was a particular emphasis on more traditional forms of pedagogy, 'real subjects' and 'facts' – what Michael Gove called a move away from 'soft' and 'airy fairy' subjects, and towards more 'rigour' and 'the best which has been thought and said'.[2] Michael Gove also argued for more 'patriotic history', the restoration of times tables and more work on British authors in English Literature courses – resulting in the dropping of *To kill a mockingbird* and *Of mice and men* from GCSE English examinations:

Exam boards were issued with strict guidance by the Department for Education (DfE) when drawing up the new English literature GCSE, which has no coursework element, instead testing teenagers through two exams at the end of year 11. Students taking the OCR exam [Oxford, Cambridge and RSA Examinations] from 2015 will be required to study a pre-20th century novel, Romantic poetry and a Shakespeare play. (*The Independent*, 2014)

Bethan Marshall, a senior lecturer in English at King's College London, told *The Sunday Times*: 'It's a syllabus out of the 1940s and rumour has it Michael Gove, who read literature, designed it himself. Schools will be incredibly depressed when they see it'.[3]

The coalition also invoked a decidedly Conservative narrative of moral atrophy and social malaise, which was re-emphasised following the 'London riots' in 2011. This formed a part of the government's 'broken society agenda', which, in education, among other things, centred on 'poor pupil behaviour' as a policy problem, with a related call for stronger discipline and authority in schools, classrooms and the wider society. There has also been a focus on 'troubled families' and 'bad parenting', a point we return to again later with reference to specific policies (see also Chapters Eleven and Twelve):

Do we have the determination to confront the slow-motion moral collapse that has taken place in parts of our country these past few generations? Irresponsibility. Selfishness. Behaving as if your choices have no consequences. Children without fathers. Schools without discipline. Reward without effort. Crime without punishment. Rights without responsibilities. Communities without control. Some of the worst aspects of human nature tolerated, indulged – sometimes even incentivised – by a state and its agencies that in parts have become literally de-moralised.… In my very first act as leader of this party I signalled my personal priority: to mend our broken society. (Speech by David Cameron, 2011[4])

We will increase the authority of classroom teachers and support them to discipline pupils appropriately. We will strengthen powers to search pupils, issue detentions and use reasonable force where necessary. We will support head teachers to maintain a culture of discipline and respect. (DfE, 2010, p 33)

Together, this ostensibly contradictory philosophical approach constituted a key tension in coalition policy, but also articulates, naturalises and embeds what Apple (2000) calls 'conservative modernisation' in social policy, a phenomenon that has a global significance. However, this tension between a weak but strong state, and between freedom and control, liberty and authority, is not new and can, in fact, be traced back, in its current iteration, to the 'landmark' Education Reform Act in 1988. This key event in the recent history of education sutured together an ideological mix – sometimes referred to as the New Right – which set in motion a pronounced commitment to both marketisation and central command and control, constituting the new 'common sense' of policy (Apple, 2014). This 'common-sense' approach continued through New Labour, albeit in some different ways and with some divergent emphases, and again through the coalition's time in office. Stevenson (2011, p 179) describes this as 'the realisation of the "1988 project"', and the 'long shadow' of Thatcherism in social and educational policy.

While the neoliberal influences on coalition policy can be attributed to both the Conservatives and the Liberal Democrats, as noted, with both parties' pre-election manifestos in 2010 being rather similar in their emphasis on market freedoms as an organisational and moral principle, the renewed and reinvigorated one nation neo-conservatism that has been seen over the past five years can be credited to the more dominant Conservative bloc of the coalition. This has been particularly significant given that it was Conservative ministers who occupied most of the major posts in the cabinet, including the ministerial position of Secretary of State for Education (initially held by Michael Gove and towards the end of the coalition government by Nicky Morgan). Other key individuals in the DfE included: the Conservative politician Nick Gibb, the Minister of State for Education, who courted some controversy when he declared shortly after his appointment that 'I would rather have a physics graduate from Oxbridge without a PGCE [Postgraduate Certificate in Education] teaching in a school than a physics graduate from one of the rubbish universities with a PGCE' (Williams, 2010); the former businessman and financier, and Conservative Party donor, Lord Nash, Parliamentary Under Secretary of State for Schools and particularly involved in the Academies and Free Schools programmes (Nash also sits on the board of the Conservative think-tank the Centre for Policy Studies, and is co-founder of the charity Future, which sponsors academies); and David Laws, the Minister of State for Schools, alongside his predecessor Sarah Teather, the only Liberal Democrat politicians who occupied high-ranking positions in the department (Laws' tenure was also rather brief).

Policy (dis)ensemble and policy (dis)continuity

One of the first things that the coalition did was to rebrand the central department responsible for education, broadly conceived. New Labour's more holistic Department for Children, Schools and Families (DCSF) was replaced by the 'Department for Education' and the other areas of responsibility were redistributed to other departments. This was a significant initial development in that it embodied a further shift away from New Labour's arguably more social-democratic Every Child Matters framework for child and family support services, and towards a more narrowed focus on educational 'outcomes'. Stewart and Obolenskaya (2015) describe this as a shift in approach from 'well-being' to 'achievement'. Despite earlier pledges by the Conservatives to maintain support for Sure Start, a New Labour initiative to improve child and family welfare through local and joined-up support services, spending on this programme has been reduced since 2010, following the removal of its ring fence shortly after the election in 2010, and a number of centres have closed and/or been merged and reorganised – reducing both accessibility and interventionist scope (for a detailed analysis, see Stewart and Obolenskaya, 2015). On the other hand, there has also been a shift towards more punitive family interventions, over and against economic and resource distribution. As noted, there has been a policy emphasis on families and parenting, with the rolling out of a 'Troubled Families Programme' in 2012, and the publishing of the Allen Report (Cabinet Office, 2011), an 'independent' and cross-party review into the social and emotional well-being of children in the early years (0–5), with recommendations for evidenced-based interventions, especially into the home environment (see Chapter Twelve):

> Troubled families are those that have problems and cause problems to the community around them, putting high costs on the public sector. The government is committed to working with local authorities and their partners to help 120,000 troubled families in England turn their lives around by 2015. We want to ensure the children in these families have the chance of a better life, and at the same time bring down the cost to the taxpayer.[5]

> In July 2010, the Prime Minister asked me to lead a review on Early Intervention. I was glad to accept. I have a long-standing personal interest in policies to break the cycle of deprivation and dysfunction from generation to

generation.... Getting this wrong has impacts way beyond the individual and family concerned: every taxpayer pays the cost of low educational achievement, poor work aspirations, drink and drug misuse, teenage pregnancy, criminality and unfulfilled lifetimes on benefits. But it is not just about money – important as this is, especially now – it is about social disruption, fractured lives, broken families and sheer human waste. (Cabinet Office, 2011, p ix)

Although the more punitive and authoritarian focus on dysfunctional families, communities and individuals is an example of the coalition's neo-conservative agenda, this apparent change in policy trajectory was also characterised by continuity with New Labour's Every Child Matters initiative. While the latter did frame the pursuit of social justice and equity within a wider narrative of common goals, commitments and rights, it was also a 'composite' economic and disciplinary policy (Ball, 2010, p 190), which both problematised 'troublesome' sections of the population as requiring moral intervention, and subsumed equity (and education) within economic goals and purposes. Lister (2000, p 97) described New Labour's approach as 'a marked retreat from greater equality as an explicit goal.... In their place [was] the objective of "redistribution of opportunity", through education, training and paid employment'.

Other early moves included cancelling New Labour's Building Schools for the Future (BSF) programme and abolishing the Education Maintenance Allowance (EMA), which provided up to £30 a week for students from low-income households to encourage their participation in further education. Nonetheless, money has been invested in other areas, and especially into the Free Schools programme and the Pupil Premium, the latter of which has been saved from other areas of spending (see the coalition government's *Programme for government* [Cabinet Office, 2010]). Following their introduction by New Labour in 1998, tuition fees in higher education were raised by the coalition, with higher education institutions now able to charge up to £9,000 a year. The raising of tuition fees was particularly damaging for the Liberal Democrats as it broke their pre-election manifesto pledge to abolish them. The teaching of synthetic phonics in schools was extended, and a new statutory phonics test was introduced for children at the end of Year One – a key influence here being the Conservative Education Minister, Nick Gibb (see later). Despite some differences in approach and rationalisation,[6] the coalition vastly expanded New Labour's academies programme, with over half of state-maintained schools in England now 'enjoying' the 'freedoms' of academy status, operating outside of local government control – the new Conservative government has also published its Education and Adoption Bill in 2015 to make it easier to academise schools in 'special measures' or considered to be 'coasting', and without any form of local consultation. The first free schools – schools that can be established by civil society groups and outside of local government control – were approved shortly after the general election in 2010, with a handful opening their doors in the autumn of 2011, and in 2015, despite a number of well-publicised problems, David Cameron announced their further expansion alongside more academies:

> Over 4,000 schools are already benefitting from academy status, giving them more power over discipline and budgets. And nearly 800 of the worst-performing primary schools have been taken over by experienced academy sponsors with a proven track record of success. This is improving education for our children. So we will continue to expand academies, free schools, studio schools and University Technical Colleges. Over the next parliament, we will open at least 500 new free schools, resulting in 270,000 new school places. And we will introduce new powers to force coasting schools to accept new leadership. (Conservative Party, 2015)

There were also significant policy developments in teaching and teacher training, with further moves towards more school-based teacher preparation (Schools Direct, Teach First) and a continuing deregulation of teacher supply (see later) – all of which have begun to residualise the traditional higher education route into teaching.

Coalition education ministers made considerable use of performance management and governance-by-numbers techniques to steer the system. They changed key performance indicators, both introducing the English Baccalaurate (E-Bac) and eliminating over 2,000 courses that had previously contributed to the General Certificate of Secondary Education (GCSE) indicator, and raised the benchmark targets for all schools. A-levels were restructured and their system of grades was changed, and a new set of applied and technical A-level programmes were introduced. These changes have had a very direct impact on the school curriculum and classroom pedagogy (Ball et al, 2012). The coalition also increased the funding for apprenticeships and launched Studio Schools and University Technical Colleges.[7]

This very brief overview of policy developments under the coalition gives a sense of the policy terrain across some of the different educational sectors. We now focus down on some specific areas and attend to them in some more detail. This will include the academy and free school programmes, and teacher and teacher training policy.

Free-er and Free-er?

In neoliberal mode, the coalition began its term in office by introducing a range of supply-side measures designed to 'set education free', introducing yet more new providers and new choices, wresting yet more schools away from local authorities by creating many more academies, cutting red tape, scrapping quasi-autonomous non-governmental organisations (quangos), and creating a streamlined funding model where government funding follows the learner and is dispensed directly to schools from central government. As noted earlier, much of this was signalled in the Conservatives' election manifesto in 2010. Forms of alternative provision have been dramatically expanded in a drive to introduce further 'flexibilities' into the education system. This has been mainly done by gradually enabling all schools (including primary schools and those judged as 'outstanding' and 'good' by Ofsted), if they wish, to become academies in a series of policy moves initiated with the Academies Bill of July 2010. In November 2010, the possibility of schools applying for academy status was extended to those deemed 'satisfactory' by Ofsted, if partnered by an 'outstanding' school – with similarities here to New Labour's Foundation Trust policy, which awarded 'earned autonomy' in finance and decision-making to hospital trusts deemed by the government to be performing well. Subsequently, many 'poor-performing schools' have been forced into academisation and some have been 'brokered' to sponsors. In turn, 'outstanding' schools have been encouraged to form relationships with poorly performing schools and executive heads have been parachuted in to 'save' such schools through the creation of federations. Former Secretary of State Michael Gove (2010–14) expected that academies would become the norm among English schools, an expectation enhanced by the fact that where a need for a new school is identified, local authorities must now seek proposals for academies or free schools, as legislated in the coalition's Education Act 2011.[8] As of February 2015, there were 4,461 academies open in England.[9] These figures are compared to a total of 203 academies open in May 2010. Academies are not bound by national agreements on pay and conditions, they have greater freedom to vary the National Curriculum than other schools, and they receive additional funding (which in surveys is shown to be the primary reason for most head teachers to consider academy conversion):

> In England, the current Conservative-led coalition has taken the academies programme initiated by Labour and greatly expanded it, meanwhile ratcheting up Labour's regime of a narrow curriculum, high stakes testing, school league tables and heavy handed external teacher inspection for schools that refuse to join the academies club. (Alexander, 2014, p 10)

In addition to academies, the government legislated for the creation of free schools (Academies Act 2010 and Education Act 2011). Free schools are 'all-ability state-funded schools set up in response to what local people say they want and need in order to improve education for children in their community'.[10] They may be set up by a wide range of proposers – including charities, universities, businesses, educational groups, teachers and groups of parents – with the same freedoms and flexibilities as academies. The introduction of free schools synthesises a number of aspects of coalition education policy: both greater choice for parents and more competition between schools, but also a further iteration of traditionalism (inasmuch as a significant number of schools celebrate traditional pedagogies, curricula and relationships, although others make a point of innovation and experimentation – and, again, there is a tension evident here between neoliberal and neo-conservative ideology). Both programmes have also opened up new opportunities for education businesses.[11] What is also significant about the academies and free schools programmes in governance terms is that they are specifically intended to bring about a further diminution and residualisation of local authorities, in continuity with the Education Reform Act 1988. At the same time, they also contribute to a general change in the labour conditions of teaching, that is: the 'remodelling' and 'flexibilisation' of the teaching profession begun by New Labour, which under the coalition, involved the establishing of a relationship between pay and performance; the devolution of contract negotiations to the institutional level; and the deregulation of the work of teaching to allow non-registered, non-qualified staff to undertake classroom activities (a 'freedom' originally granted to free schools that was extended to academies in 2012):

> Unlike local authority schools and academies, free schools
> can employ teachers without teaching qualifications and,
> like academies, they can ignore national agreements on
> pay and conditions. Stem Academy Tech City near the
> Angel in London came to attention last year when some
> of its staff went on strike after the school announced its
> intention to introduce zero-hours contracts for teachers.
> The enormous amount of time teachers spend marking and
> planning lessons would go unpaid, and they would only
> receive a salary at all during term-time. (Foster, 2015, p 9)

At the same time, universities have lost their monopoly of teacher
education as various new kinds of entry into teaching have been
established – in particular, Schools Direct (schools-based training)
and Teach First (a social enterprise funded by the DfE and corporate
sponsors).[12]

Arguably, the coalition's academies and free schools programmes
articulate with different aspects of the overall Conservative project of
reform: on the one hand, the Big Society, as 'a power shift away from
central government to the people, families and communities of Britain'
(Deputy Prime Minister Nick Clegg, quoted in HM Government,
2010, p 1); and, on the other, a free market, business orientation and
the possibility of schools run for profit by large corporations. There
are parent and teacher and community groups founding their own
free schools, as against the development of academy chains, some of
which are aiming to run dozens of schools – Academies Enterprise
Trust (AET) is the largest provider, with 80 schools.

Both academies and free schools were created as responses to what
has been presented, by all governments since the 1980s, as the low
standards of performance of some state schools, especially in areas of
social disadvantage. These new kinds of schools, it is argued by their
sponsors,[13] will bring creativity and energy to bear upon entrenched
social and educational inequalities. Some of these new schools perform
well, but: a number of academies and free schools have been deemed
by inspection and performance outcomes as 'underperforming'; some
chains of academies have been found to be unable to manage their
schools effectively; some chains of academies and free schools appear
to be indulging in dubious financial practices; the free schools were
supposed to be targeted at areas of social disadvantage, but recent
research by Higham (2014) indicates that their distribution does not
reflect this aim –indeed, DfE figures indicate that the majority of the
24 free schools that opened in 2011 have a lower proportion of children

eligible for free school meals than the local average (*The Guardian*, 2012); 18 academy chains are now 'paused' – that is, concerns related to their performance and management abilities mean they cannot take on further schools (the list includes AET, the largest academy chain, with 80 schools, and E-Act, which runs 34); and 68 academies have received pre-warning letters and seven warning letters from the DfE about their poor performance. Indeed, Lupton and Thomson (2015, p 5) note that this will be a key issue for the new government: 'Ways of managing the new fragmented system are still evolving and will be a key challenge for the next government.... The next government will inherit a school system in flux and key issues of equity and achievement still unresolved'.

The Ofsted assessment of E-Act academies reported an 'overwhelming proportion of pupils … not receiving a good education'. Inspectors visited 16 of E-Act's 34 academies over a two-week period – one was judged outstanding, four were good, six were judged as requiring improvement and five, including Hartsbrook E-Act Free School in London, were deemed inadequate. Hartsbrook has now been closed twice and has its third sponsor. Key weaknesses in the 16 academies inspected included:

1. poor-quality teaching;
2. work not matched to pupils' abilities;
3. weak monitoring;
4. poor use of assessment data; and
5. insufficiently challenging lessons for more able pupils.

Inspectors also discovered that E-Act had deducted a proportion of Pupil Premium funding from each Academy until 1 September 2013. Ofsted was unclear how the deducted funding was being used to help disadvantaged pupils.

Four free schools of the 41 that had judgements published as of April 2014 have been rated 'inadequate' by the inspectorate – this is 9.7%, compared with the national average for all schools of 3%. Overall, 79% of state schools are rated good or outstanding, compared with only 68% of free schools.[14]

In December 2014, the Chief Inspector of Schools, Sir Michael Wilshaw, a one-time academy 'superhead', stated in his annual report that struggling schools are 'no better off' under academy control and that there could be little difference in school improvement under an academy chain or a council. Imagining the position of a head teacher of a newly converted academy, he said: 'In fact, the neglect you suffered at the hands of your old local authority is indistinguishable from the neglect you endure from your new trust' (*The Guardian*, 2014).

In response to these deficits, a new layer of school governance made up of Regional Commissioners, appointed by the Secretary of State, and Boards, elected by local head teachers, has been established. The Regional School Commissioners (RSCs) and their Boards (made up mostly of head teachers) are intended to act as regulators, interveners, advocates and animators, and are responsible for both managing and growing the academies programme, towards ex-Secretary of State Michael Gove's goal that every school become an academy. The RSCs also mark another move in the almost total displacement of local authorities from education policy responsibility, while mimicking some of their previous roles. They also suggest an odd and unclear relationship to Ofsted.

Very briefly, there were also a complex set of changes to Ofsted and other forms of regulation under the coalition. While the scope and complexity of these changes cannot be mapped here, it is worth noting that there was dissatisfaction with the quality and consistency of Ofsted inspections throughout the coalition's time in office, and Sir Michael Wilshaw announced in 2014 plans to renationalise them (through a curtailment of third-party contracting). The coalition also proposed a renewed 'core purpose' for Ofsted, with inspections now focused on a more limited set of educational concerns: pupil achievement, teacher quality, leadership and management, and the safety and behaviour of pupils. This was set against the Ofsted framework under New Labour, which graded schools against a wider set of outcomes, including the cultural, moral and social development of pupils. There were also changes to the terminology of school grading – 'requires improvement' replacing 'satisfactory' – and a new 'proportionate' approach to inspection was proposed. According to Clarke and Lindgren (2015, p 150), the latter is about 'releasing outstanding schools from the burden of inspection but intensifying inspection for weaker/inadequate schools'. These actual and proposed changes, and the relationship between Ofsted and the new Conservative government, deserve further and ongoing scrutiny.

From 'great expectations' to 'managing expectations'?

Alongside the coalition's emphasis on moral decline and social entropy was a skilful but myopic colonisation of the debate around social (in)justice and social (im)mobility. This was arguably a form of 'compassionate conservatism' – part of the rebranding exercise undertaken by the Conservatives following their election failure in 2005 – which has seen educational reform and social mobility reframed within a rhetoric of moral necessity, even moral outrage. In particular, *The importance of teaching* (DfE, 2010) White Paper outlined the coalition's 'compassionate' commitment to addressing the link between economic deprivation and educational attainment, with a particular focus on the 'soft bigotry of low expectations' in schools:

> [N]o country that wishes to be considered world class can afford to allow children from poorer families to fail as a matter of course. For far too long we have tolerated the moral outrage of an accepted correlation between wealth and achievement at school; the soft bigotry of low expectations. Children on free school meals do significantly worse than their peers at every stage of their education. They are just half as likely to get good GCSEs as the average. More children from some private schools go to Oxbridge than from the entire cohort of children on free school meals. (DfE, 2010, p 4)

In 2012, Nick Gibb delivered a speech on the 200th anniversary of Charles Dickens's birth, in which he played on the title of *Great expectations* to enforce this point, while, at the same time, championing the cause of curriculum reform, including the introduction of synthetic phonics in primary schools:

> We need – if you'll forgive the Dickens pun – much greater expectations of children in reading. And this is why the Government is absolutely determined to help all children, from all backgrounds, to become fluent and enthusiastic readers.
>
> We already know how to tackle reading failure from the youngest ages. High quality international evidence has demonstrated that the systematic teaching of synthetic phonics is the best way of making sure young children acquire the crucial skills they need to read new text, so driving up standards in reading. Children are taught the sounds of the alphabet and how to blend those sounds into words.
>
> Taught as part of a language rich curriculum, systematic synthetic phonics allows problems to be identified early and rectified before it is too late. (Gibb, 2012)

While the coalition positioned tackling inequality as a key policy focus, its approach was to allocate responsibility for this to individual schools and teachers, and families themselves, at the same time as undertaking other reforms to the welfare system that saw incomes reduced for the most disadvantaged families (changes to the benefits system and tax credits) and local government support services severely curtailed. In a certain sense, the moral debate around education and inequality has been appropriated by and subsumed within the 'skills debate' and the logics of the market – what Shamir (2008) calls the 'moralisation of the economic action', and Brookes et al (2009) call the shift from 'correcting for' to 'connecting to' the market:

> The CBI surveyed 500 employers and found that 42 per cent were dissatisfied with school leavers' use of English. While at the end of last year, army recruiting officers revealed that hundreds of would-be soldiers are being turned away because they cannot pass the most basic literacy and numeracy tests – that is, because they have a reading age of less than an 11-year-old.
>
> The net result? We have tumbled down the world rankings for literacy from 7th to 25th and the reading ability of GCSE pupils in England is now more than a year behind the standard of their peers in Shanghai, Korea and Finland. And at least six months behind those in Hong Kong, Singapore, Canada, New Zealand, Japan and Australia....
>
> The government is determined to change what we expect of young people and schools that teach them. Great Expectations may have come to Philip Pirrip – but it's high expectations that we need for every child in the country regardless of background or ability. (Gibb, 2012)

Not only is the need for 'basic skills' increasingly promoted as a form of human capital development (for the poor), but the market is also on hand to provide the resources and expertise necessary for its effective implementation, with further implications for the work of the teacher and teacher training. In her review of the form and costing of the coalition's literacy policy, Margaret Clark (2014, p 14) noted the commercial opportunities being opened up for various educational companies:

> Over the period September 2011 to October 2013 DfE made match-funding available for schools that either

purchased commercial materials or training courses from 'The Importance of Phonics' catalogue. The match-funding programme was managed for the Government by a group of five organisations known as Pro5; an agreed commission was included in the catalogue sale price.... Over that period a total of £23,593,109 match-funding was provided for schools. A breakdown of those receiving the largest amounts within the training programme of approximately £1,095,733 showed that £546,614 went to Ruth Miskin Literacy Ltd. Sounds Write Ltd received £129,734 and Ann Foster Literacy £73,654. The remaining 27 providers listed received the rest of the money.

Together with curriculum changes and school reform, the coalition also rolled out its flagship Pupil Premium policy, which initially formed a cornerstone of the Liberal Democrats' election manifesto in 2010. The Pupil Premium is designed to provide extra money to schools in the form of per capita funding for students eligible for Free School Meals, a proxy indicator of deprivation. The government did not dictate how this money is to be used by schools, and there is a lack of clarity over how this is actually being spent, with some concerns that it may be being used to offset the effects of other budget cuts.

It is worth noting that the Pupil Premium, while ostensibly a more social-democratic form of policy intervention that aims to distribute extra resources according to need, can also be viewed as a form of economisation. Ball (2006) has noted that one of the outcomes of the Education Reform Act 1988 has been the emergence of an 'economy of student worth', whereby schools compete to attract students deemed capable of adding 'value' in the form of good test scores. These (largely middle-class) students pose less risk to schools and are less likely to require additional support, which might be expensive. The Pupil Premium is interesting in this respect as it assigns a market value to those students who are less attractive to schools, and can hence be considered an instance of neoliberal policy.[15] However, as noted earlier, tackling inequality, for the coalition, was the responsibility of schools and teachers, rather than the state, and it is for this reason that the Pupil Premium must be contextualised within the wider process of welfare and educational reform:

But despite the passion, to date there has been only one policy directly focused on addressing inequality, and that is the so-called 'pupil premium', which provides additional school funding for students from poorer backgrounds. But because of overall cuts in school budgets as a result of the recession, the vast majority of schools, even those with large numbers of disadvantaged students, are facing substantial cuts rather than increases in their budgets. Therefore, if a reduction in inequality is to be achieved, it will be done as an outcome of other strategies aimed at more general educational improvement. (Furlong, 2013, p 41)

There is real irony, then, in the coalition's attempt to manage expectations around social mobility, which has also been on the agenda in the first 100 days of the new Conservative government. This can be observed in the Conservatives' 'character education' policy, which is being piloted in a number of schools and could be rolled out over the course of the new administration. The push and pull to 'upskill' the disadvantaged student through academic rigour and tougher examinations is now being coupled with an ethico-disciplinary policy that aims to impart character and behaviour traits that will supposedly enable them to 'thrive in modern Britain' (DfE, 2015). While 'character education' is to include virtues such as civic engagement and community spirit, it also, and perhaps disconcertingly, includes valued capabilities like 'resilience' and 'grit', and equally disturbing is the new government's commitment to finding ways to *measure* character.[16] Thriving in modern Britain appears to be being premised upon an ability to negotiate and 'survive' an uncertain and unpredictable future where work, opportunity and social mobility are not guaranteed, and in which the provision of security and well-being is no longer seen as a task of the state. Indeed, character education is another aspect of the coalition's clever but strategic redefinition of social justice and equity in that it constructs the individual – their aspirations, personal worth and ethical character – as both the causes and solutions to intractable social problems. As Michael Apple (2014, pp 19–20) puts it:

> Equality, no matter how limited or broadly conceived, has become redefined. No longer is it seen as linked to past group oppression and disadvantagement. It is now simply a case of guaranteeing individual choice under the conditions of a 'free market'.... [Underachievement] once again increasingly is seen as largely the fault of the student.

Conclusions: looking ahead

As noted earlier, the new Conservative government indicated that it would further pursue many of the Conservative-dominated coalition's education policies – from more free schools and academies, and the continued emphasis on 'tougher standards' and 'rigour', to Nicky Morgan's interest in character education.

Having achieved a modest majority in the 2015 general election, the Conservatives have continued the drive towards further fragmentation and disarticulation of the education state. This has been pursued in the first 100 days of the new Conservative administration, with the Queen's Speech introducing the previously noted Education and Adoption Bill, which will make it easier for the government to convert schools judged to be 'inadequate' or coasting' into academies by removing, according to Nicky Morgan (2015), 'bureaucratic and legal loopholes'. The Conservatives' 2015 manifesto signalled their intention to further expand and accelerate academisation and to open more free schools. It also continued the emphasis on 'standards' and 'rigour', in part, through an expectation that 11 year olds 'know their times tables off-by-heart' (Conservative Party, 2015, p 33), tackling 'grade inflation' by making examinations more difficult, and requiring pupils to take 'core' subjects – English, maths, science – at GCSE. Schools that 'refuse' to teach these subjects at GCSE will now be unable to achieve the highest Ofsted rating.

Perhaps what is most notable, however, is the relative inattention to education issues in the Conservative election campaign and the government's initial plans, aside from a pledge to protect per pupil funding and 'Zero tolerance for failure' – with renewed attention on 'failing' and 'coasting' schools. Little or nothing that is new appears to be being considered. An agenda is already in place based on dissolution, disarticulation and diversity, on the one hand, and a moral centrism, on the other – a political approach that further embeds and nourishes the orthodoxy of the New Right in educational thinking, practice and governance (as detailed in Table 1.1 in Chapter One of this volume). What is also striking is the total disconnect between inequality, educational disadvantage and austerity. In this sense, the attempt to disconnect education from the economy in terms of 'inputs' is matched by a thoroughgoing reconnect between education and the economy in terms of 'outputs', or human capital.

The new governing space of education in England is an incoherent, ad hoc, diverse, fragile and evolving network of complex relations. It contains possibilities, inconsistencies and contradictions – both business and religion, localism and corporatism, equity and privilege. New Right market policies, and 'freedoms' of various sorts, are set alongside a traditional One Nation values-driven vision of the curriculum – the latter now increasingly inflected by concerns about security and radicalisation. Conservative education policy rests on a 'messy' combination of regulation, competition and performance management. The process of public sector 'modernisation' or transformation involved here is both creative and destructive, a process of attrition and reinvention. Although the transformation process may sometimes appear to be disjointed, it has an internal logic, a set of discernible, if not necessarily planned, facets.

Notes

[1] Brown and Carasso (2013) explore recent developments in higher education, and especially its ongoing marketisation. Stewart and Obolenskaya (2015) present a detailed account of the coalition's record in the early years. Daley, Orr and Petrie's (2015) edited volume explores further education policy and its ideological context.

[2] See: https://www.gov.uk/government/speeches/michael-gove-speaks-about-the-future-of-education-reform

[3] See: http://www.independent.co.uk/news/education/education-news/michael-gove-axes-to-kill-a-mockingbird-and-other-american-classics-from-english-literature-gcse-9432818.html

[4] Available at: https://www.gov.uk/government/speeches/pms-speech-on-the-fightback-after-the-riots

[5] See: https://www.gov.uk/government/publications/2010-to-2015-government-policy-support-for-families/2010-to-2015-government-policy-support-for-families

[6] New Labour's academies programme was initially targeted at struggling secondary schools, particularly in deprived urban areas. The coalition's approach was different in that it extended the policy to primary schools and encouraged 'good' and 'outstanding' schools to convert.

[7] Both are distinctive forms of free school that have a vocational/technical emphasis. University Technical Colleges must be sponsored by a university, which has input into curriculum and staff professional development. Studio Schools are designed for students between the ages of 14 and 19, and are an alternative to Further Education Colleges.

[8] Under the Academy/Free School Presumption of the said Act. The new Conservative government changed this to the Free School Presumption, which signals their post-election regard for all new academies as free schools. This presumes that most new schools will be free schools/academies but does not discount the possibility of community schools being opened where a suitable proposal for an alternative has not been identified.

[9] Department for Education, Transparency data. Open academies and academy projects in development, last updated 20 February 2015. Available at https://www.gov.uk/government/publications/open-academies-and-academy-projects-in-development

[10] See: https://www.gov.uk/government/policies/

[11] The Confederation of British Industry (CBI, 2010) has called for chains of schools to be set up and managed by businesses, but the role of profit-making in direct schools provision remains controversial and unclear. There is a considerable interest from business in the possibilities of profit from involvements, of various kinds, in free schools, and there is a list of 'approved providers' of services to free schools. Secretary of State for Education Michael Gove indicated that he had 'no ideological objection' to private firms running schools. However, on 4 September 2014, current Secretary of State Nicky Morgan told a TES [Times Educational Supplement] webchat: 'I think we are very clear and that the sector is very clear about the importance of not for profit. [For profit] is something I'm happy to have lots of further advice and emails on. I suspect that most people may not be very keen on it, but it's something … well, you'd have to think very carefully'. Three weeks later, Ms Morgan seemed to indicate that the idea is completely off her agenda: 'I don't think that there is a place for the profit element in education', she told the *Financial Times* on 26 September.

[12] More of the training of teachers is intended to be based in schools. The coalition piloted a programme called Schools Direct to enable Teaching Schools to bid for teacher training places, and increased the funding to Teach First to facilitate the expansion of the scheme into primary schools, the early years and across the country.

[13] See, for example: http://arkonline.org/our-approach

[14] See: http://www.watchsted.com/analysis

[15] The Pupil Premium can be traced back to Chubb and Moe's (1990) proposals for an education market in the US, which suggested using 'premium' payments to make students with educational 'deficits' more attractive to providers. A similar approach has also been advocated as a form of 'market socialism' by Julian Le Grand (1989),

Professor of Public Policy at the London School of Economics and former senior policy advisor to Tony Blair.

[16] For an analysis of resilience as an approved capability in relation to the teacher, see Bailey (2015).

References

Alexander, R. (2014) 'Visions of education, roads to reform: PISA, the global race and the Cambridge primary review'. Available at: http://www.robinalexander.org.uk/wp-content/uploads/2014/05/Alexander-Malmo-140204.pdf (accessed 15 March 2015).

Apple, M.W. (2000) 'Between neoliberalism and neoconservatism: education and conservatism in a global context', in N.C. Burbules and C.A. Torres (eds) *Globalization and education: critical perspectives*, Abingdon: Routledge, pp 57–77.

Apple, M.W. (2014) *Official knowledge: democratic education in a conservative age*, London: Routledge.

Bailey, P. (2015) 'Consultants of conduct: new actors, new knowledges and new "resilient" subjectivities in the governing of the teacher', *Journal of Educational Administration and History*, 47(3): 232–50.

Ball, S.J. (2006) *Education policy and social class. The selected works of Stephen J. Ball*, New York, NY: Routledge.

Ball, S.J. (2008) 'The legacy of ERA, privatization and the policy ratchet', *Educational Management Administration & Leadership*, 36(2): 185–99.

Ball, S.J. (2010) *The education debate*, Bristol: The Policy Press.

Ball, S.J., Maguire, M. and Braun, A. (2012) *How schools do policy: policy enactments in secondary schools*, Abingdon: Routledge.

Brooks, S., Leach, M., Lucas, H. and Millstone, E. (2009) *Silver bullets, grand challenges and the new philanthropy*, STEPS Working Paper 24, Brighton: STEPS Centre.

Brown, R. and Carasso, H. (2013) *Everything for sale? The marketisation of UK higher education*, Abingdon: Routledge/Society for Research in Higher Education.

Cabinet Office (2010) *The coalition: our programme for government*, London: Cabinet Office.

Cabinet Office (2011) *Early intervention: the next steps, an independent report to Her Majesty's Government*, London: Cabinet Office.

CBI (Confederation of British Industry) (2010) *Fulfilling potential: the business role in education*. Available at: http://www.cbi.org.uk/media/951143/fulfilling_potential_2010.pdf

Chubb, J.E. and Moe, T.M. (1990) *Politics, markets, and America's schools*, Washington, DC: Brookings Institution Press.

Clark, M. (2014) 'Whose knowledge counts in government literacy policies and at what cost?', *Education Journal*, 186: 13–16.

Clarke, J. and Lindgren, J. (2015) 'The vocabulary of inspection', in S. Grek and J. Lindgren (eds) *Governing by inspection*, Abingdon: Routledge, pp 137–58.

Conservative Party (2015) *Stronger leadership, a clear economic plan, a brighter, more secure future*, London: Conservative Party.

Cook, C. (2015) 'A coming budget squeeze on schools'. Available at: http://www.bbc.co.uk/news/education-32595377 (accessed 17 September 2015).

Daley, M., Orr, K. and Petrie, J. (eds) (2015) *Further education and the twelve dancing princesses*, Stoke-On-Trent: Institute of Education Press.

DfE (Department for Education) (2010) *The importance of teaching: the schools White Paper*, London: The Stationery Office.

DfE (2015) 'Character education: apply for 2015 grant funding'. Available at: https://www.gov.uk/government/news/character-education-apply-for-2015-grant-funding (accessed 18 September 2015).

Foster, D. (2015) 'Free schools', *London Review of Books*, 37(9): 8–9.

Furlong, J. (2013) 'Globalisation, neoliberalism, and the reform of teacher education in England', *The Educational Forum*, 77(1): 28–50.

Gibb, N. (2012) 'Speech by Nick Gibb: greater expectations'. Available at: https://www.gov.uk/government/speeches/nick-gibb-on-reading-greater-expectations

Higham, R. (2014) 'Free schools in the Big Society: the motivations, aims and demography of free school proposers', *Journal of Education Policy*, 29(1): 122–39.

HM Government (2010) *Decentralisation and the Localism Bill: an essential guide*, London: The Stationery Office.

Kingdon, J.W. (1995) *Agendas, alternatives, and public policies*, New York, NY: Harper-Collins.

Le Grand, J. (1989) *The strategy of equality: redistribution and the social services*, London: Routledge.

Lister, R. (2000) 'To Rio via the 3rd way: Labour's welfare reform agenda', *Renewal: a Journal of Labour Politics* (online), 8: 9–20.

Lister, R. (2001) 'Work for those who can, security for those who cannot', in R. Edwards and J. Glover (eds) *Risk and citizenship: key issues in welfare*, London: Routledge, pp 96–110.

Lupton, R. and Thomson, S. (2015) *The coalition's record on schools: policy spending and outcomes 2010–2015*, working paper, London: The University of Manchester/London School of Economics.

Morgan, N. (2015) 'Up to 1,000 failing schools to be transformed under new measures', Department for Education press release, 3 June. Available at: www.gov.uk/government/news/up-to-1000-failing-schools-to-be-transformed-under-new-measures (accessed 15 September 2015).

Rizvi, F. and Lingard, B. (2010) *Globalizing education policy*, Abingdon: Routledge.

Shamir, R. (2008) 'The age of responsibilization: on market-embedded morality', *Economy and Society*, 37(1): 1–19.

Stevenson, H. (2011) 'Coalition education policy: Thatcherism's long shadow', *Forum*, 53(2): 179–94.

Stewart, K. and Obolenskaya, P. (2015) *The coalition's record on the under fives: policy, spending and outcomes 2010–2015*, Social Policy in a Cold Climate Working Paper WP12, London: Centre for Analysis of Social Exclusion, LSE.

The Guardian (2012) 'Most free schools take fewer deprived pupils than local average, figures show', 23 April. Available at: http://www.theguardian.com/education/2012/apr/23/free-schools-deprived-pupils-average (accessed 11 May 2014).

The Guardian (2014) 'Ofsted chief says struggling schools 'no better off' under academy control', 10 December. Available at: http://www.theguardian.com/education/2014/dec/10/ofsted-sir-michael-wilshaw-struggling-schools-academy-neglect

The Independent (2014) 'Michael Gove 'axes' American classics including To Kill and Mockingbird from English literature GCSE syllabus', 27 May. Available at: http://www.independent.co.uk/news/education/education-news/michael-gove-axes-to-kill-a-mockingbird-and-other-american-classics-from-english-literature-gcse-9432818.html (accessed, 13 February 2015).

Williams, R. (2010) 'New minister Nick Gibb upsets teachers – already', *The Guardian*, 17 May. Available at: http://www.theguardian.com/education/mortarboard/2010/may/17/nick-gibb-upsets-teachers (accessed 11 July 2015).

SEVEN

Coalition housing policy in England

Peter Somerville

Introduction

Conservative–Liberal Democrat coalition government housing policy in England from 2010 to 2015 was virtually indistinguishable from Conservative housing policy. As Tunstall (2015, p 13) points out:

> The two Liberal Democrat manifesto pledges that were most distinctive and ideologically distant from those of the Conservatives, the pledge to investigate changing public sector borrowing requirement accounting rules to allow local authorities to borrow more, and the pledge to scale back the HomeBuy scheme, did not make it into the [coalition] Agreement.

The influence of the Liberal Democrats on coalition housing policy was, in fact, negligible – the housing ministers, for example, were all Conservative (Grant Shapps, Mark Prisk, Kris Hopkins and Brandon Lewis). For reasons of space, the chapter does not discuss housing policy in Scotland or Wales, nor has it been possible to devote as much attention as I would have liked to the geographical variation in housing-related problems and needs across England (eg much more serious shortages of housing in the South than in the north [Dorling, 2014]).

Background

The number of homes in England has risen over the years since the Second World War, but the rate of increase has varied roughly according to the trade cycle, slowing down from 300,000 per year in the 1950s and 1960s to 200,000 in the 1980s, to not much over 100,000 in the 1990s, recovering in the later 1990s and 2000s, falling to its lowest point (24,000) in the year after the financial crisis in 2008/09, and showing a fluctuating but rising trend since then (see Table 7.1). Table 7.1 shows that the numbers of owner-occupiers in

England rose year on year, from 9.7 million (57%) in 1980 to 14.7 million (71%) in 2003, then remained at more or less the same level until 2007 (70%), after which they started to fall year on year, from 14.6 million (68%) in 2008/09 to 14.3 million (63%) in 2013/14. In contrast, the numbers of private renters fluctuated between 1.7 million and 2.1 million (9–12%) from 1980 to 2001 but then rose year on year to 4.4 million (19%) in 2013/14 (see also Figure 7.1). The proportion of households who are social renters (renting from a local authority or housing association) fell from 31% in 1980 to 17% in 2013/14 (see Figure 7.1); among social renters, those renting from a local authority has fallen year on year since 1980 (mainly due to Right to Buy but also due to the transfer of housing to housing associations and to the lack of additional council housing provision), while those renting from a housing association has increased year on year, but at a slower rate, at least up until very recently.

Table 7.1: Trends in tenure, 1980 to 2013/14, England

Thousands of households with tenure	Outright owner-occupiers (1)	Owner-occupiers buying with mortgage (2)	All owner-occupiers (1 + 2)	Private renters	Social renters	All tenures
1980	N/A	N/A	9,680 (57%)	2,043 (12%)	5,378 (31%)	17,101
1991	4,795	8,255	13,050 (68%)	1,824 (9%)	4,436 (23%)	19,310
2001	5,885	8,473	14,359 (70%)	2,061 (10%)	3,983 (20%)	20,403
2003	6,158	8,542	14,701 (71%)	2,234 (11%)	3,804 (18%)	20,739
2008/09	6,770	7,851	14,621 (68%)	3,067 (14%)	3,842 (18%)	21,530
2009/10	6,828	7,697	14,525 (67%)	3,355 (16%)	3,675 (17%)	21,554
2010/11	7,009	7,441	14,450 (66%)	3,617 (17%)	3,826 (18%)	21,893
2011/12	6,996	7,392	14,388 (65%)	3,843 (17%)	3,808 (17%)	22,040
2012/13	7,152	7,184	14,337 (65%)	3,956 (18%)	3,684 (17%)	21,977
2013/14	7,386	6,933	14,319 (63%)	4,377 (19%)	3,920 (17%)	22,617

Source: DCLG (2015d), adapted from Annex Table 1.1 of the English Housing Survey (see also DCLG, 2015g, 2015h).

Figure 7.1: Trends in tenure, 1980 to 2013/14

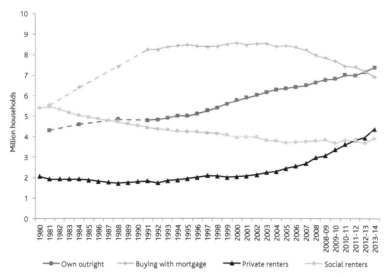

Base: all households

Note: Underlying data are taken from the following sources: 1980 to 1991: DOE Labour Force Survey Housing Trailer; 1992 to 2008: ONS Labour Force Survey; 2008-09 onwards: English Housing Survey, full household sample

Source: DCLG (2015c, p 12; 2015h).

Despite the increasing number of homes, housing shortages in England have continued and worsened, at least in the South of the country, over a period of decades (Barker, 2004; Stephens et al, 2005; Hills, 2007; Meek, 2014; Dorling, 2014, 2015; Lyons, 2014). The shortage of affordable housing impacts particularly on young people, with many forced to live with their parents because they cannot afford to rent or buy their own home (Shelter, 2014; see also Pennington et al, 2012). Currently, not much more than 100,000 homes a year are being built when more than 200,000 are required to meet existing and growing housing need (245,000 households, according to Holmans [2013], based on 2011 Census data).

Moreover, despite the Conservative Party (2015, p 51) claiming to be 'the party of home ownership', the numbers of owner-occupiers declined year on year while the coalition was in power. This fall in owner-occupation more or less coincided with the rise in private renting associated with the boom in buying to rent out; it seems likely that the increased competition resulting from the entry of buy-to-letters into the market will have 'crowded out' those who want to buy homes to live in (particularly first-time buyers), as well as exerting inflationary pressure on house prices, keeping them higher than would be expected. Housing markets are intimately related to mortgage markets – fewer people getting a mortgage means less demand to buy housing, and therefore lower house prices. With fewer owner-occupiers having a mortgage (down from 8.5 million in 2003 to 6.9 million in 2013/14), one would normally expect house prices to fall, but, of course, most buy-to-letters are also buying with a mortgage, so the overall demand to buy housing has remained more or less constant. Similarly, the 'bank of mum and dad' (Fearn, 2015) is also important in exerting upward pressure on house prices. The rents in the private sector are also relatively high, but many of the tenants will be in receipt of Housing Benefit and many will be sharing accommodation. For those newly forming households that cannot rely on the bank of mum and dad, and that are unable to access social rented accommodation, there may be no other option but to rent privately.

Similar trends of a decline in owner-occupation and a rise in private renting have been observed in other countries, such as the US, Japan and Australia (Forrest and Hirayama, 2015, pp 239–41), driven by falling real incomes, corporate investment in rented accommodation and the lack of renting alternatives, as well as buy-to-lets. It is likely, therefore, that this unprecedented change in tenure patterns reflects the wider impact of the global financial crisis, which has resulted in 'austerity' for lower-income households (Lowndes and Pratchett, 2012; O'Hara, 2015; Perry et al, 2015) combined with new opportunities for higher-income households.

The English Housing Survey provides a useful overview of the housing situation, but there can be many reasons why the numbers of housed households change (including household dissolution, new builds, demolitions, conversions of houses into flats, changes of living arrangements, changes of tenure, etc). Unfortunately, the way in which government statistics are presented does not make it easy to determine the effects of government policies in this area. For example, statistics on housing starts and completions show only the numbers of new homes provided by different sectors (private, housing association and local authority), not for what tenure they are provided (for renting or owner-occupation). The number of homes started by the private sector in England, after falling from 84,710 in 2010/11 to 82,630 in 2012/13, rose sharply to 116,290 in 2014/15 (the period of coalition government), an increase of 41% over the last two years, and the number completed rose from 83,180 to 96,740 over the same period (DCLG, 2015a, 2015e). It is likely that the vast majority of these were for owner-occupation, although it is not possible to be certain about the exact number.

Separately from the English Housing Survey, the government publishes statistics on what it calls 'affordable housing supply'. These figures show that the numbers of new social rented homes in England built through funding from the Homes and Communities Agency (HCA) and Greater London Authority (GLA) (which basically means those provided by housing associations) declined from 30,830 in 2010/11 (the highest since 1995/96) to 6,370 in 2013/14 (the lowest since the 1970s) (DCLG, 2015i). However, the numbers of newly built *affordable* rented homes (basically, social rented homes let at higher rents – up to 80% of market rents) increased from 5,500 in 2012/13 (the first full year of the programme) to 13,890 in 2013/14 (DCLG, 2015i). Figures from the HCA for 2014/15 indicate further decline in its new-build social rented provision (from 4,477 in 2013/14 to 3,139 in 2014/15) and a substantial rise in its new-build affordable rented provision (from 17,694 in 2013/14 to 31,053 in 2014/15); interestingly, however, the HCA reported a fall in affordable renting starts from 25,486 in 2013/14 to 21,879 in 2014/15 (HCA, 2015).[1] Meanwhile, after an initial sharp rise to 2,540 in 2010/11 (the highest since 1992), new social rented homes provided by local authorities fell back down again to 590 in 2013/14, although new affordable rented provision rose from 160 in 2012/13 to 760 in 2013/14 (DCLG, 2015i).

Coalition housing policies

The main coalition housing policies were set out in the coalition agreement (Cabinet Office, 2010), the Localism Act 2011, *Laying the foundations* (HM Government, 2011) and the Welfare Reform Act 2012. The policy aims were to: increase the number of available homes; help people to buy their home; transform social renting; improve the energy efficiency of homes; increase options for local housing authorities; and reduce the cost of Housing Benefit (see Table 7.2). More punitive policies later emerged for squatters[2] and Gypsies/Travellers.[3] Overall, however, with one or two notable exceptions, the emphasis was on 'government getting out of the way' to allow others (local authorities, developers and communities) to meet these aims.

Increasing the number of available homes and helping people to buy their home[4]

The New Homes Bonus, introduced in 2010, 'rewarded' local authorities for new homes made available in their area by providing funding equivalent to the council tax raised on those homes for a period

Table 7.2: Coalition housing policies 2010–15

Policy aims – what the coalition said it would do	Policies – what the coalition actually introduced
Increase the number of available homes, largely through local incentives rather than national or regional targets or strategies ('localism')	New Homes Bonus
Planning reform, eg, general presumption in favour of sustainable development, abolition of regional spatial strategies and housing targets	
Community Right to Build	
Housing zonesa	
Empty Homes Initiative	
Help people to buy their home	Help to Buy
Enhanced Right to Buy	
100,000 'starter homes' – developers exempted from charges on brownfield land in return for them offering 20% discount to first-time buyers under 40 (introduced in 2014)	
Right to Buy for housing association tenants (introduced in 2015)	
Move towards a freer market in renting ('neoliberalism')	Affordable Homes Programme
Reduced government funding for new affordable homes	
'Pay to stay' – rents to increase towards market rents for social housing tenants earning over £30,000 (£40,000 in London) (from 2017)	
Reduce cost of government-provided benefits, especially housing benefit ('austerity')	Abolition of 'spare bedroom subsidy' ('bedroom tax')
Benefits cap – at £26,000 per year from 2013, reduced to £20,000 per year (£23,000 in London) from 2016	
Reduction in social rents of 1% per year for four years (from 2016)	
Abolition of housing benefit for under-21 year olds (from 2017)	
Increase options for local housing authorities ('localism')	Abolition of housing revenue account
Flexible tenure	
Reform of access to and allocation of housing	
Improve the energy efficiency of homes	'Green deal'b

Notes: a Housing zones are areas of brownfield land where the government is providing a total of £400 million of funding to kickstart housing development (such as for infrastructure, site acquisition and leaseholder buyouts) on condition that the developer and local authority commit to providing a certain level of affordable and private housing. Twenty zones outside London were confirmed in March 2015, which will provide 34,000 new homes, and 11 zones in London. The government has also directly commissioned a £400 million pilot scheme for 10,000 homes for sale in Northstowe, Cambridgeshire (Apps, 2014). b The Coalition promised to be 'the greenest government ever' (Cameron, 2010) but ended up being even less green than its predecessor, with the erosion and final abandonment of the zero carbon target of 2016 for new-build housing set by the previous Labour government.

of six years. This policy looks successful because the total amount of funding provided so far is £3.4 billion, associated with the delivery of 700,000 new homes and conversions, and with bringing over 100,000 empty homes back into use (*Inside Housing*, 2015). However, as noted by Somerville (2011, p 123; see also Wilson, 2014), this funding continues to be top-sliced from the annual grant to local authorities, which has been cut by about 40% between 2010/11 and 2015/16. The main result of the New Homes Bonus has therefore been a substantial general redistribution of government funding from lower-council tax, lower-build council areas (especially Northern England and Yorkshire and Humberside) to higher-council tax, higher-build areas (mainly in London and South-East England), where arguably more homes need to be built (DCLG, 2014, p 3). Also, a few commentators have noted that the Bonus does not directly contribute to the actual cost of providing new homes, but is simply an incentive to local authorities to be favourably disposed towards such provision. It is impossible to say how many of these new homes and conversions would have been provided in the absence of the Bonus. Local authorities have mainly spent the bonuses they have received to support their general fund (to offset the cuts they have had to make to their services). Some of the receipts have been used to support housing growth, but not specifically to fund additional affordable homes (DCLG, 2014, p 4).

The general presumption in favour of sustainable development is enshrined in the *National planning policy framework* (NPPF) (DCLG, 2012). Every local planning authority must have a local plan that sets out the strategic development priorities for its area. If it does not have a plan, it must grant permission for development unless it can show that the net impact of the development goes against the NPPF. The coalition government's intention was that the planning system would become a facilitator of new housing development rather than the obstacle that it was perceived to be (see, eg, Cheshire, 2014). Currently, however, 76% of local planning authorities outside London and national parks still do not have a local plan in place (Youde, 2015). At the same time, government ministers continue to preach one thing and do another, advocating new housing development in principle but often opposing it in practice, especially in their own constituencies. In the run-up to the 2015 general election, Eric Pickles, the then Secretary of State for Communities and Local Government, blocked the development of 9,200 homes by rejecting a total of 18 applications, six of which had already been recommended for approval by independent planning inspectors. In spite of the policy that applications should be refused only on the material planning considerations set out in the NPPF (DCLG, 2012), nine of Pickles' refusals were based on 'landscape'.

The Community Right to Build, introduced in the Localism Act 2011 and in force since April 2012, allows local communities to give themselves permission to develop small, single sites for new housing on the basis of a local referendum. This flagship policy, championed by Grant Shapps (Housing Minister from 2010 to 2012), and encouraged by £17 million of funding, has so far resulted in just eight applications, three Right to Build Orders, one referendum (in which three quarters voted in favour of all three orders, on a 45% turnout) and no new housing (Communities and Local Government Committee, 2015, p 19 – the committee also described the Right as 'complicated, adversarial and risky' [2015, p 20]).

Help to Buy commenced in April 2013 and is of three types: an equity loan (available up to 2020), in which the government lends up to 20% of the value of a new-build home, interest-free for the first five years (enabling people to buy with a minimum of 5% deposit); a mortgage guarantee (available up to December 2016), which government gives to lenders (in return for a fee) for providing mortgages to people buying a property for owner-occupation with a deposit of between 5% and 20%; and NewBuy, in which private developers and investors work with government to enable any household to buy a new-build home with a 5% deposit (see gov.uk policies list).[5] In its first two years, 47,018 properties were bought under the equity loan scheme (representing approximately a quarter of the total private sector completions over the same period [DCLG, 2015a, 2015e]), mostly (82%) to first-time buyers (DCLG, 2015b), and from October 2013 to December 2014, 40,079 mortgages were completed with the support of the mortgage guarantee scheme, again mostly (78%) for first-time buyers (HM Treasury, 2015a). Under the NewBuy scheme, originally launched in March 2012, the total number of house purchases up to the end of March 2015 was 5,706 (DCLG, 2015b).

It seems, therefore, that the Help to Buy equity loan scheme has helped to stimulate the house-building industry, resulting in new home starts additional to those due to generally improving economic conditions (Tunstall, 2015, p 37). It is actually a classic quasi-Keynesian case of using housing market intervention to resuscitate the economy and lift the country out of recession. The same cannot be said, however, of the mortgage guarantee scheme, which is open to purchasers of existing homes, and therefore increases demand in relation to supply, resulting (counterproductively) in increased house prices and a high risk of yet another boom and bust (Chandler and Disney, 2014; Wilcox et al, 2015; Birch, 2014). Help to Buy as a whole involves increased indebtedness and increased financial risk, which some Conservatives have opposed (Gimson, 2013) and have noted that this is what got us into the housing crisis in the first place (Adam Smith Institute, 2014, p 4). In contrast, the government clearly believes that the risk is worth taking and that, in the long term, the mortgages will all be repaid and so the taxpayer will lose nothing from this policy. As the Adam Smith Institute (2014) points out, however, the taxpayer is already losing out: in the short term, with the equity loan scheme, as no interest payments are made for the first five years; and in the long term, as house prices that are already too high become increasingly unaffordable. The Help to Buy equity loan is therefore the only policy that can be shown to have achieved the coalition's aim of increasing the number of available homes to buy, but to what extent is not entirely clear. On its own, however, this policy seems unlikely to result in further increases in either starts or completions in later years, particularly if house prices rise across the country and the Help to Buy mortgage guarantee is extended. In the absence of other measures to increase housing supply, therefore, housing shortages will continue, at least in Southern England. Arguably, also, the main limitation of policies like Help to Buy is that they do not help those who cannot afford to buy even with a 5% deposit – which includes large numbers of low- to middle-income households (Alakeson and Cory, 2013, p 33).

In summary, the New Homes Bonus purported to be an example of roll-out neoliberalism (Peck and Tickell, 2002), in which government actively intervenes to make the (housing) market work better. However, evidence that it is working better is lacking. The NPPF and the Community Right to Build are examples of roll-back neoliberalism (Peck and Tickell, 2002), in which government relaxes restrictions on market forces and offers new opportunities for self-help by individuals and communities. Yet, little has changed in terms of either planning permissions or community empowerment. The Help to Buy schemes are examples of roll-out neoliberalism (and also of subsidised individualism, in that government funding goes directly to individual households [Forrest and Murie, 1986]). The equity loan scheme has had some effect as intended, but is strictly limited in terms of timescale and types of beneficiary, while the mortgage guarantee scheme and Help to Buy ISA are risky and wasteful policies that serve only to make the housing market work worse.

The Right to Buy for council tenants (introduced by the Conservatives in 1980) is an example of roll-back neoliberalism *and* subsidised individualism, and it is notorious because it subsidises tenants to buy, but only at the cost of loss to the social rented stock (roll-back). In 2012, the government raised the maximum discounts available to purchasers from £38,000 to £75,000, with successive housing ministers making empty promises that any additional homes sold would be replaced on a 'one-for-one' basis. Most local authorities expect to replace only half or fewer of their homes lost to Right to Buy (CIH et al, 2015); 26,185 homes have been sold since 2012, of which 16,000 have been estimated as 'additional' homes, but only 2,712 replacements have been started over the same period (Apps, 2015a). The new Right to Buy for housing association tenants only serves to confirm the position of the current Conservative government as the heirs of Thatcher in this respect.[6]

Towards a freer market in renting

The coalition government followed an apparently contradictory path on rented housing. On the one hand, they had policies that reduce the number of available homes to rent, such as increasing the discounts available under the Right to Buy and cutting back the public funding of housing associations – and after the Conservative election victory in 2015, extending the Right to Buy to housing association tenants, and reducing social rents by 1% per year for the next four years. On the other hand, they allowed housing associations to develop so-called 'affordable' housing, whose rents rise to 80% of market levels (instead of the 50% that has traditionally applied to social housing rents), making it more attractive to develop new rented housing. In reality, however, these different policies all form part of a wider neoliberal agenda to move towards a more free housing market, in which homes are freely bought and sold, rents are unregulated, landlords compete freely with one another to provide housing for tenants and the government does not fund housing, either directly or indirectly.[7] The government and their supporters believe that such a free housing market, in which housing supply rises to meet housing demand, will deliver more homes, both to rent and to buy, than a system in which the government plays a more directive role – even though historically, at least in the UK, substantial increases in housing supply have been achieved only through government funding and public provision. England is therefore to be subjected to a more thoroughgoing neoliberal 'experiment', whose outcome is uncertain, to say the least (comparable to the decontrol of private renting from 1957 to 1965 and again since 1988).

Although buy-to-let is not an official Conservative policy, all neoliberal parties[8] (Conservative, Liberal Democrat and Labour) have looked benevolently on this peculiarly English phenomenon as an example of free market operation. This has been in spite of the fact that buy-to-let drives up house prices and adds nothing to housing supply, and the private rented sector continues to contain the worst housing conditions and to be the worst managed tenure (33% of its homes are non-decent and it has the highest incidence of dampness problems [DCLG, 2015c; Hohmann, 2015, pp 4–5]; according to an analysis of the English Housing Survey, 16% of privately rented homes contain a 'category 1 hazard', such as a risk of falls and excess cold that presents 'a severe threat to health or safety' [Citizens Advice and New Policy Institute, 2015, p 12]). Again, although there is no official policy to fund private landlords, a freedom of information request to HMRC (Her Majesty's Revenue and Customs) from Shelter found that they enjoyed a record £14 billion in tax breaks in 2013 (including £6.3 billion tax relief on their mortgage interest payments) (Pegg, 2015), and this does not include £9.3 billion of Housing Benefit paid to their tenants, which they receive in rent (Osborne, 2015). Added to this, one could mention the unknown extent of tax evasion by private landlords who do not declare to HMRC the rent paid to them in cash (see Collinson, 2014). Unofficially, therefore, private landlords are subsidised by government to an extent comparable with local authorities and housing associations (perhaps even more if account is taken of rent pooling in the public sector, whereby the rents on older properties, with lower historic costs, subsidise the rents on newer ones, which have higher historic costs).

In 2010, the coalition government proposed to allocate only £1.3 billion of new money for housing association rented housing during 2011–15, compared with £7.8 billion in the previous four years (Tunstall, 2015, p 29). Consequently, only 8,800 homes were built in the first two years of this programme (Frontier Economics, 2014, p 14); the number for the second two years is not yet known. For the 2015–18 programme (now extended to 2020), a further £1.7 billion is being made available (HCA and DCLG, 2014), but this seems unlikely to be able to reverse the long-term trend of increasing shortages of affordable housing. Hence, housing associations are increasingly relying on their own sources of funding (eg London & Quadrant [Apps, 2015b] and Genesis [Apps, 2015c]) – which is, ultimately, what the government wants them to do anyway. Macmillan (2013, p 17) refers to this as a 'partial decoupling' of the state from the third sector. These sources have certainly grown over the years, with housing association surpluses increasing nearly tenfold, from £203 million in 2009 to just under £2 billion in 2013, mainly as a result of increases in traditional social rents (not affordable rents, which make up less than 2% of housing association homes). This growth, however, looked set to reverse in the light of the Conservative government's decision to reduce social housing rents (see later).

What the government calls 'affordable' rents, however, are patently not affordable for lower-income households. It is already well known that private rents are beyond the reach of poorer families. Alakeson and Cory (2013, p 3) found that 'there are no local authorities where a low income family can meet the costs of a basic standard of living as defined by the Minimum Income Standard and afford rent on a two bedroom property'.[9] Even 'affordable' rents, however, fail to meet this standard in many areas of England. Heywood (2013), for example, found that affordable rents in London were typically 40% higher than social rents, and the properties were being allocated mainly to tenants on benefits, resulting most obviously in an increase in the Housing Benefit bill for government. Various estimates have shown that, particularly in Southern England, rents at 80% of market rates are unaffordable for any household with below average income. Data collected by the Valuation Office Agency, for example, showed that in 2013, for a three-bedroom home, this equates to a weekly rent of £655 in Westminster, £198 in Havering, £218 in Sevenoaks, £247 in Brighton, £233 in Oxford and £179 in Bristol (Wiles, 2014). So, the shift away from traditional social rented housing to affordable rented housing has achieved the termination of housing opportunities for low-income households, at the cost of increasing the Housing Benefit bill for government, which the coalition government aimed to reduce (see next section). Clearly, the commitment to a 'free market' overrides all other considerations.

Since the 1980s, a large proportion of local housing authorities have been subsidising government rather than the other way round, with 75% of their capital receipts from council house sales being clawed back by the Exchequer, and with surpluses on their housing revenue accounts being used to defray the costs of their tenants' Housing Benefit for much of this period. With the abolition of the housing revenue account in 2012, local housing authorities were supposed to be self-financing, that is, free to make their own decisions, including on rent levels, repairs, refurbishment and new-build, and this was of net benefit to most local authority housing departments (Wilcox et al, 2014). However, this new freedom has turned out to be largely illusory as they continue to be subject to a cap on how much they can borrow, which makes large-scale building projects impossible, and increases in their rent levels continue to be restricted according to a formula based mainly on the type and size of property (DCLG, 2013).[10] Now, with the four-year 1% rent cut, even small-scale development looks impossible (Duxbury, 2015).[11]

Reducing the Housing Benefit bill

In 2010, the coalition government said that it would cut spending on welfare (except pensions) by £19 billion, and Housing Benefit is by far the next largest welfare expenditure heading. However, the cost of Housing Benefit actually rose in real terms from £23.0 billion in 2010/11 to £24.3 billion in 2014/15 (DWP, 2015a, Table 1b) (faster than during Labour's rule), though it is forecast to fall to £23.9 billion by 2019/20. So, officially, by 2020, even after 10 years of Conservative rule, 'austerity' and the shrinking of 'big government', the state will be spending nearly 1 billion pounds more on Housing Benefit than in 2010. This was to be expected given the government's commitment to raising traditional social housing rents in real terms up to 2015 and increasing the number of social tenants on affordable rents, and its support for increased private renting at market rents. A high rents policy (which, incidentally, and contrary to government intentions, tends to increase disincentives to work and creates an 'employment trap' [Tunstall et al, 2013]) in a highly unequal society can be viable only if supported by high levels of government subsidy, which only goes into the pockets of landlords anyway. Things now look very different with the 1% per year reductions in social rents, which will significantly reduce the Housing Benefit bill, but the government's pledge to reduce the overall benefit bill (again, excluding pensions) by £22 billion still seems, at best, unrealistic.

In terms of the effects of Housing Benefit 'reform' on those at the receiving end, particular attention has been focused on the so-called 'bedroom tax'. Since April 2013, for all working-age social rented tenants, Housing Benefit entitlement has been reduced by 14% for one additional bedroom and 25% for two or more additional bedrooms. Since most tenants are unable to move to smaller properties because such properties are not available, this causes hardship. Department for Work and Pensions (DWP) analysis of data from May to December 2013 shows that fewer households were initially affected than expected (559,000 rather than 660,000), with most people then coming off the tax for a variety of reasons, most commonly, an increase in bedroom entitlement (due to changes in family circumstances) (32% of cases) and downsizing within the social rented sector (10%), with only 2% moving to the private rented sector (Gambarin, 2014; see also Clarke et al, 2014; Wilcox, 2014), and only about 3% getting into work (Gambarin,

2014, p 6). Most of those who remained got into arrears with their rent (by August 2013, 39% had paid only part of the charge and 20% nothing at all [Clarke et al, 2014] – Wilcox [2014, p 3] states: 'Different surveys show slightly different results, but in broad terms suggest that close to a half of all tenants affected by the Housing Benefit size criteria are in rent arrears'. This situation appears to be ongoing [see NFA et al, 2014]); most of them had cut back on household essentials – the dilemma of whether to 'heat or eat' (Clarke et al, 2014; Power et al, 2014); the majority, being unemployed or in low-paid service jobs, found it very difficult to pay (Clarke et al, 2014), citing problems of poverty, anxiety, debt and health problems (Power et al, 2014); and most of those who had looked for work had been unsuccessful, due to having a disability, being the sole carer of young children or having been out of the workplace for a long time (Clarke et al, 2014; Power et al, 2014). The bedroom tax has also caused problems for landlords, such as difficulties in letting larger properties and increased waiting times for smaller properties; the single room restriction on Housing Benefit for under-35 year olds has also made it more difficult to secure move-on accommodation from hostels for homeless people (Clarke et al, 2014; for more detail on landlords' responses to the bedroom tax, see also McCabe, 2014; for further evaluation of the impact of the bedroom tax, see Gibb, 2015).[12]

Conclusions

Overall, the housing policies of the coalition and Conservative governments show little evidence of understanding the 'big picture' of how the housing market works, particularly in relation to how to resolve the difficulties faced by ordinary people in finding their way through that market. It sometimes seems as if we are being ruled by a firm of estate agents, full of glossy brochures and shiny specifications, but who cannot be trusted to give an accurate account of our 'broken' housing system, let alone come up with any plan for mending it. Not surprisingly, it is the poorest and weakest in our society who bear the brunt of this 'retrogression', as the United Nations rapporteur, Raquel Rolnik, called it (quoted in Gentleman, 2013), evidenced by increasing hardship, homelessness (eg GLA, 2015b) and the (illegal) use of bed and breakfasts (Douglas, 2015; Hohmann, 2015, p 4).

Coalition housing policies have been said to mark 'the return of class war conservatism' (Hodkinson and Robbins, 2013), in the sense that the coalition clearly took the side of property owners (and 'aspiring' property owners) against the propertyless (eg the bias towards helping owner-occupiers and providing tax relief for private landlords and developers, while cutting rent relief for tenants). Certainly, there is ample evidence of the denigration and stigmatisation of social housing estates and social housing tenants in many countries and over many years now (Damer, 1974, 1989; Hastings, 2004; Cooper, 2005; Card, 2006; Hanley, 2007; Johnstone and Mooney, 2007; Blokland, 2008; Watt, 2008; Paton, 2009; Law et al, 2010; Jones, 2011; Somerville, 2011, p 134; HM Government, 2011, p 22; Hodkinson and Robbins, 2013, pp 69–70; McKenzie, 2015). Some Conservative policies, however, such as the recent reduction in social rents and even the Right to Buy and Help to Buy, cannot easily be represented as 'class war', and are more consistent with an approach of 'divide and rule'. Some Conservatives (such as Blond, 2010; Norman, 2010) also recognise that many people *need* social housing, and that it can make both economic and political sense to build more of it – for the benefit of the house-building industry, to bring down house prices and rents, to house low-paid workers, to reduce upward pressure on wages, and to provide a housing safety net for all (which, in turn, reduces the costs arising from *not* building social housing, in terms of health, education, homelessness, crime, etc).

Rather than seeing the politics of housing as involving a stark choice between commodified and decommodified provision (Harloe, 1982; Hodkinson et al, 2013, p 12) or between privatisation and socialisation (Smyth, 2013), or even between 'austerity localism' and 'progressive localism' (Featherstone et al, 2012), therefore, we need to recognise both that social housing is an integral part of the capitalist system and that owner-occupied housing represents a significant material gain for many working-class households. Under capitalism, every home, whether rented or owned, is a living contradiction in that it has both use value (to be enjoyed) and market value (rent or price). Capitalist states have to compete with one another on a global scale, and this involves finding new markets for capitalists to exploit and reducing the cost of labour in existing markets, all in order to extract increasing amounts of profit. In some respects, this can mean commodifying a decommodified form of provision, as in privatisation programmes, but in other respects, it can mean government intervention, for example, to reduce the cost of labour (through in-work subsidies such as tax credits but also, indirectly, through Housing Benefit) or to make labour more productive (through education).

The problem for capitalist states in relation to housing is, then, how to balance the move towards high rents and high house prices (to maximise the profits for landlords, homeowners, developers and investors) with the drive to keep wages down and productivity up (to maximise the profits to employers). For most capitalist states, this is a no-brainer: housing being only a small (though significant) part of the system, the emphasis has to be on wages and productivity, so that rents and house prices have to be kept low. In England, however, labour productivity, especially in the construction industry, remains low by international standards, while house prices remain high (in spite of the recession) and rents are now rising beyond the reach of those on below average incomes. This is an imbalance that the coalition and Conservative governments have been slow to recognise (perhaps because a quarter of Conservative MPs are private landlords) and, in some respects, have exacerbated.

There seems to be no shortage of solutions to the current housing crisis: credit controls such as maximum loan-to-value ratios on mortgages (Stephens and Williams, 2012); rent controls such as rent freezes and rent regulation; the deregulation of housing associations (Treanor, 2015); removing the cap on local authority borrowing; property tax reform (Mirrlees et al, 2011; Dorling, 2014); and so on. Fearn and Gulliver (2015) propose a 'new deal for tenants', based on Standing's (2014) 'precariat charter'. These proposals, which I have no space to discuss, mostly contradict one another, by either increasing or reducing borrowing, stimulating or depressing investment in housing. This housing crisis could be solved relatively easily by an increase of 2% in the basic rate of income tax, ending tax incentives for private landlords, the imposition of a statutory living wage (So far, so good!) and the mutualisation of social housing ownership and management (on 'tenants' mutuals', see Handy and Gulliver, 2015). Raising taxes for social housing, however, is unpopular with most people who benefit from the shortage of housing, which inflates the value of their properties. Maybe the current rise of housing activism (Duxbury and McCabe, 2015) will have some tangible effect. To succeed, the struggle for decent, affordable housing for all must form part of a wider struggle within, against and beyond the capitalist state (Mathers and Taylor, 2005, p 29).

Notes

[1] The GLA does not break down its affordable housing programme in terms of amounts of affordable renting or social renting but reports a rise in affordable housing completions overall, from 3,905 in 2013/14 to 13,306 in 2014/15. However, as with the HCA, it also reports a fall in the number of affordable housing starts, from 6,312 in 2013/14 to 1,260 in 2014/15 (GLA, 2015a).

[2] Squatting in residential properties was made a criminal offence in section 144 of the Legal Aid, Sentencing and Punishment of Offenders Act 2012, thus punishing homeless people for finding their own solution to their housing problem. For more commentary on the criminalising of squatting, see O'Mahony et al (2015).

[3] The Conservative Party originally proposed to scrap funding for site provision within three years, criminalise staying on land that is not privately owned, evict people from their own land and close down sites with temporary permits. Once in power in 2010, it removed the obligation on local authorities to meet pitch targets for Gypsies/Travellers, but also decided to make £60 million available from 2010 to 2013 to provide sites for them (Ryder, 2015). Few sites have been secured, however, mainly due to reluctance on the part of local authorities and to vociferous opposition from local residents where potential sites have been identified. The vast majority of local authorities continue to fail in their duty to identify and provide sites, and the government does nothing about it.

[4] These policy aims are discussed together because of the considerable overlap between them.

[5] A further policy, the Help to Buy Individual Savings Account (ISA), was introduced in the 2015 pre-election budget, under which first-time buyers have their savings topped up by a maximum of £3,000 by the government to help them buy a home, at an estimated cost of £2.1 billion over five years (HM Treasury, 2015). Widely criticised by housing commentators (the National Housing Federation said that the same level of investment would have enabled housing associations to build 69,000 affordable homes [Brown, 2015]), this policy is reminiscent of the Labour government policy of 1978, which provided a grant towards a deposit on a home, the advantage of which was soon wiped out by house price increases. In housing policy, it seems, the same mistakes are repeated over and over again, memories are ever short and lessons are never learned. Predictably, perhaps, rather than rejecting this blatant giveaway in a time of supposed 'austerity', the Labour Party immediately accepted it and stated only that they would require the companies that hold these ISAs to invest the money in providing new homes (it is not clear how this would work).

[6] Neoliberal governments have long abandoned the pretence that housing associations are part of a marketed 'independent rented sector', which is how some housing associations like to think of themselves, and also how some defenders of council housing have seen them. Still, no doubt some housing associations will now be considering deregistering with the Homes and Communities Agency and 'going it alone' (see later).

[7] It may seem impossible for both raising and lowering rents to be part of the same neoliberal agenda but the government's aim is actually to lower rents for poorer tenants

while increasing rents for those who can afford to pay them (hence the new 'pay to stay' policy, too). Social rents need to be low enough so that they are affordable both to those on a 'living wage' and to those in receipt of a state retirement pension, without the need to apply for Housing Benefit – this is probably the only way to achieve substantial reductions in the Housing Benefit bill. The government probably also expects housing associations and local authorities to expand their provision of affordable housing so that, in the course of time, they will be able to assist their social housing tenants out of their own funds (by cross-subsidising poorer tenants from the rents paid by better-off ones), with no contribution from the government.

[8] By this, I mean a party in which the majority of members believe in free markets and that governments have a role in supporting and promoting free market capitalism. However, the election of Jeremy Corbyn as Labour leader in 2015 appeared to suggest that this may change.

[9] The Minimum Income Standard (MIS) defines an 'adequate' income based on what the public think people need for a minimum acceptable living standard. The proportion of people living in households with an income below MIS increased by nearly a third between 2008/09 and 2012/13, due to higher unemployment, stagnant wages, rising living costs and cuts to in-work benefits (Padley et al, 2015). For more on the impact of 'austerity', see O'Hara (2015).

[10] Research has shown that without the caps on borrowing, local authorities could develop an extra 12,000 homes per year (NFA et al, 2012). In 2013, the coalition allowed local authorities to borrow £300 million over their limit but only £122 million extra was borrowed by October 2014 because of the tight application timetable and the requirement to provide homes at affordable rents (Apps and Douglas, 2014).

[11] A further serious threat comes from the government's decision to fund replacements for housing association sales under the new Right to Buy by requiring local housing authorities to sell their more expensive housing and transfer the receipts to the Exchequer. It would be difficult to imagine a more anti-localist policy than this. It would accelerate the residualisation of the sector and lead to the exclusion of council tenants from areas of higher-priced housing – a new form of 'social cleansing' (see Hilditch, 2014). A similar argument applies to the lowering of the benefit cap (see Butler and Arnett, 2015).

[12] On the positive side, the DWP has continued to make *discretionary housing payments* available to local authorities to help people meet their housing costs as a result of the recent changes to the benefits they receive. According to the July 2015 Budget, these will amount to £800 million over the next five years. However, for the second year

running, most local authorities have spent less than their allocation (£165 million in 2014/15) (DWP, 2015b).

References

Adam Smith Institute (2014) *Burning down the house: government is not the solution to the housing crisis*, London: Adam Smith Institute.

Alakeson, V. and Cory, G. (2013) *Home truths: how affordable is housing for Britain's ordinary working families?*, London: Resolution Foundation.

Apps, P. (2014) 'Coalition intervenes to build new homes', *Inside Housing*, 5 December, pp 2–3.

Apps, P. (2015a) 'Government embarrassed over Right to Buy figures', *Inside Housing*, 27 February, p 3.

Apps, P. (2015b) 'L&Q to launch 50,000 home drive', *Inside Housing*, 2 April, p 9.

Apps, P. (2015c) 'Interview with Neil Hadden, Genesis chief executive', *Inside Housing*, 31 July, p 12.

Apps, P. and Douglas, D. (2014) 'Osborne's £300m scheme founders', *Inside Housing*, 17 October.

Barker, K. (2004) *Review of housing supply*, London: HM Treasury.

Birch, J. (2014) 'Help to Buy unlocked', *Inside Housing*, 11 April, pp 20–25.

Blokland, T. (2008) '"You've got to remember you live in public housing": place-making in an American housing project', *Housing, Theory and Society*, 25(1): 31–46.

Blond, P. (2010) *Red Tory: how Left and Right have broken Britain and how we can fix it*, London: Faber and Faber.

Brown, C. (2015) 'Sector dismay as Budget ignores supply', *Inside Housing*, 19 March.

Butler, P. and Arnett, G. (2015) 'Lower benefit caps "will exclude poor families from large parts of England"', *The Guardian*, 20 July.

Cabinet Office (2010) *The coalition: our programme for government*, London: Cabinet Office.

Cameron, D. (2010) Speech to civil servants, quoted in *The Guardian*, 14 May.

Card, P. (2006) 'Governing tenants: from dreadful enclosures to dangerous places', in J. Flint (ed) *Housing, urban governance and anti-social behaviour*, Bristol: The Policy Press, pp 37–56.

Chandler, D. and Disney, R. (2014) 'Housing market trends and recent policies', in C. Emmerson, P. Johnson and H. Miller (eds) *The IFS green budget: February 2014*, London: IFS.

Cheshire, P. (2014) 'Turning houses into gold: the failure of British planning', *CentrePiece*, Spring, Centre for Economic Performance, London School of Economics and Political Science, London. Available at: http://cep.lse.ac.uk/pubs/download/cp421.pdf (accessed 3 September 2015).

CIH (Chartered Institute of Housing), LGA (Local Government Association) and NFA (National Federation of ALMOs [Arms-Length Management Organisations]) (2015) *Keeping pace: replacing Right to Buy sales*, Coventry: CIH/LGA/NFA.

Citizens Advice and New Policy Institute (2015) *A nation of renters: how England moved from secure family homes towards rundown rentals*, London: Citizens Advice.

Clarke, A., Hill, L., Marshall, B., Monk, S., Pereira, I., Thomson, E., Whitehead, C. and Williams, P. (2014) *Evaluation of removal of the spare room subsidy: interim report*, London: Department for Work and Pensions.

Collinson, P. (2014) 'Millionaire landlords Fergus and Judith Wilson begin evicting large families', *The Guardian*, 31 October.

Communities and Local Government Committee (2015) *Community rights*, London: House of Commons.

Conservative Party (2015) *The Conservative Party manifesto 2015*, London: Conservative Party.

Cooper, C. (2005) 'Places, "folk devils" and social policy', in P. Somerville and N. Sprigings (eds) *Housing and social policy*, London: Routledge, pp 69–102.

Damer, S. (1974) 'Wine Alley: the sociology of a dreadful place', *Sociological Review*, 22(2): 221–47.

Damer, S. (1989) *From Moorepark to Wine Alley*, Edinburgh: Edinburgh University Press.

DCLG (Department for Communities and Local Government) (2012) *National planning policy framework*, London: DCLG.

DCLG (2013) *Guidance on rents for social housing: draft for consultation*, London: DCLG.

DCLG (2014) *Evaluation of the New Homes Bonus*, London: DCLG.

DCLG (2015a) *House building: March quarter 2015, England*, Housing Statistical Release, 21 May, London: DCLG.

DCLG (2015b) *Help to Buy (equity loan scheme) and Help to Buy: NewBuy statistics: April 2013 to March 2015*, London: DCLG.

DCLG (2015c) *English housing survey headline report 2013 to 2014*, London: DCLG.

DCLG (2015d) *English housing survey headline report 2013 to 2014: section 1 household tables*, London: DCLG.

DCLG (2015e) *Live tables on housebuilding, house building: permanent dwellings started (Table 208) and completed (Table 209), by tenure*. London: DCLG.

DCLG (2015g) *English housing survey households 2013–14*, London: DCLG.

DCLG (2015h) *Trends in tenure*, London: DCLG.

DCLG (2015i) *Live tables on affordable housing supply: Table 1000*, London: DCLG.

Dorling, D. (2014) *All that is solid: the great housing disaster*, Harmondsworth: Penguin.

Dorling, D. (2015) 'Policy, politics, health and housing in the UK', *Policy & Politics*, 43(2): 163–80.

Douglas, D. (2015) 'Government ends term with 55% rise in illegal B&B use', *Inside Housing*, 26 March, p 6.

Duxbury, N. (2015) 'Rent changes burn £42bn hole in plans', *Inside Housing*, 17 July, pp 1–3.

Duxbury, N. and McCabe, J. (2015) 'Rise of the housing activist', *Inside Housing*, 1 May, pp 20–21.

DWP (Department of Work and Pensions) (2015a) *Benefit expenditure and caseload tables 2015, outturn and forecast: Budget 2015*, London: DWP.

DWP (2015b) *Use of discretionary housing payments Great Britain – analysis of end of year returns from local authorities, April 2014 –March 2015*, London: DWP.

Fearn, H. (2015) 'The bank of mum and dad: Britain's best lender and creator of inequality', *The Guardian*, 17 April.

Fearn, H. and Gulliver, K. (2015) *A new deal for tenants: scoping a precariat charter for social housing*, Birmingham: Human City Institute.

Featherstone, D., Ince, A., Mackinnon, D., Strauss, K. and Cumbers, A. (2012) 'Progressive localism and the construction of political alternatives', *Transactions of the Institute of British Geographers*, NS 37: 177–82.

Forrest, R. and Hirayama, Y. (2015) 'The financialisation of the social project: embedded liberalism, neoliberalism and home ownership', *Urban Studies*, 52(2): 233–44.

Forrest, R. and Murie, A. (1986) 'Marginalization and subsidized individualism: the sale of council houses in the restructuring of the British welfare state', *International Journal of Urban and Regional Research*, 10(1): 46–66.

Frontier Economics (2014) *Assessing the social and economic impact of affordable housing investment: a report prepared for G15 and the National Housing Federation*, London: Frontier Economics Ltd.

Gambarin, A. (2014) *Removal of the spare room subsidy: analysis of changes in numbers subject to a reduction in Housing Benefit award*, London: DWP.

Gentleman, A. (2013) 'UK's bedroom tax and housing crisis threaten human rights, says UN expert', *The Guardian*, 11 September.

Gibb, K. (2015) 'The multiple failures of the UK bedroom tax', *International Journal of Housing Policy*, 15(2): 148–66.

Gimson, A. (2013) 'Help to Buy is immoral because it encourages ordinary people to risk ruin', 14 November. Available at: www.conservativehome.com/thetorydiary/2013/11/help-to-buy-is-immoral-because-it-encourages-ordinary-people-to-risk-ruin.html (accessed 9 September 2015).

GLA (Greater London Authority) (2015a) *GLA funded housing starts on site and completions – London (to end of June 2015)*, London: GLA.

GLA (2015b) *Rough sleeping in London rockets 37% in a year*, press release, 11 March, London: GLA.

Handy, C. and Gulliver, K. (2015) 'Towards a one nation housing policy', *Thinkpiece*, no 77, London: Compass. Available at: http://www.compassonline.org.uk/wp-content/uploads/2013/07/One-Nation-Housing-Thinkpiece-77.pdf (accessed 22 September 2015).

Hanley, L. (2007) *Estates: an intimate history*, London: Granta.

Harloe, M. (1982) 'Towards the decommodification of housing? A comment on council house sales', *Critical Social Policy*, 2(4): 39–42.

Hastings, A. (2004) 'Stigma and social housing estates: beyond pathological explanations', *Journal of Housing and the Built Environment*, 19(3): 233–54.

HCA (2015) *Housing statistics 1 April 2014–31 March 2015*, London: HCA.

HCA and DCLG (Department of Communities and Local Government) (2014) *Affordable homes programme 2015 to 2018: prospectus*, London: HCA.

Heywood, A. (2013) *The affordable rent model in London: delivery, viability, potential*, London: Future of London.

Hilditch, S. (2014) *So what's not to like about social renting?*, Coventry: Chartered Institute of Housing.

Hills, J. (2007) *Ends and means? The future roles of social housing in England*, Case Report 34, London: CASE, LSE.

HM Government (2011) *Laying the foundations: a housing strategy for England*, London: The Stationery Office.

HM Treasury (2015a) *Help to Buy: mortgage guarantee scheme quarterly statistics 8/10/13–31/12/14*, London: HM Treasury.

HM Treasury (2015b) *Help to Buy: ISA – scheme outline*, London: HM Treasury.

Hodkinson, S. and Robbins, G. (2013) 'The return of class war conservatism? Housing under the UK coalition government', *Critical Social Policy*, 33(1): 57–77.

Hodkinson, S., Watt, P. and Mooney, G. (2013) 'Introduction: neoliberal housing policy – time for a critical re-appraisal', *Critical Social Policy*, 33(1): 3–16.

Hohmann, J. (2015) *Protecting the right to housing in England: a context of crisis*, London: Just Fair.

Holmans, A. (2013) *New estimates of housing demand and need in England, 2011 to 2031*, Tomorrow Series Paper 16, London: Town and Country Planning Association.

Inside Housing (2015) 'Bonus funding for new homes', 6 February.

Johnstone, C. and Mooney, G. (2007) '"Problem" people, "problem" places? New Labour and council estates', in R. Atkinson and G. Helms (eds) *Securing an urban renaissance*, Bristol: The Policy Press, pp 125–39.

Jones, O. (2011) *Chavs: the demonization of the working class*, London: Verso.

Law, A., Mooney, G. and Helms, G. (2010) 'Urban "disorders", "problem places" and criminal justice in Scotland', in H. Croall, G. Mooney and M. Munro (eds) *Criminal justice in Scotland*, Abingdon: Routledge/Willan, pp 43–64.

Lowndes, V. and Pratchett, L. (2012) 'Local governance under the Coalition government: austerity, localism and the Big Society', *Local Government Studies*, 38(1): 21–40.

Lyons, M. (2014) *The Lyons housing review: mobilising across the nation to build the homes our children need*, London: Labour Party.

Macmillan, R. (2013) *Decoupling the state and the third sector? The 'Big Society' as a spontaneous order*, Birmingham: Third Sector Research Centre.

Mathers, A. and Taylor, G. (2005) 'Contemporary struggle in Europe: "anti-power" or counter-power?', *Capital & Class*, 85: 27–30.

McCabe, J. (2014) 'Learning curve', *Inside Housing*, 17 April, pp 23–7.

McKenzie, L. (2015) *Getting by: estates, class and culture in austerity Britain*, Bristol: The Policy Press.

Meek, J. (2014) 'Where will we live?', *London Review of Books*, 36(1). Available at: www.lrb.co.uk/v36/n01/james-meek/where-will-we-live (accessed 28 March 2014).

Mirrlees, J., Adam, S., Besley, T., Blundell, R., Bond, S., Chote, R., Gammie, M., Johnson, P., Myles, G. and Poterba, J. (2011) *Tax by design*, Oxford: Oxford University Press. Available at: www.ifs.org.uk/mirrleesReview/design (accessed 21 September 2015).

NFA (National Federation of ALMOs [Arms-Length Management Organisations]), ARCH (Association of Retained Council Housing), CIH (Chartered Institute of Housing) and the LGA (Local Government Association) (2012) *Let's get building: the case for local authority investment in rented homes to help drive economic growth*, York: NFA.

NFA (National Federation of ALMOs), ARCH (Association of Retained Council Housing) and the CWAG (Councils with ALMOs [Arms-Length Management Organisations] Group) (2014) *Welfare reform survey – 2013/14 quarter 2 and quarter 3 update: summary of responses*, York: NFA.

Norman, J. (2010) *The Big Society: the anatomy of the new politics*, Buckingham: University of Buckingham Press.

O'Hara, M. (2015) *Austerity bites: a journey to the sharp end of cuts in the UK*, Bristol: The Policy Press.

O'Mahony, L.F., O'Mahony, D. and Hickey, R. (eds) (2015) *Moral rhetoric and the criminalising of squatting: vulnerable demons?*, London: Routledge.

Osborne, H. (2015) 'Private landlords gain £26.7 billion from UK taxpayer, says campaign group', *The Guardian*, 9 February.

Padley, M., Valadez, L. and Hirsch, D. (2015) *Households below a minimum income standard: 2008/09 to 2012/13*, York: Joseph Rowntree Foundation.

Paton, K. (2009) 'Probing the symptomatic silences of middle class settlement: a case study of gentrification processes in Glasgow', *City*, 13(4): 432–50.

Peck, J. and Tickell, A. (2002) 'Neoliberalising space', *Antipode*, 33(3): 380–404.

Pegg, D. (2015) 'Landlords enjoy £14bn tax breaks as figures reveal buy-to-let expansion', *The Guardian*, 26 May.

Pennington, J., Ben-Galim, D. and Cooke, G. (2012) *No place to call home: the social impacts of housing undersupply on young people*, London: Institute for Public Policy Research.

Perry, J., Purcell, L. and Cooper, N. (2015) *Restoring faith in the safety net*, Manchester: Church Action on Poverty.

Power, A., Provan, B., Herden, E. and Serle, N. (2014) *The impact of welfare reform on social landlords and tenants*, York: Joseph Rowntree Foundation.

Ryder, A.R. (2015) 'Gypsies and Travellers: a big or divided society?', *Policy & Politics*, 43(1): 101–17.

Shelter (2014) *The clipped wing generation*, London: Shelter.

Smyth, S. (2013) 'The privatization of council housing: stock transfer and the struggle for accountable housing', *Critical Social Policy*, 33(1): 37–56.

Somerville, P. (2011) 'Conservative housing policy', in H. Bochel (ed) *The Conservative Party and social policy*, Bristol: The Policy Press, pp 119–44.

Standing, G. (2014) *A precariat charter: from denizens to citizens*, London: Bloomsbury.

Stephens, M. and Williams, P. (2012) *Tackling housing market volatility in the UK: a progress report*, York: Joseph Rowntree Foundation.

Stephens, M., Whitehead, C. and Munro, M. (2005) *Lessons from the past, challenges for the future for housing policy*, London: Office of the Deputy Prime Minister.

Treanor, D. (2015) *Housing policies in Europe*, Treanor Books. Available at: www.m3h.co.uk/publications

Tunstall, R. (2015) *The coalition's record on housing: policy, spending and outcomes 2010–2015*, Working Paper 18, York and London: Centre for Housing Policy, University of York, Centre for Analysis of Social Exclusion, London School of Economics and Political Science, and Joseph Rowntree Foundation.

Tunstall, R., Bevan, M., Bradshaw, J., Croucher, K., Duffy, S., Hunter, C., Jones, A., Rugg, J., Wallace, A. and Wilcox, S. (2013) *The links between housing and poverty*, York: Joseph Rowntree Foundation.

Watt, P. (2008) '"Underclass" and "ordinary people" discourses: representing/re-presenting council tenants in a housing campaign', *Critical Discourse Studies*, 5(4): 345–57.

Wilcox, S. (2014) *Housing benefit size criteria: impacts for social sector tenants and options for reform*, York: Joseph Rowntree Foundation.

Wilcox, S., Perry, J. and Williams, P. (2014) *UK Housing Review*, Coventry: Chartered Institute of Housing.

Wilcox, S., Perry, J. and Williams, P. (2015) *UK housing review*, Coventry: Chartered Institute of Housing.

Wiles, C. (2014) 'Affordable housing does not mean what you think it means', *The Guardian*, 3 February. Available at: www.theguardian.com/housing-network/2014/feb/03/affordable-housing-meaning-rent-social-housing (accessed 6 March 2015).

Wilson, W. (2014) *The New Homes Bonus scheme*, Commons Library Standard Note 26, London: House of Commons Library.

Youde, K. (2015) 'Planning shortfall could hit 180,000 homes', *Inside Housing*, 7 May.

EIGHT

Social security under the coalition and Conservatives: shredding the system for people of working age; privileging pensioners

Stephen McKay and Karen Rowlingson

Introduction

In this chapter, we consider the changes made to social security – increasingly known as 'welfare' – during the period of the Conservative–Liberal Democrat coalition government, and in the early days of the majority Conservative government. First, we set the context in terms of the amount of spending on social security policy. As the largest single budget of any government department, social security was clearly a key target for a coalition government determined to reduce public spending. However, policies were driven not just by fiscal goals, but also ideological aims in terms of changing individual behaviour and reducing the role of the state in preference to the market.

The chapter then gives an overview of the key social security reforms before focusing separately on policies relating to those of working age and those over state pension age. This has become an increasingly important distinction since 2010, with those of working age (whether or not with children) being the key target for reform, leaving pensioners relatively protected from austerity cuts.

The chapter then reviews the impacts of the reforms alongside the key themes of reform, identifying the influence of the Liberal Democrats on coalition policy. It then compares these recent reforms with those of the previous New Labour governments (1997–2010) and the prior Conservative governments (1979–97). We conclude that there is much continuity but also some radical change, not least the introduction of benefit caps and the effective abandonment of policy to reduce child poverty. An intensification of the neoliberal project is further being pursued by the 2015 Conservative majority government.

Background: the 2010 context

Following the 2008 financial crisis, the New Labour government provided the banks with £124 billion in the form of loans or share purchases, which required a transfer of cash from the government to the banks (National Audit Office, 2011). At the same time, social security expenditure was increasing due to rises in unemployment. The coalition government came into power with a key focus on reducing the public sector deficit and national debt. As the largest single budget of any government department, social security spending would be a key target. At £210 billion in 2010/11, or over 13% of gross domestic product (GDP), spending on social security was around twice as large as spending on the National Health Service (NHS). As well as being large in scale, several notable benefits had also increased rapidly in spending during the years of New Labour, partly as a matter of policy (to reduce child poverty and pensioner poverty) and partly as a response to the recession, which had caused lower earnings and higher unemployment, and hence greater pressure on spending for tax credits and unemployment. Two other longer-term drivers of higher spending were an increasing number of older people and rising rents for those receiving Housing Benefit, particularly in the private sector.

Added to this increased spending, and perhaps because of it, attitudes towards social security spending had tended to become rather more negative than on health. Clery, Lee and Kunz (2013) identify drops in support for welfare spending over time, with the greatest decreases occurring among Labour supporters and for young people (see also Chapter Four). There was also concern expressed – in certain parts of the media, at least – that social security spending had been creating a 'welfare-dependent' class or lifestyle. In the *Daily Mail*, for example, there were several reports during 2008–10 about the rise of a 'Shameless generation'.[1]

While the economic context is clearly vital in understanding coalition social security policy, ideological goals are also key. These goals were developed partly, in opposition, by the Centre for Social Justice, which produced a number of analyses of 'Breakdown Britain' in a series of reports in 2006 covering indebtedness, addiction, educational failure, family breakdown and 'economic dependency' (Centre for Social Justice, 2006), which it regarded as the most important 'pathways to poverty'. A year later, a set of reports under the heading of 'Breakthrough Britain' proposed various solutions, and in 2009, the report *Dynamic benefits* (Centre for Social Justice, 2009) proposed a single allowance for those of working age – the Universal Credit. This was enthusiastically adopted by the Conservative Secretary of State for Social Security, Iain Duncan Smith, becoming a key element of longer-term reform.

Another important part of the context for social security policy is that it remains a 'reserved power' for Westminster, that is, with little devolution, except in respect of Northern Ireland, which has generally pursued a policy of parity (see Chapter Fifteen). Nevertheless, despite the limited scope for any differences, resources were found by the Scottish government to increase discretionary housing payments to effectively eliminate the 'bedroom tax' in Scotland. However, social security policy was generally uniform across the UK during the periods that we consider.

Key coalition policies

Overview

As noted earlier, spending on social security forms a major part of all public expenditure and it has been increasing, for pensioners at least, quite dramatically from 1997/98 to 2010 (see Figure 8.1). Spending on those of working age was much flatter over the same period, although there was a noticeable increase during 2009/10. In looking at these overall trends in spending, it is, of course, important to distinguish between the trends associated with ongoing demographic factors and economic shocks, and those due to deliberate policy changes. The long-run increase in spending on older people is linked to increases in the number of older people, recently moderated by more rapid increases in state pension ages. The clear uptick in spending on benefits of working age partly resulted from the great recession that followed the banking crisis, which led to fewer people being in paid work and more receiving benefits.

In Table 8.1, we look at some of the key reforms enacted between 2010 and 2014, considering the savings made through various benefit cuts in the 2014/15 financial year. One of the biggest cuts/savings was the change in indexation (uprating) of various benefits/tax credits such that they now go up in line with the Consumer Prices Index (CPI) rather than the Retail Price Index (RPI). This reform received little media attention, not least because it is rather technical. Furthermore, while it has affected many millions of people, the amounts involved have been relatively small compared with some other cuts. By contrast, the so-called 'bedroom tax' saved much less but had a much higher public profile.

Figure 8.1: Spending on benefits by working age and pensionable age since 1997/98

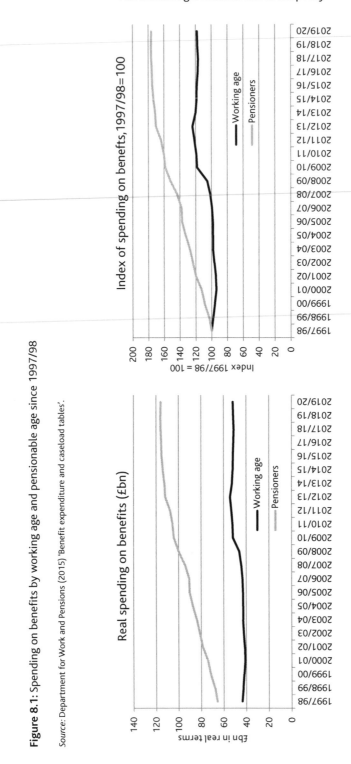

Source: Department for Work and Pensions (2015) 'Benefit expenditure and caseload tables'.

While the vast majority of reforms to social security for working-age people involved cuts to benefits, some involved 'giveaways' that necessitated extra government spending, such as the 'triple lock' for the Basic State Pension, which cost significant amounts (see Table 8.1). Another substantial and costly reform was the increase in the income tax threshold from £6,475 in 2010/11 to £10,600 from April 2015, at an annual cost of over £5 billion (Browne, 2012). This rise was much faster than either price inflation or income growth and helped those on relatively low incomes. However, it did nothing for the poorest, who were below the income tax threshold, and did less for those receiving means-tested in-work benefits.

Table 8.1: Key reforms to social security 2010–14

Measure	Date (last updated)	Saving calculated in 2014/15
Benefits, tax credits and public service pensions: switch to CPI indexation from 2011/12	Budget 2011	£10,595 million
Child Benefit: remove from families with a higher-rate taxpayer from January 2013	Budget 2012	£2,370 million
Working-age discretionary benefits and tax credits: increase by 1% for three years from 2013/14	Budget 2013	£1,685 million
Contributory Employment and Support Allowance: time limit for those in the Work Related Activity Group to one year	Budget 2012	£1,335 million
Tax credits: first and second withdrawal rates: increase to 41% from 2011/12	Budget 2011	£755 million
Disability Living Allowance: reform gateway from 2013/14	Budget 2013	£660 million
Local Housing Allowance: set at the 30th percentile of local rents from 2011/12	Budget 2011	£475 million
Social sector: limit working-age entitlements to reflect size of family from 2013/14 ('bedroom tax'/'spare room subsidy')	Budget 2013	£465 million
		Extra spending calculated in 2014/15
Basic State Pension: introduce triple guarantee from 2011/12	Budget 2011	£1,530 million

Source: 'Welfare reform: collated costings, Budget 2010 to Budget 2014' (available at: https://www.gov.uk/government/statistics/welfare-reform-collated-costings-2010-to-2014).

One of the key features of coalition policy was the division between policies for those of working age and policies for those of state pension age. The next section therefore reviews coalition reforms for these groups.

Social security for those of working age

The coalition government introduced a huge number of reforms to social security for people of working age, across a number of different areas. One of the 'flagship' policies (Sainsbury, 2014) was the introduction of Universal Credit. Unlike many of the reforms to working-age benefits, this has perhaps attracted the most support across the political spectrum, at least initially, even by those concerned at its slow implementation: 'We continue to support the policy objectives of UC [Universal Credit], particularly improving incentives to work and smoothing the transition from benefits into work' (Work and Pensions Select Committee, 2014, p 3). This reform is a radical change to simplify the benefit system. It brings together what were previously six different means-tested benefits and tax credits (including Housing Benefit) into a single payment. It is paid directly to one recipient in the family (likely to be the man in most cases), including any Housing Benefit for rent. Universal Credit is an ambitious reform that has been beset by various information technology (IT) and implementation difficulties and design challenges. It was first introduced for a small number of claimants in April 2013. By October 2014, only 18,000 were receiving it rather than the 2 million originally intended by then (see Hills, 2015), let alone the 7.7 million eventually intended recipients.

The focus on a single recipient, and inclusion of Housing Benefit, has prompted concerns about effects on budgeting and the gender distribution of income (Bennett, 2012). More recently, commentators have expressed more concerns about whether Universal Credit will achieve its objectives irrespective of the implementation problems (Millar, 2015), anxieties likely to have been exacerbated by the 2015 Summer Budget, which reduced the generosity of provision.

Claimants have to apply online and have their benefit paid into a bank account. Part of the rationale for Universal Credit was to increase work incentives by removing the rule on the minimum number of hours required to qualify for in-work support. On the other hand, those working part-time may have to try to increase hours as a condition of entitlement.

A key and novel policy reform was the introduction of two benefit caps: one relating to overall spending on social security benefits (excluding the state pension and Jobseeker's Allowance); and another relating to the maximum that any particular family may receive – the latter 'benefit cap' perhaps receiving more attention (see McKay, 2012). For couples not in work, in the first round of reform, the maximum amount of benefits they may receive was £500 per week, with £350 for single adults. This policy is based on the idea that no non-working family should receive in benefits more than the average wage. Those affected by this cap tend to have larger families or very high housing costs. Those in work or with disabled family members (a group who may also have a large benefit entitlement) are exempt, as are those above state pension age and those recently made unemployed. In a common pattern, the amount saved by this policy (at around £260 million, a tiny proportion of total spending not even registering in Table 8.1) is arguably rather lower than the attention it has received. However, the concept of comparing a particular level of benefits to average earnings (rather than past earnings) is novel.

An underlying debate is whether social security is about providing only a temporary respite from short-lived economic difficulties, or is instead supporting those choosing a 'lifestyle' on benefits. The introduction of a benefits cap may be seen as an attempt to engineer greater fairness into the payment of social security (between workers and non-workers), but in its initial form, it affected relatively few families, albeit often to a high degree.

Conversely, restrictions on uprating benefits have had perhaps the largest effects on total spending but have received rather less attention than the benefit cap and, indeed, the 'bedroom tax', which we discuss later. Most benefits had previously been uprated in line with RPI but for most working-age benefits, this was changed to the CPI, which is almost always lower. On some estimates, this saved over £3 billion in 2012/13 alone, with successively larger cumulative amounts each year (see earlier).

An overall cap was then placed on the uprating of benefits such that if the CPI was higher than 1%, benefits would nevertheless not be increased by more than 1% for three years from 2012/13 – saving about £1.5 billion by 2014/15. Hills (2015, p 16) has argued that this is more akin to working-age people getting 'the lower of prices and earnings' in contrast to the treatment for pensioners (see later). Part of the justification for such restrictions has been the low level of wage inflation over the period of the coalition government, with drops in real earnings.

Since Beveridge, the 'problem of rent' has beset the social security system. The coalition government's response has been to cut Housing

Benefit further, not least so that it now only covers the lowest 30% of local rents rather than the median (see also Chapter Seven). Housing Benefit for those in social housing was also cut by 14% for those deemed to be 'under-occupying' their homes (eg having a 'spare' bedroom). Those with two 'spare bedrooms' lost 25% of their housing benefit. Such a rule already existed for tenants in private renting, but the introduction of the infamous 'bedroom tax' (or removal of the 'spare room subsidy', as the government tried to label it) in social renting received considerable media attention, and even the Conservative Mayor of London, Boris Johnson, said that it would lead to 'Kosovo-style social cleansing' in the capital.[2]

Tax credits were a key part of policy under New Labour, with the new tax credits (Working Tax Credit and Child Tax Credit) being a key element of moves to reduce child poverty. Spending on such tax credits almost quadrupled between 1997 and 2010 (see Figure 8.2).

Figure 8.2: Spending on tax credits under different regimes since 1997/98

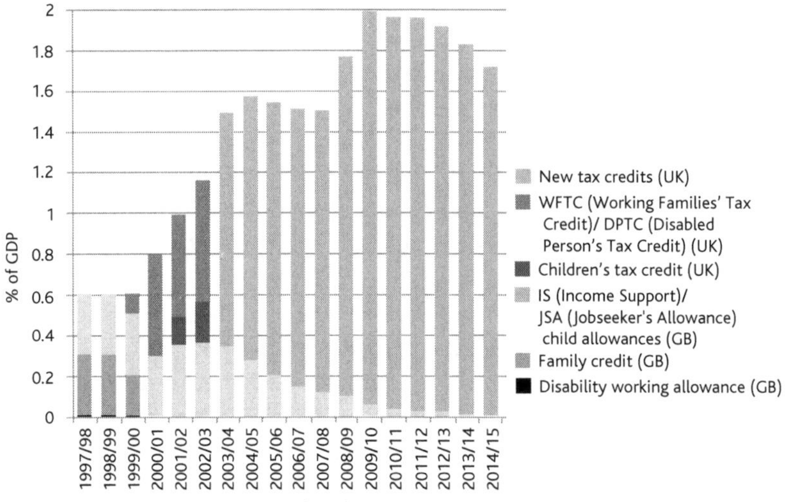

Source: Office for Budget Responsibility (2014).

The policy towards tax credits, prior to 2015, was to introduce a number of cuts and changes to what appear to be quite technical (or at least lesser-known) provisions. So, such measures include: reducing the disregard for in-year income rises from £25,000 down to £5,000 (saving about £0.5 billion a year); reducing the support for childcare costs from 80% to 70% (about £0.3 billion); increasing the withdrawal rate to 41% (£0.7 billion); and removing the 'baby element' of provision (about £0.3 billion). These imply quite widespread reductions in the generosity of tax credits, following a period of strong expansion.

Significant reforms also took place in relation to disability benefits; indeed, this was one of the most active areas of reform under the coalition, although disabled people were exempted from some changes (like the benefits cap). However, the move from Incapacity Benefit to Employment and Support Allowance included a change to just one year linked to contributions before being means tested. Disability Living Allowance is also being replaced by Personal Independence Payments – which are aimed to reach fewer people (Wood and Grant, 2010; UNISON, 2013).

While the benefit caps and changes to the 'mainstream' social security benefits have received much public attention, reforms to Council Tax Benefit and the Social Fund have also made a major difference to people. A cut of 10% was made to provision for paying council tax when Council Tax Support (previously Council Tax Benefit) was devolved to local authorities, each then applying different rules for entitlement. The Social Fund was also 'localised' in this manner from April 2013, with local authorities given freedom to make changes (many opting for loans and vouchers), but without (in time) any financial support for provision.

Alongside these attacks on universal and insurance benefits, Child Benefit was removed from those families with an earner receiving £60,000 a year, and started to reduce at £50,000. Finally, reforms have effectively abandoned any 'asset-based welfare' policies introduced or planned by the New Labour government. Child Trust Funds are no longer to be issued to new children (although accounts remain in place for those who already had them), and the planned roll-out of Saving Gateway was abandoned.

Benefits for those of pensionable age

The situation of older people receiving benefits has been much more protected than that of younger people, as the overall trends tend to indicate (see Figure 8.1). They have not been part of key new policies (the bedroom tax, benefit cap or even Universal Credit). Under the stewardship of the Liberal Democrat minister Steve Webb (a former social policy professor), a number of reforms have provided a degree of simplification of a rather complex system.[3]

First, despite cuts to benefits for working-age people, benefits for pensioners have not only been protected from cuts, but actually increased, providing close to a minimum income standard for this group (Hirsch, 2015). While there are various caps on increases to working-age benefits (see earlier), the coalition government introduced the 'triple lock' on the uprating of the state pension, such that this benefit increases each year by either 2.5%, average earnings or the CPI, whichever is highest. Thus, an insurance-based benefit is increasing in value for pensioners while such benefits play an ever-decreasing role for those of working age. Moreover, the gap between benefit levels for otherwise similar people of different ages is extremely high and projected to increase over time.

Having said all this, people are having to wait longer to get their state pension as the age at which people become entitled to it is rising over the next few decades, currently planned to reach 68 for those born in 1978 (ie in 2046). This reform, coming on top of the previous equalisation of state pension age between men and women, will particularly affect women born in the years around 1954, who will now wait up to 10 years after those born four years earlier.

While the basic state pension is becoming more generous – in terms not only of the amounts received, but also the credits needed to gain entitlement to the full pension, the earnings-related parts of the state pension will gradually disappear as the single-tier pension will be introduced from April 2016 (see Department for Work and Pensions, 2012). People will no longer be able to build up a state second pension (or benefit from National Insurance relief if they opt out of this). Introduced at zero net cost, some of those with more average earnings will lose out compared with the previous system, and, indeed, Crawford, Keynes and Tetlow (2013) explain that the new system is less generous to almost everyone in the long run, especially today's younger people.

More recently, new 'pension freedoms' have been granted for those with Defined Contribution pensions. Under the new reforms (from April 2015), people with Defined Contribution pension pots will be able to take the full amount saved and use it as they wish, though they will be subject to tax if they take out more than 25% of the fund value. Previously, most people in such schemes were obliged to purchase an annuity with the fund value.

There have also been reforms of private pensions, in particular, the introduction of auto-enrolment into workplace pensions. This continues the process of reform introduced by New Labour following the recommendations of the Pensions Commission (2005).

The impacts of reform

The coalition government's social security reforms, particularly for working-age people, appear radical on the surface, but what difference have they made in practice? During the first two years of the coalition (2010–12), the social security system remained largely the same – reform takes time. Indeed, during this period, benefits were uprated with RPI while real earnings fell. Thus, the social security system worked, as intended, to provide a safety net in a time of recession. Relative poverty rates actually fell over that period (although some measures of absolute poverty showed an increase). However, then the coalition's significant reforms were introduced and various projections suggested that these reforms would hit the poorest hardest, although, again, with a major distinction between those of working age (including families with children), on the one hand, and pensioners, on the other (Browne and Elming, 2015; Hills, 2015; Hood and Phillips, 2015).

As we have seen, the overall size of the benefits bill did not seem to change much in response to government policy. Given the coalition's mission to cut public spending and, hence, public debt, these figures appear to suggest that little had changed. However, this is due to a number of factors. First, the recession meant that unemployment was high and social security spending therefore went up to support people out of work or on reduced incomes (particularly in the first couple of years of the coalition before the cuts hit). Second, there was an increasing number of pensioners receiving increasingly large payments of state pension (although some of this was offset by a corresponding reduction in Pension Credit). Overall, the changes to the (direct) tax and benefit system were fiscally neutral (in other words, they gave away as much as they took back) but regressive (as the bottom half of the income distribution lost out). Income data lags behind change but it is expected that child and working-age poverty will be higher in 2014/15 than 2012/13 (Hills, 2015). One impact of coalition policies has been the growth of in-work poverty (Belfield et al, 2015). The proportion of poor children whose parents work has risen. Thus, work is clearly no guarantee of avoiding poverty.

Underlying themes and features

We can detect a number of key themes running through these reforms. First, as highlighted earlier, the reforms were often justified in terms of the need to cut the public sector deficit and national debt. However, alongside this apparently economic driver, there were also particular ideological motives that influenced the nature of reform. For example, the Conservatives, in particular, argued that people of working age should not be relying on 'welfare', but should, instead, take paid work and increase their hours and pay until they no longer qualified for means-tested support. Those reliant on such benefits should not expect them to increase, or to approach the earnings of those in paid work, whatever their circumstances. Furthermore, people should only have large families if they can afford to provide for them without recourse to public funds. Hence, there was a renewed (see later) emphasis on (individual) 'responsible behaviour' in terms of work and family life. Where such behaviour was not seen as being appropriate, conditions and sanctions were increased, and the benefit cap was aimed at either deterring people from having large families 'on benefits' or further encouraging them to find financial support outside the welfare state. The focus on the labour market rather than the welfare state as a source of support was therefore intensified, even if this could not guarantee that people avoided poverty.

Fairness was a key theme under the coalition, although Hills (2015) points out that this was a different idea of 'fairness' compared with the previous New Labour government as it was partly about 'those with the broadest shoulders [bearing] the greatest burden' (as George Osborne had put it), but also partly about 'desert', with desert linked to (the right) behaviour. There was therefore an increased focus on family breakdown and alcohol and drug addiction.

Apparent simplification/centralisation (eg through Universal Credit) was another theme, but this was accompanied by growing complexity/localisation in other areas (the Social Fund, Council Tax Benefit). Indeed, implementation may differ in some parts of the UK. For example, Scotland effectively nullified the 'bedroom tax' by giving out discretionary payments, and seems to have similar plans for 2015 onwards (see also Chapter Fifteen).

Another key theme was the distinction between pensioners and those of working age. Those above pension age were not subject to any of the kind of reasoning described earlier, remained exempt from most of the controversial measures and enjoyed an enhanced expectation of uprating. It is not entirely clear why this distinction has been drawn so tightly. It could be due to political expediency – the desire to retain or capture a large proportion of votes from a group that is more likely to vote (and to vote Conservative) than younger people. Or, it could be more ideological, in the sense that those over state pension age are not expected to work (any longer), and are seen as more deserving of state support. However, it seems somewhat arbitrary that just because someone reaches a particular birthday, they turn from someone potentially requiring conditions and sanctions to secure state support to someone who thoroughly deserves a much higher level of state support without conditions or sanctions.

One of the striking features of the coalition government was the continuity of political leadership in relation to social security. Iain Duncan Smith remained as secretary of state for the whole period of the coalition (and, indeed, into the Conservative government). He had also served as shadow secretary of state from 1997 to 1999, and ran the Centre for Social Justice for a time, so had a clear commitment and expertise in social security matters. By contrast, secretaries of state under New Labour came and went with great frequency: there were no fewer than eight from 2001 to 2010. This, without doubt, gave Gordon Brown, as Chancellor, then Prime Minister, more power over social security policy. Iain Duncan Smith used his power to focus on what he saw as fundamental issues of behaviour, rather than just trying to cut costs, as George Osborne in the Treasury might have preferred.

The Pensions Minister, Steve Webb, from the Liberal Democrat side of the coalition, also remained in his post for the duration of the coalition government. A former economist at the Institute for Fiscal Studies and academic at the University of Bath, he also had strong authority in his role and managed to argue for many Liberal Democrat policies (see later). Some have also suggested a shared Christian faith between Webb and Duncan Smith as potentially important (Nelson, 2014).

The influence of the Liberal Democrats

The Liberal Democrats appear to have had a major influence on reforms in two key areas. The first was the increase in the income tax allowance – originally to £10,000 and estimated to cost £16.8 billion in the Liberal Democrat manifesto. This was hugely expensive at a time when the government was focusing on reducing public debt. The other reform was also expensive – the triple lock on the state pension from 2011 and protecting other benefits for pensioners. The Conservatives accepted both of these reforms and also dropped their plan to increase the Inheritance Tax threshold to £1 million. While the increase in the tax threshold was a Liberal Democrat policy, it was certainly part of the economic liberalism that many Conservatives could easily sign up to. Cutting taxes is certainly compatible with Conservative ideology. A particular wing of the Liberal Democrats, associated with *The orange book* (Marshall and Laws, 2004), could also sign up to economically liberal policies.[4] Thus, the impact of the Liberal Democrats was perhaps not as dramatic as it might seem. The policy to increase the level of the state pension might be seen as less Conservative perhaps (see later), although this reform partly emanated from the cross-party consensus following the work of the Pensions Commission in the early 2000s. It is also a policy that appeals to pensioners, a core part of the Conservative vote.

Otherwise, there was little in the coalition agreement on working-age benefits. In their manifesto, the Conservatives had said that they would look into: ways of simplifying the benefit system; making people 'work for the dole' if they were long-term unemployed; and reassessing all Incapacity Benefit claims. However, again, there had been little detail and it seems that the Conservatives were left largely free to craft working-age social security policy (via Iain Duncan Smith), while the Liberal Democrats focused on pension policy (via Steve Webb). However, at different times, it is possible that pressure from the Liberal Democrats may have tempered even more radical cuts in working-age benefits, and certainly more draconian cuts followed once the Conservatives won a majority in the House of Commons in 2015 (see later).

Comparison with the previous Labour governments (1997–2010)

The New Labour governments of 1997–2010 cut poverty, particularly child poverty and pensioner poverty (for an overview, see McKay and Rowlingson, 2008). The focus for the anti-poverty strategy for the working-age population was on 'education, education, education', alongside early intervention, training for young people and making work pay (through tax credits) and possible (through various New Deals). A National Minimum Wage was introduced in 1999 and work obligations increased, particularly for lone parents, who had previously been able to claim means-tested benefits with no obligation to work until their youngest child left school. Gordon Brown, as Chancellor, redistributed income to those on the lowest incomes 'by stealth', through quiet manipulation of the tax credit system. Following Tony Blair's pledge to eradicate child poverty, it fell (by a third before housing costs and by a fifth after housing costs). By contrast, Labour was not particularly concerned about people of working age without children. Poverty among this group actually increased under New Labour (see MacInnes et al, 2014).

As far as pensions were concerned, the Pension Acts of 2007/08 set in motion the increases in the state pension age while, at the same time, widening entitlement to it. Automatic enrolment into workplace pensions was also established in the legislation, as was the link between the value of the state pension and earnings from 2013. Pensioner poverty fell by 30% before housing costs and by half after housing costs under New Labour (for the latest figures, see Department for Work and Pensions, 2015).

As the banking crisis hit and the recession followed, New Labour withdrew tax-free income tax personal allowances from those earning £100,000 plus and also introduced a 50% rate of tax on earnings over £150,000. Before leaving power, the government introduced the Child Poverty Act in 2010 to bind any successor to maintaining its commitment to child poverty reduction. However, while child and pensioner poverty reduced under New Labour, income inequality changed little over the period, not least because the rich saw no curbs on their income and wealth. However, tax and benefit policies were 'modestly' redistributive (Hills, 2015).

In their early review of coalition policy, McKay and Rowlingson (2011) suggested that the coalition had important aspects of continuity but also areas of difference when compared with New Labour. For example, the 'p' word – poverty – was still being used by the coalition, although the causes were seen as more individual and behavioural rather than structural. Both coalition and New Labour governments shared a belief that paid work was the best route out of poverty, with ever-increasing conditionality and sanctions for those not apparently trying hard enough to find a job. As mentioned earlier, there was much continuity in relation to pensions policy given the consensus following the Pensions Commission of the early 2000s.

However, some years on, it is clear that there is also much discontinuity from the previous New Labour government. First of all, poverty may have been mentioned and monitored by the coalition government but it was clearly not a priority to meet the existing income-based poverty measures. The introduction of Universal Credit also marks a radical departure from New Labour. This 'Holy Grail' of social security policy is something that New Labour may have accepted ideologically but simply did not get round to doing given many of the challenges it faces (which the current policy may still not be able to overcome). By contrast, New Labour's Asset Based Welfare policies (Child Trust Fund and Saving Gateway) have been abandoned by the coalition. On the surface, there is much to commend these to Conservative ideology, but they had little support from the Liberal Democrats and were perhaps too closely associated with New Labour to survive.

Comparison with previous Conservative governments (1979–97)

The last Conservative government prior to the current (2015–) government was in power from 1979 to 1997. That government certainly heralded a major change from the post-war consensus that preceded it, with cuts across the social security board, including for pensioners (for an overview, see McKay and Rowlingson, 1999). In this respect, the coalition government was quite different as it protected pensioners and, indeed, restored the link between uprating state pensions and earnings/inflation (or, indeed, 2.5%). It was in 1980 that this link had been broken, and state pensions were then uprated with inflation, which lagged significantly behind earnings in the 1980s.

The cuts in pensions and other social security benefits in the late 1970s/early 1980s were partly pragmatic, due to the recessionary times, but this also soon became a matter of ideology, with private pensions incentivised, for example. Alongside these cuts in contributory state pensions, there were corresponding cuts in contributory benefits and earnings-related additions for those of working age. The Conservative government focused on means testing. Once again, this aimed to save money but was also, perhaps, part of an ideological agenda to reduce social security to something for 'the poor', rather than as a more universal system that all could rely on at different points in their lives. One group that received additional support over this period, however, was working families (eg through the introduction of, and reforms to, Family Credit). However, young people lost out during this time, with most 16–17 year olds losing eligibility to Income Support or Jobseeker's Allowance. Simplification was certainly an aim of the Conservative government as the Fowler Review introduced Income Support to replace Supplementary Benefit through the Social Security Act 1986. Housing Benefit reform was also aimed at simplification.

With the arrival of John Major as Prime Minister in 1990 came the introduction of new disability benefits: Disability Living Allowance and Disability Working Allowance. These were part of the growing recognition at the time of disability discrimination and the need to ensure that disabled people are supported with the extra costs they face. On the other hand, in 1995, Invalidity Benefit was replaced with the less generous Incapacity Benefit. The introduction of Jobseeker's Allowance to replace Unemployment Benefit also demonstrated a renewed focus on placing conditions on people who were unemployed to look for work. The Major government also flirted with welfare-to-work for lone parents, with a couple of prototype projects, but it was New Labour who started significantly down this particular road when it came to power in 1997.

The key areas of continuity between the 1979–97 Conservative governments and the coalition can be seen as around: increases in means testing; cuts in benefits, though spending increased due to recession; benefit simplification; residualisation of social housing; and poverty (and perhaps inequality) being likely to increase.

A key area of discontinuity was the treatment of pensioners, with the triple lock maintained by the coalition government compared with the dissolution of the link between pensions and earnings from 1980 onwards. The whole array of new benefit caps for people of working age also appears to be a major difference from the Thatcher and Major governments. There was also some redistribution from pensioners to children during 1979 to 1997, which is the reverse of the position under the coalition and the Conservative government.

Conservative majority government (2015–)

As part of its 2015 manifesto, the Conservative Party said that it aimed:

> to create a fairer welfare system where benefits are capped to the level that makes work pay.... Where people really cannot work, they must be supported – but where they are able to work, they should ... we have capped benefits so no household can take more in out-of-work benefits than the average household earns by going out to work. (Conservative Party, 2015, p 25)

This signalled a continuation and, indeed, intensification of the policies of the coalition, with a warning that 'The days of something for nothing are over' (Conservative Party, 2015, p 25).

In terms of the policy details, the manifesto said that it aimed for 2 million more jobs and 3 million new apprenticeships to be created, with ministers being required to report annually to Parliament (though with little detail about how these targets would be achieved). Furthermore, young people would be required to 'earn or learn', and automatic entitlement to Housing Benefit for 18–21 year olds would be scrapped. According to the Institute for Fiscal Studies (2015) this would affect about 20,000 people and save about £0.1 billion.

Another money-saving measure in the manifesto was to cap overall welfare spending, lower the amount that any household can receive to £23,000 – saving £0.1 billion, with 24,000 families losing another £3,000 and 70,000 families losing less, according to the Institute for Fiscal Studies (2015). There was also a commitment to continue the roll-out of Universal Credit. Working-age benefits would be frozen from April 2016 for two years (with exemptions for disability and pensioner benefits and statutory maternity and sick pay, etc), affecting 11 million people according to the Institute for Fiscal Studies (2015) and saving £1 billion.

The manifesto did argue that the government would work to eliminate child poverty 'by recognising the root causes of poverty: entrenched worklessness, family breakdown, problem debt, and drug and alcohol dependency' (Conservative Party, 2015, p 28). However, there was also another warning that if people refused recommended medical treatment 'we will review whether their benefits should be reduced' (Conservative Party, 2015, p 28). The use of conditions and sanctions is therefore likely to increase still further.

In terms of 'giveaways' rather than cuts, the Conservative Party planned to increase the tax-free personal allowance to £12,500 and the 40% income tax threshold to £50,000 (although it was not clear when this would be introduced). Neither of these measures would support people in poverty.

Pensioners look likely to continue to be protected, as would some extra-cost disability benefits. The Conservatives still support the triple lock, not least because 'Our pensioners have made this country what it is, and we believe that, in return, younger generations owe it to them to ensure they have dignity and security in their old age' (Conservative Party, 2015, p 65).

Manifestos are clearly political documents and not necessarily implemented in full, but the 2015 Summer (July) Budget gave an even clearer indication of the new government's direction of travel, with the surprise introduction of a so-called National Living Wage for over 25s of £7.20 in 2016, rising to £9 in 2020. This focus on 'making work pay' came after criticism that support through tax credits merely subsidised low-paying employers. According to the Institute for Fiscal Studies (Hood, 2015), this was a regressive Budget, with those in the second-poorest income decile losing 7% of their already low income. The new government has also signalled a rethink on measuring child poverty, which it has referred to as strengthening the measure.[5] This new measure aims to include data on worklessness, educational attainment, family breakdown, debt and addiction. All of these changes signal a downgrading in any commitments to redistribute income towards the poorest families. An increased minimum wage will be welcome by many but cannot offset the scale of reductions made to tax credits.

Conclusions

This chapter has provided an overview of key coalition policies and compared them with those of previous governments. It has also given an indication of the new Conservative government's direction of travel. As we have argued, there are some long-running continuities in social security policy since 1979, regardless of whether governments have been Conservative, Labour or coalition. A broad neoliberal consensus has emphasised the importance of work rather than 'welfare', alongside a particular focus on individual behaviour rather than social rights. While New Labour accepted much of this approach, they did, at the same time, directly tackle child and pensioner poverty. The coalition government most certainly did not, introducing a range of benefit caps, conditions and sanctions for people of working age (including those with children) that marked a major break from the past. While the economic conditions of the time provided a public defence for these measures (perhaps contra the reality, see Blyth, 2013), it is clear that ideological drivers were equally, if not more, important. Furthermore, it appears to be these ideological drivers that are paramount for the new Conservative government. The desire to reduce the role of social security in favour of the (private) labour market and an even greater focus on individual behaviour is clear. While some Conservatives may believe that this will ultimately reduce poverty, it seems that the direct impact of reform on poverty is much less of a concern now than it has been since 1997. Poverty and inequality are likely to increase over the course of this new government as a result of both coalition and new Conservative policies. The 'neoliberal project' has, for now at least, survived the Global Financial Crisis of 2008, and looks set to enter a more intense stage from 2015.

Of course, this mostly applies to those of working age, and it remains a partial paradox that pensioners remain so well protected given the apparent economic constraints. The electoral power of pensioners is clearly important, but that also applied before 2010, when pensioner benefits were not so well protected. The rationale for protecting these benefits, compared with other groups, is not impervious to challenge, and, indeed, the picture for social care is rather different (see Chapter Ten).

In terms of the framework set out in Chapter One, the coalition's approach to social security reform, certainly for those of working age, most certainly resembled the New Right. The Liberal Democrat influence on policy added to this given the economic liberalism of many of the Liberal Democrat ministers who contributed to the *Orange book* (including Steve Webb). Reforms to pensions embodied both generosity (increases via the triple lock) but also retrenchment (via a more rapidly increased state pension age), and a continued faith in market solutions (workplace pensions) and individual decision-making (pensions freedom).

Notes

[1] For example: http://www.dailymail.co.uk/news/article-1209072/Five-million-job-Labour--raising-fears-Shameless-generation-benefit-addicts.html; http://www.dailymail.co.uk/news/article-1310220/7-million-live-jobless-households-works.html; http://www.dailymail.co.uk/news/article-1318978/The-rise-Shameless-generation-drop-court-cases-Labour-government.html; http://www.dailymail.co.uk/news/article-1019616/Generation-born-shameless-parents-lessons-layabout-TV-character-Frank-Gallagher.html

[2] See: http://www.theguardian.com/society/2012/apr/25/boris-johnson-kosovo-style-cleansing-poor

[3] For a guide to the system as a whole, see the Pensions Policy Institute's excellent pensions primer, available at: http://www.pensionspolicyinstitute.org.uk/pension-facts/pensions-primer-a-guide-to-the-uk-pensions-system

[4] In addition to the editors, Laws and Marshall, the contributors were Vince Cable, Nick Clegg, Ed Davey, Chris Huhne, Susan Kramer, Mark Oaten and Steve Webb/Jo Holland. Laws, Cable, Clegg, Davey, Huhne, Kramer and Webb all became ministers during the coalition; Marshall and Holland are not MPs; Oaten did not stand in 2010.

[5] See: https://www.gov.uk/government/news/government-to-strengthen-child-poverty-measure

References

Belfield, C., Cribb, J., Hood, A. and Joyce, R. (2015) *Living standards, poverty and inequality in the UK: 2015*, London: Institute for Fiscal Studies. Available at: http://www.ifs.org.uk/uploads/publications/comms/R107.pdf (accessed 4 September 2015).

Bennett, F. (2012) 'Universal Credit: an overview and gender implications', in M. Kilkey, G. Ramia and K. Farnsworth (eds) *Social policy review 24*, Bristol: The Policy Press, pp 15–34.

Blyth, M. (2013) *Austerity: the history of a dangerous idea*, Oxford: Oxford University Press.

Browne , J. (2012) 'A £10,000 personal allowance: who would benefit, and would it boost the economy?', *Observations*. Available at: http://www.ifs.org.uk/publications/6045

Browne, J. and Elming, W. (2015) *The effect of the coalition's tax and benefit changes on household incomes and work incentives*, London: IFS. Available at: http://www.ifs.org.uk/uploads/publications/bns/BN159.pdf (accessed 4 September 2015).

Centre for Social Justice (2006) *Breakdown Britain: interim report on the state of the nation*, London: Centre for Social Justice.

Centre for Social Justice (2009) *Dynamic benefits: towards welfare that works*, London: Centre for Social Justice.

Clery, E., Lee, L. and Kunz, S. (2013) *Public attitudes to poverty and welfare 1983–2011: analysis using British Social Attitudes data*, London: National Centre for Social Research.

Conservative Party (2015) *The Conservative Party manifesto 2015*, London: Conservative Party.

Crawford, R., Keynes, S. and Tetlow, G. (2013) *A single-tier pension: what does it really mean?*, Report R82, London: Institute for Fiscal Studies.

Department for Work and Pensions (2012) *Single-tier pension: a simple foundation for saving*, London: The Stationery Office.

Department for Work and Pensions (2015) *Households below average income: an analysis of the income distribution 1994/95–2013/14*, London: Department for Work and Pensions.

Hills, J. (2015) *The Coalition's record on cash transfers, poverty and inequality, 2010–2015*, London: CASE.

Hirsch, D. (2015) 'A minimum income standard for the UK in 2015'. Available at: https://www.jrf.org.uk/report/minimum-income-standard-uk-2015 (accessed 4 September 2015).

Hood, A. (2015) 'Benefit changes and distributional analysis', online presentation. Available at: http://www.ifs.org.uk/uploads/publications/budgets/Budgets%202015/Summer/Hood_distributional_analysis.pdf (accessed 5 September 2015).

Hood, A. and Phillips, D. (2015) *Benefit spending and reforms: the coalition government's record*, London: Institute for Fiscal Studies. Available at: http://www.ifs.org.uk/uploads/publications/bns/BN160.pdf (accessed 4 September 2015).

Institute for Fiscal Studies (2015) *The parties' plans*, London: Institute for Fiscal Studies.

MacInnes, T., Aldridge, H., Bushe, S., Tinson, A. and Born, T. (2014) *Monitoring poverty and social exclusion 2014*, York: JRF/NPI.

Marshall, P. and Laws, D. (eds) (2004) *The orange book: reclaiming liberalism*, London: Profile Books.

McKay, S. (2012) 'If the cap fits? The introduction of a cap on UK welfare benefits', *The Birmingham Brief*. Available at: http://www.birmingham.ac.uk/news/thebirminghambrief/items/2012/03/welfare-benefits.aspx (accessed 9 September 2015).

McKay, S. and Rowlingson, K. (1999) *Social security in Britain*, Basingstoke: Palgrave Macmillan.

McKay, S. and Rowlingson, K. (2008) 'Social security and welfare reform', in M. Powell (ed) *Modernising the welfare state: the Blair legacy*, Bristol: The Policy Press, pp 53–71.

McKay, S. and Rowlingson, K. (2011) 'Social security', in H. Bochel (ed) *The Conservatives and social policy*, Bristol: The Policy Press, pp 145–60.

Millar, J. (2015) 'Policy briefing: Universal Credit – is it worth it?', *Discover Society*, issue 16. Available at: http://discoversociety.org/2015/01/03/policy-briefing-universal-credit-is-it-worth-it/ (accessed 4 September 2015).

National Audit Office (2011) *The comptroller and auditor general's report on accounts to the House of Commons*, London: HM Treasury.

Nelson, F. (2014) 'It shouldn't be a surprise that David Cameron has got religion', *The Daily Telegraph*, 18 April. Available at: http://www.telegraph.co.uk/news/religion/10772993/It-shouldnt-be-a-surprise-that-David-Cameron-has-got-religion.html (accessed 4 September 2015).

Office for Budget Responsibility (2014) 'Welfare trends report, October 2014'. Available at: http://budgetresponsibility.org.uk/wordpress/docs/Welfare_trends_report_2014_dn2B.pdf (accessed 5 September 2015).

Pensions Commission (2005) *A new pension settlement for the twenty-first century: the second report of the Pensions Commission*, London: The Stationery Office.

Sainsbury, R. (2014) 'Universal Credit: the story so far ...', *Journal of Poverty and Social Justice*, 22(1): 11–13.

UNISON (2013) 'Welfare reform changes affecting disabled people'. Available at: https://www.unison.org.uk/content/uploads/2013/07/On-line-Catalogue217093.pdf (accessed 4 September 2015).

Wood, C. and Grant, E. (2010) *Destination unknown*, London: Demos.

Work and Pensions Select Committee (2014) *Universal Credit implementation: monitoring DWP's performance in 2012–13*, London: House of Commons.

NINE

Welfare and active labour market policies in the UK: the coalition government approach

Anne Daguerre and David Etherington

Introduction

From the mid-1980s onwards, the UK social security system has become increasingly residual in nature, with the language of contracts pervading most areas of welfare, as evidenced by the creation of Jobseeker's Allowance (JSA) in 1995/96. By the mid-1990s, a cross-party consensus had emerged concerning the need to move away from a passive welfare system based on entitlement to unemployment benefits towards an active welfare model based on responsibilities, encapsulated in the notion of the moral obligations of citizenship. There has been a marked shift away from an approach based upon the duty of the state to support its citizens towards one concerned with the enforcement of a citizen's obligation to participate in the labour market (Harris, 2010). Under the new welfare contractualism (White, 2000; Freedland and King, 2003; Griggs and Bennett, 2009), social rights can be understood as consisting of rights to reasonable access to benefits, rather than unconditional rights to welfare benefits as such. This new welfare contractualism has become a strong area of bipartisan consensus, not least because New Labour under Tony Blair had promoted a 'work-first' approach based on the active monitoring of claimants. Work over welfare (Haskins, 2006), or how to enable the non-working poor to enter or re-enter the world of paid employment, has been at the heart of welfare reform changes over the past three decades. Here, we can identify two different views of the causes and cures for welfare dependency of the issue, which gave rise to different sets of policy prescriptions in the 1980s and 1990s:

- Behavioural deficiencies – economic inactivity, underemployment and long-term unemployment (all different phenomena in labour market terms) are the result of a lack of work ethic and/discipline on the part of the non-working poor. From this perspective, entry-level jobs are available and welfare claimants need a combination of hassle and help to take them up. The issue of unemployment is explained in terms of behavioural deficiencies. The portrayal of the non-working poor as lacking the drive and motivation to take up available jobs means that there is an emphasis on churning people into low-paid jobs or maintaining them in a perpetual state of job-readiness (Peck, 2001, p 12). The policy instruments deployed for getting people into jobs rely on a mix of sticks (in the form of benefit sanctions in case of non-compliance with work-related activities, time-limited benefits, close monitoring of claimants to ensure that they comply with the requirements and incentive reinforcement) and carrots (such as in-work credits or income disregards, or transitional and or passport benefits).

- Human capital – while work-first measures rely on rapid attachment to the labour force, with an emphasis on stick and carrots and with strong disciplinarian and authoritarian tendencies, human capital approaches insist on the importance of individual barriers to employment, such as a lack of professional skills. From this perspective, there is a fierce competition for jobs that places people who lack skills at a severe disadvantage, not simply because they find it increasingly difficult to access entry-level jobs, but also because they can only take up unstable, low-paid employment, leading to a pattern of 'labour market churning', whereby people cycle back and forth between low-paid, low-skilled employment and welfare benefits. The lack of relevant skills in a highly selective labour market is seen as the primary cause of long-term unemployment and, increasingly, the widespread experience of economic marginality. There is an emphasis on upskilling the labour force (Bonoli, 2012) by providing on-the-job training, basic skills sets (including literary and numeracy) or postgraduate diplomas.

Between 1997 and 2010, successive Labour administrations had pledged to rebuild the welfare state along the logic of mutual obligations on the part of the state and its citizens, with a corresponding emphasis on paid work as the best way to combat poverty. There was not much emphasis on skills, however; instead, Labour endeavoured to make work pay through the introduction of the National Minimum Wage and in-work tax credits, which became more generous in 2003.

The Labour governments endorsed a 'workfarist' approach, and gradually extended work-search requirements to categories of the working-age population who had in the past been exempted from such requirements – essentially lone parents and people with health conditions. The expansion was achieved in stages through the implementation of various New Deals (Daguerre, 2007; Driver, 2009). The Welfare Reform Act 2009 realised the vision of the Gregg (2008) report, according to which conditionality (the principle that entitlement to benefits should be dependent on satisfying certain conditions) should be extended to the vast majority of the working-age population so that virtually no one may claim benefits without taking active steps to address their barriers to work. The aim was to establish a personalised conditionality regime tailored to the individual needs of jobseekers regardless of administrative classification. The legislation was couched in a strong personal responsibility language, with the key notion that there was a need for a much clearer sanction regime for those who failed to attend an interview or failed to sign on without a good reason (Daguerre and Etherington, 2014).

To a large extent, welfare reforms post-2010 have strengthened the dominant work-first logic, where the focus is on strict job search, the key element of which is to increase labour supply. This emphasis on the obligation to take up work as a condition of receiving benefits was laid out by the future Prime Minister David Cameron when describing the Conservative welfare contract:

> We're going to change the whole way welfare is done in this country so everyone takes responsibility and plays their part. This is our new welfare contract: do the right thing and we will back you all the way. But fail to take responsibility – and the free ride is over. (Cameron, 2010)

The welfare-to-work system was designed to condition and coerce benefit claimants into jobs through tougher and more widespread benefit sanctions for those who are closest to the labour market (JSA claimants). This was the policy announced by the Conservative manifesto in 2010. The manifesto stipulated that:

> Anyone on Jobseeker's Allowance who refuses to join the Work Programme will lose the right to claim out-of-work benefits until they do, while people who refuse to accept reasonable job offers could forfeit their benefits for up to three years. (Conservative Party, 2010, p 15)

This chapter seeks to characterise the policies of the Conservative-led coalition government between 2010 and 2015. The chapter is divided into three sections. First, we briefly summarise the main reforms to the tax and benefit systems (cuts to tax credits, a tougher conditionality regime and the introduction of Universal Credit) (see also Chapter Eight). We also examine the characteristics of work-for-your-benefit schemes, which represent workfare in the strictest sense of the word since welfare claimants have to work for their benefits. Second, we argue that the coalition's welfare-to-work agenda was, to a large extent, dominated by a traditional Conservative discourse based on the stigmatisation of welfare dependency on moral and economic grounds. Participation in paid work was portrayed as a moral duty of citizenship (Larkin, 2014), with social assistance being concentrated on the most 'vulnerable' and 'deserving' individuals. Third, we conclude that the Liberal Democrats did exert a moderating influence in some areas of social policy, mainly in relation to welfare policies for young people and cuts to tax credits.

The reforms

As noted by Hills (2015), the coalition government agreement (Cabinet Office, 2010) was relatively vague and succinct in relation to welfare and employment policies. However, three main principles underpinned the new government's approach. First, the tax and benefit system should positively encourage participation in paid work, which meant that out-of-work benefits should be kept at a bare minimum and even reduced; this justified both the introduction of in-work conditionality through Universal Credit and the benefit cap. Indeed, a major change compared with New Labour's policies was the cuts to tax credits that had subsidised low-paid workers since the 2000s. Second, taxpayers' money was to be spent wisely on both the most deserving and the most vulnerable; in particular, the threat of benefit sanctions in the form of cuts to out-of-work benefits was geared to promote behavioural change on the part of benefit claimants so that they would fulfil their part of the bargain, that is, engage in paid work whenever possible. Of course, the idea that the benefit system could be used to steer behavioural change and instil a work ethic among welfare recipients had also been a central tenet of New Labour policies, but the main difference between the approaches of Labour and the coalition was that the latter put a much greater emphasis on sticks (financial sanctions in case of non-compliance with work requirements), as opposed to carrots, both in terms of rhetoric (as illustrated by the previous quote from David Cameron) and in actual policies. Third, the coalition government was committed to reducing the role and the size of the state through the generalisation of the contracting out of employment and training services to private providers (elements of privatisation and contracting out had already been introduced by New Labour under the Flexible New Deal, but the Work Programme (WP) was much more ambitious in this respect). We will review the main changes to the benefit system with a particular emphasis on benefit sanctions (as encapsulated by the Welfare Reform Act 2012), as well as the expansion of work-for-your-benefit schemes (see also Chapter Eight).

The coalition government's tax and benefit policies were spelled out in the 2010 Green Paper, *21st century welfare*, and the White Paper, *Universal Credit: welfare that works* (DWP, 2010a, 2010b). The most radical reform consisted of the unification of several means-tested benefits (Income Support [IS], Employment and Support Allowance [ESA], JSA and Housing Benefit) and tax credits (Working Tax Credit and Child Tax Credit) in order to simplify a complex and confusing system and ensure that work always pays through the introduction of Universal Credit (Patrick, 2014, p 61). In this respect, the coalition were following the 1997–2010 Labour administrations' attempts to simplify the welfare system, when Labour established the Benefit Simplification Unit in 2006 (Harris, 2013, pp 18–19). The model for in-work conditionality had been introduced by the Centre for Social Justice (CSJ), and was explained at length in the document *Dynamic benefits* (CSJ, 2009). Universal Credit involves in-work conditionality, with the requirement for claimants to attain an 'earnings threshold' set at the level of effort that it is reasonable for an individual to undertake. Working-age adults are subject to conditionality until they work full-time (35 hours) at the National Minimum Wage. If someone is earning below the conditionality cut-off point, they will be expected to 'look for work, more work or better-paid work'. Exceptions to this are those with caring responsibilities and those with health conditions (Tarr and Finn, 2012). Universal Credit is being introduced in stages, starting with the most simple cases (single unemployed claimants), and followed by more complex cases, essentially couples and families. The trials and delays associated with Universal Credit are beyond the scope of this chapter, but the scheme has suffered several setbacks due to the introduction of a number of ambitious reforms at a time of spending cuts, thus affecting the capacity of the Department for Work and Pensions (DWP) to carry out reforms within rigid time frames (National Audit Office, 2015).

Other changes in the tax and benefit system included the introduction of a cap of £26,000 per year in the total amount of benefits that working-age people and their families can receive (excluding those on certain disability benefits or working enough hours to qualify for Working Tax Credit). Crucially, tax credits, a central component of making work pay under New Labour, were also made less generous through various means, notably, the abolition of the 'baby element' of Child Tax Credit (Hill, 2015, pp 16–17), The decisions to freeze major out-of-work benefits, to cut and freeze tax credits, and to restrict access to disability benefits represent fundamental, cumulative changes to the tax and benefit system.

The coalition also built upon previous Labour policies by extending work-search requirements to other groups of benefit claimants who had been subjected in the past to moderate work-search requirements, namely, single parents on IS and people with health conditions who had been either on Incapacity Benefit (IB) or, in some cases, IS on the grounds of disability.

IB is traditionally determined within a framework of rules and without a specific limit on budgets. Two sets of rules determine the eligibility: a test of incapacity to work and an assessment of benefit eligibility, based either on national insurance contributions or on means testing. The Work Capability Assessment (WCA) devised in 2007/08 led to a reduction in the range of conditions that enabled people to qualify for IB. It essentially restricted eligibility criteria for IB receipt and introduced a kind of employability test (Gulland, 2013, pp 71–3). Claimants can be placed in the Work Related Activity Group (WRAG) if they are unwell but may still be able to do some work. Claimants are expected to attend a work-focused interview and training, and will have regular reassessments to decide if they should claim JSA instead of ESA. Once placed in the Support Group, claimants do not have to attend work-focused interviews and training unless they would like to. The coalition government wanted to accelerate the migration of IB claimants onto ESA, and initially aimed to move 1.5 million IB claimants onto ESA between 2010 and 2014 (Patrick, 2014, p 60). They were, however, unable to meet this ambitious target, in part, because a higher than expected volume of IB claimants were found incapable of some form of work-related activity, and also because the screening process carried out by the private company ATOS resulted in a large number of appeals from claimants who had been found fit for work: 40% of new claimants found fit for work appealed, with almost 40% of those appeals being successful (Hood and Phillips, 2015, p 25).

The coalition government also subjected more lone parents to the requirements of JSA by moving them off IS. The reform, known as the Lone Parent Obligation (LPO), started in 2008 under Labour, and as a result, lone parents whose youngest child was aged 12 were subjected to a work-search requirement. The age condition was reduced to 10 from October 2009, to seven from October 2010 and to five from May 2012 (Hood and Phillips, 2015, p 28).

The new policy framework for benefit sanctions was consolidated in the Welfare Reform Act 2012 and subsequent regulations. Although the drive towards the adoption of a more stringent sanctions regime had started well before 2010, there was a significant qualitative and quantitative difference between the benefit sanction regime prior to 2010 and the policy framework post-2012. The length of sanction periods was extended at the end of 2012, with the minimum sanction period being increased from one week to four weeks and the maximum from 26 weeks to three years. Higher-level sanctions represent a 'very much more stringent sanctions regime than those previously applicable' (Wood et al, 2015, p 93). The new sanctions were applied to JSA claimants from October 2012.

In practice, the coalition clearly delivered on its promise to implement a tougher sanctions regime, with JSA sanctions reflected as a proportion of claimants after reconsiderations and appeals having stabilised at 5.5% and 6% of claimants per month, compared to an average of 2.2% of claimants between 2000 and 2006. There was an upward trend in JSA sanctions between 2007 and 2008, from 2.2% to 3.5%, followed by a sharp decline with the start of the intense economic recession. JSA sanctions rates then increased from 2.2% in April 2010 to 4.3% in December 2010, which corresponded to the increased use of sanctions once the coalition government took office. This was then followed by a sharp decline in JSA sanctions in 2011, when WP providers become responsible for monitoring JSA claimants. However, from 2011, and especially as a result of the implementation of the new sanctions regime under the Welfare Reform Act 2012, JSA sanctions increased from a low of 3.5% in April 2012 to 5.8% in December 2013, and then fell slightly to 5.4% in December 2014 (Webster, 2014).

Another policy change was the widespread expansion of work-for-your-benefit schemes, mainly the Jobseeker's Allowance (Mandatory Work Activity Scheme) Regulations (SI 2011/688), the Jobseeker's Allowance (Employment, Skills and Enterprise) Regulations 2011 (SI 2011/917) (known as ESE), which replaced the Jobseeker's Allowance (Work for Your Benefit Pilot Scheme) Regulations 2010 (SI 2010/1222) introduced as part of the Welfare Reform Act 2009. The 2011 Regulations were made in terms of section 17 of the Jobseeker's Act 1995. The ESE scheme initially covered four initiatives: (1) Skills Conditionality was aimed at improving the take-up of help and support for those claimants with an identified skills need – Jobcentre Plus was to refer claimants to a skills training provider; (2) Service Academies aimed to support jobseekers who were close to the labour market but who would benefit from participating in pre-employment training and work experience leading to a guaranteed interview to help them move into sustained employment; (3) the New Enterprise Allowance aimed to promote self-employment under the guidance of a business mentor, providing access to a weekly financial allowance and business start-up loan finance; and (4) the WP provided back-to-work support for a wide range of claimants, including JSA, ESA, IB and IS claimants. The other work-for-your-benefit scheme was the Mandatory Work Activity Regulation. Its purpose, as explained by the Explanatory Notes to the Mandatory Work Activity Regulations 2011, was:

> to target the small number of customers who do enough to meet the conditions of their claim while at the same time continually failing to demonstrate the focus and discipline that is a key requirement of finding, securing and retaining employment. (Explanatory Notes to the Mandatory Work Activity Regulations 2011 [SI 2011/688])

The language of the Explanatory Notes made it clear that there were a minority of JSA claimants who failed to engage with employers, and who did not have the work ethic or the discipline that was required to find, secure and retain employment.

Under the WP, private providers could decide to place people in work-related activities such as work experience placements. The WP is, in most cases, a mandatory programme: individuals aged 18–24 are referred to the WP after the nine-month point of their claim, while those aged 25 and over are placed on to the WP after claiming JSA for 12 months. The WP was emblematic of the governmental strategy of opening up the public sector to the market. Prime contractors (generally from the private sector) were appointed to deliver in localities (contract areas) on the basis of plans and strategies that were generally negotiated directly between the contractor and the DWP. The WP extended the contracting model and the role of private providers in the delivery of previous welfare-to-work programmes (Crighton et al, 2009). Providers were funded on a 'payments by results basis', structured in relation to initial attachment to the programme, job outcomes and job sustainability, with additional payments made for higher-performing contractors.

The other work-for-your-benefit scheme was the Work Experience Scheme, which is targeted at 18–24 year olds with little or no experience of work. Young people can participate in the scheme after they have been claiming JSA for three months, but before they join the WP. Work Experience Schemes started in January 2011, and entry was voluntary but, as with the other work-for-your-benefit schemes, participation became compulsory after the individual began his/her placement. Table 9.1 provides a summary of the main work-for-your-benefit schemes under the coalition government.

Table 9.1: Main work-for-your-benefit schemes

Title	Eligibility	Length of placement	Mandatory or voluntary?
Work experience	Young people on JSA for three months, no work experience	Up to 8 weeks	Voluntary, originally risk of sanction if leaving. Became voluntary after February 2012
Sector-based work academy	Any age on JSA	Up to 6 weeks	Deciding whether or not to take part is voluntary but once placement starts, participation is mandatory
Work Programme (if referred to work experience)	Participant in Work Programme	Up to 4 weeks	Mandatory
Mandatory Work Activity	Any age on JSA	Up to 4 weeks	Mandatory
Help to Work (post Work Programme provision)	JSA claimants who complete 104 weeks on the Work Programme	Placement of 30 hours a week for up to 26 weeks	Mandatory

Source: CESI 'Government work experience schemes, what are the differences?' (available at: http://www.cesi.org.uk/keypolicy/government-work-experience-schemes-what-are-differences).

Work experience represented the single most important workfare scheme under the coalition, with 300,290 placements between January 2011 and November 2014 (Dar, 2015). Work Experience Schemes, which were originally mandatory, became completely voluntary at the end of February 2012 following negative media coverage and employers dropping out of the scheme. As a result, Work Experience Schemes no longer qualify as workfare. Work-for-your-benefit schemes have been subjected to intense scrutiny in the courts, as shown by the number of legal challenges surrounding the work-for-your-benefit regulations (Larkin, 2013; see also Daguerre and Etherington, 2014).

The Conservative-led coalition government's approach

How can we characterise the coalition government's policies, and to what extent did they differ from what might have emerged from a traditional Conservative majority government? To what extent, if any, did the Liberal Democrats exercise a moderating influence? In general, Conservative ministers took the lead on welfare reform within the DWP (see also Chapter Eight). Indeed, a division of labour occurred between the Conservatives and the Liberal Democrats, with Iain Duncan Smith, as Secretary of State for Work and Pensions, and his personal advisers (notably, Philippa Stroud, from the CSJ), taking the lead on welfare and employment, and Steve Webb, a Liberal Democrat, in charge of pension reform.

In general, as indicated by Bochel and Powell in Chapter One of this volume, the coalition government's approach to welfare reform was characterised by a New Right philosophy, with a strong emphasis on the responsibilities of citizenship (see Powell, 1999). Indeed, the focus was on the obligation to take up paid employment as a condition of citizenship. In fact, the goal of welfare reform under the coalition government was to produce self-reliant, autonomous citizens, whose dependency on the public purse should be reduced to a minimum. To help achieve this, the coalition believed that benefit levels should be kept at a low level, as evidenced by cuts to tax credits and the introduction of the benefit cap. Although the coalition espoused the logic of making work pay promoted by New Labour, its main policy instrument to promote participation in the labour market was sticks instead of carrots. In line with the goal of reducing welfare spending and ultimately the size of the state, the coalition first and foremost used negative financial incentives in the form of benefits sanctions and low benefit levels to encourage people to either stay off benefits or to leave cash assistance.

The rhetoric of personal responsibility was one of the most prevalent principles underpinning the Welfare Reform Act 2012, especially through the claimant commitment. According to the Welfare Reform Act 2012, the claimant commitment 'is a record of a claimant's responsibilities in relation to an award of universal credit', and 'is to be in such form as the Secretary of State thinks fit'. In general, the claimant commitment includes an expectation that claimants will comply with a 35-hour work-search rule, although the DWP may agree a reduced time if claimants have impairments or caring disabilities. The claimant commitment was part of the 'cultural transformation' introduced by Universal Credit, whereby jobseekers 'will have to account more clearly for their efforts to find work and will be given a weekly timetable of tasks to complete' (DWP, 2013).

With reference to the claimant commitment, Iain Duncan Smith declared:

> Through the 'claimant commitment', which deliberately mirrors a contract of employment, we are making this deal unequivocal. Those in work have obligations to their employer; so too claimants a responsibility to the taxpayer: in return for support, and where they are able, they must do their bit to find work. (Duncan Smith, 2014)

The good citizen is viewed as first and foremost economically self-reliant. From this perspective, there is no entitlement to public assistance.

In terms of the mixed economy of welfare, the coalition opened up the welfare-to-work market to contracted-out providers; indeed, the WP effectively privatised training and employment services. Central to this approach was the view that public service provision should be kept at a low level.

One of the most influential intellectual inputs to government thinking was the work conducted by the CSJ, the think tank founded in 2004 by Iain Duncan Smith. The CSJ was commissioned in 2006 by David Cameron to examine the causes of poverty in the UK. The report *Breakdown Britain* (CSJ, 2006) was hailed as evidence-based and identified five 'pathways to poverty' (see also Chapter Twelve): family breakdown, educational failure, economic dependence, indebtedness and addiction. This document is interesting because it set out a 'modern' Conservative vision, which drew on classic authors and political Conservative political figures such as Adam Smith (including in relation to notions of relative poverty), Disraeli and Churchill, while at the same time paying tribute to the work of *Guardian* columnist Polly Toynbee (2003), the Child Poverty Action Group and the academic John Hills's report on economic inequality (Hills et al, 2010). However, the document primarily gave a contemporary twist to the notion of an underclass culture based on drug and alcohol addiction, the breakdown of marriage and family relationships, the rise of fatherless families, and the lack of male role models for young people. The report stated:

> We reject the comfortable mantra that policy can or should be wholly morally neutral on the grounds that this is unworkable in practice.... The failure to form a durable

bond between a mother and father often leads to welfare dependency. This report makes clear the extent to which families suffer financially after family breakdown.... Family breakdown is both contributor to and a consequence of poverty and most other social problems. (CSJ, 2006, pp 29–32)

In effect, Iain Duncan Smith reverted to a traditional Conservative moral underclass discourse that attributed poverty and unemployment to essentially individual and moral failings. Poverty and unemployment were portrayed as being caused by individual behaviour, such as alcohol and drug addiction, chaotic lifestyles, and a lack of purpose (dissolution). The structural causes of poverty, such as a lack of available jobs in the aftermath of the recession, tended to be overlooked or marginalised. Moral arguments regarding an intergenerational culture of worklessness were also embraced with a renewed vigour, as pointed out by Shildrick et al (2012, p 9).

New paternalism approaches based on the close supervision of benefit recipients (Mead et al, 1997; MacGregor, 1999) also played an important role in government thinking. The Secretary of State for Work and Pensions spelled out a vision almost exclusively centred on the individual and the family, with a marked emphasis on the need to strengthen family life and stable relationships as the best way to provide children with a loving, stable environment. The aim was to deliver 'life change' because spending on benefits, referred to as a 'poverty-plus-a-pound' approach, which was seen as characterising Labour's antipoverty and social exclusion policies, did not address the root cause of the problems, whether it be addiction, low expectations or, most importantly, family breakdown. At the heart of Iain Duncan Smith's vision is a system of monitoring individual behaviour as early as possible in the life cycle:

> This must be based on prevention throughout someone's life, intervening early to tackle the root causes of problems before they arise rather than waiting to treat the symptoms. That starts with the family, the most important building block in a child's life. When families are strong and stable, so are children. (Duncan Smith, 2012)

In general, the Conservative-led coalition government used divide-and-rule rhetoric, along the lines of the hard-working majority versus the minority living on welfare benefits, in order to justify both tougher benefit sanctions and the expansion of workfare schemes. Although the divide between the deserving and the undeserving poor is a classical theme in the history of social security, especially in the field of social assistance and unemployment benefits (Deacon, 1976), ministers devised a new theme around the idea of 'fairness to the taxpayer'. This narrative has been at the heart of the Conservative Party rhetoric on the unemployed and social security since the 1980s. For instance, in 1987, the Conservative Secretary of State for Social Security, John Moore, justified targeting social spending on those in greatest needs in these terms:

> The indiscriminate handing out of benefits not only spreads limited resources too thinly, it can also undermine the will to self-help, and builds pools of resentment among the taxpayers who are footing the bill, often from incomes barely larger from the money benefit recipients receive. By targeting our welfare resources we will be able to provide more real help where need is greatest. (Moore, 1987, cited by King, 1995, p 180).

In particular, under the coalition, the notion that the 'taxpayer' directly pays jobseekers to look for employment and accept job offers was consistently used as a powerful rhetorical device to justify tougher benefit sanctions, as spelled out by Iain Duncan Smith in May 2010:

> The Job Seeker's Allowance has a sanction at present. It just has not been used. If you simply are not going to play ball, then the taxpayer has a right to say: 'You need to know there is a limit to the amount of support we are going to give you'. The sanction comes into play. (Duncan Smith, 2010, quoted by Wintour, 2010)

One of the fundamental tenets of the Conservative-led welfare-to-work programme was the portrayal of income maintenance as a privilege or 'advantage' 'unfairly' enjoyed by claimants to the detriment of those who abide by the rules, taxpayers and full-time workers who are not being helped with living costs. This representation of life on welfare as a lifestyle choice fundamentally different from the life of the general population represented the main moral justification for implementing a much stricter benefit sanction regime. This narrative had no real equivalent under the previous Labour governments. Conservative ministers advocated the implementation of a conditionality regime that strictly mirrored 'life in the real world', especially employment contracts. In particular, ministers held that people on welfare should be subjected to exactly the same requirements and conditions as those who were in full-time work by spelling out that individuals should spend up to 35 hours a week looking for work because 35 hours a week is the average working week in the UK.

The coalition enjoyed widespread public support in relation to its welfare-to-work policies, especially the benefit cap and the stricter conditionality regime backed by tougher financial sanctions. These policies were supported by the electorate, as measured by public attitude surveys and focus groups. Indeed, public attitudes towards the unemployed have considerably hardened, with most people now 'firmly believing that JSA claimants could get a job if they really wanted one' (Deeming, 2015, p 879; although see also Chapter Three). In this context, the coalition was able to portray harsher benefit sanctions as essentially 'fair'.

Conclusion

To conclude, what emerges under the WP and the escalating sanctions regime is the image of an authoritarian workfare state that delegates much of its sanctioning powers to contracted-out welfare-to-work providers, while, at the same time, eroding some of the support services that are at the heart of active labour market policies. Welfare beneficiaries are being subjected to increased monitoring and surveillance in what appears to be an unbalanced welfare contract. As MacLeavy (2011, pp 362–3) observes:

> The allotment of state resources to encouraging work through these programmes serves to discipline citizens in politically and economically expedient ways.... Austerity, in this sense, provides a means of legitimating the coalition government's arrangements to expand programmes to orientate state assistance towards work, which increases levels of state control over welfare recipients' lives, at the same time as dampening public expectations regarding citizenship entitlements.

Taken together, the cumulative impact of the reforms – benefit caps, higher benefit sanctions, changes in benefit rules and conditions of entitlement, accelerated migration of IB claimants onto ESA through the WCA, and additional requirements for benefit claimants –

corresponds to a recasting of the UK's welfare state, with an erosion in terms of substantive social rights, both through statutes, regulations and policy implementation.

The record so far of the Conservative government post-2015 suggests that the Liberal Democrats did exert a moderating influence on their coalition partners in relation to workfare policies for young people and cuts to tax credits and disability benefits. The Conservative Party manifesto of 2015 singled out young people aged 18–21 for stronger work requirements, with the suppression of JSA and the introduction of a time-limited (six months) youth allowance, 'after which young people will have to take an apprenticeship, a traineeship or do daily community work for their benefits', the justification for which is framed in terms of 'fairness to the taxpayer', so that 'it is not fair – on taxpayers, or on young people themselves – that 18–21 year-olds with no work experience should slip straight into a life on benefits without first contributing to their community' (Conservative Party, 2015, p 18). During the coalition government, the Liberal Democrats had opposed ending Housing Benefit for young people, which had been a key objective of the Prime Minister between 2010 and 2015. Indeed, cuts to social security payments for young unemployed people have been one of the key ideological characteristics of Conservative Party's social policies since the 1980s. As in the 1980s, Conservative policy post-2015 aims to deliberately prolong the dependence of the young unemployed on their families (Harris, 1988, p 518). In July 2015, the Conservatives' Budget stated that:

> To prevent young people slipping straight into a life on benefits, from April 2017 the Budget will also remove the automatic entitlement to housing support for new claims in Universal Credit from 18–21 year olds who are out of work. This will ensure young people in the benefits system face the same choices as young people who work and who may not be able to afford to leave home. (HM Treasury, 2015, p 41)

Other measures announced in the summer 2015 Budget included cutting the rate of ESA for new claimants in the WRAG to the lower JSA rate in order to promote full employment (the objective is to remove any financial incentive to claim sickness benefits over JSA), cuts to tax credits through reducing the level of earnings at which a household's tax credits and Universal Credit award starts to be withdrawn for every extra pound earned, and removing tax credits for non-disabled claimants without children (HM Treasury, 2015, p 37).

The Conservative government post-May 2015 has therefore resumed with renewed fervour a policy of residual welfarism (Wintour, 2015). The announcement of a 'National Living Wage' is likely to only partially offset the cuts to tax credits in a radical departure from the previous Labour administrations' approach to making work pay through generous in-work benefits.

References

Bonoli G. (2012) 'Active labour market policy and social investment: a changing relationship', in N. Morel, B. Palier and J. Palme (eds) *Towards a social investment state*, Bristol: The Policy Press, pp 181–204.

Cabinet Office (2010) *The coalition: our programme for government*, London: Cabinet Office.

Cameron D. (2010) 'Ending the free ride for those who fail to take responsibility'. Available at: http://www.conservatives.com/News/News_stories/2010/04/Ending_the_free_ride for_those_who_fail_to_take_responsibility.aspx (accessed 15 December 2010).

Conservative Party (2010) *Invitation to join the government of Britain: the Conservative manifesto 2010*, London: Conservative Party.

Conservative Party (2015) *The Conservative Party manifesto 2010*, London: Conservative Party.

Crighton, M., Turok, I. and Leleux, C. (2009) 'Tensions in localising welfare to work in Britain's cities', *Local Economy*, 24(1): 46–67.

CSJ (Centre for Social Justice) (2006) *Breakdown Britain: interim report on the state of the nation*, London: Centre for Social Justice.

CSJ (2009) *Dynamic benefits*, London: Centre for Social Justice.

Daguerre, A. (2007) *Active labour market policies and welfare reform: Europe and the US in comparative perspective*, Basingstoke: Palgrave Macmillan.

Daguerre, A. and Etherington, D. (2014) 'Workfare in 21st century Britain'. Available at: http://workfare.org.uk/images/uploads/docs/Workfare_in_21st_century_Britain_Version_2.pdf (accessed 17 September 2015).

Dar, A. (2015) *Work experience schemes*, House of Commons Briefing Paper 06249, London: House of Commons.

Deacon, A. (1976) *In search of the scrounger*, London: G. Bell and Son.

Deeming, C. (2015) 'Foundations of the workfare state – reflections on the political transformation of the welfare state in Britain', *Social Policy and Administration*, 49(7): 862–86.

DWP (Department for Work and Pensions) (2010a) *21st century welfare*, London: The Stationery Office.

DWP (2010b) *Universal Credit: welfare that works*, London: The Stationery Office.

DWP (2013) 'Claimant commitment to spell out what jobseekers must do in return for benefits', press release, 29 August.

Driver, S. (2009) 'Work to be done? Welfare reform from Blair to Brown', *Policy Studies*, 30: 69–77.

Duncan Smith, I. (2012) 'Transforming lives', speech, Department for Work and Pensions. Available at: https://www.gov.uk/government/speeches/social-justice-transforming-lives (accessed 17 September 2015).

Duncan Smith, I. (2014) 'Speech on welfare reform', Centre for Social Justice, London. Available at: http://blogs.spectator.co.uk/coffeehouse/2014/01/iain-duncan-smiths-speech-on-welfare-reform-full-text/ (accessed 17 September 2015).

Freedland, M. and King, D. (2003) 'Contractual governance and illiberal contracts: some problems of contractualism as an instrument of behaviour', *Cambridge Journal of Economics*, 27(3): 465–77.

Gregg, P. (2008) *Realising potential: a vision for personalised conditionality and support: an independent report to the Department for Work and Pensions*, London: The Stationery Office.

Griggs, J. and Bennett, F. (2009) *Rights and responsibilities in the social security system*, Social Security Advisory Committee, occasional paper no 6, London: Social Security Advisory Committee.

Gulland, J. (2013) 'Ticking boxes: decision-making in Employment and Support-Allowance', *Journal of Social Security Law*, 18(2): 69–86.

Harris, N. (1988) 'Social security and the transition to adulthood', *Journal of Social Policy*, 17(4): 501–23.

Harris, N. (2010) 'Conditional rights, benefit reform and drug users: reducing dependency?', *Journal of Law and Society*, 37(2): 223–36.

Harris, N. (2013) *Law in a complex state*, Oxford: Hart Publishing.

Haskins, R. (2006) *Work over welfare*, Washington, DC: Brookings Institution Press.

Hills, J. (2015) *The coalition's record on cash transfers, poverty and inequality 2010–2015*, Working Paper 11, CASE, London: LSE.

Hills, J., Brewer, M., Jenkins, S., Lister, R., Lupton, R., Machin, S., Mills, C., Modood, T., Rees, T. and Riddell, S. (2010) *An anatomy of economic inequality in the UK – report of the National Equality Panel*, London: Centre for Analysis of Social Exclusion, LSE.

HM Treasury (2015) *Summer Budget 2015*, London: The Stationery Office. Available at: https://www.gov.uk/government/uploads/system/uploads/attachment_data/file/443232/50325_Summer_Budget_15_Web_Accessible.pdf (accessed 17 September 2015).

Hood, A. and Phillips, D. (2015) *Benefit spending and reforms: the coalition government's record*, IFS Briefing Note BN160, London: Institute for Fiscal Studies.

King, D. (1995) *Actively seeking work: the politics of unemployment and welfare in the United States and Great Britain*, Chicago, IL: University of Chicago Press.

Larkin, P. (2013) 'A permanent blow to workfare in the United Kingdom or a temporary obstacle? Reilly and Wilson V Secretary of State for Work and Pensions', *Journal of Social Security Law*, 20(3): 110.

Larkin, P. (2014) 'The new puritanism: the resurgence of contractarian citizenship in common law welfare states', *Journal of Law and Society*, 41(2): 227–56.

MacGregor, S. (1999) 'Welfare, neo-liberalism and new paternalism: three ways for social policy in late capitalist societies', *Capital and Class*, 23(1): 91–118.

MacLeavy, J. (2011) 'A "new politics" of austerity, workfare and gender? The UK coalition government's welfare reform proposals', *Cambridge Journal of Regions, Economy and Society*, 4(3): 355–67.

Mead, L.M., Lewis, J. and Webb, R. (eds) (1997) *The new paternalism: supervisory approaches to poverty*, Washington, DC: Brookings Institution Press.

Moore, J. (1987) 'Secretary of State for Social Security, speech 26 September, Conservative Party conference', *Conservative Party News*, London.

National Audit Office (2015) *Welfare reform, lessons learned*, London: The Stationery Office.

Patrick, R. (2014) 'Welfare reform and the valorization of work', in M. Harrison and T. Sanders (eds) *Social policies and social control*, Bristol: The Policy Press, pp 55–70.

Peck, J. (2001) *Workfare states*, New York, NY: The Guildford Press.

Powell, M. (1999) 'Introduction', in M. Powell (ed) *New Labour, new welfare state*, Bristol: The Policy Press, pp 1–27.

Shildrick, T., MacDonald, R., Furlong, A., Roden, J. and Crow, R. (2012) *Are 'cultures of worklessness' passed down the generations?*, York: Joseph Rowntree Foundation.

Tarr, A. and Finn, D. (2012) *Implementing Universal Credit: will the reform improve the services for users?*, London: CESI. Available at: http://www.cesi.org.uk/publications/implementing-universal-credit-will-reforms-improve-service-users (accessed 15 September 2015).

Toynbee, P. (2003) *Hard work: life in low-pay Britain*, London: Bloomsbury.

Webster, D. (2014) 'Evidence submitted to House of Commons Work and Pensions Committee'. Available at: http://www.publications. parliament.uk/pa/cm201314/cmselect/cmworpen/479/479vw36. htm (accessed 17 September 2015).

White, S. (2000) 'Review article: social rights and the social contract – political theory and the new welfare politics', *British Journal of Political Science*, 30(3): 507–32.

Wintour, P. (2010) 'Coalition government sets out radical welfare reforms', *The Guardian*, 26 May. Available at: http://www. theguardian.com/politics/2010/may/26/coalition-welfare-reforms-duncan-smith (accessed 15 September 2015).

Wintour, P. (2015) 'Osborne's first Budget without Lib Dems likely to hit welfare state hard', *The Guardian*, 2 July. Available at: http:// www.theguardian.com/uk-news/2015/jul/02/osbornes-first-budget-without-libdems-likely-to-hit-welfare-state-hard (accessed 17 September 2015).

Wood, P., Wikeley, M.A., Bonner, D. and Mesher, J. (2015) *Social security legislation. Volume 2, Income Support, Jobseeker's Allowance, State Pension Credit and the Social Fund*, London: Sweet & Maxwell.

TEN

'It ain't what you do, it's the way that you do it': adult social care under the coalition

Jon Glasby

Introduction

'Adult social care' is a broad term to describe the practical assistance that is provided to people over the age of 18 who are assessed by a social worker as needing various forms of care and support. This can often be to do with activities of daily living, such as getting up, getting washed, eating and other personal care needs. Typically, groups of people using such services include older people, disabled people, people with mental health problems and people with learning difficulties, and traditional services have often taken the form of home care, day care, meals services and residential care. Whereas a qualified social worker would typically assess people's need for support, any subsequent services might be provided by social care providers in the public, private or voluntary sector. Given that so much care and support is provided within families, adult social care also works with family carers to help meet their needs and those of the person being cared for. However, issues such as child protection, work with so-called 'troubled families' and welfare rights advice would typically be provided by other services, and these are covered elsewhere in this book.

Of all the service areas explored in this edited collection, adult social care is arguably one of the most neglected and the least well understood. While the National Health Service (NHS), for example, is usually seen as a service that provides care to people when they are most in need, adult social care has tended to have a more mixed reputation, based on a combination of 'care' but also of state 'control'. With origins in the Poor Law and in the workhouse, it is based, in part, on a history of stigma, of segregation and of potentially very intrusive attempts to distinguish between 'deserving' and 'undeserving' poverty (for an overview of the history and nature of adult social care, see Means and Smith, 1998; Means et al, 2002; Payne, 2005; Glasby, 2012). Whereas health services are provided free at the point of delivery to people we see as being 'sick', people who are somehow merely frail or disabled are left to rely on local authority adult social care services, which are means-tested and typically incur significant user charges. Over time, adult social care has come to focus primarily on those with the most severe needs and with very low incomes, so that many people in moderate and significant need are shocked to find that they are not eligible for any publicly funded support (often when they are in a crisis and feeling particularly vulnerable and therefore let down by services). As a qualified social worker myself, the acid test is the reaction of people at parties when they ask what you do for a living. While a doctor, a nurse or a teacher would usually get a (predominantly) sympathetic response, saying that you are a social worker tends to attract a more ambiguous reaction.

After a brief review of the Conservative–Liberal Democrat coalition government's overall track record on adult social care, this chapter focuses on the main policy priorities identified in the coalition agreement of 2010 (namely, the funding of long-term care, the relationship between health and social care, developing a preventative approach, and the personalisation agenda). To this list is added a further topic (the scale of which has been truly breathtaking and has arguably dwarfed all other changes): the impact of massive cuts in the local government budget. Given the scale of the funding challenges facing local government and the long-standing nature of debates around the funding of long-term care, it is these two topics that form the bulk of the chapter (with more succinct reviews of topics such as integrated care, personalisation and prevention, where there was much greater continuity between the coalition and New Labour). In the process, the chapter seeks to comment on some of the major influences on coalition policy with regards to adult social care, to highlight the main similarities to and differences from New Labour's policies and approaches, and to consider the implications of developments under the coalition for the future. In the process, it argues that there is significant consensus between the main three political parties, and that apparently similar policy proposals have been, and are likely to be, pursued by the 1997–2010 New Labour governments, the coalition government (2010–15) and the Conservative government elected in 2015. What differs, perhaps, is the underlying value base and tactics behind such reforms – hence the title of this chapter ('It ain't what you do, it's the way that you do it').

Adult social care under the coalition: from initial neglect to the Care Act 2014

Given the ambiguous and poorly understood nature of adult social care, it is perhaps unsurprising that social care did not feature strongly in the development of Conservative Party thinking in the run-up to the 2010 general election. As Box 10.1 suggests, commentators, practitioners and service users wondering what a potential Conservative government might do in office would have been hard pushed in the late 2000s to know what to expect. The Conservative Party's (2010) ambitiously entitled *Invitation to join the government of Britain* (their 2010 general election manifesto) mentioned social care just three times in 131 pages, and all of those were subsumed in a chapter on the NHS. These included a desire to integrate health and social care funding as part of an expansion of personal budgets, and a rejection of what was described as New Labour's 'death tax' (Conservative Party, 2010, p 48) – committing to reform the funding of long-term care on the basis of a voluntary one-off insurance premium for people wishing to guard against having to sell their home in order to meet the costs of a care home placement. Nor did the Liberal Democrats have much more to add. Their manifesto contained only two key references to adult social care, pledging to 'integrate health and social care to create a seamless service, ending bureaucratic barriers and saving money to allow people to stay in their homes for longer rather than going into hospital or long-term residential care' (Liberal Democrats, 2010, p 41), as well as to avoid the funding of long-term care being treated as a 'political football' by establishing an 'independent commission to develop future proposals for long-term care that will attract all-party support and so be sustainable' (Liberal Democrats, 2010, p 53).

In contrast, the 2010 Labour manifesto did at least contain a degree of detail on the steps it would take to create what it described as a:

> new National Care Service to ensure free care in the home for those with the greatest care needs and a cap on the costs of residential care so that everyone's homes and savings are protected from care charges after two years in a care home. (Labour Party, 2010, s 6.2)

While consensus on funding would be reached via establishing a 'Commission', the early part of this process would be financed, in part, by 'our decision to freeze Inheritance Tax Thresholds until 2014–15' (Labour Party, 2010, s 6.6). However, many people would suggest that New Labour had neglected the reform of long-term care funding for most of its three terms of office, producing a flurry of policy proposals in the late 2000s when it was potentially too late for any of these to actually be implemented. As a result, it is hardly surprising that New Labour could provide a degree of detail as it had already done the background work needed to produce a 'case for change', a subsequent Green Paper and a 2010 White Paper (HM Government, 2008, 2009; Department of Health, 2010a). While Labour seemed to say more about adult social care in their manifesto, critics might argue that they ought to have had much more to contribute having been in government for so long but done so little to reform long-term care funding in practice.

> **Box 10.1: Conservative Party silence on community care in the late 2000s (extract from Glasby, 2011, pp 186–7)**
>
> In April 2008, the Conservative Party website had no separate section under 'policy' for social care, adult services or children's services. Although there are a number of policy papers available on the NHS, none had yet been published for social care. While there was a section on families, this referred mainly to issues such as financial help, flexible working and health visiting. Similarly, the schools section referred primarily to education.
>
> Also at this time, the Party had 13 campaigns. Of these, 2 focused on the NHS ('Save your local GP' and 'Stop Brown's NHS cuts') while others sought to save 'the great British pub', save local newspapers and keep post offices open. None related to adult social care or to community care.
>
> Where social care and social work were mentioned on the website, many were very brief news items and a significant proportion were focused on children's services following a series of child protection scandals....
>
> Where community care does appear, it tends to be in a very brief comment on current events, critiquing New Labour's record without articulating a potential alternative. Thus, in January 2008, the Shadow Health Minister responded to a review of eligibility criteria for adult social care by suggesting that 'there is no evidence that the Government are going to do anything more than talk about social care' (Conservative Party website, News, 29 Jan 2008). Around the same time, the same person saw a negative Public Accounts Committee report on dementia as evidence of 'the Government's ongoing failure to bring forward wider solutions for social care' (24 January 2008).

Following the creation of the Conservative–Liberal Democrat coalition government, adult social care was once again conspicuous by its absence from the bulk of the coalition's *Programme for government* (Cabinet Office, 2010; see also Box 10.2). While there was an entry on 'social care and disability', this took up less than one column in a 36-page document, and social care itself was only mentioned three times. 'Health', in contrast, was mentioned 36 times and had an entry that spanned three pages, in addition to a separate entry on 'public health' and several mentions in other policy areas. Perhaps more significantly, the single entry on social care said very little beyond emphasising the importance of dignity and respect, and making brief reference to ongoing debates about the funding of long-term care, health and social care partnerships, prevention, personal budgets and direct payments (all of which had also been long-standing policy priorities under New Labour). Indeed, reading the *Programme for government*, a social care practitioner or service user would almost certainly have been unable to identify which of the three main political parties had drafted it, as the language and commitments were almost entirely in keeping with all major policy pronouncements on adult social care (probably at least as far back as the community care reforms of the early 1990s, and certainly since 1997).

> **Box 10.2: Extract from the coalition's *Programme for government* (Cabinet Office, 2010, p 30)**
>
> **28. SOCIAL CARE AND DISABILITY**
> The Government believes that people needing care deserve to be treated with dignity and respect. We understand the urgency of reforming the system of social care to provide much more control to individuals and their carers, and to ease the cost burden that they and their families face.
>
> • We will establish a commission on long-term care, to report within a year. The commission will consider a range of ideas, including both a voluntary insurance scheme to protect the assets of those who go into residential care, and a partnership scheme as proposed by Derek Wanless.
> • We will break down barriers between health and social care funding to incentivise preventative action.
> • We will extend the greater roll-out of personal budgets to give people and their carers more control and purchasing power.
> • We will use direct payments to carers and better community-based provision to improve access to respite care.

• We will reform Access to Work, so disabled people can apply for jobs with
funding already secured for any adaptations and equipment they will need.

The main social care reforms introduced by the coalition came late
in its term of office with the passage of the Care Act 2014. One of
the Act's main contributions was to modernise, consolidate and tidy
up the current legal framework (which had evolved piecemeal over
many decades with a series of one-off pieces of legislation, reviews, a
growing body of case law and increasing calls for reform over time).
As a review by the Law Commission (2011, p xvii) argued:

> It is now well over 60 years since the passing of the
> National Assistance Act 1948 which remains to this day the
> bedrock of adult social care. Since then, adult social care
> law has been the subject of countless piecemeal reforms
> including new Acts of Parliament and a constant stream of
> regulations, circulars, directions, approvals and guidance.
> The intervening years have also seen the implementation of
> the Human Right Act 1998, devolution, the restructuring
> of social services departments and numerous landmark
> legal judgements. It is of little surprise that not only does
> the law perplex service users and social workers, but also
> the judiciary. Adult social care law ... has been described
> as 'piecemeal ... numerous', 'exceptionally tortuous',
> 'labyrinthine' and as including some of the 'worst drafted'
> subordinate legislation ever encountered.

However, in addition to this general updating, the Care Act also
introduced a series of changes and new duties, including:

- a duty to promote 'well-being';
- great emphasis on prevention;
- a duty to provide information and advice (including for people with
  lower-level needs who do not qualify for formal care services); and
- a series of changes to the funding of long-term care (for further
  discussion, see the following).

Of course, all this came at a time when funding was constrained, when
needs were increasing and when demand and expectations were rising
– arguably creating some of the most difficult financial and policy
circumstances ever experienced, as discussed further in the following.

The impact of austerity

As reflected elsewhere in this book, the scale of the expenditure cuts faced by local government since 2010 has been unprecedented. This has not only been bad for people using adult social care, but also impacted on other services (with concerns that more frail older people will be admitted to hospital on an emergency basis if their needs are unmet in the community and/or that such patients will find their subsequent discharge from hospital delayed). While many local authorities have tried to protect their children's services and adult social services as much as possible, the result has nevertheless been a situation in which all other areas of adult social care policy have been overshadowed by the sheer size of the funding challenge. As the Local Government Association (LGA, 2014, p 3) explains:

> Councils are currently half way through a scheduled 40 per cent cut in funding from central government. Having delivered £10 billion of savings in the three years from 2011/12, local authorities have to find the same savings again in the next two years. As a result of these cuts councils in many areas will not have enough money to meet all their statutory responsibilities. Our future funding outlook model predicts that the amount of money available to deliver some of the most popular local services will shrink by 66 per cent by the end of the decade.

This has been described by one prominent council leader as 'the end of local government as we know it' (quoted in Dudman, 2012), and has led one London borough to produce an analysis known as the 'Barnet graph of doom' (predicting that over the next 20 years, councils will have nothing left to spend on any service other than adult social care or children's services [see Brindle, 2012]).

According to the National Audit Office (2014, p 7):

- *Adults' care needs are rising.* Adults with long-term and multiple health conditions and disabilities are living longer. The number of adults aged 85 or over, the age group most likely to need care, is rising faster than the population as a whole....
- *Local authorities' total spending on adult social care fell 8 per cent in real terms between 2010–11 and 2012–13 and is projected to continue falling...* Our analysis shows that

around three-quarters of the fall in spending since April 2010 has been achieved by reducing the amount of care provided, which could reflect the effective prevention of need for care, changes in eligibility criteria or reductions in service. The rest has been achieved through paying less to provide care, for example through reducing back-office costs, or through changes to and improvement in the commissioning of care....

- *Local authorities have reduced the total amount of state-funded care provided through individual packages of care every year since 2008–09.*

As they conclude (National Audit Office, 2014, p 11):

> Pressures on the care system are increasing. Providing adequate adult social care poses a significant public service challenge and there are no easy answers. People are living longer and some have long-term and complex health conditions that require managing through care. Need for care is rising while public spending is falling, and there is unmet need. Departments do not know if we are approaching the limits of the capacity of the system to continue to absorb these pressures.

For the Association of Directors of Adult Social Services (ADASS, 2014, p 1):

> Despite everything that is being done to prioritise Adult Social Care – the cash invested in Adult Social Care will reduce by a further 1.9% (£266m) in 2014–15 to £13.68bn. This is the third year of continuing cash reductions and the fifth year of real terms reductions in spending. These five years of real terms reductions in Adult Social Care spending continues to contrast sharply with the Health Service, which has received real term protection of its spending over this same period.... Since 2010 spending on Adult Social Care has fallen by 12% in real terms at a time when the population of those looking for support has increased by 14%. This is leading to fewer people receiving support, with councils over the last 4 years making savings to Adult Social Care budgets totalling £3.53bn.

As is often the case, the scale of these cuts might be a mix of pragmatism and ideology. Politically, it is hard to see the local government financial settlement as anything other than an attempt to 'roll back the boundaries of the welfare state' by significantly reducing the funding available for a wide range of local services (entirely consistent with previous New Right governments and with the approaches set out in Table 1.1 in Chapter One). In many respects, the austerity agenda may prove to be even more effective at this than previous, more explicit, attempts under the Thatcher governments of 1979–90. However, at the same time, it is important to note that governments of all persuasions have tended to target spending pressures onto local government (not least so as to avoid blame centrally for unpopular decisions), a practice known colloquially as 'passing the axe'. Viewed from this angle, the scale of the local government cuts might therefore be seen as an ideologically motivated attempt to reduce public service expenditure, coupled with a more pragmatic attempt to transfer the subsequent blame away from central government.

Long-term care

In the run-up to the 2010 general election, there was widespread consensus that the funding of long-term care for older people and disabled adults needed to be reformed, with a growing sense that this politically difficult issue had been ignored for far too long (for discussion of the New Labour legacy and the build-up to the 2010 general election, see Glasby, 2011). Prior to the election, there had been a series of attempts to develop a longer-term consensus about the issues at stake, with debates becoming increasingly bad-tempered and polarised as the election loomed. In many ways, this dates back to the Conservatives' community care reforms of 1990–93, when adult social care was given responsibility for assessing the needs of older and disabled people and for funding the cost of residential and nursing care for those needing institutional forms of support. Although those reforms talked about the importance of choice, independence and support for families, they were widely interpreted as an attempt to transfer responsibility for a rapidly escalating central budget to cash-limited local authorities, knowing that they would have to bring such budgets back under control in order to stay solvent. This has been described anecdotally as 'the only thing Thatcher gave local government' (Glasby, 2011), and represents a classic example of the tactic noted earlier of 'passing the axe'.

In many ways, the success of local government in bringing spending back under control was one of the unsung achievements of the 1990s. However, the financial tensions inherent in this agenda did not go away, and began to re-emerge in the late 1990s and throughout the 2000s. To make ends meet, local government was increasingly forced to concentrate its resources on people with the most severe needs, with many people left without any access to publicly funded adult social care. The funding arrangements behind the community care reforms also meant that anyone who owned their own home would be liable for the full cost of their care (typically, many hundreds of pounds a week) unless their assets reduced to around £23,250 (the upper threshold in 2014), at which point the state would begin contributing until the person's assets (savings, income and property) reached £14,250 (when the full cost of care would be met by the local authority, provided the home charged rates already agreed by the council). Given a widespread expansion of home-ownership over time, together with rapidly rising property prices, this meant that the vast majority of people had to fund the bulk of their own care – a politically very unpopular situation that involved people having to sell their home or place a charge on their property to be redeemed after their death. While New Labour set up a Royal Commission on Long-term Care following their 1997 manifesto commitment, they baulked at the spending implications and did not implement the main recommendation of their own review (see Royal Commission on Long-term Care, 1999). They also failed to act on an independent analysis carried out by Sir Derek Wanless, who had previously conducted an official and highly influential review of NHS finances and of public health spending (see Wanless, 2002, 2004, 2006), and only produced a White Paper on their desire to create a 'National Care Service' in 2010, far too late in the day to be able to implement this in practice (Department of Health, 2010a).

As public anxiety and anger over the funding of long-term care continued to mount, a series of debates took place behind the scenes in order to explore scope for cross-party consensus around what everyone knew was a long-term issue that needed significant continuity of thinking in order for a solution to be sustainable. However, such attempts broke down as the 2010 general election approached, with many commentators feeling that New Labour's proposals were rushed and ill-thought through, and with the Conservatives labelling some of the funding options being considered a 'death tax' (a hard-hitting description that arguably does little to further sensible and measured political debate). As we have already seen, this was an allegation repeated in the 2010 Conservative manifesto (along with a less than subtle poster campaign depicting a grave stone inscribed 'R.I.P.' and the caption 'Now Gordon wants £20,000 when you die').

After the 2010 general election, the coalition appointed Sir Andrew Dilnot to review the long-term care funding issue yet again. Reporting in 2011, he proposed a series of detailed and carefully crafted changes, including a cap on the maximum that individuals could be asked to pay towards the cost of their care (Dilnot, 2011). A figure between £25,000 and £50,000 was explored, with £35,000 emerging as a suggested maximum. Although most commentators felt that this issue was almost immediately kicked into the long grass, the proposal was later enacted under the Care Act 2014, albeit with a crucial difference: rather than the maximum £35,000 modelled in the initial review, the figure actually implemented was £72,000. Straight away, this changed the nature of the offer, and the fear is that relatively few people will ever incur sufficient costs to benefit, and that the careful thinking that had gone into the initial Dilnot proposals had been overturned in an instant. If younger people owning their own property were given the chance to save £35,000 (whether through savings or some sort of insurance), it is possible that some would choose to prepare more fully than at present for potential care costs in older age (if this meant that they could then retain the money invested in their homes for their families). This might stimulate more of a market for relevant financial products and would help to move away from the current situation where too few people prepare for older age, and subsequent costs are potentially devastating for individuals in a crisis, who inevitably feel betrayed and let down by the system. At a stroke, this potential was lost with a cap that simply feels too high – if this is the maximum, then is it worth people's while preparing in advance, or would they be better off not being ready for future costs and, in very stark terms, hoping that they die before too much of their estate is whittled away?

Quite how this 'solution' was reached remains unclear (and seems a little at odds with the characteristics of the coalition government set out in Table 1.1 of this book). At face value, a policy that encouraged people to prepare for older age, to be more self-sufficient and to consider some form of insurance policy to meet future costs would seem consistent with previous Conservative policies and with ideas around citizens taking greater responsibility for their own care. There were also rumours that the insurance industry was lobbying for some form of compulsory scheme (which might have appealed to the traditional New Right emphasis on markets and competition, but would have been inconsistent with the emphasis on deregulation if made compulsory). Certainly, there was a strong desire not to add to existing public expenditure by making a generous financial settlement, and the policy appears to do little to benefit people on very low incomes (who would have received state-funded care under the previous system), but might instead benefit people with significant assets to pass on to their family.

In the end, what emerged was so underwhelming that it is difficult to avoid the conclusion that: (1) this may have been a pragmatic attempt to be seen to be responding to a long-standing but contentious issue in a way that effectively kicks the topic into the long grass again; and/or (2) that the Liberal Democrats might have been able to soften potential Conservative proposals behind the scenes. Ultimately, it may be that the funding of long-term care was simply not seen as important enough to justify the amount of hostility that would be created by whatever solution was put forward. Rather than this being an ideologically charged issue, most governments over time seem to have concluded that it is just too hard, and that being seen to do something about it without really doing something about it is the best way forward (for more recent developments following the general election of May 2015, see the conclusion at the end of this chapter). Whether this is what older people want or need from their political leaders is perhaps another question, but finding a long-term solution to these issues seems as elusive as ever.

Joint working between health and social care

Away from the funding of long-term care, there has been significant continuity in terms of the ongoing emphasis placed on the greater integration of services (both within the NHS and between health and social care). Over time, the coalition government created new Health and Well-being Boards (see also Chapter Five) to help coordinate care at the local level, introduced a 'Better Care Fund' to fund joint health and social care priorities, identified a series of 'integrated care pioneer' sites to fast-track local reform and emphasised the need for new, more integrated, service models as part of NHS England's (2014) *Five year forward view* (for an overview of recent policy developments, see Glasby and Dickinson, 2014). While policymakers have tended to describe this as 'integrated care', it feels very similar in aspiration and nature to the emphasis that New Labour placed on 'partnership working' and on 'joined-up solutions' to 'joined-up problems' (see, eg, Glendinning et al, 2002). Indeed, the coalition's 'integrated care pioneers' seem very similar to New Labour's 'integrated care organisation' pilots, and the early indications are that the former will struggle to join up services in a meaningful way in a system not designed with integration in mind in exactly the same way as the latter did (see RAND Europe and Ernst and Young, 2012; PIRU, 2015).

What is most interesting here is not so much this apparent continuity, but the unusual way in which 'integrated care' became a key policy priority. A search of the 2010 White Paper reveals no direct reference to the phrase 'integrated care', with much of the document concentrating instead on 'liberating the NHS' (from central and from managerial control). Indeed, there is only one reference to the word 'integrated' and only four fairly non-specific references to 'integration', with paragraph 3.11 (as an example) acknowledging that:

> It is essential for patient outcomes that health and social care services are better integrated at all levels of the system. We will be consulting widely on options to ensure health and social care works seamlessly together to enable this. (Department of Health, 2010b, para 3.11)

However, after widespread protest, the initial legislation was 'paused' and an 'NHS Future Forum' was established under the leadership of Professor Steve Field (former Chair of the Royal College of General Practitioners and subsequently Chief Inspector for general practice with the health and social inspectorate, the Care Quality Commission) (see Chapter Five). In contrast to the White Paper, the Forum focused on the importance of integration in significant detail, devoting a specific working group to the topic (NHS Future Forum, 2012). This seems to have been extremely successful in securing recognition of the importance of integration, and coalition policy subsequently emphasised the need for more integrated care on a regular basis. In one sense, the sudden 'conversion' by the Conservatives to the concept of integration is significantly different to the Liberal Democrats, who supplied both Care Services Ministers during the coalition, each of whom had a prior and long-standing reputation for recognising and promoting the importance of joint working in previous roles as well as when in office.

Interpreting this turn of events is difficult, but it is possible that the Conservatives were happy to adopt the language of integrated care when this seemed to offer a way of reducing the criticism that they were receiving for their proposed health reforms, and when this way of framing the issues at stake helped them avoid allegations of privatisation and fragmentation. Whereas the two Liberal Democrat ministers arguably had a long-standing and more genuine commitment to inter-agency working, the Conservatives' championing of this cause felt more than a little half-hearted at various stages, and a matter of rhetoric rather than reality. Whether or not a Conservative government would have pursued a policy of integrated care without being in coalition, or without the intervention of the Future Forum, must remain a matter of conjecture – but from the analysis in Chapter One of this book, it seems unlikely.

Prevention

As suggested earlier, the need to develop a more preventative approach was a key feature of the Care Act, as it had been a feature of a series of previous initiatives under New Labour. Over time, many commentators have argued that the adult social care system has become increasingly focused on those with very high needs and with very low incomes, leaving most other people ineligible for support and effectively on their own (for a summary, see Allen and Glasby, 2010, 2013; see also: www.scie.org.uk/prevention-library). This has long been recognised as a poor outcome for those in need, but also as an inefficient way of organising services (as those with low-level needs who need minor support are left unaided until a major crisis occurs and they qualify for much more intensive and expensive services). Instead, most key stakeholders recognise the need for a more preventative approach, helping people to stay healthy and independent for as long as possible. Over the years, this has been described in terms of breaking out of a 'vicious cycle' by the former Audit Commission (1997, 2000), or of 'inverting the triangle of care' by the Association of Directors of Adult Social Services and the Local Government Association (ADASS and LGA, 2003).

Of course, actually doing this in practice is much harder than committing to the concept rhetorically (for further discussion, see Allen and Glasby, 2010, 2013; Allen et al, 2013). Adult social care budgets have long been hard-pressed, but recent cuts have decimated them in many areas of the country. In such a situation, the main priority (legally, practically and ethically) has to be to support people with the most severe and urgent needs, with any money left over potentially available to spend on prevention. Preventative services have also often suffered from difficulties in generating robust evidence about effectiveness, whether because they operate over longer timescales than is feasible in political or media terms, or because of the challenges of proving that something has been prevented. As a result of all of this, many attempts at prevention have taken the form of time-limited pilots, struggling to prove their worth, to secure mainstream funding and to rebalance the system as a whole away from its traditional crisis focus.

Under the coalition government, these long-standing trends continued. While the Care Act and other initiatives placed significant emphasis on developing a more preventative approach, it is difficult to see how this can be achieved in practice. Not only have the traditional barriers not gone away, but the current financial situation could easily make the situation much worse. While it has always been difficult to fund prevention, it could prove almost impossible in the current financial context. Against this background, a charitable interpretation would be that the coalition's commitment to prevention is well-meaning and genuine, but ultimately naive. A more cynical interpretation might be that the rhetoric of prevention is one way of significantly reducing local authority budgets while, at the same time, avoiding public outcry and direct legal challenge by being able to argue that individual councils could free up resources to meet all local needs if they chose to strategically invest in prevention. This would then make any subsequent funding problems, service gaps and local protest the responsibility of 'incompetent' local authorities, rather than of a long-standing policy tension that no amount of local pilots could hope to solve. Which interpretation one chooses will probably vary according to the reader.

Personalisation

A final policy priority – again suggesting significant continuity with New Labour – is around the personalisation of adult social care (and potentially other public services as well). In one sense, this began with the passage (by a Conservative government) of the Community Care (Direct Payments) Act 1996, enabling local councils to make payments to disabled people in lieu of directly provided services. This way of working had been invented by disabled people themselves and had long been campaigned for by disabled people's organisations (for a summary, see Glasby and Littlechild 2009). For these groups, direct payments were a route to greater choice, control and independent living: a form of citizenship and the product of a hard-fought civil rights campaign. For the government of the day, such approaches were consistent with neoliberal concepts of consumerism, personal responsibility and the rolling back of the boundaries of the welfare state. Although the initial legislation passed, this tension between citizenship and consumerism has continued ever since.

Under New Labour, direct payments spread, were extended to a range of other user groups (including older people) and became a mainstream option for everyone using adult social care. From the mid-2000s, this way of working was supplemented by (and, in some senses, subsumed into) the broader concept of a 'personal budget'. Here, the local authority is clear with the person upfront how much money is available to spend on meeting their needs, thus enabling the person and the worker to be more imaginative and creative because they have a greater sense of how much is available. The person can then receive the money in a range of different ways, from receiving a direct payment through to the social worker managing the money on the person's behalf. Other options include a friend or family member administering the personal budget, a trusted service provider taking on this role, or the use of a broker or independent living trust. Invented by a social innovation network known as 'In Control', this was piloted with a small number of people with learning difficulties in a number of local authorities, initially generated very positive findings and quickly became national policy (for results of the initial national evaluation, see Glendinning et al, 2008). There were also a series of attempts to introduce similar approaches in other settings by integrating money from a number of funding streams (eg disability benefits, employment support, equipment funding, etc) and by piloting in areas of the NHS.

Under the coalition, these developments continued, and, indeed, increased. While New Labour stated that all social care would be delivered by a personal budget (except in an emergency), the coalition argued that the default position should be that this personal budget takes the form of a direct payment wherever possible. Although New Labour piloted personal health budgets, the coalition embraced them enthusiastically, rolling them out in a number of different areas of health care (for an introduction, see Alakeson, 2014). At the time of writing, a national survey by the Association of Directors of Adult Social Services, completed by 132 councils in England (87% of eligible councils), found that some 370,000 people (80% of all people using community-based services) were supported by personal budgets, representing around 70% of all spending on community-based services (ADASS, 2014). However, these numbers arguably mask a range of complexities, with many commentators concerned that personal budgets have been implemented in a period of austerity with insufficient funding to meet assessed need and in a way that pays lip service to personalisation while actually enabling traditional services to continue in the same way as in the past (see, eg, Needham and Glasby, 2014). For Duffy (2014, p 178), one of the initial inventors of the concept of personal budgets, what we now have is a form of 'zombie personalisation' (a pale and potentially sinister imitation, but with any genuine scope for innovation watered down as the old system seeks to reinvent itself). For him, this is partly about the ability of existing systems to resist radical change, but also about what he sees as a massive assault on the rights and quality of life of disabled people, with widespread cuts in welfare benefits, social care budgets and housing completely incompatible with notions of citizenship, independent living and empowerment. Drawing upon the analysis in Table 1.1 in Chapter One, this seems to be a case of a policy that could be pursued as part of a broader civil rights campaign being appropriated by a government in order to justify deregulation, greater personal responsibility, greater use of market mechanisms, a more mixed economy of care and a reduction in the basic safety net available to people with social care needs.

Conclusions: reflections on the coalition government

In seeking to take stock of the coalition government's approach to adult social care, there seems at first glance to be significant continuity with the language and approaches adopted by New Labour. Certainly, governments of all persuasions have emphasised the importance of integration, prevention and personalisation, and have also tended to struggle to implement genuine and long-term solutions to ongoing debates about the funding of long-term care. Behind the rhetoric, however, there may be less continuity than at first appears. Despite emphasising the importance of 'integrated care', the coalition seemed a relatively late convert to the idea, and it is hard to avoid the conclusion that the subsequent championing of this cause may have been the result of genuine commitment by the Liberal Democrats, but also of pragmatism on the part of a Conservative Party seeking to deflect criticism of its health reforms. While prevention has been an aspiration for successive governments, it has proved difficult to achieve in practice. Once again, stressing the importance of prevention could be a helpful contribution to the debate, but could equally be a way of arguing that local authorities are sufficiently well resourced if only they could more strategically invest in prevention. Finally, the personalisation of services was an aim of both the New Labour and coalition governments, but it is possible to call for personalisation out of a desire for greater citizenship and civil rights, on the one hand, or as a way of rolling back the frontiers of the welfare state, on the other. In any case, any practical progress with regards to any of these agendas has almost certainly been undermined by the draconian funding cuts experienced by local government. Reflecting on five years of the coalition, therefore, it may be a question of adopting similar approaches to New Labour, but arguably of different underlying tactics and values behind the rhetoric – a question of 'It ain't what you do, it's the way that you do it'.

Under a majority Conservative government, it now remains to be seen how much of the 2010–15 experience was the result of having to seek compromise behind the scenes with Liberal Democrat partners, and what happens when that potential buffer is no longer there. Certainly, the early signs post-election have not been promising, with nothing of any significance on adult social care in the 2015 Queen's Speech, in the new government's 'first 100 days' or in the July 2015 Budget. Indeed, the situation deteriorated significantly with the bankruptcy of the College of Social Work (the national body set up to raise the status of the social work profession) after the responsibility for assessing and accrediting advanced child and family practitioners was contracted out to a consortium led by a major international consultancy and the government concluded that the College was 'no longer wanted or needed' (Whitehall source, quoted in McNicoll, 2015). While the College also faced significant additional problems, it is hard to imagine a similar body in a profession such as medicine or nursing being allowed to fail in such a way. Around the same time, the new government announced that it would be delaying the lifetime cap on care costs introduced under the Care Act until 2020, despite this being a manifesto commitment – effectively kicking the matter into the (by now very) long grass once again (Brindle, 2015). Given the broader policy shifts described in this edited collection, adult social care has probably never been more important, but it is possible that it may struggle even more from 2015 to 2020 than it did between 2010 and 2015.

References

ADASS (Association of Directors of Adult Social Services) (2014) 'ADASS Budget survey report 2014: final'. Available at: http://www. adass.org.uk/adass-budget-survey-2014/ (accessed 18 July 2014).

ADASS and LGA (Local Government Association) (2003) *All our tomorrows: inverting the triangle of care*, London: ADSS.

Alakeson, V. (2014) *Delivering personal health budgets: a guide to policy and practice*, Bristol: The Policy Press.

Allen, K. and Glasby, J. (2010) *'The billion dollar question': embedding prevention in older people's services – 10 high impact changes*, Policy Paper 8, Birmingham: Health Services Management Centre.

Allen, K. and Glasby, J. (2013) 'The "billion dollar question": embedding prevention in older people's services – ten "high-impact" changes', *British Journal of Social Work*, 43(5): 904–24.

Allen, K., Miller, R. and Glasby, J. (2013) *Prevention services, social care and older people: much discussed but little researched?*, London: School for Social Care Research.

Audit Commission (1997) *The coming of age: improving care services for older people*, London: Audit Commission.

Audit Commission (2000) *The way to go home: rehabilitation and remedial services for older people*, London: Audit Commission.

Brindle, D. (2012) 'Graph of doom: a bleak future for social care services', *The Guardian Society*, 15 May. Available at: http://www.theguardian.com/society/2012/may/15/graph-doom-social-care-services-barnet (accessed 18 July 2014).

Brindle, D. (2015) 'Plan for lifetime cap on care costs deferred until 2020', *The Guardian*, 17 July. Available at: http://www.theguardian.com/society/2015/jul/17/lifetime-cap-care-costs-deferred-2020 (accessed 11 August 2015).

Cabinet Office (2010) *The coalition: our programme for government*, London: Cabinet Office.

Conservative Party (2010) *Invitation to join the government of Britain*, London: Conservative Party.

Department of Health (2010a) *Building the national care service*, London: The Stationery Office.

Department of Health (2010b) *Equity and excellence: liberating the NHS*, London: The Stationery Office.

Dilnot, A. (2011) 'Fairer care funding: the report of the Commission on Funding of Care and Support' (the Dilnot Review). Available at: http://webarchive.nationalarchives.gov.uk/20130221130239/https://www.wp.dh.gov.uk/carecommission/files/2011/07/Fairer-Care-Funding-Report.pdf (accessed 18 July 2014).

Dudman, J. (2012) 'The end of local government?', *The Guardian Society*, 30 October. Available at: http://www.theguardian.com/society/2012/oct/30/end-of-local-government (accessed 18 July 2014).

Duffy, S. (2014) 'After personalisation', in C. Needham and J. Glasby (eds) *Debates in personalisation*, Bristol: Policy Press, pp 167–84.

Glasby, J. (2011) 'The Conservative Party and community care', in H. Bochel (ed) *The Conservative Party and social policy*, Bristol: The Policy Press, pp 181–95.

Glasby, J. (2012) *Understanding health and social care* (2nd edn), Bristol: The Policy Press.

Glasby, J. and Dickinson, H. (2014) *Partnership working in health and social care: what is integrated care and how can we deliver it?* (2nd edn), Bristol: The Policy Press.

Glasby, J. and Littlechild, R. (2009) *Direct payments and personal budgets: putting personalisation into practice* (2nd edn), Bristol: The Policy Press.

Glendinning, C., Powell, M. and Rummery, K. (eds) (2002) *Partnerships, New Labour and the governance of welfare*, Bristol: The Policy Press.

Glendinning, C., Challis, D., Fernandez, J., Jacobs, S., Jones, K., Knapp, M., Manthorpe, J., Moran, N., Netten, A., Stevens, M. and Wilberforce, M. (2008) *Evaluation of the individual budgets pilot programme*, York: Social Policy Research Unit.

HM Government (2008) *The case for change: why England needs a new care and support system*, London: Department of Health.

HM Government (2009) *Shaping the future of care together*, London: The Stationery Office (TSO).

Labour Party (2010) *The Labour Party manifesto*, London: Labour Party.

Law Commission (2011) *Adult social care*, London: The Stationery Office.

LGA (Local Government Association) (2014) *Under pressure: how councils are planning for future cuts*, London: LGA.

Liberal Democrats (2010) *Liberal Democrat manifesto 2010*, London: Liberal Democrats.

McNicoll, A. (2015) 'College of Social Work faced £240,000 annual deficit before closure, leaked report reveals', *Community Care*. Available at: http://www.communitycare.co.uk/2015/06/22/college-social-work-faced-240000-annual-deficit-closure-leaked-report-reveals/ (accessed 11 August 2015).

Means, R. and Smith, R. (1998) *From Poor Law to community care*, Basingstoke: Macmillan.

Means, R., Morbey, H. and Smith, R. (2002) *From community care to market care? The development of welfare services for older people*, Bristol: The Policy Press.

National Audit Office (2014) *Adult social care in England: an overview*, London: National Audit Office.

Needham, C. and Glasby, J. (eds) (2014) *Debates in personalisation*, Bristol: The Policy Press.

NHS England (2014) *NHS five year forward view*, Leeds: NHS England.

NHS Future Forum (2012) *Integration – a report from the NHS Future Forum*, London: NHS Future Forum.

Payne, M. (2005) *The origins of social work: continuity and change*, Basingstoke: Palgrave.

PIRU (Policy Innovation Research Unit) (2015) *Early evaluation of the integrated care and support pioneers programme: interim report*, London: PIRU.

RAND Europe and Ernst and Young (2012) *National evaluation of the Department of Health's integrated care pilots*, Cambridge: RAND Europe.

Royal Commission on Long-term Care (1999) *With respect to old age: long term care – rights and responsibilities*, London: The Stationery Office.

Wanless, D. (2002) *Securing our future health: taking a long-term view – a final report*, London: HM Treasury.

Wanless, D. (2004) *Securing good health for the whole population – final report*, London: HM Treasury.

Wanless, D. (2006) *Securing good care for older people: taking a long-term view*, London: King's Fund.

ELEVEN

Family policy: the Mods and Rockers

Rosalind Edwards and Val Gillies

Introduction

Conservative–Liberal Democrat coalition government family policy was characterised by, on the one hand, a social and economic liberalism subscribed to by both the Conservatives and Liberal Democrats, and, on the other, a traditional moralism championed by many Conservatives. It was informed by battles and uneasy alliances of political perspectives that *The Times* (1998) once referred to as 'The Tory Mods and Rockers', with the former embracing a 'modernising' and investment agenda for change and the latter seeking to conserve established doctrines. In coalition family policy, Mod and Rocker tensions and alliances can be demonstrated in the socially liberal opening up and moral universalisation of marriage, and the economically liberal and morally categorical dividing off of particular sorts of families as in need of targeted early or turnaround intervention to turn them into responsible worker-citizens (see Table 1.1 in Chapter One). Under the coalition government, families became a cipher for the state of British society generally. There were 'hard-working families', and the other sort: the shirker and scrounger families of Broken Britain who had lived off welfare benefits for generations rather than get a job, where parents had no idea how to bring up their young children properly, and neither knew nor cared what their feral teenage children were up to, leaving them free to truant and riot. These distinctions appear repeatedly in this book (see, eg, Chapters Eight, Nine and Twelve).

These images underpinned a range of developments in coalition government policy, and specifically in family policy, as we consider here. While hard-working families were lauded and received some rhetorical pats on the back (in practice, they became hard-hit by policy developments), the policy prescription for supposed shirkers and scroungers conjured poverty into the fault of poor families themselves through asserting their intergenerational culture and biological deficit as causal in their disadvantage. Attention was drawn away from broader structural and economic risks facing families. A seemingly progressive and moral focus on improving the lives of children and families to the benefit of society has been subject to party-political consensus. Although there were some differences with the previous New Labour government's policies towards disadvantaged families, in the coalition's preoccupation with targeting, the main thrust has been strong continuities and extrapolations (Bond-Taylor, 2015a). Indeed, it is notable that several key review reports that provided a justification for coalition family policies were commissioned from or chaired by Labour MPs. Examples include: *Preventing poor children becoming poor adults* by Frank Field (2010); *Early intervention: the next steps* and *Early intervention: smart investment, massive savings* by Graham Allen (2011a, 2011b); and *Social mobility and child poverty in Great Britain* by Alan Milburn (Social Mobility and Child Poverty Commission, 2013).

In what follows, we briefly review the nature of the similarities and differences between the New Labour and coalition governments' family policies, before going on to consider the source and features of coalition Mod and Rocker approaches to families, and to explore their universalist and targeted nature. In particular, we do this through consideration of, first, the treatment of marriage and stability in and for families, and, second, two key forms of social investment in families: early intervention so as prevent poverty and disadvantage in the next generation; and interventions to turn around dysfunctional families who must be made to help themselves.

From New Labour to the coalition

When the Conservative–Liberal Democrat coalition government was formed in May 2010, it came into a family policy field shaped by New Labour over a 13-year period. While families, and especially how mothers and fathers bring up their children, have long been an issue of social political concern, linked to the state of the nation (Rose, 1987), the advent of the New Labour government in 1997 pushed parenting practice in particular to the centre stage of social policy (Edwards and Gillies, 2004). It did so in a distinct form; while other European countries also demonstrate concern with supporting families, the New Labour emphasis on normative and standardised interventions and parenting education packages stands out (Boddy et al, 2011). 'Parents', generally, were posed as in need of expert help to empower and support them in carrying out the vital work of fostering and transmitting crucial values to their children, which protected and reproduced the common good. New Labour family policy aimed to change cultural understandings through the provision of advice and services that were relevant to all parents regardless of their circumstances (Home Office, 1998, p 7). Authoritative advice was available to all through the National Family and Parenting Institute and the Parentline Plus telephone helpline, with the Sure Start programme providing parenting education and support, as well as subsidised childcare, toy libraries, drop-in groups and cafes in local Children's Centres. In a rolling out of economic liberalism that has shaped the family policy landscape beyond the New Labour government, childcare was redrawn as a motor of meritocracy, with family conceived as the formative site through which well-parented children would grow up better able to navigate and capitalise on the new post-industrial economic landscapes (Gillies, 2014). The Child Trust Fund, where government provided a kick-start child savings account for family members to top up regularly, symbolised the social investment approach in which children were positioned primarily as worker-citizens of the future (Lister, 2003), as human capital that required investment. Poverty for families and children was to be ended through this investment, rather than redistribution. As part of the New Labour 'Third Way' modernising public sector reform agenda of dismantling state bureaucracy, such investment included private financing, where investors would receive returns when public service targets were met. Indeed, New Labour's policy initiatives stimulated a major expansion of state and third sector professionals and services aimed at supporting parenting through inculcating expert-approved parenting practices (Boddy et al, 2011).

At this level, the New Labour government approach to family policy was ostensibly universal. It shaded into subtle targeting and further into authoritarian control however, heralding the stronger focus on targeting subsequently adopted by the coalition. Where parents (in reality, mostly poor mothers) who were judged to need support did not seem to accept and enact their moral responsibility for preventing their children's anti-social behaviour, they were fined, jailed and compelled to attend intensive parenting skills classes. Deterministic notions of transmitted deprivation accompanied the conviction that family and parenting were at the core of persistent anti-social behaviour and could be subjected to enforced intervention in the quest to produce a more meritocratic society (Milbourne, 2009; Millie, 2009). In particular, Family Intervention Projects, delivered through key workers in local outreach and residential units, crossed between the parenting support and criminal justice system as part of New Labour's anti-social behaviour strategy and 'Respect' agenda. The strategy focused on 'a small minority[1] of high cost/high risk problem families' (Home Office,

2006), and involved time-limited contracts, sanctions, tough support and a 'whole family' approach (Nixon et al, 2006).

It is this preoccupation with transmitted problems and highly dysfunctional families, and the targeted and harsh response in New Labour family policy, that has chimed with and driven coalition approaches (see also Chapter Twelve). This continuation was not much of a stretch for the coalition government given the moralistic and neoliberal economic approach pursued by the New Labour administration. The approach was, however, ramped up under the coalition to include a dismantling of the universal aspects of family service provision, which was justified through the need for public expenditure cutbacks in the context of austerity. Indeed, as noted in Chapter One of this volume, spending per child on early education, childcare and Sure Start services fell by a quarter between 2009/10 and 2012/13 (Lupton, 2015), while child and family poverty was reframed as more than mere 'symptomatic' household income level. The causal features of poverty were identified as 'low achievement, aspirations and opportunity across generations ... worklessness and educational failure and ... family and relationship breakdown' (Department for Work and Pensions and Department for Education, 2011), and the Child Poverty Commission set up by New Labour was renamed the Social Mobility and Child Poverty Commission to emphasis this focus on causes rather than symptoms. New Labour's blanket expansion of a veritable industry of parenting and family support provisions was characterised by the coalition government not only as expensive and ineffective, but also as morally corrosive in its 'nanny state' encouragement of dependency and discouragement of familial and personal responsibility (Bamfield, 2012). The 'inverted culpability' premise that the need for austerity and dismantling of universal family support services is a consequence of a 'something for nothing' culture has become the accepted construction of the political economy across most of the political spectrum (Serougi, 2015).

The mood music of coalition government family policy was largely dominated by the Tory Mods and Rockers, where (as this volume shows) the Conservatives held most of the relevant major cabinet posts. There are exceptions, however. For example, the social liberality that saw the universalisation of marriage that we discuss later was an approach that Liberal Democrats could go along with. However, the traditional moralism that underlay Conservative Party manifesto commitment to reward marriage in the tax system was not. There was determined Liberal Democratic opposition and they managed to delay and constrain the measure until towards the end of the Coalition government, when a limited tax break of £212 per annum was introduced in April 2015. Yet, similarly traditional and moralistic targeted and punitive Conservative policy prescriptions did hold sway, such as a cap of £26,000 on the amount of benefit that a family can claim to ensure that they did not have more to live on than 'hard-working families'. Such measures had their roots, in particular, in Iain Duncan Smith's angst-driven enquiries into the causes of poverty and social breakdown and initiation of the Centre for Social Justice (CSJ) think tank in 2004, consequent upon his ousting from the Conservative Party leadership the previous year (Slater, 2012). The CSJ has been key in promoting the idea that 'welfare' is a lifestyle choice for dissolute families. It has been the crucible for ideas about benefit cuts, conditionality and intervention to disrupt supposed cycles of intergenerational worklessness and the literal and metaphorical reproduction of underachievement. These ideas were enacted in the rolling back of the welfare state policies that Duncan Smith has pursued as Secretary of State for Work and Pensions under the coalition and, since 2015, Conservative governments. For a short period, the Liberal Democrat MP Sarah Teather was Minister of State for Children and Families at the Department for Education. She introduced a lighter-touch Early Years Foundation Stage, and focused on progress checks and early intervention for young children in deprived families, especially to promote school-readiness. Beyond that social investment approach to promote social mobility, the Liberal Democrats had little distinct effect on coalition government family policy. Indeed, sacked after two years in post, Teather revealed that she was critical of the 'immoral and divisive' policies that the coalition was pursuing (*The Observer*, 2012). The cracks in the coalition and its contradictory Mod and Rocker social sensibilities can be seen in the fate of the 'Childhood and Families Taskforce'. Announced by Nick Clegg as Liberal Democratic Deputy Prime Minister, and involving leading Conservative and Liberal Democrat ministers, it aimed to produce policy proposals that would remove barriers to success for children and families. However, no reports appeared.

Under the coalition, the New Labour-instituted Department for Children, Schools and Families was dismantled, and different aspects of family-relevant policy were variously located in the Departments for Education, Communities and Local Government, and Health. In addition to discrete responsibility for the early years curriculum in Education, targeted family intervention programmes were located in the respective departments through which they were delivered, each with a slightly different intervention emphasis. Turnaround intervention was delivered through the Department of Communities and Local Government, and early preventive intervention through the Department of Health, both of which were headed by Conservative secretaries of state.

New Labour's featuring of marriage as a preferential state (see Barlow et al, 2002) was pushed further by the CSJ, which became the crucible for ideas about encouraging and rewarding marriage as a panacea for familial and thus social ills. Marriage was promoted as a moral virtue and a means of achieving better human capital outcomes. Correlations between parents who were married and relationship stability, higher income, educational achievement and so on were reworked as causal, with the conclusion that marriage created these benefits (as opposed to such advantages leading couples to marry precisely because they are in propitious circumstances) (Hayter, 2015). Iain Duncan Smith exemplifies the way that Mod social liberality and Rocker conservative moralistic traditionalism were dragooned into an alliance as (presumably through gritted teeth) he espoused the extension of marriage to same-sex couples on the grounds that it would promote stability in relationships (*Pink News*, 2012).

Stable marriage and stable families

A focus on stable marriage and family was a key feature of the Conservative-dominated coalition's family policy, with a Mod and Rocker skirmish with respect to same-sex marriage. On the Mod side, liberalisation of the economic sphere and modernisation of state provision was extended to a liberal approach to people's lifestyle choices, while on the Rocker side, more traditional moral values of marriage and family were advocated. A long-standing feature of tension in Conservative politics (Hayton, 2015; Hayton and McEnhill, 2015), these two dogmas were shoehorned into coalition government family policy to institute equal marriage rights for same-sex couples. The extension of the institution of marriage to same-sex couples gave the impression of a socially progressive Mod Conservative–Liberal Democratic coalition government alongside retention of a traditional Conservative Rocker emphasis on its moral and social value at one and the same time. As a founder of both the CSJ and the Conservative Home blog put it: 'Because it is so beneficial an institution it should be enlarged rather than fossilised. Whereas some people see the gay marriage issue as primarily about equal rights, I see it as about social solidarity and stability' (Montgomerie, 2012). The internal Mod and Rocker split was still in evidence, however, as a majority of Conservative MPs voted against the policy.

A less fraught Mod and Rocker combination was also apparent in the coalition government's focus on reform of the Adoption Statutory Guidance, where the supposed overly bureaucratised process of recruiting and training adopters and the ethnic matching of adopters and children in care was castigated by the then Conservative Secretary of State for Education Michael Gove as old-fashioned social engineering: a politically correct barrier to children's universal need for a (colour-blind) stable family life.[2] Where the majority of children in care likely to be placed for adoption are from black groups and poor backgrounds, and it is white middle-class parents who are regarded as being prevented from adopting them, this initiative racialised rather than deracialised the adoption process, at the same time as it ignored the wider question of why disproportionate numbers of black and minority ethnic children are taken into care (Ali, 2014). More widely, the number of 'looked-after' children has increased by 12% over the past five years (Harker and Heath, 2014), linked to the early intervention stricture we discuss later.

Rhetorical support for family stability was underlined by the introduction of a 'family test' for coalition government policies, championed again through Duncan Smith (Department for Work and Pensions, 2014). A series of criteria were published to guide policymakers on considering the impact that new initiatives might have on the formation of strong, stable families, parenting and caring duties, and the risk of family breakdown and separation. Generally, in a conflation of stable families with stable couple relationships, resources were ploughed into couple relationship education in order to prevent relationship breakdown (Van Acker, 2015), and 'important signals' were sent about support for the institution of marriage through enacting policies devised by the CSJ.

One of the groups for whom stable parents and family life was not regarded as important was migrants, where family-related migration was regarded as undermining immigration controls and selective immigration policies. The coalition government introduced a series of changes that extended probationary settlement periods for spouses and partners, and raised the gross income threshold required to sponsor admission for children, along with removing the full right of appeal against the refusal of a family visit visa. The main impact of this coalition reform, Kilkey (2015) points out, was not on 'them' but on 'us', where over half of sponsors of partner visas are UK-born British citizens, and it was on a particular 'us' – the poorer in society who cannot meet the income threshold. However, we should also note that those affected may not be considered 'us' in terms of ethnicity, even if UK-born.

Another group whose family life was not supported was lone-parent families (see also Chapter Twelve). Indeed, coalition government policy threatened lone mothers who receive Income Support, and thus are not a 'hard-working family', with losing 40% of their benefit if they did not demonstrate that they were actively seeking work once their youngest child reached five years of age. Coalition Child Benefit policy was also at the expense of poorer families generally, with a failure to keep Child Benefit levels in line with inflation meaning that the benefit lost over 15% of its value from the advent of the coalition (CPAG, 2014). Further, Child Benefit is taxed where a parent earns over £50,000 per annum. Thus, a lone parent who earns just over £50,000 has their Child Benefit taxed, while couple parents who each earn just under the threshold do not. While this measure hit fairly affluent lone parents, however hard-working, what it did was to reinforce the idea that welfare benefits are targeted not universal, only for the poor and with conditionality attached to them.

Indeed, poor families themselves were the focus of 'social mobility' and poverty strategies under the coalition government, rather than the inequalities and deprivation that they suffered, following the CSJ idea that low income is a symptom rather than cause of poverty. Continuing and ramping up New Labour preoccupations, the coalition laying the moral responsibility for their own and their children's disadvantage at the door of poor parents meant a focus on their supposedly flawed causal parenting practices, behaviours and attitudes, and intervention to deal with them.

Targeting: early and turnaround intervention

The coalition's focus on children as human capital continued the New Labour social investment emphasis. The 2011 *Open public services White Paper* (Cabinet Office, 2011) set out a modernising agenda for public sector reform that rolled out payment by results, where an intervention is commissioned and funded wholly or partially on the basis of results achieved rather than the cost of the service. Similarly, social impact bonds were regarded as a way of encouraging private investment, with the bond investment in providing improved social outcomes operating over a fixed period and profit repayment to investors dependent on the achievement of the specified outcomes (see also Chapter Three). Each form of human capital investment is well embedded in the family and children field, with targeted interventions provided by both the voluntary and private sectors.

A hooking together of Mod social liberal values and Rocker traditional moral authoritarian conservatism wove its way through targeted intervention policies to ensure that the poor were 'empowered' to take control of their own lives through responsibilisation. Mothers were empowered through recognising and accepting their family and parenting responsibilities, managing themselves and their children competently, and pursuing the transformation of their lives through appropriate aspirations (Bond-Taylor, 2015b; Gillies, 2014). Intervening to support mothers and fathers to ensure better material, social and behavioural outcomes for children seems both progressive and morally authoritative. It is also morally judgemental and embeds social divisions in its ideas about biological deficits and damaging intergenerational cultures.

Targeted family intervention policies took two main forms under the coalition government. One emphasis was on early intervention, where the family relationships of poor and young families were subject to the rhetoric of preventing the transmission of material, cultural and aptitude deprivation to the next generation. The other was on intervention to turn around families that were supposedly deeply complicit in their own deprivation, having not had the benefit of earlier intervention. In each case, an effective rhetorical wedge was driven between 'hard-working' and achieving families, and the dysfunctional and undeserving families living off benefits at their expense.

Targeting disadvantaged working-class families

Family and parenting support under the coalition government was characterised by the further embedding of normative and standardised education and training programmes. This reframed the New Labour parenting curriculum to explicitly target particular social groups. Early intervention through such programmes was promoted in the belief that pregnancy and the earliest years of life are crucially important for future social mobility (eg Leadsom et al, 2013). The ideal was to pre-empt rather than react to social, educational and behaviour deficiencies, with intervention in families in the early years promoted as an evidenced, boundaried and cost-limited policy approach (eg Allen 2011a, 2011b). Evidence from social indicators was used to identify particular categorial groups in which 'poor parenting' was said to be leading to 'poor outcomes' for children. New parents (overwhelmingly mothers) in the category were targeted for intervention so as to disrupt the transmission of dysfunctional parenting practices they learnt at their own mother's knee. For instance, the Family Nurse Partnership delivers interventions with pregnant teenage and first-time mothers, and Parent–Infant Partnerships offer psychotherapeutic attachment intervention. The minutiae of everyday interactions between mothers and their children were held up as deeply significant and capable of overcoming structurally ingrained disadvantages. Indeed, the Prime Minister, David Cameron, described the 'realisation' of the significance of parenting above socio-economic status as 'one of the most important findings in a generation' (Cameron, 2011).

This ostensibly progressive, Mod, coalition family policy of improving children's life chances through 'supporting' parents to learn how to better handle their children was built on a social investment model that galvanised cross-party support. In practice, it personalised and normalised inequality alongside reducing broad and universal state support for families. It also biologised it (Edwards et al, 2015; Macvarish et al, 2015). Early intervention policies were reinforced by the claim that advances in neuroscience provide incontrovertible evidence that parenting is absolutely formative in the first years after birth. Reports and reviews detailed the apparent physical damage that inadequate parenting inflicts on infant brains, with the poorest in society at most risk of damaging their children's brains (eg Allen 2011a, 2011b; Leadsom et al, 2013). Such claims justify gendered, race and social inequalities. They reflect an essentialist turn towards viewing mothers as the sole architects of outcomes for their children, judged according to the quality of their maternal responsiveness. They laud and promote Eurocentric and middle-class values and assumptions about parenting practices and ideal family life, and propose a meritocratic construction of the wealthy and privileged as having better-developed brains through optimal mothering (Edwards et al, 2015).

The majority of early interventionist parenting support programmes are commercial enterprises (eg the Family Nurse Partnership programme is licensed to deliver the US-based David Olds Nurse Family Program), and unsurprisingly express the neoliberal Mod objectives of self-discipline and self-transformation. Poor disadvantaged mothers must remedy their 'parenting deficit' through managing themselves as a self-directed and responsible, 'authoritative' parent. They are then better able to regulate their child, who needs to be school-ready so as to develop the required cognitive, social and emotional skills required for the productive 'worker-citizen' of the future (Hendrick, 2003) (see Table 1.1 in Chapter One regarding citizenship). The Troubled Families programme has a similar self-regulating premise, keying into wider processes of neoliberal state-crafting undertaken by the coalition (Crossley, 2015a).

Targeting troubled and multiple problem families

A more explicit authoritarian and moralistic Rocker agenda is evident in the Troubled Families Programme (albeit initially including Mod rhetoric about 'empowerment'). The programme was implemented by the coalition government in the aftermath of the 2011 English riots, but has its roots in the New Labour Family Intervention Projects discussed earlier. The 2011 civil unrest was identified by the Prime Minister, David Cameron, in a post-riot speech, as carried out by 'failing' and undisciplined young people who were products of 'welfare reliant single mothers', and as caused by 'what some people call problem and others call troubled families' (Cameron, 2011). A specific target group of 120,000 families was identified as 'both troubled and causing trouble', in that they exhibited a particular set of three problem behaviours and were in need of intensive intervention to 'turn' them around (DCLG, 2012): a family member involved in criminal and anti-social behaviour; children's truancy or exclusion from school; and a family member claiming out-of-work benefits (including disability and carers benefits). There is also a 'local discretion filter', where local authorities can identify families who meet two of the criteria above and who also meet local criteria of concern, such as under-18 conceptions and drug and alcohol misuse.

The figure of 120,000 'troubled' families and ideas about their characteristics have been revealed as erected on extremely shaky statistical ground, drawn from a 'spurious' reading of survey data and bearing little resemblance to the set of three 'troubled families' criteria through encompassing families with broader multiple disadvantages (such as poverty, inadequate housing, disability and mental ill health) rather than anti-social fecklessness (Levitas, 2012). Nonetheless, the 'evidence' providing a justification for intervention in families' lives was key in holding together a consensus on the policy among liberal and authoritarian factions within the Conservative Party, the coalition and across the political spectrum. The responsibilities of the state were focused firmly on the role of (coercive) moral educator, rather than addressing underlying structural factors impeding families, and poor families were cast in terms of their social pathology (Bond-Taylor, 2015b).

A dedicated Troubled Families Unit was set up, with Louse Casey appointed to head a programme that continued in the vein of the time-limited, goal-oriented 'tough love' Family Intervention Projects approach using a family keyworker. Tellingly, Casey's antecedents were with New Labour's Respect Task Force and Antisocial Behaviour Unit.

Central government funding was made available on a payment-by-results basis: local authorities were funded per family to work with a target number of troubled families in their area and a set of measurable improvements to achieve. Families have to enter into a contract at the start of the intervention that lays out expectations and sanctions if they fail to engage with or participate in the programme, such as loss of tenancy. Further Rocker-type punitive and authoritarian plans to pay benefits to those identified as troubled families by a smart card that could only be used for essential purchases or to pass control of benefits to a troubled family's key worker were apparently blocked by the Liberal Democrat ministers in the coalition (Stratton, 2013). By 2014, it was claimed that over 70% of the target number of families had been 'turned around' (DCLG, 2014a). The meeting of targets for troubled families was hailed as such a success – despite concerns again expressed about the basis for measures of that success – that the coalition government announced an 'Extended Troubled Families Programme', expanding the target group of families requiring intervention to include 'children who need help' and 'parents and children with a range of health problems' (DCLG, 2014b). One year later, it was announced that 105,000 of the 120,000 families had been turned around, with savings of over £1 billion.[3] Both the 2014 and 2015 claims have been challenged as extrapolating from a small sample size, as involving selection bias and deadweight (where families' circumstances would have changed anyway without intervention), and for the implications for the data collected from local authorities of their payment by results (Crossley, 2015b; Portes, 2015).

Rather confusingly, there is also a Department for Work and Pensions (DWP)-led Families With Multiple Problems initiative, which aims to tackle 'entrenched' worklessness in families. Provision is aimed at families with 'multiple problems and complex needs', where at least one member of a family receives a DWP working-age benefit and either no one in the family is working or there is a history of worklessness across generations.[4] Unlike the Troubled Families Programme, participation is voluntary and is administered through centrally contracted 'providers'. The Families With Multiple Problems programme is funded by the European Social Fund, so perhaps that is why its existence is downplayed. Indeed, Iain Duncan Smith's remarks portraying worklessness and other 'associated' family troubles as part of a pernicious lifestyle culture within deprived families and communities that are passed down the generations are often assumed to apply to the Troubled Families Programme. Notably, Duncan Smith (2009) first made the claim that there were housing estates where three generations of families had never had a job, and who often had more than four children, with Conservative Minister for Work and Pensions Chris Grayling then upping this to four generations.[5] As with challenges to the statistics underlying the Troubled Families Programme, extensive research into the existence of three-generation workless families in deprived neighbourhoods has failed to find evidence for them or for a culture that discourages employment (Shildrick et al, 2012).

An unfettered Conservative government

In 2015, the coalition was superseded by a Conservative government. The unfettered Tories came to power on a manifesto that evoked family as an individualised worker-citizen unit, with sections headed 'An economic plan to help you and your family' and 'The best schools and hospitals for you and your family' (Conservative Party, 2015). A cap on overall welfare spending was promised to 'save your money'. The manifesto and Conservative government actions in its first 100 days continued the emphasis on stable marriage through promises of an increased tax-free working income transfer and investment in relationship support. The worker-citizen unit is to be supported in its responsible endeavour through the manifesto commitment to double the hours of free childcare for three and four year olds to 30 hours a week for parents in employment. Distinctions between the striver worker-citizen family units and the shirker troubled families were further entrenched through a series of measures set out in the Conservative government's Welfare Reform and Work Bill. The Bill posed the overriding aim of the welfare benefit measures it contained as reducing expenditure and to 'support the policy of rewarding hard work while increasing fairness with working households' (Kennedy, 2015, p 5). Legal targets on the eradication of child poverty will be abandoned, replaced only by a statutory duty of reporting on 'life chances' (notably, including children living in 'workless households', despite the fact that two thirds of poor children currently have at least one parent in work [Belfield et al, 2015]). The child poverty element of the Social Mobility and Child Poverty Commission was dropped, as its name and remit was changed (once again) to become the Social Mobility Commission. The Welfare Reform and Work Bill also requires government to report on the Troubled Families Programme, thus legislating for the commitment to targeted intervention. An extensive raft of changes to welfare benefits and tax credits affecting families has been introduced, with a lowering of the total benefit cap threshold, a freezing of working-age benefit levels for four years and a limiting of support through Child Tax Credits. Welfare conditionality for lone mothers is subject to tighter requirements. The Rocker moralisation of family policy seems ascendant.

Free of the Liberal Democrat constraint on rewarding marriage through the tax system during the coalition, the Conservative government has made an increased transferable tax allowance of £1,000 available to married couples and civil partners where one partner stays at home or earns very little, the Married Couple's Allowance. Symbolism appeared to be the issue, however, given the fact that under a third of married couples are eligible, a third of whom are pensioners (Toynbee, 2015). More contradictorily regarding the institution of marriage, but clear about strengthening the distinction between families where parents are in employment and those where they are not, 'hard-working' and 'hard-pressed' two-parent families where both are in paid work and earn less than £150,000 receive up to £2000 in 'Tax-Free Childcare' payments for each child. Thus, with these two measures, families headed by a couple, whether with one breadwinner or with both parents in work and whether married or not, are prioritised at the expense of lone-parent families, however hard-working and hard-pressed they may be.

Families where parents are not in employment are subject to rigid conditionality. The Welfare Reform and Work Bill proposes a ramping up of the pressure on lone mothers (the vast majority of lone parents are mothers), lowering the age threshold of their children at which they are subject to work-related requirements to two years. Other punitive measures have already been implemented. The manifesto pledge to lower the total benefit income cap even further, to £20,000 (£23,000 within London), has been implemented. Furthermore, benefits for asylum-seeker families, where parents are not allowed to work their way out of poverty, has been subject to a £16 per week cut in the amount allocated for a child, exacerbating already strained circumstances (Asylum Support (Amendment) Regulations 2015[6]).

At the same time, however, the Conservative government has also hit the hard-working alongside the supposed scrounger families. Working Tax Credit and Child Tax Credit are to be cut and child benefit has been frozen for four years. A parent who works full-time on the 'National Living Wage' (minimum wage) has been calculated to lose money as a result of these measures (Johnson, 2015). 'Large' families are to be treated as somehow complicit in creating their own poverty, whether in work or out of it. Under the Welfare Reform and Work Bill, families with more than two children will not receive tax credits or Housing Benefit for their third or subsequent children, even should they have had their two or more children prior to needing to claim any benefits, and the measure may also affect situations where two lone parents form a step-family. Families with any young people who are of working age are also hit hard; young people aged 18 to 21 will not be able to claim tax credits or Housing Benefit, forcing them into reliance on their parents. There is barely a mention that this affects young people even where they may themselves be earning parents heading a family.

The manipulation of data is set to play a key role in family policy under the Conservative government. On the one side, as welfare benefits are cut further, the annoyances caused by the current rising levels of child poverty are to be solved by a redefinition of its measurement under the Welfare Reform and Work Bill. Income-based measures of poverty are downgraded in favour of supposed 'root cause' indicators, such as family breakdown, problem debt and drug and alcohol dependency. If only those poor parents would marry, not buy items like a bed with payday loans or attempt to dull immiseration and enjoy themselves, they would not be poor. On the other side, targeted investment in human capital through the Troubled Families and other parenting intervention programmes will be aided by developments in data availability and use, with the collection and analysis of biosocial data, and the ability to link across administrative data sets. The Department of Communities and Local Government is set to link personal data that local authorities hold about families with 'multiple problems' to information collected by various central government departments, so as to monitor progress under the Troubled Families Programme. There are, however, questions about whether and how the initiative will comply with the Data Protection Act 1998 in gaining consent from the data subjects to have their information processed in this way (Marrs, 2015). It is not inconceivable that families deemed to be shirkers and scroungers will somehow be placed outside of a citizenship that accords them data privacy rights. Further, the increased ability to identify and track people and families through the exploitation of biosocial data and administrative data linkage developments may well support an even wider extension of the numbers of troubled families in order to provide families for the payment-by-results services, and profits for the private sector businesses supplying them. It was all very well identifying 120,000 troubled families and turning them around, but that cannot be the end of the supply in a marketised welfare economy.

Looking further into the future of a continued Conservative government, the explicit emphasis on marriage as a stable family life and the concomitant implicit lack of support for lone mothers seems set to continue. Recently, Steve Hilton (2015), often referred to as Cameron's 'former guru', argued that a culture of father-headed families and stable family life will counter poverty and deprivation, crime, the need for social housing, worklessness and welfare dependency, and children accessing pornography. Intervention may be pushed forward firmly into pregnancy. The US context provides us with warnings here, with a creeping criminalisation of pregnant women. Mothers-to-be using alcohol and drugs have been arrested, and mothers losing their unborn babies through stillbirth have been accused of murder under chemical endangerment laws. Finally, the emphasis on instilling 'character' in pupils in schools, lauding the values of self-confidence, respect and leadership, traits of resilience and grit, and a sense of aspiration, seems ripe ground for entrenching further divisions between families.[7]

The coalition government laid the foundations for family policy under the subsequent Conservative government. It set in place the construction of a sharp distinction between hard-working, hard-pressed families and scrounging, troubled families. The coalition planted a strategy of reduced tax payments by well-off families and reduced welfare benefits for poor families that is now being assiduously nurtured by the Conservative government. The cartoon depiction of striver versus shirker families has meant that welfare benefits have become synonymous with supporting the shirkers in the face of the reality that they are a safety net for the strivers in an insecure labour market. Increasingly, state spending and public services are residual, only for the poor and undeserving families, not for the likes of 'us'.

Note

[1] Estimates of the exact number of this minority shifted around over the years of the New Labour government (see: https://akindoftrouble.wordpress.com/troubled-families-timeline).

[2] See: http://www.theguardian.com/society/2012/feb/23/legislation-adoption-racial-lines

[3] See: https://www.gov.uk/government/news/more-than-105000-troubled-families-turned-around-saving-taxpayers-an-estimated-12-billion

[4] See: https://www.gov.uk/government/publications/european-social-fund-esf-support-for-families-with-multiple-problems

[5] Grayling made these comments in an interview on BBC2's *Newsnight* programme on 15 February 2011.

[6] See: http://www.legislation.gov.uk/uksi/2015/645/made

[7] See: https://www.gov.uk/government/news/measures-to-help-schools-instil-character-in-pupils-announced

References

Ali, S. (2014) 'Governing multicultural populations and family life', *British Journal of Sociology*, 65(1): 82–106.

Allen, G. (2011a) *Early intervention: the next steps. An independent report to Her Majesty's Government*, London: HMSO.

Allen, G. (2011b) *Early intervention: smart investment, massive savings. The second independent report to Her Majesty's Government*, London: The Stationery Office.

Bamfield, L. (2012) 'Child poverty and social mobility: taking the measure of the coalition's "new approach"', *The Political Quarterly*, 83(4): 830–37.

Barlow, A., Duncan, S. and James, G. (2002) 'New Labour, the rationality mistake and family policy in Britain', in A. Carling, S. Duncan and R. Edwards (eds) *Analysing families: morality and rationality in policy and practice*, London: Routledge, pp 110–28.

Belfield, C., Cribb, J., Hood, A. and Joyce, R. (2015) *Living standards, poverty and inequality in the UK: 2015*, Institute for Fiscal Studies Report (R107), London: Institute for Fiscal Studies.

Boddy, J., Smith, M. and Statham, J. (2011) 'Understandings of efficacy: cross-national perspectives on "what works" in supporting parents and families', *Ethics and Education*, 6(2): 181–96.

Bond-Taylor, S. (2015a) 'The politics of "anti-social" behaviour within the "Troubled Families" programme', in S. Pickard (ed) *Anti-social behaviour in Britain: Victorian and contemporary perspectives*, Basingstoke: Palgrave Macmillan, pp 141–54.

Bond-Taylor, S. (2015b) 'Dimensions of family empowerment in work with so-called "troubled" families', *Social Policy and Society*, 14(3): 371–84.

Cabinet Office (2011) *Open public services White Paper*, London: The Stationery Office.

Cameron, D. (2010) *Speech to Demos think tank*, London, 11 January.

Cameron, D. (2011) 'PM's speech on the fightback after the riots'. Available at: https://www.gov.uk/government/speeches/pms-speech-on-the-fightback-after-the-riots (accessed 10 September 2015).

Conservative Party (2015) *The Conservative Party manifesto 2015*, London: Conservative Party.

CPAG (Child Poverty Action Group) (2014) 'Policy note 2: uprating and the value of children's benefits'. Available at: http://www.cpag.org.uk/sites/default/files/CPAG-Uprating-childrens-benefits-policy-note-Dec-14.pdf (accessed 7 September 2015).

Crossley, S (2015a) 'Realising the (troubled) family, crafting the neoliberal state', *Families, Relationships and Societies* (forthcoming).

Crossley, S. (2015b) 'Policing "troubled families" through "algorithmic regulation"'. Available at: https://akindoftrouble.wordpress.com/2015/03/18/policing-troubled-families-through-algorithmic-regulation/ (accessed 7 September 2015).

DCLG (Department for Communities and Local Government) (2012) *The Troubled Families programme: financial framework for the Troubled Families programme's payment by results scheme for local authorities*, London: DCLG.

DCLG (2014a) *Troubled Families: progress information at end of September 2014 and families turned around at end of October 2014*, London: DCLG. Available at: https://www.gov.uk/government/publications/troubled-families-progress-information-at-september-2014-and-families-turned-around-at-october-2014 (accessed 7 September 2015).

DCLG (2014b) *Estimating the number of families eligible for the expanded Troubled Families programme*, London: DCLG. Available at: https://www.gov.uk/government/publications/estimating-the-number-of-families-eligible-for-the-expanded-troubled-families-programme (accessed 7 September 2015).

Department for Work and Pensions (2014) *The family test: guidance for government departments*, London: DWP.

Department for Work and Pensions and Department for Education (2011) *A new approach to child poverty: tackling the causes of disadvantage and transforming families' lives*, London: The Stationery Office.

Duncan Smith, I. (2009) 'Conservatism and society', address to the Heritage Foundation's Margaret Thatcher Center for Freedom, Washington USA, 9 March. Available at http://www.conservativehome.blogs.com/torydiary/files/ids_heritage_address.pdf (accessed 27 November 2015).

Edwards, R. and Gillies, V. (2004) 'Support in parenting: values and consensus concerning who to turn to', *Journal of Social Policy*, 33(4): 627–47.

Edwards, R., Gillies, V. and Horsley, N. (2015) 'Brain science and early years policy: hopeful ethos or "cruel optimism"?', *Critical Social Policy*, 35(2): 167–87.

Field, F. (2010) *The Foundation Years: Preventing poor children from becoming poor adults – The report of the Independent Review on Poverty and Life Chances*, London: Cabinet Office.

Gillies, V. (2014) 'Troubling families: parenting and the politics of early intervention', in S. Wragg and J. Pilcher (eds) *Thatcher's grandchildren*, Basingstoke: Palgrave Macmillan, pp 204–24.

Harker, R. and Heath, S. (2014) *Children in care in England: Statistics*, London: House of Commons Library.

Hayton, R. (2015) 'Cameronite conservatism and the politics of marriage under the UK coalition government', *Families, Relationships and Societies*, 4(1): 151–6.

Hayton, R. and McEnhill, L. (2015) 'Cameron's Conservative Party, social liberalism and social justice', *British Politics*, 10(2): 131–47.

Hendrick, H. (2003) *Child welfare: historical dimensions, contemporary debate*, Bristol: The Policy Press.

Hilton, S. (2015) 'Come on, Dave, it's time to stand up for marriage', *Mail Online*, 21 May. Available at: http://www.dailymail.co.uk/debate/article-3090327/Come-Dave-s-time-stand-marriage-writes-PM-s-close-friend-former-guru-STEVE-HILTON.html (accessed 28 June 2015).

Home Office (1998) *Supporting families: A consultation document*, Home Office and Voluntary and Community Unit, London: The Stationery Office.

Home Office (2006) *Respect action plan*, London: Home Office.

Johnson, P. (2015) 'Summer post-Budget briefing', Institute for Fiscal Studies, 9 July. Available at: http://www.ifs.org.uk/uploads/publications/budgets/Budgets%202015/Summer/opening_remarks.pdf (accessed 7 September 2015).

Kennedy, S. (2015) 'Welfare Reform and Work Bill [Bill 51 of 2015–16]', House of Commons Library Briefing Paper No. 07252. Available at: http://services.parliament.uk/bills/2015-16/welfarereformandwork/documents.html (accessed 7 September 2015).

Kilkey, M. (2015) '"Getting tough" on the family-immigration route: a blurring of the "them" and "us" in anti-immigration rhetoric', in L. Foster, A. Brunton, C. Deeming and T. Haux (eds) *In defence of welfare 2*, Bristol: Policy Press, pp 49–51.

Leadsom, A., Field, F., Burstow, P. and Lucas, C. (2013) '1001 critical days: the importance of the conception to age two period. A cross-party manifesto'. Available at: http://www.andrealeadsom.com/downloads/1001cdmanifesto.pdf (accessed 7 September 2015).

Levitas, R. (2012) 'There may be "trouble" ahead: what we know about those 120,000 "troubled" families', Poverty and Social Exclusion in the UK Policy Response Series No 3, University of Bristol. Available at: http://www.poverty.ac.uk/system/files/WP%20Policy%20Response%20No.3-%20%20'Trouble'%20ahead%20(Levitas%20Final%2021April2012).pdf (accessed 7 September 2015).

Lister, R. (2003) 'Investing in the citizen-workers of the future: transformations in citizenship and the State under New Labour', *Social Policy and Administration*, 37(5): 427–43.

Lupton, R., with Burchardt, T., Fitzergerald, A., Hills, J., McKnight, A., Obolenskaya, P., Stewart, K., Thomson, S., Tunstall, R. and Vizard, P. (2015) *The coalition's social policy record 2010–2015*, Summary Research Report 4, January, London: Trust for London.

Macvarish, J., Lee, E. and Lowe, P. (2015) 'Neuroscience and family policy: what becomes of the parent?', *Critical Social Policy*, 35(2): 248–69.

Marrs, C. (2015) 'Troubled Families data sharing project announced', PublicTechnology.net, 25 August. Available at: https://www.publictechnology.net/articles/news/troubled-families-data-sharing-project-announcedhttps://www.publictechnology.net/articles/news/troubled-families-data-sharing-project-announced (accessed 7 September 2015).

Milbourne, L. (2009) 'Remodelling the third sector: advancing collaboration or competition in community-based initiatives?', *Journal of Social Policy*, 38(2): 277–97.

Millie, A. (2009) *Antisocial behaviour*, Milton Keynes: Open University Press.

Montgomerie, T. (2012) 'A conservative case for gay marriage'. Available at: http://www.conservativehome.com/thetorydiary/2012/02/a-conservative-case-for-gay-marriage.html (accessed 25 November 2015).

Nixon, J., Hunter, C. and Parr, S. (2006) *Anti-social behaviour intensive family support projects: an evaluation of six pioneering projects*, London: Department for Communities and Local Government. Available at: http://webarchive.nationalarchives.gov.uk/20100405140447/http:/www.communities.gov.uk/documents/housing/pdf/hrs230.pdf (accessed 7 September 2015).

Pink News (2012) 'Iain Duncan Smith defies Catholic church to back marriage for gay couples', 28 April. Available at: http://www.pinknews.co.uk/2012/04/08/iain-duncan-smith-defies-Catholic-church-to-back-marriage-for-gay-couples/ (accessed 26 November 2015).

Portes, J. (2015) 'A troubling attitude to statistics', National Institute of Economic and Social Research. Available at: http://www.niesr.ac.uk/blog/troubling-attitude-statistics#.VctymBtRGvE (accessed 7 September 2015).

Rose, N. (1987) 'Beyond the public/private division: law, power and the family', *Journal of Law and Society*, 14(1): 61–76.

Serougi, N. (2015) 'Austerity as ideology', *Discover Society*, 1 April. Available at: http://discoversociety.org/2015/04/01/austerity-as-ideology/ (accessed 7 September 2015).

Shildrick, T., MacDonald, R., Furlong, A., Roden, J. and Crow, R. (2012) *Are 'cultures of worklessness' passed down the generations?*, York: Joseph Rowntree Foundation. Available at: https://www.jrf.org.uk/report/are-cultures-worklessness-passed-down-generations (accessed 7 September 2015).

Slater, T. (2012) 'The myth of "Broken Britain": welfare reform and the production of ignorance', *Antipode*, 46(4): 948–69.

Social Mobility and Child Poverty Commission (2013) *State of the Nation 2013: Social Mobility and Child Poverty in Great Britain*, London: HMSO.

Stratton, A. (2013) 'Plan to divert benefits of troubled families scrapped', BBC News, 26 September. Available at: http://www.bbc.co.uk/news/uk-politics-24286726 (accessed 7 September 2015).

The Observer (2012) 'Demonisation of the poor is taking place ... horrible things will happen', 17 November. Available at: http://www.theguardian.com/politics/2012/nov/17/demonisation-poor (accessed 25 November 2015).

The Times (1998) 'The Tory Mods and Rockers', 6 July.

Toynbee, P. (2015) 'Iain Duncan Smith's family values won't help the poor', *The Guardian*, 11 March. Available at: http://www.theguardian.com/commentisfree/2015/mar/10/iain-duncan-smith-family-values-married-couples-allowance-tax (accessed 7 September 2015).

Van Acker, L. (2015) 'Investing in couple relationship education in the UK: a gender perspective', *Social Policy and Society*, 14(1): 1–14.

TWELVE

One step forward, two steps back: children, young people and the Conservative–Liberal Democrat coalition

Harriet Churchill

Introduction

After 13 years of Third Way reforms under Labour, the formation of the Conservative–Liberal Democrat coalition government in 2010 signalled change, continuity and uncertainty. The coalition's *Programme for government* (Cabinet Office, 2010) espoused a firm commitment to the Conservatives' deficit reduction plan and neoliberal welfare state reforms. However, the coalition also pledged to work towards the 2020 child poverty targets that Labour had established. There were also plans to introduce child and youth reforms that took forward the coalition parties' shared policy goals and constituted dimensions of change and continuity in childcare, early intervention, education, public health, parenting and family services, and work–family policies. However, there remained much scope for conflict between the coalition partners. Prior to the 2010 election, the Liberal Democrats had called for more extensive investment and reform in welfare state support and services for children, youth, parents and families (Marshall and Laws, 2004). The Conservatives' agenda, in contrast, sought reduced and rationalised welfare state support (Conservative Party, 2010). Moreover, many child-centred and youth-focused Conservative policies were framed in terms of their 'Broken Britain' campaign, which emphasised 'five main pathways to poverty' – 'welfare dependency, educational failure, family breakdown, severe debt and poor health' (CSJ, 2006, p 2; see also Conservative Party, 2010). While justifying public expenditure cutbacks and pro-market welfare state reforms, this agenda also incorporated increasing interest among Conservatives in early childhood and parenting and family interventions and services (CSJ, 2006). The coalition's *Programme for government* primarily promoted Conservative agendas in these areas (Cabinet Office, 2010), but the Liberal Democrats were influential in shaping subsequent policy developments.

To review the coalition years, this chapter initially situates this period within a broader context of prior developments and debates. It then examines the coalition government's initial programme and subsequent policy developments. The analysis highlights three aspects of policy change and reform: reductions in cash support for children, young people and families; the reframing of child poverty in terms of the Conservatives' 'five pathways to poverty' thesis, the Liberal Democrats' social mobility agenda and early intervention developments; and child protection and children's social care reforms. The analysis highlights change and continuity, conflicts and contradictions, in social policies for children and young people during the coalition period. It recognises some constructive developments, but critiques the detrimental implications of the reductions in welfare state support and services for many children and young people, and their diminished social citizenship.

Labour's Third Way child-centred approach

During the 1980s and 1990s, there were growing concerns about children, young people and families in the UK. Relative child poverty sharply rose between 1983 and 1993, from 15% of families living on incomes half the national average to 29% (Brewer et al, 2011). Only 45% of 16 year olds achieved five GCSE qualifications at grades C and above in 1997, and while unemployment overall fell from 1994, youth unemployment (of 16–24 year olds) continued to rise, standing at 14% in early 1998 (Lupton and Obolenskaya, 2013). There were stark social class differences in life expectancy, physical and mental health, and teenage pregnancy. The numbers of children and young people on the Child Protection Register, in care and in custody increased.

Oriented towards absolute notions of poverty, the New Right-influenced Conservative government of 1979–97 had dismissed concerns about relative poverty. Rather, many trends were explained with reference to 'the collapse of the family' and 'an emerging social underclass', both of which were associated with increasing rates of welfare dependency, the latter defined by Murray (1996, p 19) as incorporating 'undesirable behaviour, including drug taking, crime, illegitimacy, failure to hold down a job, truancy from school and casual violence'. To address these problems, the Conservatives curtailed welfare rights and sought to promote parental responsibilities, employment and marriage as part of a broad agenda of New Right social policies, incorporating New Public Management and marketisation, and economic and labour market deregulation. The 'family breakdown' and 'social underclass' discourses deflected attention away from many social policies and socio-economic changes contributing to social problems, including: economic and labour market restructuring (such as economic globalisation, a decline in manufacturing, wider income inequality and an increase in low-paid and more precarious lower-skilled employment); social inequalities related to ethnicity, citizenship, disability, age and gender; and gendered responsibilities in relation to family, children and social care (Churchill, 2011). However, from 1989, there were developments in support for working mothers/parents (eg Family Credit, childcare vouchers), and youth services, child welfare, family support and children's rights (including the Children Act 1989 and the 1989 United Nations Convention on the Rights of the Child).

New Labour (1997–2010) then introduced major changes, pursuing Third Way, centre-left, evidence-based 'modern' social policies, summed up as 'social justice ends via market means', and promoting social inclusion (Powell, 2002). Building on New Right developments, they took forward economic deregulation and expanded New Public Management and marketisation (Powell, 2002). Compared to the New Right, however, social policies addressed many social disadvantages, including labour market disadvantage, low pay, social discrimination, educational disadvantages, area-based deprivation and access to, and standards in, public services (Churchill, 2011). However, informed by centre-left social underclass theories, problems of welfare dependency, personal and parental irresponsibility, social deviance, anti-social behaviour, and low aspirations were understood as key behavioural reasons for social exclusion. Notions of the undeserving poor also incorporated concerns about immigration and citizenship claims (Equalities Commission, 2007). Labour's discourse of 'rights and responsibilities' crystallised these concerns (Powell, 2002). Greater welfare state support and higher investment in public services was combined with disciplinary and active social policies.

The Labour years saw major child-centred developments. First, this was because poverty was understood in relative and absolute terms, and children were positioned as the deserving poor (although not some children, as indicated earlier). Labour pledged to halve child poverty by 2010, and to eradicate it by 2020. Second, Labour increasingly sought multiple social policy goals via child-centred social investments and reforms. Third, these two agendas, and Labour's Third Way approach, generated new imperatives to support, activate, regulate and enforce parental responsibilities as adult worker-citizens and as parents.

Several policies sought to increase family incomes, promote mothers' employment and promote work–family balance (tax credits, benefit increases, work-related conditions to benefit receipt, welfare-to-work programmes, childcare rights and family-friendly employment policies). Others supported young people's post-16 education opportunities (Education Maintenance Allowance [EMA] and legislation raising the school leaving age). Measures expanded legal notions of parental responsibility and introduced statutory powers to discipline irresponsible parents in these respects, especially around school attendance and youth behaviour. Tough youth crime prevention included lowering the age of criminal responsibility to 10 years. Labour increased investment in universal and targeted children's services, setting national standards and monitoring performance closely. Free part-time pre-school provision was introduced for three and four year olds and early years' services and parenting education initiatives were expanded. New duties were placed on local children's services to promote child well-being. Reforms sought better-coordinated children's services via comprehensive record keeping and information sharing, common needs and risk assessment frameworks, and integrated service models, such as children's centres and extended schools. From 1998 to 2005, there were many positive trends, with falling child poverty, rising educational standards, better health trends and falling rates of youth offending (Equalities Commission, 2007; Brewer et al, 2011). However, from 2004/05, many trends stagnated or reversed. In addition, some problems, such as poor mental health and child neglect, appeared to continue to rise.

From a progressive perspective, there were many problems with Labour's approach. Disadvantages and discrimination faced by vulnerable young people, disabled people or minority ethnic groups were not sufficiently addressed, while market-led childcare expansion was associated with variable quality and rising costs (Equalities Commission, 2007). Access to specialist support remained limited due to rising needs, social stigma and restrictive eligibility criteria (Churchill, 2011). Children and young people tended to be conceptualised as 'future adult citizens' rather than 'child citizens' in their own right, the latter being important to enhancing rights to 'participation, provision and protection'.

Developments from 2006 incorporated progressive reforms (such as the Equalities Act 2010 and the Child Poverty Act 2010), especially at local and devolved government levels, as well as further disciplinary measures. There was greater concern about 'deep social exclusion', symbolised by long-term welfare receipt, 'anti-social problem families', 'chaotic lifestyles' and families with 'entrenched complex, multiple problems' (Social Exclusion Taskforce, 2006). Stricter welfare-to-work conditions were introduced alongside more interventionist family services, such as Family Intervention Programmes (FiPs), targeted at 'the most socially excluded families', providing intensive and assertive 'whole family' support and delivered on the basis of behaviour change conditions. After the 2007/08 financial crisis, the banking sector bailout and subsequent economic downturn, Labour's economic and social policies were more strongly criticised. In addition, the death of a young boy known to children's social care services led to a highly political media critique of local services and Labour's children's services reforms. Ministers strongly blamed local services and initiated social work reforms.

Towards the coalition's Programme for government

The 2010 election was dominated by economic recovery concerns. The Conservatives emphasised 'urgent action' to 'reduce the record public deficit' (Conservative Party, 2010, pp 7–8). They criticised Labour's 'big government' approach and stated that they would 'rebalance the economy', 'reducing reliance on public sector jobs' and promoting 'private sector-led economic recovery' (Conservative Party, 2010, p 5). Their 'big government to Big Society' discourse incorporated other concerns about citizen–state–market relations, proposing more localism, decentralisation, de-bureaucratisation, deregulation, community social action and independent sector provision (Conservative Party, 2010, p 41; see also Chapter Three). The Liberal Democrats proposed to halve the public deficit, while they also sought to reduce 'bureaucracy and regulation' and promote localism and decentralisation in public services, as well as to address threats to civil liberties (Liberal Democrats, 2010).

Informed by these agendas, the Conservatives and Liberal Democrats set out similar and different child and youth policies, informed by recent party policy reviews. Under David Cameron, the Conservatives had 'modernised' family policies and were more supportive of developments in childcare and work–family policies. However, reflecting the longer-standing concerns about an emerging social underclass and problems of 'family breakdown', the Conservatives developed their 'social breakdown' critique of Labour's approach (CSJ, 2006). This critique emphasised 'five main pathways to disadvantage': family breakdown, educational failure, economic dependency, indebtedness and addiction. Policy proposals focused on the first three problems. Family breakdown was defined as 'family dissolution and dadlessness' and 'family dysfunction', and was associated with many 'acute social problems' (CSJ, 2006, p 17). Policy proposals sought to favour 'couples and marriage' in the benefits and tax system, as well as to maintain investment in evidence-based parenting, family intervention and relationship support services, with preference for independent sector provision (Conservative Party, 2010). To tackle 'education failure', the Conservatives proposed a Pupil Premium, funding to schools for struggling pupils, and expansion of Labour's academies programme (more independently operating schools, encouraged to secure private and charity sector sponsorship). To 'tackle economic and welfare dependency', welfare benefits and tax credits would be restricted, work-related welfare conditions would be enhanced, and welfare-to-work schemes would be replaced by a new Work Programme, delivered by independent providers paid by results. Informed by all of these concerns, the Conservatives became more interested in early intervention approaches, particularly 'long-term investments' in 'early childhood' and 'parental interventions' targeted at the 'most disadvantaged and dysfunctional families', as cost-effective policies to reduce 'intergenerational cycles of poverty' (Allen and Duncan-Smith, 2008, p 15). The Conservatives therefore pledged to: 'take a new approach to early intervention'; refocus children's centres on supporting 'the neediest families'; encourage private and voluntary sector provision delivered on a payment-by-results basis; expand universal heath visiting; and take 'a new approach to families with multiple problems' (Conservative Party, 2010, p 41). Several aspects of the Conservatives' agenda have been described as incorporating recent developments in neoliberal paternalism, summed up by Parton (2014, p 140) thus:

> Under neoliberal paternalism, the reform of the state, and state welfare in particular, is informed by the new public management practices of contracting out and 'payment by results' together with a much greater emphasis on a coercive paternalism that strives to strengthen labour discipline and social behaviour, particularly among the social underclass.

In addition, this agenda incorporated greater interest in early childhood policies, services and programmes as measures to promote 'readiness for school' and to reduce intergenerational cycles of 'disadvantage and dysfunction'. This resonated with developments under Labour, but reframed early intervention more narrowly as tackling the problems associated with the social underclass.

The Liberal Democrats had also developed their policies significantly. Resonating with Labour and the Conservatives, *The Orange Book*, written by leading Liberal Democrats (Marshall and Laws, 2004), emphasised that 'the early years of a child's life are critical' and that 'the home environment and family background are the strongest influence on children, particular young children' (Webb and Holland, 2004, p 237). However, 'family processes, family relationships and good parenting are key', 'not family form' (Webb and Holland, 2004, p 239). Webb and Holland (2004) detailed proposals to: scrap the welfare-to-work obligations for mothers with children under 11 years old; scrap lone-parent employment targets; improve support for disabled children; extend paternity and parental leave rights; extend flexible working rights; invest in high-quality and more subsidised childcare; provide free childcare for children from 18 months old; extend duties to provide youth services; invest in more parenting and relationship education services for parents and young people; and strengthen children's rights. At the 2010 election, however, some of these policies were not taken forward. Instead, as part of austerity measures, reduced tax credits for better-off families were outlined. Proposals did however include free part-time (20 hours a week) childcare for children from 18 months old, and better shared parental leave and flexible working rights (Liberal Democrats, 2010). They also set out plans for a Pupil Premium scheme with £2.5 billion funding (Liberal Democrats, 2010, p 34). There would be youth-focused reforms, including 'scrapping university tuition fees', a minimum wage rate for 16–18 year olds, more support for post-16 education and stronger statutory duties to provide youth services. The manifesto also promised child protection reforms and to legislate to bring the UN Convention on the Rights of the Child fully into UK law.

Following the formation of the coalition government, the *Programme for government* stated that 'the most urgent task is to tackle our record public deficit', 'mainly to be achieved by reducing public spending' (Cabinet Office, 2010, p 15). However, 'those on low incomes' would be protected and the commitment to the 2020 child poverty targets would be maintained (Cabinet Office, 2010, p 15). The Conservatives' welfare state and 'social breakdown' reforms figured prominently. There were pledges to introduce a Pupil Premium and shared parental leave, but no mention of the Liberal Democrats' policies for post-16 education, youth, children's rights, childcare or child protection reforms.

The severity of the public expenditure cuts soon became apparent. In June 2010, the Emergency Budget set out targets to eliminate the structural deficit (see also Chapter Two), to reduce public expenditure overall by 19% by 2014/15 and to reduce the public deficit as a proportion of gross domestic product (GDP) from 11% to 1.1% by 2015/16 (HM Treasury, 2010a, p 16). The 2010 Spending Review then stated that the budget of the Department for Work and Pensions would fall by 26% by 2014/15, including £11 billion savings in welfare spending (later increased to £18 billion) (HM Treasury, 2010b). Central government funding to local authorities would fall by 27% by 2015 (HM Treasury, 2010b). Schools (5–16 years) and National Health Service (NHS) spending were to increase, but the Department for Education (DfE) budget was to fall overall by around 3% by 2015, while the Department of Health (DH) was to make £20 million efficiency savings. In June 2010, however, Nick Clegg announced that he would be chairing a 'Childhood and Families Taskforce', indicating a potential leading role for the Liberal Democrats in this policy domain.

Reduced cash support for children and young people

Under the coalition government, there were significant changes in cash support for children, families and young people. EMA, the financial support for disadvantaged young people to remain in post-16 education in England, was abolished and replaced with a less generous bursary distributed by education providers. Tax credits for families with children were restricted and reduced via rate freezes and reductions, changes to eligibility and reduced support for childcare costs (reduced to 70% of childcare costs during 2011–15). The coalition also controversially withdrew universal Child Benefit. Both party leaders had declared that Child Benefit would not be means-tested, but subsequently argued that high earners needed to make economic sacrifices given the public deficit. Critical of the proposals, the Liberal Democrats pressed for less severe cuts, with final changes leading to families on household incomes of £50,000–£60,000 per annum gradually losing Child Benefit via the tax system (rather than all higher-rate taxpayers). It could be argued that relatively better-off families lost small amounts of income. However, Child Benefit has been an important source of child-centred expenditure. Moreover, collectively, the Child Benefit and tax credit changes substantially reduced family incomes, especially for lone-parent families, who lost around £1,600 per annum during 2011–13, while couple families lost around £1,300 per annum (Reed and Elson, 2014). However, tax reforms raised incomes for married couples, low earners and working parents via the new marriage tax allowances, an increase in the tax threshold (to £10,600 per annum by 2015) and childcare tax breaks.

Welfare benefit cutbacks and reforms significantly targeted children, young people and families. Welfare benefits were reduced via low annual benefit uprates, reduced Housing Allowance (HA) (cash support for low-income private rental tenants), reduced Housing Benefit (HB) eligibility for 25–35 year olds, 'unoccupied bedrooms' deductions to HB for social housing tenants (the 'bedroom tax') and the new benefit cap (total annual household benefits to not exceed £26,000 per annum). The coalition reassessed all disability and incapacity benefit recipients using stricter medical assessments in an attempt to reduce claimant numbers. From 2013, Universal Credit was introduced, a new welfare system replacing Working and Child Tax Credits, Income Support, Employment Support Allowance (ESA), HB and HA (see Chapter Eight). It provided a basic allowance, with additional payments for children, disability, housing and childcare, for those out of work and in paid work but on low incomes. It also introduced a stricter system of work-related conditions and benefit sanctions requiring engagement in the Work Programme, the new welfare-to-work programme (National Audit Office, 2014). Lone parents with children aged under one constituted the 'no work conditions' group, while young people (16–24 years) and lone parents with children aged five and over were in the 'full work conditions' group. The rationales for these changes were the deficit reduction plan and tackling welfare dependency (HM Treasury, 2010b). The Work Programme, however, performed poorly in the initial years, but then improved its results, particularly in respect of supporting youth employment (National Audit Office, 2014). Overall, there were increases in youth employment under the coalition, and youth unemployment fell to 13.1% by June 2015, but there were concerns about the extent to which youths took up part-time, lower-paid and less secure employment. Young people also saw their median incomes fall by around 14% from 2007/08 to 2012/13, more than double the fall in adult earnings (National Audit Office, 2014). Support for lone parents and those affected by disability was criticised as limited and insufficient via the Work Programme and in respect of help with childcare costs. The welfare reforms, in many ways, constituted further moves towards 'workfare' for unemployed young people and lone parents with children age five and over. The Liberals Democrats, however, claimed they prevented more severe welfare and benefit cuts.

Although these reforms led to significant savings in Child Benefit, tax credits and Jobseeker's Allowance expenditure from 2010 to 2015 (although below target), spending on housing and disability benefits actually rose due to increasing housing rents, levels of need and the costs of appeals and reforms (Hood and Phillips, 2015). However, the detrimental impacts on children's and teenagers' material security were potentially severe. Hood and Phillips (2015) reported that 600,000 families were affected by the bedroom tax, 68% of which were affected by poor health or disabled, and 50% of which were in rent arrears six months later. Reed and Elson (2014) estimated that 89% of households affected by the benefit cap included children, losing an average of £70 a week. A longitudinal study of families in receipt of HB in London captured the qualitative effects (Chowdhury and Cass, 2014). Parents reported that benefit reductions, rent increases and increased living costs combined to severely restrict their expenditure, which led to prioritising paying for bills and necessities and reducing spending on social activities, transport and 'non-necessities'. Some were in rent arrears, under threat of eviction. Moving to cheaper housing was a difficult and distressing choice to make – due to moving costs, a lack of housing availability and disruption to children's school and family lives. Others were evicted and living in temporary housing, placing costs on councils and stress on families. Recent figures have also shown an increase in absolute child poverty (after housing costs) from 27% to 31% between 2010 and 2014 (Department for Work and Pensions, 2015, p 53). Seventy per cent of children in workless households were classified as in absolute poverty in 2013/14 (Department for Work and Pensions, 2015).

Reframing childhood disadvantage, refocusing social investment

According to the coalition government, the changes just discussed were necessary. They were driven by the Conservatives' welfare state reform agenda and its 'five pathways to poverty' thesis (Conservative Party, 2010). This section illustrates how these agendas, alongside Liberal Democrat social mobility policies, sought to reframe the problem of child poverty under the coalition. This reframing was informed by three policy reviews about early years and early intervention commissioned in 2010. One review was completed by the Labour MP Frank Field (2010, p 5), whose Inquiry into Life Chances and Poverty set out a 'new approach to child poverty', focused on 'preventing poor children becoming poor adults'. This approach emphasised that 'children's life chances are heavily predicated on their development in the first five years of life', and argued that in comparison to 'money', 'health in pregnancy, maternal health, family background, parental education, loving parenting with good boundaries, and opportunities for child learning and development' were the crucial factors (Field, 2010, pp 5–6). Field proposed redirecting welfare savings to investments in 'Foundation Years' services – health, parenting, childcare, early education and children's centres. He also proposed new 'early child development' and 'family risk' indicators to improve data about children's life chances.

Another influential review was Allen's (2011) Review into Early Intervention, which reiterated arguments set out in his joint publication with Duncan-Smith (Allen and Duncan-Smith, 2008). Similarly to Field, there was reference to brain development research that, for Allen (2011), suggested that young children with problems became 'emotionally wired' to have long-term psychosocial difficulties and disorders. Targeted early childhood and parenting interventions (in the first three years of childhood) were urgently needed, 'before it is too late', while remedial interventions were 'more costly and least effective' (Allen, 2011, p 6). Allen recommended: a Foundation Years strategy; child development and readiness for school checks for 0–5 year olds; evidence-based programmes; a National Parenting Campaign; an Early Intervention Foundation; 15 early intervention place-based pilots; and pooled community budgets and public–private social investment finance schemes.

While wide-ranging support and high-quality childcare, parenting and family support services are valuable early childhood social investments, both of these reviews marginalised the role of socio-economic factors (including income, wealth, social capital and cultural capital) in intergenerational patterns of socio-economic advantage and disadvantage. They also provided a limited understanding of the multiple factors, contexts and relationships that shape parental practices and child development and well-being, including children's own agency in these processes, and the value of social investment throughout childhood and youth (McAuley and Rose, 2010). Further, there have been strong criticisms of the brain development research most cited (eg Featherstone et al, 2014).

Nevertheless, these reviews informed policy developments. As required by the Child Poverty Act 2010, in early 2011, the coalition published its Child Poverty Strategy (HM Government, 2011a). This was launched by Iain Duncan Smith, as Secretary of State for Work and Pensions. On the same day, Nick Clegg launched the Social Mobility Strategy (HM Government, 2011b). The Child Poverty Strategy reframed the problem of child poverty in terms of the

Conservatives' 'five pathways to poverty' thesis. It criticised Labour's approach of reducing relative child poverty rates via tax credits and benefit increases, claiming that this approach 'trapped claimants in a culture of welfare dependency' (HM Government, 2011a, p 8). Rather than relative child poverty measures, new 'severe child poverty' and 'childhood circumstances' measures were later adopted. Resonating with Labour's social inclusion approach, poverty was defined as 'a lack of opportunities, aspirations and skills' (HM Government, 2011a, p 4). The strategy, however, refocused on the 'root causes of childhood disadvantage' – 'educational failure, worklessness, family breakdown, severe debt and poor health, including alcohol and drug addiction' (HM Government, 2011a, p 63). Reforms largely took forward Conservative policies in welfare, schools, health, early intervention, parenting and family policy areas. The Social Mobility Strategy (HM Government, 2011b), however, complemented the Conservatives' 'five pathways policies' with Liberal Democrat policies to promote social mobility. It set out 'a life cycle framework' to 'breaking intergenerational cycles of disadvantage' (HM Government, 2011b, p 5), incorporating Liberal Democrat work–family, education, early years and youth policies. The same year, a Foundation Years Strategy was published (Department for Education and Department of Health, 2011). This stated that the aim of the foundation years' services was to ensure that children were 'ready to learn at school', and summarised the key reforms already described in the two strategies above (Department for Education and Department of Health, 2011, p 6). New pre-school learning summaries (for two year olds from childcare providers) and child health checks (0–5) would be introduced.

The government's response to the August 2011 summer riots further shaped these agendas. Rhetorically, this strongly emphasised the Conservatives' social underclass and family breakdown discourses. Subsequently, the Troubled Families Programme (TFP) was launched, with £450 million, to 'turn around the lives of 120,000 of the most troubled families in England' (DCLG, 2012; see also Chapter Eleven). The programme provided local funding for family intervention services, primarily targeted at families with co-occurring problems of long-term welfare reliance, poor school attendance and youth anti-social behaviour. The scheme operated on a payment-by-results basis, with local authorities receiving funding for engaging target families and then securing specified family outcomes (DCLG, 2012). Additionally, £10 million was provided to 33 areas to develop youth crime and gang reduction schemes based on locally devised strategies and inter-agency partnerships.

Having illustrated the reframing of the problem of child poverty around the Conservatives' 'five root causes' thesis and the Liberal Democrats' early years and social mobility policies, this section now selectively reviews several main developments. While a number of valuable reforms were introduced, there were many limitations. Further, funding cutbacks and the emphasis on independent sector provision led to the loss of many valuable services and sources of expertise, reducing child and youth access to support services.

From 2011, several funding streams for early intervention services (including children's centres, parenting support, disabled children, youth crime prevention and family intervention services) were combined and provided to local authorities as the Early Intervention Grant (EIG). This provided more local budgetary control but was less generous, 11% lower compared to 2010 (FPI, 2012). Coupled with the fall in spending to local authorities overall, there were therefore severe budgetary constraints on services, especially: children's centres; public health services; youth offending/youth services; family support workers; parenting initiatives; child and youth mental health services (CAMHS); and community services, such as recreation and leisure (FPI, 2012; UNISON, 2014).

Investment in the foundation years, though, included the introduction of free part-time (15 hours weekly) childcare for disadvantaged two year olds, with plans to provide places for 40% by 2015 (Department for Education and Department of Health, 2011). Ofsted (2015) reported that where two year olds received high-quality provision, they were likely to benefit, particularly in their speech, language, numeracy, literacy and social development. Overall, according to Ofsted (2015, p 9), quality ratings improved in childcare and pre-school provision, with 13% rated as outstanding, 72% good and 13% requiring improvement, while 1% was inadequate. However, concerns remain about average quality standards in poorer areas. Further, 42% of two year olds (113,000) did not take up the free childcare available by 2015 (Ofsted, 2015), and with the emphasis on independent sector provision, children's centres were no longer required to provide childcare. This led to a fall in what was generally well-respected high-quality childcare provision by around a third by 2013 (CRAE, 2013).

Foundation years' reforms included investment in parenting programmes: Family Nurse Partnership (FNP) programmes (intensive multi-agency support led by family nurses for young mothers with infant children); health visitors with an extended role (and a target of 4,200 new staff by 2015); and voluntary sector parenting, family and relationship support services (HM Government, 2011a, p 63). The

Early Intervention Foundation was launched in 2013. Parenting and FNP evaluations reported beneficial outcomes for maternal and child health, but also highlighted challenges in parental engagement, high levels of poverty among families and gaps in specialist support services (Barnes and Henderson, 2012). After considerable criticism about welfare cuts in particular, there were several announcements about early years support from Nick Clegg in 2013/14. These included free school meals for infant schoolchildren (then up to seven year olds), an important measure, as well as an increase in childcare costs support via tax credits and new tax breaks for working parents (from 2015). In addition, the Liberal Democrats were central to the shared parental leave reforms, which from 2015, provided mothers and fathers with more extensive paid leave entitlements.

School reforms included the expansion of academies, encouraging more schools in England to receive funding directly from central government, secure independent sector sponsors and have more autonomy (see Chapter Six). 'Failing' schools were required to become academies. Free schools were also encouraged, enabling educators, parents or charities to set up more autonomous schools. By December 2014, there were 4,344 academy schools (mainly secondary schools) and around 280 free schools (Education Select Committee, 2015). Academies overall improved GCSE attainment rates more than state-maintained schools from 2010 to 2013, but the strategies behind the figures were debated. The Academies Commission (2013) criticised selective admissions procedures and higher rates of school exclusions among academies.

The Pupil Premium was introduced, amounting to £1,300 per pupil by 2014. Ofsted (2013) evidenced that many schools targeted this funding well, but raised concerns about whether the funding was being spent in the most cost-effective ways. Further, the TFP contributed to a reduced risk of school exclusion for many young people (DCLG, 2014). Although not without problems, these were all valuable developments in targeted pupil support. However, contradictory pressures (the move away from extended schools and funding cutbacks) led to reduced school-based and area-based health and social care services (CRAE, 2013). Given the accessible nature of school support services for young people, however, many local authorities took steps to maintain developments. The Welsh government placed a statutory duty on schools to provide counselling and health services.

Youth reforms included the post-16 education bursary that replaced EMA, more vocational education for 14–19 year olds, youth apprenticeship schemes and the National Citizens Service

(HM Government, 2011b). In contrast, further education suffered an estimated 33% reduction in funding from 2010 to 2015 (CRAE, 2013), the well-known Connexions service for 13–19 year olds was abolished and, as noted earlier, youth services were particularly affected by spending cuts (UNISON, 2014).

Child protection and children's social care reforms

The coalition period was a time of heightened child protection concerns, and several social work and social care reforms were introduced. Taking forward Labour's reforms initiated in 2009, in 2010, the coalition government commissioned Eileen Munro (2011) to undertake a *Review of child protection*. Munro's report criticised the bureaucratic procedural approach to children's social work, where administration had come to dominate practice, and performance was measured in terms of procedural compliance – meeting timescales for referral responses and assessments, completing paperwork, accounting for the number of family visits completed, and the speed of case closure. Munro felt that there was inadequate engagement and direct work with children, youth and families, and limited focus on the quality of services and better outcomes for children, issues compounded by gaps in specialist support, rehabilitation and therapeutic services. Her report called for more effective and responsive 'early help' services delivered via multi-agency and inter-professional safeguarding teams led by advanced social workers, and stronger entitlements to early help and family support. The coalition responded with revised *Working together* guidelines for inter-agency responses to child welfare concerns (HM Government, 2013). Local authorities were given more autonomy to develop their approaches in support services, child welfare needs and risk assessments, and timescales for assessments. There were also major changes to social work education and professional training. In addition, the coalition launched an action plan to reduce violence against girls and women (HM Government, 2012). This included measures to improve police and legal responses and investigations, introduce legal changes, and fund voluntary sector sexual violence support services. The action plan also encouraged schools to provide better sex and relationships education, covering issues of sexism, bullying and sexual consent. Further action was taken to attempt to detect and prosecute abusive images and material on the internet. This was accompanied by sexual health and sex education guidelines for schools to promote awareness of sexual health, consent and services, although CRAE (2013) criticised the failure to introduce stronger duties on schools for sexual health, sex education and relationships education, especially given the autonomy granted to academies and free schools over these aspects of the curriculum.

Although many local authorities introduced child protection and child welfare changes, a report by the Education Select Committee (2012) was critical of progress. It reported rising demand for children's social care and increasing thresholds, with concerns that the thresholds for responses to child neglect were too high, limiting preventative and protective actions (Education Select Committee, 2012, p 3). It was critical of the fact that the safeguarding needs of teenagers, including youths in care, were not taken seriously enough because of a greater focus on safeguarding young children, and because social workers tended to focus on problematic behaviour rather than consider signs of neglect, abuse and exploitation. The Education Select Committee also criticised an inadequate focus on young people who perpetrate abuse and domestic violence. It called for more school-based and community initiatives to raise awareness of children's rights and respectful relationships, and reiterated Munro's call for better entitlements to support and services. Subsequently, Scotland introduced child and youth entitlements to advocates in child welfare and social care services, as will Wales from 2016 (NSPCC, 2015).

During the coalition years, there were several high-profile child abuse scandals, including the discovery of decades of child sexual abuse orchestrated by the late Jimmy Savile, other prosecutions of historical abuse perpetrated by celebrity figures and contemporary child protection scandals about child sexual exploitation. These led to public inquiries and government interventions in councils. They are also likely to have driven the major increases in disclosures and reports of child sexual abuse, with recorded offences up by 39% in England from 2014 to 2015 and calls to the NSPCC (National Society for the Prevention of Cruelty to Children) about this issue up 128% (NSPCC, 2015). The NSPCC (2015) was critical of the government's response as being reactive and narrowly focused on local poor practice and child protection training initiatives. Instead, the NSPCC called for more extensive investment and reform to assist victims with more advocacy and therapeutic services, as well as further police and court reforms. It called for a national child sexual abuse prevention strategy. Such a strategy would require serious assessment of the gendered dimensions of various forms of child sexual abuse, as well as the relationship to power relations in society more broadly, including vulnerabilities associated with being a young person, socio-economic disadvantage, having a learning disability, being in care and having limited social support.

Finally, the coalition introduced several social care reforms via the Children and Families Act 2014. These included reforms that sought to increase adoption rates, reduce delays and increase placement rates. In some ways, alarmist early intervention arguments led to a greater focus on adoption for young children as families involved in the child protection system were characterised as overwhelmingly harmful to children and specialist family support as less effective and more expensive (Loughton, 2014). Adoption was described as more beneficial for young children at risk, removing them from birth families 'before it's too late' (Loughton, 2014). The problem with this view is that decisions should be based on comprehensive needs and risk assessments for each case, and taking account of children's views and wishes. The Children and Families Act 2014 also introduced new special educational needs assessments and provided more support to young people in care, such as a higher level of Pupil Premium. However, it did not take forward many recommendations of the Care Inquiry (2013), which called for improvements in listening to and engaging with children and youth, and more mental health and advocacy services.

Conclusions

This chapter has examined changes and continuities in social policies for children and young people under the coalition government, illustrating the retreat in, and refashioning of, welfare state support for children and young people. It has highlighted areas of consensus and conflict between the coalition partners and critically evaluated selected reforms. In many respects, the coalition years were detrimental to children and young people, reducing their access to welfare state support and increasing socio-economic vulnerabilities. Following the 2015 election, the newly formed Conservative government is continuing to target cutbacks in family benefits and youth welfare rights.

In other areas, the coalition introduced new targeted support measures – such as via the Pupil Premium, early intervention funding, youth crime prevention measures and the reforms of the Children and Families Act 2014 – oriented to promoting social mobility and 'protecting the vulnerable'. While many children and young people benefitted from these, some measures were time-limited initiatives rather than longer-lasting service reforms. Further, this chapter has questioned the extent to which the coalition achieved and fulfilled their policy goals, especially given the increase in absolute child poverty, the need for investment in support services for high-need groups and ongoing trends in precarious employment for youth.

In addition, under the coalition, there were major welfare reforms that extended work-related welfare conditions and workfare policies, and the Conservative government is consolidating these. There were also developments in childcare provision and support, benefitting many young people and working parents, although take-up for the subsidised places for disadvantaged two year olds was not as extensive as the government had anticipated. Access to childcare has continued to receive attention under the Conservative government.

Although it is clear that, in some areas, the Liberal Democrats were successful in influencing the coalition government's approaches and policies, many reforms were significantly informed by the Conservatives' 'five root causes of poverty' thesis and early intervention discourses – agendas that, unsurprisingly, will continue to restructure the welfare state for children and young people under the current administration.

References

Academies Commission (2013) *Unleashing greatness: getting the best out of an academised system*, London: Academies Commission.

Allen, G. (2011) *Early intervention: the next steps*, London: Department for Education.

Allen, G. and Duncan-Smith, I. (2008) *Early intervention: good parents, great kids, better citizens*, London: Centre for Social Justice.

Barnes, J. and Henderson, J. (2012) *Summary of the formative evaluation of the first phase of the group-based Family Nurse Partnership programme*, London: Department of Health.

Brewer, M., Browne, J. and Joyce, R. (2011) *Child and working age poverty from 2010–2020*, York: Joseph Rowntree Foundation.

Cabinet Office (2010) *The coalition: our programme of government*, London: Cabinet Office.

Care Inquiry (2013) *Making not breaking: building relationships for our most vulnerable children*, London: Care Inquiry. Available at: https://thecareinquiry.files.wordpress.com/2013/04/care-inquiry-full-report-april-2013.pdf (accessed 20 August 2015).

Chowdhury, R. and Cass, N. (2014) *The experiences of families claiming Housing Benefit during times of cuts and changes in benefits*, London: Citizens Advice Bureaux.

Churchill, H. (2011) *Parental rights and responsibilities: analysing social policy and lived experiences*, Bristol: The Policy Press.

Conservative Party (2010) *Invitation to join the government of Britain*, London: Conservative Party.

CRAE (Children's Rights Alliance for England) (2013) *The state of children's rights in England 2013*, London: CRAE.

CSJ (Centre for Social Justice) (2006) *Breakdown Britain: interim report on the state of the nation*, London: Centre for Social Justice.

DCLG (Department for Communities and Local Government) (2012) *The Troubled Families Programme: financial framework for the Troubled Families Programme's payment by results scheme for local authorities*, London: Department for Communities and Local Government.

DCLG (2014) *Troubled families: progress information at end of September 2014 and families turned around at end of October 2014*. Available at: https://www.gov.uk/government/publications/troubled-families-progress-information-at-september-2014-and-families-turned-around-at-october-2014 (accessed 26 December 2014).

Department for Education and Department of Health (2011) *Supporting families in the foundation years*, London: The Stationery Office.

Department for Work and Pensions (2015) *Household below average earnings: an analysis of the income distribution 1994/5 to 2013/14*, London: The Stationery Office.

Equalities Commission (2007) *Fairness and freedom: the final report of the equalities review*, London: The Stationery Office.

Education Select Committee (2012) *Children first: the child protection system in England*, London: The Stationery Office.

Education Select Committee (2015) *Academies and free schools*, London: The Stationery Office.

Featherstone, B., Morris, K. and White, S. (2014) 'A marriage made in hell: early intervention meets child protection', *British Journal of Social Work*, 44(7): 1735–49.

Field, F. (2010) *The foundation years: preventing poor children becoming poor adults: the report of the Independent Review on Poverty and Life Chances*, London: Cabinet Office.

FPI (Family and Parenting Institute) (2012) *Families on the frontline? Local spending on children's services in austerity*, London: Family and Parenting Institute.

HM Government (2011a) *A new approach to child poverty: tackling the causes of disadvantage and transforming family lives*, London: The Stationery Office.

HM Government (2011b) *Opening doors, breaking barriers: a strategy for social mobility*, London: The Stationery Office.

HM Government (2012) *Call to end violence against women and girls*, London: The Stationery Office.

HM Government (2013) *Working together to safeguard children*, London: The Stationery Office.

HM Treasury (2010a) *Emergency Budget 2010*, London: The Stationery Office.

HM Treasury (2010b) *Spending review 2010*, London: The Stationery Office.

Hood, A. and Phillips, D. (2015) *Benefit spending and reforms: the coalition government's record*, IFS briefing note BN160, London: IFS.

Liberal Democrats (2010) *Change that works for you: building a fairer Britain*, London: Liberal Democratic Party.

Loughton, T. (2014) *The state our children are in*, speech at the 4Children 30th anniversary event, London: 4Children.

Lupton, R. and Obolenskaya, P. (2013) *Labour's record on education: policy, spending and outcomes 1997–2010*, Working Paper Series 3, London: CASE/LSE.

Marshall, P. and Laws, D. (eds) (2004) *The Orange Book: reclaiming liberalism*, London: Profile Books.

McAuley, C. and Rose, W. (eds) (2010) *Child well-being: understanding children's lives*, London: Jessica Kingsley Publishers.

Munro, E. (2011) *The Munro review of child protection: final report – a child-centred system*, London: The Stationery Office.

Murray, C. (1996) 'The emerging British underclass', in P. Alcock, M. David, M. Phillips and S. Shipman (eds) *Charles Murray and the social underclass: the developing debate*, London: IEA Health and Welfare Unit, pp 23–53.

National Audit Office (2014) *The Work Programme*, London: National Audit Office.

NSPCC (National Society for the Prevention of Cruelty to Children) (2015) *How safe are our kids?*, London: NSPCC.

Ofsted (2013) *The Pupil Premium: how schools are spending the funding successfully to maximise achievement*, Manchester, Ofsted.

Ofsted (2015) *Early years annual report*, London: Ofsted.

Parton, N. (2014) *The politics of child protection*, Basingstoke: Palgrave.

Powell, M. (ed) (2002) *Evaluating New Labour's welfare reforms*, Bristol: The Policy Press.

Reed, H. and Elson, D. (2014) *An adequate standard of living: a child-rights-based quantitative analysis of tax and social security policy changes in the Autumn Statement 2013 and the Budget 2014*, London: Office of the Children's Commissioner.

Social Exclusion Taskforce (2006) *Reaching out: social exclusion action plan*, London: The Stationery Office.

UNISON (2014) *The UK's youth services: How cuts are removing opportunities for young people and damaging their lives*, London: UNISON.

Webb, S. and Holland, J. (2004) 'Children, the family and the state: a liberal agenda', in P. Marshall and D. Laws (eds) *The Orange Book: reclaiming liberalism*, London: Profile Books.

THIRTEEN

The coalition and criminal justice

Peter Squires

Introduction

A lot can happen in five years: the Conservative Party manifesto for the 2010 general election insisted that 'Britain needs change', and went on to claim that our 'communities are shattered by crime and abuse' (Conservative Party, 2010, p vii). Given such an urgent clarion call in 2010, it is fascinating how far explicit discussion of crime, disorder and criminal justice had slipped from the front lines of party-political concern by 2015. The 2015 Conservative manifesto did not begin any discussion of crime until page 58, in a section headed 'Fighting crime and standing up for victims'. The Labour Party's discussion of crime, on page 51, referred to addressing crime and anti-social behaviour, and was set in the context of the insecurities facing families and communities, themes that had been set by the Blairite 'tough on crime' agenda (Labour Party, 2015). The Liberal Democrat discussion of law-and-order matters had to wait until page 117, where it comprised a number of fairly routine pronouncements on 'secure communities, Policing and Justice, and the Border Force' (Liberal Democrats, 2015, p 117). In five years of the Conservative–Liberal Democrat coalition government, therefore, law, order and criminal justice had apparently slipped from the front page to a back burner. Of course, consistently falling rates of reported and recorded crime may be part of an explanation for the 'dog that ceased to bark', except that this particular dog had fallen relatively silent[1] despite the fact that a number of high-profile law-and-order issues had arisen during the government's term.

Some similar shifts were also reflected in government spending on law, order and protective services. According to Garside and Ford, for the Centre for Crime and Justice Studies:

> UK spending on public order and safety – which largely comprises criminal justice – grew by 17 per cent in the four years to 2010. In the four years to 2014 it fell by 12

per cent. The cuts were greatest in England and Wales. (Garside and Ford, 2015, p 26)

The Institute for Fiscal Studies predicted that over the period 2010/11 to 2015/16, Home Office spending would have fallen by 24.9% and that of the Ministry of Justice by 34.3%. These were among some of the heaviest hit areas of government activity (perhaps surprisingly in light of the often close alliance perceived between Conservative governments and 'law and order'), having consequences we shall shortly consider, resulting in an overall fall in 'public order and safety' spending from 8.2% of gross domestic product (GDP) in 2000 to 6.4% of GDP in 2014 (Crawford and Keynes, 2015). Of course, the suggestion that spending simply 'fell' is something of a misnomer, a more appropriate characterisation would be that spending was 'driven down' in the face of substantial opposition in order for the government to meet its chosen austerity targets. The government's pursuit of a 'politics of austerity' was, of course, itself part of an explanation for the relegation of the law-and-order agenda – but there were others.

The coalition government had set out its programme of action in a 32-page document, *The coalition: our programme for government* (Cabinet Office, 2010). The document was a carefully negotiated programme for government; line-by-line, it set out the ambitions of the government – section 6 addressed crime and policing, and section 20 justice. Key highlights in the programme included: police reform and local accountability; supporting victims and tackling hate crime; dealing with 'legal highs' and alcohol licensing; clarifying the right to engage in non-violent protest; a review of sentencing and of legal aid; and the reform of powers to deal with persistent anti-social behaviour. The document also proposed a 'rehabilitation revolution', although the 'revolutionary' element concerned the process by which rehabilitation was to be organised, rather than any distinctive quality that the rehabilitation itself offered. Independent, although, as it turned out, largely private sector, companies would deliver community justice services within a 'payment by results' management philosophy. Echoing something of the rhetoric of the incoming Thatcher government in 1979, the last time a new Conservative-leaning government had been elected for the first time, a Treasury spokesperson, interviewed for the *Financial Times*, reflected on the significance of the forthcoming Budget, due in a couple of weeks and the first since the election: 'Anyone who thinks the spending review is just about saving money is missing the point.... This is a once-in-a-generation opportunity to transform the way that government works' (quoted in Parker and

Giles, 2010). The coalition's programme document likewise referred to making a '*radical reform* of our criminal justice system' (Cabinet Office, 2010, p 13, emphasis added).

Protest and disorder

Acknowledging these parallels between the Thatcher government and the incoming coalition helps to provide us with both some themes and context to situate and analyse the issues, agenda and concerns of the coalition, as well as helping us to account for some of the tensions it had to overcome.

In one sense, there were some striking parallels: both the Thatcher government and the coalition were confronted, shortly after gaining office, by significant popular discontent and disorder. In the coalition's case, this was occasioned by the government's decision (in the process, ditching a Liberal Democrat policy commitment) to introduce £9,000 loans for university tuition fees and to abolish Education Maintenance Allowances. These decisions prompted significant opposition, including large demonstrations around the country and, in some cases, significant disorder. These confrontations brought new police public order management tactics (protest liaison, forward intelligence management and containment and dispersal tactics) into the limelight. The new measures were something of a tactical complement to the soul-searching that had gone on in policing circles following the unlawful killing of Ian Tomlinson during the policing of the 2009 G-20 Summit protests in London (Rosie and Gorringe, 2009). Facing criticism for its handling of public order incidents, Her Majesty's Inspectorate of Constabulary (HMIC) had embarked upon a series of inquiries seeking to establish a new public order management philosophy (Lewis and Laville, 2009). The HMIC, drawing significantly upon new social psychology research findings into policing and crowd behaviour (Stott and Reicher, 1998; Drury et al, 2003; Reicher et al, 2004; Hoggett and Stott, 2010a, 2010b), developed a range of new public disorder management protocols designed to 'facilitate legitimate protest' (HMIC, 2009, 2011). Unfortunately, many of the positive developments associated with the newer and more accountable, democratic and human rights-compliant policing of public order were overshadowed by a critical focus upon police containment tactics – or 'kettling' as these became known – which many critics argued were oppressive, breaching fundamental rights of assembly and protest (Fenwick, 2009; Home Affairs Select Committee, 2009). A High Court ruling initially held that kettling could be an illegal use of force by the police to detain citizens, but this was later overturned by the Court of Appeal (Bowcott, 2012), a view also consistent with the view taken by the European Court of Human Rights (Oreb, 2013).

Even greater disturbances were to follow. The debates about the policing of disorder were still unresolved when the most serious rioting that Britain had seen for 30 years erupted. This directly followed the Metropolitan Police's ineffectual handling of family and community protests in Tottenham after a police armed response unit had shot and killed Mark Duggan,[2] although much of the ensuing commentary explored the wider causes and contexts, including a unique research collaboration between the London School for Economics (LSE) and the *Guardian* newspaper, *Reading the riots* (Lewis et al, 2011). Thirty years earlier, the Thatcher government had also been beset by riots, in St Pauls, Bristol, in 1980 and, more seriously, the following year in Brixton, London, and Toxteth, Liverpool, each occasion being prompted, in part, by perceptions of heavy-handed policing of minority ethnic communities. The riots of 2011 became subject to a wide and varied academic commentary and analysis (Stott and Reicher, 2011; Waddington, 2012; Bridges, 2012; Briggs, 2012; Treadwell et al, 2012; Winlow and Hall, 2012), including a number of government-sponsored inquiries (Morrell et al, 2011; Singh, 2012), the conclusions of which – in sharp contrast to the impact of the Scarman Report in 1981 – the government chose to completely ignore, preferring its own narrative that the riot had been the result of gangs, a claim that was later modified to suggest that 'gang culture'[3] had been responsible for the rioting. In turn, this focus upon gangs and 'gang culture' led to a core plank of coalition criminal justice strategy: *Tackling gang and youth violence* (HM Government, 2011) and *The Troubled Families Programme* (DCLG, 2012), to which we will return (see also Chapter Eleven). One aspect of the reaction to the riots that had some lasting influence upon government policy concerned the abolition of the loosely framed Section 44 police 'stop and search' powers (Protection of Freedoms Act 2012), which had contributed to the huge disproportion, in London especially, in the stopping and searching of young black and Asian men, who were five to seven times more likely to be targeted than white people.

Government and police: friends no more

Moving on from policing, riots and disorder, another area in which the governments elected in 1979 and 2010 might be compared is the relationship they had with the police. The 1979 Thatcher government, elected on a 'law and order' platform, almost as a first act implemented the generous police pay deal worked out by the Edmund-Davies Committee (Edmund-Davies, 1978); after the Brixton riots, Thatcher was fulsome in her praise and support for the police and, later, famously asserted: 'never, never, have you ever heard me say that we must economise on law and order' (Thatcher, 1985). By contrast, in 2010, the coalition government was set on doing precisely that as part of a major programme of austerity cuts, accompanied by significant changes to police pay, conditions and pensions, changes to police leadership, reform of the Police Federation, and a proposal to establish locally elected Police and Crime Commissioners to replace the existing Police Authorities. In addition, there were a number of long-standing difficulties concerning police ethics and integrity. These included the Leveson Inquiry,[4] the 'Plebgate' affair,[5] the publication of the final report into the Hillsborough disaster (which pointed to police failings and cover-ups), the dismissal of a Chief Constable for 'gross misconduct' and 10 further investigations into the behaviour of senior officers, and allegations that the crime statistics were being rigged by target-sensitive police forces (Squires, 2015). In short, there was much to preoccupy the police in their relationships with the Home Office and the Home Secretary, although few would have predicted the belligerent assault that Theresa May launched upon the police rank and file at the annual conference of the Police Federation in Bournemouth in 2014.[6]

One further aspect of the 'fallout' from the 2011 riots, which resonates with the earlier Thatcher government, concerns the symbolic performance of 'tough government' and a firm commitment to 'law and order'. As we have noted, the 1979 government embraced a strong commitment to law and order, and some commentators have regarded 1979 as a 'law and order election' (Reiner, 2007, p 120; see also Taylor, 1980). While David Cameron had attracted some attention for his 'hug a hoodie' moment in 2006, and suggested criticism of the relentless criminalisation pursued under New Labour, he had added that 'understanding' the problems leading to crime 'doesn't mean … we can't be tough when a crime is committed' (BBC News, 2006). Yet, when it came to the sentencing of people arrested during the 2011 riots, a distinct air of toughness prevailed, the sentencing was unusually severe. By August 2012, Ministry of Justice data revealed that almost 1,300 individuals had been given custodial sentences for their involvement in the riot activity. The average custodial sentence imposed was 17.1 months – almost four times longer than the typical sentence given for similar offences (Ministry of Justice, 2012).[7] In the year before the London Olympics, it may have been deemed necessary to send a message that widespread public disorder would not be tolerated during this showcase international event; in any event, further disorders seemed likely.

The uses of 'austerity'

The Thatcher governments had faced considerable social and political disorder; indeed, some would argue that Thatcher's brand of 'confrontational politics' provoked it. It was during this time that the Conservatives' image as the 'nasty party' became established. Theresa May referred explicitly to this label in a party conference speech in 2002, and in the wake of the 2010 election and George Osborne's first 'austerity budget', the label resurfaced: 'in the space of just six weeks in office, Tory nastiness has returned' (Hasan, 2010). This alleged 'nastiness' directly concerned the broader neoliberal programme of the coalition government. Both the Thatcher government and the coalition were embarking upon a programme to cut the government deficit, reduce public spending and especially welfare spending (for social, political and economic reasons), privatise further and shrink the size of the public sector. In the 1980s, the economic rationale was driven by a commitment to combating inflation by adopting monetarist (supply-side) economic methods and principles; in 2010, similar policies were driven by the government's explicit commitment to an austerity strategy to reduce the deficit resulting from the bank bailout of 2008. In other words, economic priorities prevailed over social ones: social welfare was represented as a burden and initiatives to increase equality and opportunity were considered contrary to the efficiencies of the market. This version of economic neoliberalism has always argued that inequality serves as an incentive in a healthy market economy and that what the poorest needed most was not welfare, but rather order, discipline and a healthy respect for the work ethic.

Britain has experienced three pronounced phases of such governance and the similarities between them abound. The coalition being just the most recent example, the preceding administrations were in the 1920s and 1930s, and the Thatcher administration of 1979–90. Table 12.1 depicts the salient characteristics of all three.

Each administration pursued, as a priority, an economic agenda, and in order to achieve these economic priorities, each embarked upon a substantial programme of public spending cuts and restrictions to social welfare, which hit the poor the hardest (including means testing, cuts, availability-for-work testing, workfare, welfare conditionality and benefit sanctions). For the purposes of our present discussion,

Table 12.1: Three phases of neoliberal austerity

Dates	Underlying economic issue	Politics	Social policy responses	Law and order consequences
1920s–early 1930s	Financial stability and the return to the gold standard (1925)	Baldwin and MacDonald, a hung Parliament and the national government: Churchill and Treasury financial orthodoxy in dealing with post-First World War national debt (contra Keynes); Great Depression	Widespread unemployment; public expenditure cuts ('Geddes Axe', 1922; May Committee, 1931). Cuts to wages and welfare benefits (dole), means testing and the punitive application of 'genuinely seeking work' test; labour colonies	General Strike, 1926; Hunger Marchers, Jarrow Crusade, rise of Mosley's 'Blackshirts' and the BUF (British Union of Fascists); concerns about police abuse of powers; the Public Order Act 1936
Thatcherism 1979–1980s	Monetarism, supply-side economics and controlling inflation/stagflation	Thatcherism, the rise of the 'New Right'	Three million unemployed, cuts to welfare and pensions; 'scroungermania'; social housing residualisation/sink estates; control of local government spending/capping; privatisations; industry policy and closing 'uneconomic' pits; youth training	Crime almost doubled in a decade; riots; Police and Criminal Evidence Act 1984; police public order mobilisation/paramilitarism debate; policing the miners' strike, the short, sharp shock revival; prison population rising; Public Order Act 1986; Prevention of Terrorism Act 1989; rediscovery of the 'underclass', criminalisation/racialisation – 'stop & search'; broken windows/incivilities – antisocial behaviour
Coalition 2010–2015	Austerity management, deficit reduction, major public expenditure cuts	Conservative-led coalition government	Welfare reform/cuts, abolition of Education Maintenance Allowance; 'bedroom tax', benefit sanctions/testing; public sector 'efficiency savings'; privatisations; cuts to legal aid; zero-hours contracts; the new 'precariat'	20% police cuts; riots; accountability; Police and Crime Commissioners; recorded crime falling – crime data queries; privatisation of probation; prison population rising; 'crimmigration'/detention; anti-terror and security politics

key analytical parallels of the coalition government of 2010–15 are that the economic and social policies of these respective 'austerity' governments each generated forms of dissent and disorder as they increased inequalities and unpicked important aspects of citizenship and cohesion, principles they also profoundly compromised via the deployment of often discriminatory and anti-social depictions of the idle, feckless, feral, undeserving and underclass poor, in so doing, reviving in 2010 the kinds of 'culture of poverty' arguments prevalent in the 1980s (Squires, 1990). Tyler's recent work on social abjection and the 'othering' of the poorest (Tyler, 2013) draws upon the derogatory and judgemental representations of poor and marginal lives, such as the much-criticised Channel 4 *Benefits Street* series (typical of a number of similar programmes), first broadcast in 2014, which some commentators have styled 'poverty porn' (Mooney and Hancock, 2010). In 2013, Chancellor George Osborne revealed something of his own thinking on 'dependency culture' when he commented upon the abusive and criminal lifestyle of a man who, having fathered 17 children with several different partners, had set fire to his own house, killing six of the children. Implying that the welfare state had fostered such lifestyles, he argued: 'there is a question for government and for society about the welfare state ... *subsidising* lifestyles like that, and I think that debate needs to be had' (George Osborne, quoted in Dominiczak and Winnett, 2013). The comments, and the issues they raise, are an appropriate reminder that the 'tough' and disciplinary policies of the supposed 'nasty party', to which the Liberal Democrats allied themselves in 2010, were not just related to law and order, but traversed a range of social programmes.

This analysis ties in closely with a recent reappraisal of the Thatcher administration by Farrall and Hay (2010), which has direct relevance for our assessment of the coalition. The authors develop their question regarding the Thatcher administration in terms of the seeming mismatch between popular perceptions of Thatcherism as embodying tough law-and-order governance, the outcome, as we have seen, of a 'law and order' election, and the difficulty that criminologists often have in pointing to a distinctively New Right/neoliberal agenda of criminal justice reform introduced by the Thatcher governments. Farrall and Hay resolve this apparent dilemma by noting that while the Thatcherites often 'talked tough' on law and order, invoking the 'authoritarian populist' form of discourse identified by Hall et al (1978; Hall 1985), and 'articulating concerns in a way which resonated with the electorate' (Farrall and Hay, 2010, p 565), their wider array of policies effectively produced the circumstances in which crime flourished during the 1980s and early 1990s (rising by some 80% during the decade). There is, they suggest, a deep irony in the Conservative Party's 'party of law and order' credentials because 'their policies ultimately produced greater levels of unemployment, inequality and associated crime' (Farrall and Hay, 2010, p 565). Overall, they conclude, Thatcherite policies 'had a self-fulfilling aspect to them: the social and economic changes they unleashed from 1979 onwards had the net result of demanding a more punitive response to crime' (Farrall and Hay, 2010, p 566).

The crime drop and the sceptics

Of course, it is here that, despite all the parallels we have considered, perhaps the vital *difference* between Thatcherism and the coalition arises, for while Thatcherism presided over a rapid upturn in recorded and reported crime figures, the coalition saw overall crime apparently falling consistently and continuously for the decade prior to its election and (with the exception of some recent contrary evidence relating to serious violence and sexual crime[8]) throughout its term of office (see Figure 13.1).

Figure 13.1: Falling crime 2001–14: police-recorded crime and the Crime Survey of England and Wales

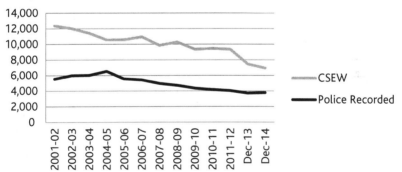

Source: Office for National Statistics, 2014

Crime falling may only be a part of the story; at least as important is the overall fall in criminal justice workloads (and therefore criminal justice spending). As Figure 13.2 shows, although the prison population has remained fairly constant, prison receptions have dipped slightly (a sign here of the lengthening of prison sentences) and the numbers of offenders proceeded against for indictable (more serious) offences has fallen since 2011. Furthermore, probation starts are falling, while out-of-court disposals (antisocial behaviour measures, penalty notices) had fallen by around 45% since 2009, suggesting that what was happening had little to do with penology's 'holy grail' of criminal justice diversion, but rather reduced rates of activity.

Figure 13.2: Criminal justice workloads, activity indicators

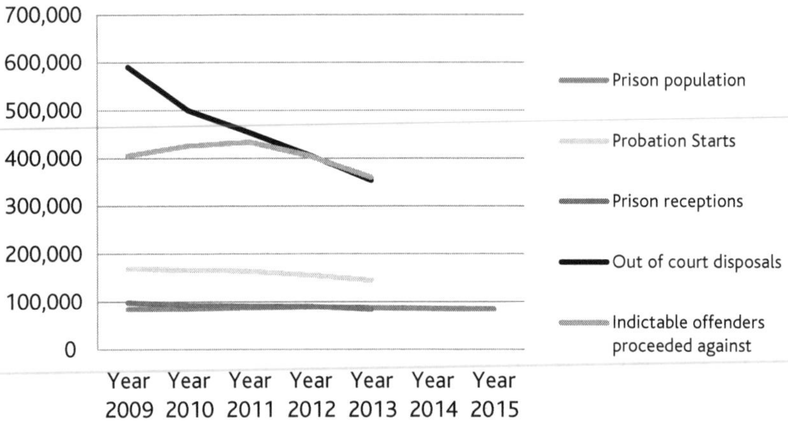

Note: Selected criminal justice process indicators (thousands).

Sources: Ministry of Justice (2014) 'Statistics bulletin' and National Offender Management Service (NOMS) 'Prison statistics'.

It was the same story within the youth justice system: arrests were down from around 90,000 in 2009/10 to 40,000 in 2013/14; first-time entrants to the youth justice system were down almost 75% over the same five years, and repeat offenders were down 60% (suggestions of effective diversion here), and the youth custody population had fallen from 2,500 to just over 1,000. Falling criminal justice workloads provide a more reliable indicator of a change in policy than falling crime statistics. In any event, many critics have argued that the apparent fall in crime was overstated, a series of arguments underpinned by continuing evidence that the police were failing to record many crimes diligently and accurately, culminating in the decision to redesignate the criminal statistics and shift responsibility for compiling them to the Office of National Statistics. The second area of dispute for the 'crime drop sceptics' has concerned the scale of internet-facilitated and online or 'cyber-'crime, many of the victims of which may not realise that they have been targeted (although some victims are significantly harmed; see Button et al, 2014; Button and Tunley, 2015), and most of which is never reported; even the volumes of identity crimes or credit card fraud that are reported to financial institutions or to Action Fraud[9] (which has identified over 150 distinct types of internet-based fraud) seldom make it to the criminal statistics. The evidence on cyber-crime, as expert witnesses told the Home Affairs Committee inquiry in 2013, suggests that it is a 'war' we are 'not winning', that the problems are getting worse and that 'this nature of crime is rising exponentially' (Home Affairs Committee, 2013, p 8). The committee also argued that the 'basket' of volume crimes that serves as Britain's national 'barometer' on crime is becoming increasingly out of date.

Separate ways

Also increasingly 'out of date', according to Garside and Ford (2015), is the notion of a coherent criminal justice system covering the entire British Isles. While separate criminal justice jurisdictions have long historical roots, they argue that, 'in the past five years ... the local distinctiveness of the three jurisdictions has, in general, become more pronounced' (Garside and Ford, 2015, p 26). Simply put, Garside and Ford argue that during the coalition government, the record can be summarised in terms of four broad 'governing strategies', which they characterise as: 'austerity' (referring to the UK as a whole); market-building, framed around the privatisations envisaged for the criminal justice sector, especially, but not entirely, the privatisation of the community justice sector (formerly known as probation) in England and Wales; nation-building (in Scotland); and peace-building (in Northern Ireland).

Beneath these 'governing strategies' were a series of 'system priorities' that found some expression in each of the separate national jurisdictions, and these included: bringing greater efficiency and effectiveness to policing; improving the effectiveness and outcomes from community justice; cutting the cost of legal aid; and addressing the crisis of the inexorably rising prison population. All such 'priorities' were underpinned by the austerity agenda; for instance, in Scotland, this entailed the establishment of Police Scotland in 2013 following the amalgamation of all eight territorial forces; in Northern Ireland, the continued winning of consent for the Police Service of Northern Ireland, established after 2001, remained a priority, involving, in Topping's (2008, p 779) terms, wresting policing from the state and 'giving it back to the people'. However, while these strategies and systems may have captured the formal outlines of coalition politics, a great deal of the tone of these changes reflected the application of a range of neoliberal austerity values.

Separate spheres of injustice?

Despite being overlain by a pretext of inclusion – 'we're all in it together' – austerity and exclusion were never far from the new values. They included: a diminishing commitment to equality and equal treatment; the demonisation of the poorest; the dispersal of more intensive discipline; and surveillance over the behaviour of those 'marginal' and 'precarious' others cast aside from 'bulimic society' (Young, 1999; Wacquant, 2008; Standing, 2011), accompanied by a growing disregard for their needs, rights and well-being. These new relations of discipline and disregard may explain the reluctance to apply the costly apparatus of criminalisation against groups for whom substantially cheaper penalties, sanctions and exclusions were available. This was especially so with the 'payment by results' regime at the heart of the supervisory Troubled Families strategy (DCLG, 2012) and the Rehabilitation Revolution, where the chief purpose of the policy was precisely to move the poor on and cut the cost of welfare and service delivery.

The Troubled Families policy (see also Chapters Eleven and Twelve) drew upon the preceding Labour government's antisocial behaviour strategy, for despite the supportive rhetoric, actual practice more closely reflected low-level enforcement activity underpinned by sanctions. In effect, conformity to a model of neoliberal family life, education and job-seeking was endorsed rather more than access to welfare, opportunities or resources. In some respects, the transition was seamless. In its long-anticipated revisions to antisocial behaviour management (Home Office, 2012), in the strategy to tackle gangs and youth violence (HM Government, 2011) and, finally, in its Troubled Families Programme, the coalition government closely followed the lead of its predecessor. Taken together, the three policy fronts comprised a powerful array of innovative low-intensity/low-cost measures to better regulate the poor.

The White Paper *Putting victims first* (Home Office, 2012) promised simplified and streamlined, faster and more effective orders, with new police powers to tackle the 'anti-social', enhanced operational discretion for antisocial behaviour management professionals and speedier evictions, as well as longer-term enforcement solutions for some of the underlying problems. Most novel of all was the 'community trigger', a measure to localise the enforcement process by allowing community members to nominate their own neighbours for enforcement intervention.

Taken together, these measures combine stigma, speed, low-intensity/high-utility intervention, local, visible, cheap, responsibility-oriented and 'entry-level' alternatives to 'costly criminalisation'. Such measures, whether 'diversions from' or 'alternatives to' criminal justice, facilitated control and containment without involving the constraints of due process, or the added costs of prosecution. They formed a new regime of perverse and antisocial incentives by which local authorities might select those to 'support' or those to neglect. All told, they comprised a neoliberal form of limited (superficial and short-term) local 'crime and disorder management' activism, making poverty pay while sidestepping the heavy symbolism of crime or the expensive requirements of justice – let alone social justice. The latest policy and practice for managing immigrants and migrants bears many similar characteristics; collectively, they have been depicted as marking the resurgence of a new 'repressive welfarism' (Phoenix, 2009), a new administrative law for the poor – a new Poor Law – inserted, rather like the old one, beneath the criminal law and the courts of justice.

For example, the coalition government very much adopted and expanded the language and practice of welfare conditionality developed under the previous Labour administration, especially as regards job-seekers, and they intensified the pressure of enforcement. The use of tough medical tests for assessing entitlement to Employment and Support Allowances was seen as particularly harsh, with ATOS, the private company contracted to undertake the work, prematurely withdrawing from its contract. Somewhat endorsing this unforgiving image of the work capability assessments was a report, based upon freedom of information requests, that some 2,380 people, roughly 90 a month, died shortly after being found capable of work and having their benefit entitlements curtailed (BBC News, 2015a).

By the end of the coalition's five-year term of office, the government was close to completing a wide-ranging restructuring of the justice system, producing a selective, segmented and more localised system of regulation specified for differing problems of governance, deviance, compliance, criminality, risk and threat. Figure 13.3 seeks to capture this new segmented hierarchy of law and discipline. In large part, although it reflects a longer history and leaves, undoubtedly, a much bigger legacy, the hierarchy, as depicted, owes much to Tony Blair's notion that the criminal justice system was not fit for purpose in the 21st century and needed 'rebalancing' (Crawford, 2009; Tonry, 2010) and streamlining. While, for the purpose of illustration, it describes the separate 'segments' of this layering of social controls, in fact, as we shall see, effective practice in one sphere might be picked up, adapted and applied in another. For example, the old Antisocial Behaviour Order (ASBO) formed the basis for gang injunctions (or GangBOs) and Control Orders, later replaced in 2011 by Terrorism Prevention and Investigation Measures (TPIMS), while the emerging field of 'crimmigration' (Aliverti, 2013) now embodies the interplay of immigration and asylum controls and the pressures and practices of criminalisation.

Figure 13.3: Separate spheres of justice and injustice

Compliance work	Welfare sanctions and conditional entitlements	'Troubled families' social controls	Antisocial behaviour and disorder management	Criminal law	Criminal 'others': gangs, immigrants	Serious and organised and counter-terror

At the lower end of the range are a series of less intrusive compliance measures, inducements to citizens to pay their taxes and the like, areas of law that are often remarkably sanction-free and where 'defendants' negotiate. Next come the three tiers of regulatory sanctions, which have flourished in the shadows at the end of the welfare state. New Labour's antisocial behaviour interventions were a novel policy invention that, as we have argued, effected a significant dispersal of discipline (Squires and Stephen, 2005) and made significant inroads into the conventional criminal law, especially following the coalition's further reforms. Welfare sanctions and conditional entitlement have always been components of the social welfare state (Squires, 1990), but it is only during the three austerity phases described in Table 13.1, and especially now, that they have come to assume such significance. Between them, drawing upon both forms of new regulation, lies the Troubled Families Programme mentioned earlier, a new tier of disciplinary welfare premised upon personal responsibility, the work ethic, behaviour modification and familial compliance linked to welfare entitlements.

However, this only accounts for the low end of the series of regulatory regimes, and the final dimensions of the segmented system of justice were only completed in 2015 by the passage of the Serious Crime Act 2015, which marked a coming together of aspects of the Tackling Violence and Gang Strategy (HM Government, 2011) and the government's evolving Counter-Terrorism Strategy.

The management of serious crime and the practice of counter-terrorist policing were both modelled upon a four-part programme of activities: Pursue, Prevent, Protect and Prepare. Each aspect involved high-level risk assessment and – relatively novel for UK law enforcement – the legal confirmation or construction of a 'serious criminal actor' identity.[10] The new identities reflect not just *legal* construction, but also moral denunciation, media vilification, character assassination, 'dangerisation' and demonisation, and the fundamental reconstruction of attributed motives around badness, in other words, the most complete othering, such as Wacquant (2009) describes of paedophiles in the US. The identities in question in the UK are (1) terrorist, (2) organised criminal (3) gang member. A little further down the scale of severity, we find further vilified identities, such as immigrant/asylum seeker, antisocial youth and benefit scrounger.

The significance of these identities lies in the way they effect a convenient legal reversal, whereby an accused person finds it necessary to prove that they are *not* culpable as charged. The effect is especially clear in the field of criminal asset recovery, whereby offenders need to prove the legitimacy of their property, or in the doctrine of 'joint enterprise' gang prosecution, which has had such a massive and disproportionate impact on the numbers of young black men serving life sentences (McClenaghan et al, 2014). As Krebs (2010) has argued, the 'common criminal purpose' that the gang member (or organised criminal) identification establishes (often upon the basis of circumstantial police surveillance information) assumes that the gang member knows of or shares in the criminal intentions of the rest of the gang, thereby changing his normative position in the eyes of the law, in the eyes of the jury and certainly in the eyes of Chris Grayling, the coalition government's Justice Secretary. Responding to a 2014 Home Affairs Select Committee recommendation that the joint enterprise law be reformed, Grayling noted:

> While academics and families of convicted offenders might disagree with me, relatives of victims and large sections of the law-abiding public ... are likely to be concerned if we were suddenly to announce a dilution of this important area of law. (Grayling, 2014)

Here we have it, 'us and them'; the allies of the guilty, on the one hand, and the law-abiding, on the other. There was no doubt about which side of this balance the government stood, or any dilution of an indiscriminate and punitive policy, despite its consequences.

Legacies

Having seemingly completed the 'Blairite' mission of tuning the systems of criminal justice to the needs of the 21st century, the coalition departed the scene in 2015, leaving a highly graded and differentiated regime of interventions and enforcements to its Conservative successor. Taken together, these entailed an often more selective and more localised response to many aspects of crime and disorder. It might seem strange, at this point, to refer back to an analysis of law and crime control dating from 1999, but Ian Taylor's (1999) book, *Crime in context: a critical criminology of market societies*, perceptively anticipated many of the developments under discussion. His starting point was the enormously criminogenic environment that neoliberal globalisation represented, compared with the capacity and political will of states to address it.

Fully developing this critique would require much more space and time, but its central elements involve the growing inequality of crime and disorder victimisation, with ultimately less support, reduced acknowledgement of the rights of the poorest and diminishing access to justice. Despite a speech by Michael Gove (BBC News, 2015b), substantial cuts are still impacting on the scale and coverage of legal aid. Government crime control strategies, however, as Taylor anticipated, will become increasingly selective and institutional, introducing new laws and rearranging enforcement practices, creating new agencies – framing institutional solutions, virtual Maginot lines of crime prevention – without grappling with the underlying social processes producing marginality and illegality. These issues are well illustrated in the criticisms, advanced earlier, of the government's three core control strategies (gangs and violence, terrorism and organised crime).

At the same time, as a number of vilified priority enforcement targets emerge, crime risks have become increasingly focused upon particular systems, especially threats to markets, governance systems, borders and communities, although the policing and security services of the austerity state, less accountable and often privatised, encounter both capacity and selectivity dilemmas. Perhaps few police forces will 'resolve' this dilemma in the manner chosen by Leicestershire Police, however, who decided to 'ration' their burglary response by only responding to calls from even-numbered houses (Hamilton, 2015), apparently with no impact upon 'victim satisfaction'. Perhaps this is a 'rebalance' too far and too arbitrary, although, in other ways, such rebalancing has already become the new justice. Crime control and crime prevention has always involved addressing some interests, rather than others, using force on the behalf of some *against* others.[11] The combined effect of neoliberal priorities and austerity selectivity has simply made these rebalances – 'them' and 'us', new versions of the 'deserving' and 'undeserving', the 'law-abiding' and the supposed 'predatory other' – more explicit, more obvious and more unjust. However, notwithstanding an increasingly selective deployment of criminalisation, ever-lengthening sentences for priority and persistent offenders imply that the prison will remain the one constant among falling crime, rebalanced justice and shifting priorities. In March 2015, Justice Secretary Grayling announced the 'green light' on the contract for Britain's first 'Titan-sized' prison (to hold 2,100 inmates), an initiative previously rejected (Travis, 2015). The new prison is anticipated to begin taking inmates in February 2017.

Notes

[1] Law-and-order politics are often characterised as a form of 'dog-whistle' politics: the whistle is blown (by politicians looking to exploit the issue), the dog (the media and electorate) start barking. In 2015, while the parties were blowing other whistles (the economy, immigration, Europe), the 'law and order' dog remained fairly quiet.

[2] Squires (2014), see also: https://theconversation.com/mark-duggan-lawful-killing-verdict-leaves-questions-over-police-use-of-lethal-force-21697

[3] In 2011, the coalition government produced a 'cross-government' strategy to tackle gang and youth violence (HM Government, 2011). The introduction to the document contained the claim that gangs had been a primary driver of the 2011 rioting. Subsequent evidence, that less than 20% of arrested rioters had any known gang affiliations, led to a backing away from this original claim. Instead, it was rather more amorphously claimed that 'gang culture' was a cause of the riots (see Hallsworth and Brotherton, 2011).

[4] The Leveson Inquiry (2012) concerned the practices and ethics of the British press, including allegations of phone hacking and, among other issues, corrupt and unethical dealings between police and journalists.

[5] The 'Plebgate Affair' concerned disputed allegations, leaked memos and dishonesty by police officers following an altercation in Downing Street in September 2012 between officers and the government chief whip, who was forced to resign.

[6] At the following year's conference, she was met by the Federation Chairman, who described their 2014 meeting as 'Groundhog Day', before continuing: 'Home Secretary, we are not good friends … police officers have to deal with whatever is thrown our

way. Our professionalism means showing toleration even in the face of provocation. We learn to put up with the criticism. The abuse. The jeering and dirty looks. The scowls of anger and derision. And that was just from you at our conference last year, Home Secretary' (quoted in Squires, 2015).

[7] According to Bell et al (2014, p 486), who analysed the riot sentencing: 'For all crimes, the immediate custody rate tripled from 12% to 36% in magistrates' courts and rose from 33% to 81% in crown courts'.

[8] According to the Office for National Statistics (2015) *Violent crime and sexual offences – overview*, published in February 2015, the Crime Survey for England and Wales continues to show steady declines in violent crime. Between the 1995 and 2014 surveys, the number of violent crime incidents fell from 3.8 million in 1995 to 1.3 million. The number of offences of violence against the person recorded by the police in 2013/14 increased 6% from the previous year, following a period of year-on-year falls. Improvements in crime recording has led to more crimes being recorded than previously. The numbers of sexual offences recorded by police (64,205) in 2013/14 was the highest since 2002/03. Improvements in recording, as well as a greater willingness of victims to come forward, are largely thought to explain this increase.

[9] Action Fraud is the UK national reporting centre for fraud and internet crime. It works in conjunction with the National Fraud Intelligence Bureau, providing a central point of contact for information about fraud and financially motivated internet crime.

[10] Until the Serious Crime Act 2015, section 45, British law had not formally adopted the notion of the 'organised criminal' as a status in itself. Enforcement had focused upon organised criminal activities, conspiracies and crimes, rather than targeting members of proscribed criminal organisations (like the Mafia). With the 2015 legislation, Britain adopted the US and European Union (EU) model, and simply participating in the activities of a criminal organisation became an offence, even in the absence of evidence of other actual crimes (rather like being a member of a proscribed terrorist organisation).

[11] According to Dixon (2004, p 252): 'wholesome notions of community ... [often] elide the adversarial aspect of policing by implying that whatever is done, is done in the interest, and with the consent, of the people ... the fact that policing is usually done to someone, as well as on someone's behalf, is conveniently forgotten'.

References

Aliverti, A. (2013) *Crimes of mobility: criminal law and the regulation of immigration*, London: Routledge.

BBC News (2006) 'Cameron defends hoodie speech', 10 July. Available at: http://news.bbc.co.uk/1/hi/uk_politics/5163798.stm (accessed 5 September 2015).

BBC News (2015a) 'More than 2,300 died after fit for work assessment – DWP figures', 27 August. Available at: http://www.bbc.co.uk/news/uk-34074557 (accessed 5 September 2015).

BBC News (2015b) 'Michael Gove: justice system fails society's poorest', 23 July. Available at: http://www.bbc.co.uk/news/uk-politics-33230552 (accessed 5 September 2015).

Bell, B., Jaitman, L. and Machin, S. (2014) 'Crime deterrence: evidence from the London 2011 riots', *Economic Journal*, 124(576): 480–506.

Bowcott, O. (2012) 'Kettling protesters is lawful, Appeal Court rules', *The Guardian*, 19 January.

Bridges, L. (2012) 'Four days in August: the UK riots', *Race & Class*, 54(1): 1–12.

Briggs, D. (ed) (2012) *The English riots of 2011: a summer of discontent*, Hook: Waterside Press.

Button, M. and Tunley, M.J. (2015) 'Explaining fraud deviancy attenuation in the United Kingdom', *Crime, Law and Social Change*, 63(1/2): 49–64.

Button, M., Lewis, C. and Tapley, J. (2014) 'Not a victimless crime: the impact of fraud on individual victims and their families', *Security Journal*, 27(1): 36–54.

Cabinet Office (2010) *The coalition: our programme for government*, London: Cabinet Office.

Conservative Party (2010) *Invitation to join the government of Britain*, London: Conservative Party.

Crawford, A. (2009) 'Governing through anti-social behaviour: regulatory challenges to criminal justice', *British Journal of Criminology*, 49(6): 810–31.

Crawford, R. and Keynes, R. (2015) 'Options for further departmental spending cuts', in C. Emmerson, P. Johnson and R. Joyce (eds) *Institute for Fiscal Studies: Green Budget, 2015*, London: Institute for Fiscal Studies, pp 151–75. Available at: http://www.ifs.org.uk/publications/7530 (accessed 10 September 2015).

DCLG (Department for Communities and Local Government) (2012) *The Troubled Families Programme: financial framework for the Troubled Families Programme's payment-by-results scheme for local authorities*, London: DCLG.

Dixon, B. (2004) 'Community policing: cherry pie or Melktert', *Society in Transition*, 35(2): 251–72.

Dominiczak, P. and Winnett, R. (2013) 'George Osborne: Why should the taxpayer fund 'lifestyles' like those of the Philpotts?', *Daily Telegraph*, 4 April.

Drury, J., Stott, C.J. and Farsides, T. (2003) 'The role of police perceptions and practices in the development of "public disorder"', *Journal of Applied Social Psychology*, 33(7): 1480–500.

Edmund-Davies, H. (1978) *Report of the Committee of Inquiry on the Police (chairman: Lord Edmund-Davies PC)*, London, HMSO.

Farrall, S. and Hay, C. (2010) 'Not so tough on crime? Why weren't the Thatcher governments more radical in reforming the criminal justice system?', *British Journal of Criminology*, 50(3): 550–69.

Fenwick, H. (2009) 'Marginalising human rights: breach of the peace, "kettling", the Human Rights Act and public protest', *Public Law*, 2009(4): 737–65.

Garside, R. and Ford, M. (2015) *The coalition years: criminal justice in the United Kingdom, 2010–2015*, London: Centre for Crime and Justice Studies.

Grayling, C. (2014) *Joint enterprise: follow-up: government response to the committee's fourth report of session 2014–15*, HC 1047, London, The Stationery Office.

Hall, S. (1985) 'Authoritarian populism: a reply to Jessop et al.', *New Left Review*, 151(1): 115–23.

Hall, S., Critcher, C., Jefferson, T., Clarke, J. and Roberts, B. (1978) *Policing the crisis: mugging, the state and law and order*, London: Macmillan.

Hallsworth, S. and Brotherton, D. (2011) *Urban disorder and gangs: a critique and a warning*, London: Runnymede Trust.

Hamilton, F. (2015) 'Police ignore break-ins at odd-numbered homes', *The Times*, 5 August.

Hasan, M. (2010) 'The Tories are still the nasty party: David Cameron came to power as a moderniser, but the Budget shows that the spirit of Thatcher lives', *New Statesman*, 24 June.

HM Government (2011) *Ending Gang and Youth Violence: A Cross Governmental Report*, Cm 8211, London: The Stationery Office.

HMIC (Her Majesty's Inspectorate of Constabulary) (2009) *Adapting to protest: nurturing the British model of policing*, London: HMIC/Central Office of Information.

HMIC (2011) *Policing public order: an overview and review of progress against the recommendations of 'Adapting to protest'*, London: HMIC.

Hoggett, J. and Stott, C. (2010a) 'Crowd psychology, public order police training and the policing of football crowds', *Policing: An International Journal of Police Strategies & Management*, 33(2): 218–35.

Hoggett, J. and Stott, C. (2010b) 'The role of crowd theory in determining the use of force in public order policing', *Policing & Society*, 20(2): 223–36.

Home Affairs Select Committee (2009) *Policing of the G20 protests. Eighth report, session 2008–09*, London: The Stationery Office.

Home Affairs Select Committee (2013) *E-crime*, London: The Stationery Office.

Home Office (2012) *Putting victims first: more effective responses to anti-social behaviour*, London: The Stationery Office.

Krebs, B. (2010) 'Joint criminal enterprise', *Modern Law Review*, 73(4): 578–604.

Labour Party (2015) *Changing Britain together*, London: Labour Party.

Leveson Inquiry (2012) *Leveson Inquiry: culture, practice and ethics of the press*, London: The Stationery Office. Available at: http://webarchive.nationalarchives.gov.uk/20140122145147/http:/www.levesoninquiry.org.uk/ (accessed 30 November 2015).

Lewis, P. and Laville, S. (2009) 'G20 report lays down the law to police on use of force', *The Guardian*, 25 November.

Lewis, P., Newburn, T., Taylor, M., Mcgillivray, C., Greenhill, A., Frayman, H. and Proctor, R. (2011) *Reading the riots: investigating England's summer of disorder*, London: LSE. Available at: http://eprints.lse.ac.uk/46297/1/Reading%20the%20riots(published).pdf (accessed 5 September 2015).

Liberal Democrats (2015) *Stronger economy, fairer society, opportunity for everyone*, London: Liberal Democratic Party.

McClenaghan, M., McFadyean, M. and Stevenson, R. (2014) *Joint enterprise: an investigation into the legal doctrine of joint enterprise in criminal convictions*, London: Bureau of Investigative Journalism.

Ministry of Justice (2012) *Statistical bulletin on the public disorder of 6th to 9th August 2011 – September 2012 update*, Ministry of Justice Statistics bulletin, London: Ministry of Justice.

Ministry of Justice (2014) *Statistics Bulletin: Criminal Justice Statistics 2013 – England and Wales*, London, Ministry of Justice.

Mooney, G. and Hancock, L. (2010) 'Poverty porn and the broken society', *Variant*, 39/40: 14–18.

Morrell, G., Scott, S., McNeish, D. and Webster, S. (2011) *The August riots in England: understanding the involvement of young people*, London: National Centre for Social Research.

Office for National Statistics (2014) *Crime in England and Wales, year ending March 2014, Statistical Bulletin*. Available at: http://www.ons.gov.uk/ons/dcp171778_371127.pdf

Office for National Statistics (2015) *Violent crime and sexual offences – overview: England and Wales*, London: Office for National Statistics.

Oreb, N. (2013) 'Case comment: the legality of "kettling" after Austin', *The Modern Law Review*, 76(4): 735–42.

Parker, G. and Giles, C. (2010) 'Cuts will affect "everyone" says Cameron', *Financial Times*, 7 June.

Phoenix, J. (2009) 'Beyond risk assessment: the return of repressive welfarism', in F. McNeil and M. Barry (eds) *Youth offending and youth justice*, London: Jessica Kingsley.

Reicher, S., Stott, C., Cronin, P. and Adang, O. (2004) 'An integrated approach to crowd psychology and public order policing', *Policing: An International Journal of Police Strategies and Management*, 27(4): 558–72.

Reiner, R. (2007) *Law and order: an honest citizen's guide to crime and control*, Cambridge: Polity Press.

Rosie, M. and Gorringe, H. (2009) 'What a difference a death makes: protest, policing and the press at the G20', *Sociological Research Online*, 14(5). Available at: http://socresonline.org.uk/14/5/4.html (accessed 5 September 2015).

Singh, D. (2012) *After the riots: final report of the Riots, Communities and Victims Panel*, London: Riots, Communities and Victims Panel.

Squires, P. (1990) *Anti-social policy: welfare, ideology and the disciplinary state*, Hemel Hempstead: Wheatsheaf Books.

Squires, P. (2014) 'Mark Duggan lawful killing verdict leaves questions over police use of lethal force', *The Conversation*, 8 January. Available at: https://theconversation.com/mark-duggan-lawful-killing-verdict-leaves-questions-over-police-use-of-lethal-force-21697

Squires, P. (2015) 'Policing & politics: no longer, "just good friends"', *British Society of Criminology Newsletter*, 76(Summer): 27–9.

Squires, P. and Stephen, D. (2005) *Rougher justice: young people and anti-social behaviour*, Cullompton: Willan Publishing.

Standing, G. (2011) *The precariat: the new dangerous class*, London: Bloomsbury Press.

Stott, C. and Reicher, S. (1998) 'Crowd action as inter-group process: introducing the police perspective', *European Journal of Social Psychology*, 28(4): 509–29.

Stott, C. and Reicher, S. (2011) *Mad mobs and Englishmen? Myths and realities of the 2011 riots*, London: Robinson.

Taylor, I. (1980) 'The law and order issue in the British general election and the Canadian federal election of 1979: crime, populism and the state', *Canadian Journal of Sociology*, 5(3): 285–311.

Taylor, I. (1999) *Crime in context: a critical criminology of market societies*, Cambridge: Polity Press.

Thatcher, M. (1985) 'Margaret Thatcher Foundation'. Available at: http://www.margaretthatcher.org/document/106113 (accessed 5 August 1985).

Tonry, M. (2010) 'Rebalancing the criminal justice system in favour of the victim: the costly consequences of populist rhetoric', in T. Bottoms and J. Roberts (eds) *Hearing the victim: adversarial justice, crime, victims and the state*, London: Routledge, pp 72–103.

Topping, J.R. (2008) 'Diversifying from within: community policing and the governance of security in Northern Ireland', *British Journal of Criminology*, 48(6): 778–97.

Travis, A. (2015) 'Britain's first titan-sized prison gets green light', *The Guardian*, 27 March.

Treadwell, J., Briggs, D., Winlow, S. and Hall, S. (2012) 'Shopocalypse now: consumer culture and the English riots of 2011', *British Journal of Criminology*, 53(1): 1–17.

Tyler, I. (2013) *Revolting subjects: social abjection and resistance in neoliberal Britain*, London: Zed books.

Wacquant, L. (2008) *Urban outcasts: a comparative sociology of advanced marginality*, Cambridge: Polity Press.

Wacquant, L. (2009) *Punishing the poor: the neoliberal government of social insecurity*, Durham: Duke University Press.

Waddington, P.A.J. (2012) 'Explaining the riots: August 2011 riots in the context of policing public order', *Criminal Justice Matters*, 87(1): 10–11.

Winlow, S. and Hall, S. (2012) 'A predictably obedient riot: post-politics, consumer culture, and the English riots of 2011', *Cultural Politics*, 8(3): 465–88.

Young, J. (1999) *The exclusive society*, London: Sage.

FOURTEEN

Equalities: the impact of welfare reform and austerity by gender, disability and age

Kirstein Rummery

Introduction

As is widely discussed in this book, policies under the post-2010 Conservative–Liberal Democrat coalition government were dominated by the spectre of the 2008 private sector financial crisis, which by 2010, had turned into a global recession, reducing economic production and seeing rises in unemployment. The UK, in common with other G20 countries, initially adopted a fiscal stimulus approach (quantitative easing), which slowed the recession but led to a sharp rise in the budget deficit, to 11.6% in 2009/10 (ONS, 2010), the highest since 1945. What had started out as a private financial crisis was very quickly turned into a crisis of public policy, particularly in countries such as Ireland and Greece, which found it difficult to borrow money at preferential rates to service their growing deficits.

The coalition government that came to power in 2010 took the position that addressing the deficit was an economic necessity, and social policy therefore followed this aim (see Chapter Two). The primary mechanism used to achieve this was cuts to public expenditure – a policy paradigm that has come to be known as 'austerity'. The 2010 Comprehensive Spending Review detailed how these cuts would be distributed across departments (see Table 14.1).

However, simply examining the scale of the cuts by department masks the fact that they fell disproportionately on certain groups of people. Those dependent on the state for a proportion or the whole of their income were more affected by the changes than the average: while an estimated 21% of people in the UK are living in poverty, they are bearing the brunt of 39% of the funding cuts. Moreover, over half the cuts fell on social security and local government, despite them making up only 27% of central government expenditure – and 60%

Table 14.1: The coalition government's plans for public expenditure, in £ billions

Department	Spending 2010/11	Spending 2014–15	Annual change (% change in real terms)
Schools	£60.6	£61.5	£0.9 (−11.1%)
National Health Service	£101.8	£114.6	£12.8 (0%)
Transport	£13.1	£12.2	−£0.9 (−19.5%)
English local authorities	£38.6	£27.3	−£11.3 (−41.9%)
Business and universities	£20	£16.1	−£3.9 (−32.1%)
Justice	£22.4	£19.6	−£3.1 (−26.4%)
Defence	£35.7	£36.8	£1.1 (−9.5%)
Foreign aid	£9.6	£12.8	£3.2 (20.7%)
Energy, environment and culture	£14.1	£12.4	−£1.7 (−24.7%)
Scotland	£28.2	£28.1	−£0.1 (−13.0&)
Wales	£14.9	£14.5	−£0.4(−15.3%)
Northern Ireland	£16	£16.4	£0.4 (−10.1%)
Tax administration	£10.7	£11.1	£0.4(−8.9%)
Treasury and quangos	£1.1	£3.9	£2.8(241.9%)
Pensions	£71.6	£80.6	£0 (0%)
Benefits and tax credits	£118.4	£111.3	−£7.1 (−18.6%)

Note: Quangos – quasi-autonomous non-governmental organisations.
Source: HM Treasury (2010).

of local government expenditure goes on social care for children and adults (Duffy, 2013). The purpose of this chapter is to examine the impact that this paradigm and the policies introduced by the coalition government had on four groups of people who are at risk of inequality, poverty and social exclusion: women, working-age disabled people, older people and young children. Data were not easily available to assess the impact of policies on people from minority ethnic groups, but, where possible, the cumulative impact of intersectionality, that is, where equalities issues such as gender, disability, age and ethnicity intersect, is discussed.

A gendered analysis of spending cuts

Adopting a policy of fiscal austerity rather than Keynesian investment in response to the crisis meant that cuts to public services were inevitable. Health was the most protected area, seeing only a 1% cut of the initial budget in 2009/10. Housing was cut by 27% of the budget, and the other hardest hit departments included further and higher education (31%), social care (20%) and early years education and care (18%). One fifth of the cut in budget came from other areas, including social security. Cutting spending meant that while 21% of the population are estimated to be living in poverty, they bore the cost of 39% of the cuts. These cuts impact differently on women, and particular groups of women, than they do on men. Twenty percent of women's income comes from social security and tax benefits, as compared to 10% of men's, and of the £26 billion of changes to benefits and tax credits since 2010, £22 billion were born by women and £4 billion by men (Fawcett Society, 2015).

Moreover, women's role as parents and carers means that they are more at risk of poverty and will feel the impact of the withdrawal or reduction of state benefits more acutely than men. For example, 92% of lone parents are women, and 95% of lone parents dependent on income support are women; 74% of people claiming Carers Allowance are women, and they make up around 60% of unpaid carers (Carers UK, 2014). In addition, the development of Universal Credit, designed to make work pay and encourage more people into the workforce, did not take childcare issues into account. As a result of changes to child benefit, the childcare element of Working Tax Credit and Income Support, low-income women with very young children were forced into looking for work, women with high-income partners lost what was often their only independent source of income, all women lost some income that was the only source targeted directly at children and access to childcare was reduced for low-income families, particularly lone parents (Poverty Alliance, 2013).

It is estimated that unpaid carers save the UK over a third of its national budget. However, Carers Allowance is currently around only 25% of the minimum wage, which makes it the lowest rate for any income replacement benefit. Around £1 billion will have been cut from carers' incomes between 2011 and 2018 (Carers UK, 2014). Women make up the majority of carers (particularly those of working age), are the majority of those providing more than 35 hours of care per week and are also more likely than male carers to be working part-time (and it should be noted that women are less likely than men to self-identify as carers, so these figures are likely to be underestimates).

Women are also more likely than men to be working as formal carers, either in the statutory or market sector (which relies heavily on services commissioned using state funding, either through local authorities or through disabled and older people using care-related benefits such as Disability Living Allowance and self-directed support payments to purchase care and support). This means that, as workers, they will bear the brunt of cuts to social care funding.

Overall, workers in the public sector numbered around 5.7 million in mid-2013, and made up just under 20% of total employment, and an estimated 1.1 million further job losses by 2018/19 would take the share of the workforce working in general government to just 14.8% (IFS, 2014). Nearly two thirds of this workforce are women, and they tend to work in the National Health Service (NHS), education and social care. Given that the NHS has been largely protected compared to other areas, this proportion will increase. In addition, the changes to the delivery of public services have also had an impact on women. There have been big increases in private sector employees delivering services historically dominated by the public sector. For example, in the mid-1990s, private sector nursery nurses and assistants accounted for around 40% of the nursery workforce, but that increased to more than 70% by 2010. In social care, the statutory workforce numbers have remained stable, while numbers in the private sector have more than doubled since 1995, and by 2010, three quarters of the social care workforce were in the private sector.

The growing use of casualisation in the workforce, and the move towards direct payments, means not only that women's jobs are subject to cuts as part of public sector spending reductions, but also that women experience substantially less job protection and higher rates of income deflation and job insecurity as their jobs are moved into the private sector. The Women's Budget Group (Reed et al, 2013; Women's Budget Group, 2013a) has estimated the cumulative effect of losses to total income (see Table 14.2).

This represents a substantial loss of control over income by women, particularly those with low incomes (Pearson and Elson, 2015). In addition, low-income families are experiencing greater food poverty (the use of food banks more than doubled between 2012 and 2014 [Mason and Butler, 2014]) due to benefits sanctions and low pay, as well as direct cuts to state-derived income. Certain groups of women have also suffered multiple discrimination: as well as being over-represented among carers, women are also over-represented among disabled people

Table 14.2: Women's Budget Group estimates for percentage of loss of income, 2008–13

Group	% loss	Disaggregated by sex
Single parents	15.1	Single mothers lose 15.6%; single fathers lose 11.7%
Single pensioners	11.6	Single women pensioners lose 12.5%; single male pensioners lose 9.5%
Couples with children	9.7	Data not available
Single childless adults	9.7	Single women lose 10.9%; single men lose 9.0%
Couple pensioners	8.6	Data not available
Childless couples	4.1	Data not available

Source: Women's Budget Group (2013b)

likely to be in full-time employment and to be earning less than disabled men – the disability pay gap for disabled men compared to non-disabled men is 11%, but for disabled women, it is 22% (Equalities and Human Rights Commission, 2010). Refugee women also experience much greater delays in accessing benefits such as Job Seeker's Allowance, Child Benefit and Child Tax Credits, and this can cause significant hardship for women (and children) without access to kinship-based networks of support (Scottish Refugee Council, 2014). In addition, the impact on older women, although yet to be fully assessed, includes the impact of the raising of pension ages (pushing older women into work activity for which they often lack the skills or training) and the 'triple lock' on the uprating of the state pension (on which women are more likely to be reliant than men).

Given that under the Equalities Act 2010, public bodies (including the government) have a statutory duty to consider the gendered impacts of any changes or cuts to the benefits or services they provide, why do we see such a large gender differential in the impact of fiscal policy? Pearson and Elson (2015) argue persuasively that this is due to two main factors. First, there is a lack of women's representation in the decision-making bodies at both supranational and national level in public sector finance. For example, women hold only 4.5% of the seats on the International Monetary Fund (IMF) board and make up only 5% of the key decision-makers in the European Central Bank (Schuberth and Young, 2011), and only three of the 19 largest European Union (EU) countries have female finance ministers (Atkins and Whiffen, 2011). Furthermore, there were no senior women in the Treasury during the coalition government's term of office. Second, the coalition government blocked or ignored challenges from the equalities sector. Pearson and Elson (2015, pp 13–14) found:

> Estimates by researchers at the House of Commons Library, at the request of Shadow Minister Yvette Cooper, found that £5.8 billion (72 per cent) of the money raised by changes to personal income tax and social security cuts would be paid by women and £2.2 billion (28 per cent) by men ... the Coalition government ignored the statutory requirement to consider the equalities impact when it drew up the austerity measures in 2010.

Challenges by the Fawcett Society (a third sector women's rights organisation) and the Equalities and Human Rights Commission were also suppressed or ignored (McKay et al, 2013). It is probably going too far to say that fiscal austerity was a policy aimed at disempowering women, but it is certainly the case that, intentionally or not, it has contributed to the growth of gender inequality in the UK.

Disability: the cumulative impact of workfare and austerity

Just as women's organisations were concerned with the coalition government's failure to take into account the gendered nature of fiscal austerity, so disability rights and other organisations were concerned about the failure to undertake a Cumulative Impact Assessment of the changes to disabled people. In particular, the combination of changes and funding cuts to social care, and cuts in income as a result of changes to benefits and taxes, has had a significant effect on disabled people in the UK. Disabled people (8% of the population) have borne 29% of the cuts, and severely disabled people (2% of the population) have borne 15% of the cuts (Duffy, 2013).

By far the largest cuts directly affecting disabled people have been to the grants awarded to English local authorities, which will have seen a 41.9% reduction in their income (see also Chapter Ten). Moreover, the cuts to Scotland, Wales and Northern Ireland will include NHS services, so if they opt (as they have done so far) to ring-fence and protect the NHS, it is social care that will suffer. Social care includes services for older people, working-age disabled people, mental health services and safeguards for disabled, abused and neglected children. Mental health services are already underfunded, and both NHS and social care struggle to meet their statutory obligations, as do children's services. Effectively, these are ring-fenced because it is not legally possible to reduce safeguarding services, which leaves an ever-shrinking pot for older and physically disabled people, those with non-life-threatening mental health issues, carers and disabled children and their families.

Although local authorities could offset some of the impact of cuts to funding by raising council tax levels, in practice, they have not done so significantly (and, indeed, in Scotland, council taxes remain frozen). Between 2010 and 2012, funding for adult social care and for children's social care in England were each cut by around £1.9 billion (ADSS, 2012; CIPFA and NSPCC, 2012). This has led to reductions in the level of funding given to voluntary organisations and advocacy services, reductions in direct support (including direct payments and personal budgets), increases in the threshold of eligibility for services (eg by stopping provision for those having low or moderate needs), and increases in social care charges (Duffy, 2013).

The cuts to social care have been matched by those to the incomes of disabled people from a complicated array of changes to benefits, some designed to increase workforce participation (workfare) and others to reduce the benefits bill (austerity). For example, the move from Disability Living Allowance to Personal Independence Payments was designed to save £1.2 billion, and time-limiting Employment and Support Allowance (ESA) to save £1.2 billion, with a further £2.6 billion coming from changes to tax credits and £1.9 billion from Housing Benefit reforms. The cumulative effect of these changes means that the austerity cuts are costing the average disabled person £4,410 per annum – nine times the national average – while severely disabled people are losing £8,832 per annum – 19 times the national average (Duffy, 2013).

Moreover, the complexity of these changes has caused significant hardship and distress, as some of the lowest-income and most vulnerable people have had to deal with income uncertainty caused by system changes, delays and sanctions (often wrongly imposed). Recent figures show that while initial assessments move around 30% of claimants off Incapacity Benefits and onto the Fit for Work group of ESA, around 30% of appeals are upheld (and this proportion is rising as claimants are entering into the second and sometimes third round of appeals); when the cost of administering the appeals is added to human cost, this is a very expensive revolving door. While the most recent figures indicate that mortality rates overall for those on ESA are lower than those on Incapacity Benefit (Department for Work and Pensions, 2014) (which supports the 'work/looking for work is good for you' hypothesis underlying the change in the system), a freedom of information request found that over 4,000 people died within six weeks of being assessed as fit to work in 2014/15 (Department for Work and Pensions, 2014; Stone, 2015), making you more likely to die shortly after being found 'fit for work' than to be murdered.

These changes also have a differential effect across different groups of disabled people. In particular, the changes affect older working-age and disabled people, who are expected to seek work. However, disabled women aged over 50 will be disproportionately affected by their lower workforce participation record due to caring commitments and by the cuts in public sector jobs, which would traditionally be where most of these women would find employment.

The impact of austerity by age

Two areas of policy have effectively protected older people from the most severe austerity cuts. The first was the decision to keep state pension levels steady, which meant that pensioners' income fell from 13% below 60% of median income to 10% over the course of the coalition government (Hills, 2015). The second was the protection and ring-fencing of NHS spending in England (and subsequent decisions in the devolved administrations to follow suit), as NHS spending on retired households is nearly double that of non-retired households (Cracknell, 2010).

However, this does mask some of the realities of older people's poverty in the UK. The first of these is that UK state pensions are among the least generous in the developed world (Pensions Commission, 2005), with around half of all pensioners in the UK eligible for means-tested income assistance (Ginn, 2013). The coalition government has done nothing to reverse the inherent inequality and poverty experienced by older people in the UK: they are caught in a trap of declining real-term incomes and rising costs (particularly fuel costs), which will impact particularly on the poorest pensioners, making post-retirement inequality even wider. The second is that, according to Age Concern, working from Department for Work and Pensions figures, many pensioners do not claim their full income entitlement from the state:

> The latest estimates of take up found that in 2009–12 around a third (up to 1.6 million) of older people who were entitled to Pension Credit were not claiming it. On average they were missing out on over £1700 a year (£33 a week).

- Up to 2.2 million older people were missing out on help with their council tax bill which, on average would have reduced their annual bill by £728.
- Up to 390,000 more older people could have claimed Housing Benefit to reduce their rent by an average of £48 a week. (Age UK, 2015)

The third is that such calculations mask the fact that poverty and inequality are experienced differently by different groups of older people. The Women's Budget Group has calculated that while the flat-rate change to pensioners' incomes are gender-neutral, in real terms, single female pensioners will see a drop in living standards of around 12%, as compared to single men of just under 10%, because not only do they live longer and are likely to be poorer, but they also experience an increased reliance on (and therefore vulnerability to cuts in) social care and other public services. This compares to an overall drop in the standard of living of only 6% for pensioner couples. Moreover, policy decisions to reduce the indexation of pensions mean that pensioners' incomes will reduce in real terms over time, which will affect women more significantly than men as they both tend to start out with a lower pension entitlement (around 75% of men's) and live longer; the differential access to private pensions and savings further exacerbates this inequality (Ginn, 2010).

At the other end of the age spectrum, the under-fives were the focus of a coalition government-commissioned review which found that investment in infrastructure and services, as well as improved monitoring, were vital in tackling child poverty and the associated reduced life chances (Field, 2010; see also Chapter Twelve). However, the poorest under-fives were particularly hard hit by the decision to reduce funding for local authorities, with the result that spending on early years education and Sure Start fell by a quarter between 2009/10 and 2012/13 (Hills, 2015), from £2,508 to £1,867 per child, partly as a result of the withdrawal of ring-fencing. Spending on Child Tax Credits also went down, with only spending on childcare vouchers (a scheme whereby working parents can chose to take part of their salary as tax-free vouchers to be spent on childcare) increasing. However, spending on the 'demand' side of childcare does not increase access for poorer families, and while the number of childcare places increased by roughly 8%, the number of day care centre places reduced substantially – and these centres are more likely to have higher-qualified staff and be able to cater for the needs of disabled and special needs children (Steward, 2015). This will impact on the ability of parents of disabled children to work, and on the early years educational experience of disabled children themselves: both of these are groups who are at significant risk of poverty and social exclusion.

The human face of austerity

Wilkinson and Pickett (2010) point out that the cost to societies of inequality are high, including in relation to infant mortality, life expectancy, violence and greater need for regulation. Growing inequality will therefore result in a need for higher state spending, counteracting both the normative and fiscal objectives of the coalition government. Office for National Statistics data point to the fact that the poorest 10% of households pay 47% of their income back to the state in taxes, whereas middle- to high-income households are paying between 5% and 25% of their income back in tax. Moreover, cuts in public sector jobs mean that there will be lower numbers of women in paid work (women currently make up around 75% of those working for local authorities), so that tax income from these two groups will fall substantially, making it even harder to balance the books and pay off the deficit.

Moreover, the qualitative impact of austerity on specific groups of people can be significant. For example, for *women experiencing or at risk of domestic abuse*: (1) the drop in income to low-income households increases stress and alcohol use, which leads to a rise in the risk of violence; (2) the loss of control over her own income gives an abused woman fewer options to avoid or escape abuse; and (3) the closure of social care services and domestic violence services, as well as cuts to funding to voluntary sector services, leads to a 'triple jeopardy' effect.

In addition, certain groups of *women at risk of or experiencing multiple disadvantage*, who have traditionally been poorly served by the state, will particularly suffer from the withdrawal of funding from key areas. For example, cuts to legal aid will disproportionately affect the poorest women, refugee women, those experiencing domestic abuse, victims of sexual violence and those challenging welfare and benefits decisions. The abolition of Sure Start will affect not only the poorest children (reversing the progress made on child poverty and child health and education outcomes by the previous Labour administrations), but also their mothers, many of whom will no longer be able to afford to work, thus exposing both themselves and their families to significant risks of poverty. Disabled and older women (who are most likely to be providing *and* receiving care and support) will be disproportionately affected by the cuts to local authority grants and social care, as well as increased workfare and conditionality in the benefits system. Cuts to transport and housing services have a significant impact on poorer and older women, as well as those living in rural areas, increasing their risk of social exclusion, isolation and poverty.

For *disabled people*, the reductions in services (including specialist childcare services for disabled children) and the higher threshold of need to access them, cuts in support for informal carers and funding for providers and voluntary sector organisations, and the reduction in income also add up to a 'triple jeopardy' impact, leading to a loss of independence and social isolation, and, in many cases, an increase in health problems (and associated costs) for themselves and their families. Moreover, when family members are forced to provide high levels of intimate personal care because there are no alternatives, this leads to a double jeopardy for both disabled people and carers, leaving both at risk of mental and physical health problems, exclusion from the labour market, poverty, social exclusion, and the breakdown of family relationships.

Although pensions and funding for the NHS have been ring-fenced, which protects *older people* from the brunt of austerity, some groups of older people are also seeing the impact of cuts in public services, particularly social care and transport – which disproportionately affects those on low incomes and women, leaving them isolated. Moreover, cuts in preventative spending, such as low- to medium-level social care, leads to a higher risk of falls and ill health needing hospital admissions, which, in turn, makes it much more likely that older people will need residential or nursing home care and be unable to live independently in the community. Cuts in support for carers and disabled people will also have an impact on older people providing care and support to spouses, siblings and parents, meaning that they will have to pick up the slack and provide more help at a time when their own health is likely to be becoming poorer. For those older people without friends and family living close by to provide low- and medium-level social care support, the risks of isolation and preventable physical and mental health problems are also acute.

The final words on the impact of austerity on their lives should come from the people themselves:

> My worst fear is having to give up my job as my husband's needs change. The last few years have been a whirlwind of hospital appointments, dealing with ill health and navigating public services which just seem to make our lives more difficult. I already work part-time. I am in a job which does

not reflect my experience. I won't have any real pension to speak of. But I enjoy working. It's important that as a carer I am able to have something that is about me. Not Carole, the carer. Losing work would be like losing part of who I am. My greatest fear is that I become dependent on benefits. I don't want to live on the absolute pittance that is Carer's Allowance – I don't want to be stigmatised by the press and politicians who say they value what carers do – then whip the rug out from under us. (Engender, 2015, p 11)

The worst thing about ESA/WCAs [work capability assessments] is the ongoing stress of assessment. I have been diagnosed with a long term chronic health condition with no cure, which is made worse by stressful situations, yet I have to be reassessed every year or two and despite filling in the form the same way every single time, the response can be totally different. (Benstead, 2015, p 9)

Whilst in refuge Ms G was informed by the Homeless Case Officer that they accepted the letter from her GP stating that the older boy required his own bedroom as he has severe ADHD and she would be given a 3 bedroom property. When Ms G was subsequently rehoused in a 3 bedroom housing association property she was informed that she would have to pay the bedroom tax for the extra room. (Engender, 2015, p 13)

Larry Newman attending a work capability assessment when a degenerative lung condition made it impossible for him to go on working. The ATOS staff member who carried out the medical test awarded him zero points. He received a letter stating that he was not eligible for ESA and would be fit to return to work within three months. Before three months was up he died from his lung problems. (Spartacus, 2013, p 13)

Conclusions

Towards the end of the coalition government's period in office, the Liberal Democrats sought to develop a rhetoric portraying themselves as mediators against the Conservatives, who they suggested would have made even deeper cuts to benefits and services without their influence. The scale of their electoral defeat in 2015 (seeing them reduced to eight seats, and virtually wiped out in Scotland, losing eight out of nine seats to the SNP) suggests that either the electorate were not convinced by this rhetoric, or that this was not a key issue for them in deciding how to vote. Certainly, the impact of fiscal austerity has been disproportionately felt, so any stated commitment to fairness or heeding equalities issues was not followed through.

It is, however, worth noting areas of policy development that have had positive outcomes in equality terms during the coalition's term in government. The Marriage (Same Sex Couples) Act 2013 allowed same-sex partners full legal marriage, and there was an extension of shared parental leave and free childcare. While the Liberal Democrats claimed these as evidence of their sway in the coalition government (Pack, 2015) the Marriage (Same Sex Couples) Act had, in fact, near-universal cross-party support – all three major parties gave their MPs a free vote and it passed 366 to 161 on its third reading, with some Liberal Democrats voting against the measure at each stage (UK Parliament, 2013). Similarly, policies on parental leave and childcare provision secured cross-party support and were not particularly Liberal Democrat-led.

It is clear from the repeated announcements of further cuts to budgets and welfare that the post-2015 Conservative government intends to pursue fiscal austerity, despite criticism from economists (eg Chu, 2015). Moreover, the ongoing reluctance to publish Department of Work and Pensions figures about numbers of claimants moving from Incapacity Benefit to Jobseeker's Allowance and their outcomes indicates a continued unwillingness to change the direction of travel. It seems that women, disabled people, the youngest and the most vulnerable and poorest will continue to be disproportionately negatively affected by the impact of the post-2008 policy framing of the hegemony of fiscal austerity. It was not low-income women, disabled people, vulnerable children or older people who caused the global financial crisis that shaped so much of the coalition government's social policies, but due to the choice to embrace the ideology and practice of fiscal austerity, it is they that bore the brunt of paying for it and are continuing to do so.

References

ADASS (Association of Directors of Adult Social Services) (2012) 'Adult social care: 2012 state of the nation report'. Available at: http://www.local.gov.uk/documents/10180/5854661/Adult+social+care+funding+2014+state+of+the+nation+report/e32866fa-d512-4e77-9961-8861d2d93238 (accessed 11 September).

Age UK (2015) 'How we can end pensioner poverty'. Available at: http://www.ageuk.org.uk/Documents/EN-GB/Campaigns/end-pensioner-poverty/how_we_can_end_pensioner_poverty_campaign_report.pdf?dtrk=true (accessed 11 September 2015).

Atkins, R. and Whiffen, A. (2011) 'FT ranking of EU finance ministers', *Financial Times*, 23 November.

Benstead, S. (2015) *Welfare that works: Employment and Support Allowance*, London: Spartacus Network.

Carers UK (2014) 'Carers and family finances inquiry: carers struggling with alarming levels of hardship'. Available at: http://www.carersuk.org/for-professionals/policy/policy-library/caring-family-finances-inquiry (accessed 12 September 2015).

Chu, B. (2015) 'Two thirds of economists say coalition austerity harmed the economy', *The Independent*, 1 April. Available at: http://www.independent.co.uk/news/business/news/two-thirds-of-economists-say-coalition-austerity-harmed-the-economy-10149410.html (accessed 12 September 2015).

CIPFA (Chartered Institute of Public Finance and Accountancy) and NSPCC (National Society for the Prevention of Cruelty to Children) (2012) 'Smart cuts? Public spending on children's social care'. Available at: http://www.nspcc.org.uk/globalassets/documents/research-reports/smart-cuts-report.pdf (accessed 11 September 2015).

Cracknell, R. (2010) 'The ageing population: key issues for Parliament 2010'. Available at: http://www.parliament.uk/documents/commons/lib/research/key_issues/Key-Issues-The-ageing-population2007.pdf (accessed 12 September 2015).

Department for Work and Pensions (2014) *Employment and Support Allowance: outcomes of Work Capability Assessments, Great Britain*, London: Department for Work and Pensions.

Duffy, S. (2013) 'A fair society? How the cuts target disabled people'. Available at: http://www.centreforwelfarereform.org/uploads/attachment/354/a-fair-society.pdf (accessed 12 September 2015).

Engender (2015) *A widening gap: women and welfare reform*, Edinburgh: Engender.

Equalities and Human Rights Commission (2010) *How fair is Britain?*, London: Equalities and Human Rights Commission.

Fawcett Society (2015) *Where's the benefit? An independent inquiry into women and Jobseeker's Allowance*, London: Fawcett Society.

Field, F. (2010) *The foundation years: preventing poor children becoming poor adults: the report of the Independent Review on Poverty and Life Chances*, London: HM Government.

Ginn, J. (2010) 'Unkindest cuts: the impact on older people', *Radical Statistics*, 103: 50–7.

Ginn, J. (2013) 'Austerity and inequality: exploring the impact of cuts in the UK by gender and age', *Research on Ageing and Social Policy*, 1(1): 28–53.

Hills, J. (2015) 'The coalition's record on cash transfers, poverty and inequality 2010–2015'. Available at: http://sticerd.lse.ac.uk/dps/case/spcc/WP11.pdf (accessed 11 September 2015).

HM Treasury (2010) *Spending review 2010*, London: The Stationery Office.

IFS (Institute for Fiscal Studies) (2014) 'Government spending on public services', presentation to The Kings Fund, London. Available at: http://www.kingsfund.org.uk/audio-video/paul-johnson-government-spending-public-services (accessed 11 September 2015).

Mason, R. and Butler, P. (2014) 'DWP advising jobcentres on sending claimants to foodbanks', *The Guardian*, 11 March. Available at: http://www.theguardian.com/society/2014/mar/11/food-bank-jobcentre-dwp-referrals-welfare (accessed 29 November 2015).

McKay, A., Campbell, J., Thomson, E. and Ross, S. (2013) 'Economic recession and recovery in the UK: what's gender got to do with it?', *Feminist Economics*, 19(3): 108–23.

ONS (Office for National Statistics) (2010) *Pocket databank*, London: HM Treasury.

Pack, M. (2015) 'What did the Liberal Democrats achieve in government?'. Available at: http://www.markpack.org.uk/libdem-infographic/ (accessed 12 September 2015).

Pearson, R. and Elson, D. (2015) 'Transcending the impact of the financial crisis in the United Kingdom: towards plan F – a feminist economic strategy', *Feminist Review*, 109: 8–30.

Pensions Commission (2005) *A new pension settlement for the twenty-first century: the second report*, London: The Stationery Office.

Poverty Alliance (2013) 'Submission from the Poverty Alliance – women and work call for evidence by the Scottish Parliament Equal Opportunities Committee', Glasgow: Poverty Alliance.

Reed, H., Elson, D. and Himmelweit, S. (2013) *An adequate standard of living: a child's rights based quantitative analysis of budgetary decisions 2010–13*, London: Office of the Children's Commissioner.

Schuberth, H. and Young, B. (2011) 'The role of gender in governance of the financial sector', in B. Young, I. Bakker and D. Elson (eds) *Questioning financial governance from a feminist perspective*, London: Routledge, pp 132–54.

Scottish Refugee Council (2014) 'Holistic integration service year 1 evaluation report'. Available at: http://www.scottishrefugeecouncil. org.uk/assets/0000/8576/Holistic_Integration_Service_-_year_1_ evaluation_report.pdf (accessed 14 September 2015).

Spartacus (2013) *The people's review of the Work Capability Assessment: further evidence*, London: Spartacus.

Stewart, K. (2015) *The coalition's record on the under fives: policy spending and outcomes 2010–2015*, London: CASE.

Stone, J. (2015) 'Thousands have died soon after being found "fit to work" by the DWP's benefit tests', *The Independent*, 27 August. Available at: http://www.independent.co.uk/news/uk/politics/over-4000-people-have-died-soon-after-being-found-fit-to-work-by-the-dwps-benefit-tests-10474474.html (accessed 14 September 2015).

UK Parliament (2013) 'Bill stages – Marriage (Same Sex Couples) Bill 2012–13 to 2013–14'. Available at: http://services.parliament. uk/bills/2013-14/marriagesamesexcouplesbill/stages.html (accessed 14 September 2015).

Wilkinson, R. and Pickett, K. (2010) *The spirit level: why equality is better for everyone*, Harmondsworth: Penguin.

Women's Budget Group (2013a) *The impact on women of the Autumn Financial Statement*, London: Women's Budget Group.

Women's Budget Group (2013b) *To ensure economic recovery for women we need Plan F*, London: Women's Budget Group.

FIFTEEN

Social policy, the devolved administrations and the UK coalition government

Derek Birrell and Ann Marie Gray

Introduction

Since the establishment of devolution for Scotland, Wales and Northern Ireland in 1999, a major feature has been the prominence of social policy in terms of the nature of devolved powers and in terms of devolved expenditure (Chaney and Drakeford, 2004; Mooney et al, 2006; Birrell, 2009). This was again demonstrated in the various programmes for government published following the 2011 elections for the devolved assemblies and the Scottish Parliament. There was originally a degree of policy continuity from the previous administrations, produced by rather similar electoral outcomes. In Scotland, the Scottish National Party (SNP) moved from a position as a minority government to forming the government with a majority (Cairney, 2011). In Wales, a Labour–Plaid Cymru coalition changed to a Labour administration, but with only 50% of the Assembly members. Northern Ireland continued with its form of compulsory coalition or power-sharing, consisting of a four-party executive, later a five-party executive, although with two parties, the Democratic Unionists and Sinn Fein, in a dominant position. The establishment of a UK Conservative–Liberal Democratic coalition brought an incongruence to the party and ideological alignments between the UK and the devolved governments and the increased possibility of major policy divergence. Three other debates were to have an important influence on the development of social policy. First, there was a debate on the future of devolution under the coalition government: this was to mean that a settled direction for the future of devolved policies and the meaning of the union was not clear (Jeffery et al, 2010). Second, there was a debate on the enhancements and changes in devolved powers: in Scotland, the debate on the powers of a Scottish government related to the campaign for independence for Scotland and the referendum; a major debate also commenced in Wales on the extension of legislative powers; while completing the devolution of justice and policing and some other limited extensions dominated the Northern Ireland debate. Third, there was an extensive debate on the financial arrangements and increasing fiscal devolution and responsibilities.

Context for proposals and action on financial and constitutional powers

A number of contextual factors were important for the operation of devolution under the coalition government in relation to social policy. These centred on proposals to introduce reform to the financial arrangements to devolution and changes to other devolved powers.

For most of this time, the financial arrangements for devolution remained unchanged, dominated by the Barnett Formula, which is used to allocate more than half of total public expenditure to the devolved administrations. The formula, used by the UK government for the last 30 years, has a partly historical base (with increments added on to the previous year's allocation), is partly population-based and is partly linked to changes to expenditure in England. The formula produced a higher per capita expenditure for Northern Ireland, followed by Scotland and Wales and then England, but it has been calculated that need in Wales is less adequately met by the formula (McLean et al, 2013). There are two additional forms of funding outside the Barnett Formula that have specific relevance for Northern Ireland. First, Annually Managed Expenditure (AME), which is demand-led and agreed annually with the Treasury, makes up some 40% of total managed expenditure. The main component is social security, which is not yet devolved in Scotland and Wales. Second, there have been instances of significant amounts of funding being provided outside of the Formula, often associated with the unique post-conflict situation in Northern Ireland (eg funding for devolving policing and justice and European Union [EU] Peace Funding) (Birrell, 2015). Under the tax variation powers agreed when the Scottish Parliament was set up in 1999, the Scottish government could vary the tax rate by up to 3p, but these powers were never used and ceased to be available from 2007. The Scotland Act 2012 gave the Scottish government further devolved tax powers: to set a Scottish rate of income tax from 2016; to introduce taxes on land transactions and on waste disposal from landfill from 2015; and powers for new taxes to be created in Scotland and for additional taxes to be devolved, subject to certain criteria (Seely, 2015).

While financial resources were largely determined by the UK government, the devolved administrations had a very wide discretion over expenditure on devolved services. During the life of the coalition government, the issue of the adequacy of funding and the need for devolved financial responsibility grew in importance. The range of devolved powers did undergo some significant changes, but a momentum for enhanced devolved powers increased, especially in Scotland and Wales, and a series of government and political inquiries, along with the Scottish independence referendum, dominated devolved politics. After the major development of full legislative powers for the National Assembly for Wales in 2011, the UK government established a commission to review its powers. The Silk Commission reported in two parts, with the first (Commission on Devolution in Wales, 2012) leading to the Wales Act 2014. This established new tax and borrowing powers and created the possibility of a reduction in income tax and a Welsh income tax subject to a referendum. The second Silk report (Commission on Devolution in Wales, 2014) resulted in recommendations largely accepted by the UK government for additional powers for the Assembly, but to be included in new legislation after the 2015 general election. In Scotland, there had been a major review of the devolution arrangements, including financial accountability, supported by the Scottish Parliament, other than the SNP, and the UK government. The recommendations of the Calman Commission (Commission on Scottish Devolution, 2009) were accepted by the UK government and became the basis for the Scotland Act 2012. The main measure, the introduction of a Scottish income tax, would not become operative until 2015, and the other enhanced powers were limited to more minor matters, including air guns, speed limits and the drink-drive limit. In the run-up to the Scottish referendum, all of the main UK parties agreed to further increase devolved powers in the event of a 'no' vote. Subsequently, the Smith Commission was set up to find agreement on further devolved powers to be enacted by Westminster after the general election. The agreed list would this time include significant social security powers, covering benefits for disabled people, carers, those who are ill and discretionary housing benefits. It also included new benefits, top-ups to reserved benefits and adjustment to the benefits cap. In addition were powers over Parliament, broadcasting, transport, elections and energy (Smith Commission, 2014). Northern Ireland originally presented a less complex scenario, with the completion in 2012 of the devolution of justice and policing powers and a debate on the possible devolution of corporation tax.

The policies of the UK government on austerity measures to reduce the deficit through a combination of cuts and the reconstitution of services (Taylor-Gooby, 2013) inevitably had what were seen as adverse impacts on the devolved administrations' resources and capacities. All three devolved governments expressed concern at the scale and consequences of the cuts and, in 2010, issued a joint declaration opposing the government's spending plans (Birrell, 2012). The austerity measures were to eventually present a more conflictual political context. In Northern Ireland, the failure of the Assembly to pass a version of the Welfare Reform Act led to a context of internal dispute and conflict with the UK government.

Operational context

A further context, which has become more important as devolution has become fully operative, has been the emergence of overlaps and entanglements. This has required agreements on intergovernmental cooperation and joint decision-making, on such topics as marine planning, misuse of drugs regulations, company law and regulation for charities, while the Scottish Parliament had to develop a closer relationship with the Health and Safety Executive (Scotland Office, 2009). UK and Scottish ministers established a joint ministerial working group on welfare to discuss the implementation of welfare reforms. It has also been necessary for the UK government to liaise with the devolved administrations to produce integrated reports and responses for the EU, for example, on social inclusion, and for the United Nations in relation to a range of conventions and treaties. In some instances, overlaps have appeared as conflicts leading to difficulties, for example, in the case of children held at Dungavel Immigration Centre in Scotland and health-care entitlements for refugees. The ultimate outcome can be the use of judicial review, as, for example, happened in Wales over powers affecting local government.

Programmes of government and policies

A commitment to particular political and social values has had a central role in underpinning devolved social policies, particularly in Scotland and Wales. This has been described by Keating (2005) as a sense of shared responsibilities and community ethos that challenges neoliberal assumptions, and as continuing strong support the welfare state and universalism (Mooney and Scott, 2012). Comprehensive universalist policies had also been seen as building civil and national solidarity and new forms of social citizenship (McEwen, 2005; Wincott, 2006; Birrell, 2012). This has seen devolution regarded as a bulwark against a 'race to the bottom' (Mooney and Scott, 2012, p 12), enhancing welfare entitlements (Keating, 2013) and combating austerity (Drakeford, 2013), with even a degree of political consensus in Northern Ireland about the need to reduce the impact of austerity measures.

The Scottish and Welsh governments each produce a programme for government, revised each year (Scottish Government, 2015 and Welsh Government, 2015 are the latest), while the Northern Ireland Programme for government is produced for the whole five-year period (see Northern Ireland Executive, 2011). The Scottish and Welsh programmes contain a rationale for the policies and legislative proposals, laid out with a preamble outlining the value position of the governments. In Scotland, the most recent programmes of the SNP government have been based on three priorities: creating a stronger economy; two social policy goals (building a fairer Scotland and tackling inequality); and pushing policy to engage people and communities. The value focus is on a stronger economy producing a fairer society and reducing poverty and all forms of inequality. This has translated into legislation on childcare, education and carers' support, and strategies on the integration of health and social care, welfare mitigation, the protection of vital public services, community engagement, and affordable housing.

The Welsh programmes for government have identified 12 main areas for programme delivery and action, with six clearly falling under a social policy heading: health, education, supporting people, homes, equality and tackling poverty. Three others relate, in part, to social policy topics: safer communities, rural communities and public service improvement. Recent legislation has been focused on social care, housing, public health and planning reform, and an innovative measure on sustainable environmental, economic and social development. There has been a continuing focus on early years, educational attainment, worklessness, health quality, support for users and carers, and collaboration between public bodies. Protecting the welfare state, social services and the public sector has, as in Scotland, been a major aspect of devolved policy.

Northern Ireland presents a different scenario, and the programme for government has to reflect the views of five different parties with widely separate interests and ideologies. This means that the degree of consensus is more limited and commitments to policies often reflect a lowest common denominator approach (Gray and Birrell, 2012). The main priority is given to an economic objective: to grow a vibrant economy that will transform people's lives. Of the five main policy priorities, only one is clearly a social policy objective – to tackle disadvantage and improve health – with one other aiming at high-quality public services. In practice, the amount of social policy legislation has been limited, with much related to the restructuring of health provision.

Social policy and the devolved administrations 2010–2015: categories of social policy development

Social policy development in the period 2010 to 2015 can be placed in categories of development: the continuation of significant divergent policies; the development of new divergence and innovation; policies introduced to combat the austerity measures introduced by the coalition government; and convergence in social policies.

Continuation of major divergent policies introduced prior to 2010

Some examples of divergence in social policy between Westminster and Scotland, Wales and Northern Ireland pre-date devolution. In health and social care, for example, the Scottish and Welsh offices had introduced some distinctive features. In Northern Ireland, the existence of a devolved Parliament at Stormont between 1922 and 1972 allowed for possibly more radical divergence, in particular, the establishment of an integrated structure of health and social care in the 1970s, which remains unique in the UK (Birrell and Gray, 2013). In the areas of education and family policy, it could be argued that devolution built on something of a legacy of distinctiveness in both policy and administration in Scotland. To a considerable extent, however, policy development in Scotland, Wales and Northern Ireland was about implementing policy made at Westminster. The market-based health reforms introduced by the Conservative governments in the 1990s were introduced across the UK, as were radical policy changes in social security and housing.

In the decade from 1998, social policy developments become more divergent and policies in Scotland and Wales, in particular, seemed to reflect a different ethos and values from those existing at Westminster. In the area of health, the first Scottish Labour–Liberal Democratic devolved government continued the policy aim instigated by New Labour of abolishing competition in health care; in 2004, it abolished health care trusts and set up community health partnerships, thereby ending the internal market in health care. In 2007, the Labour–Plaid

Cymru coalition government proposed the abolition of the internal market in health (Welsh Government, 2007), and the purchaser–provider model of health-care commissioning in Wales ended in 2008. Both Scotland and Wales moved to resource allocation systems. In Northern Ireland, while the system appeared similar to that operating in England, in practice, it was much less of a true commissioning system due to the lack of providers in the market and the small geographical scale of Northern Ireland. All three devolved countries abolished prescription charges – Wales in 2007, Northern Ireland in 2010 and Scotland in 2011.

Since 2010, while there is some evidence of shared health and social care goals – more personal care, better integration between health and social care, improvements in standards – there is growing divergence in terms of how each of the governments of the UK feels these can be achieved. Patient choice, which has had a strong focus in England, and is seen as a key driver in pushing up performance has not been seen as such a priority elsewhere in the UK. There has been increasing organisational divergence, with none of the devolved administrations moving in the direction of the radical health-care reforms introduced via the Westminster coalition government's Health and Social Care Act 2012 (see Chapter Five). Bevan et al (2014, p 19), in a study of the four health systems in the UK, argue that that while the NHS in England:

> is acting increasingly as a public insurer, funding commissioners to contract with 'any qualified' provider, and with patients empowered to exercise choice in a system in which 'money follows the patient' ... the health services in Scotland and Wales have reverted to being traditional state monopolies run by organisations funded to deliver care to their local populations.

They conclude that Northern Ireland could arguably also fall into the latter category. Although highly critical of the availability of comparable data (a situation that they argue has worsened since devolution), Bevan et al (2014, p 115) conclude that, based on the available evidence, 'increasing divergence of policies since devolution has not been associated with a matching divergence of performance'. There is, however, much debate about the actual role and operation of choice and the degree of privatisation in the NHS in England (Pollock, 2014; Powell and Miller, 2014). While the coalition government's programme for government stated that 'We will give every patient the power to choose any healthcare provider that meets NHS standards, within

NHS prices' (Cabinet Office, 2010, p 26), most patients remained loyal to local hospitals and services, and the Secretary of State for Health admitted in 2014 that patient choice was not the key to improving performance (West, 2014).

Significant differences emerging in adult social care and education were maintained after 2010, including the decision by the Scottish government in 2002 to introduce free long-term personal care for the over-65s. Despite concerns about future affordability and unmet need, this has remained a key aspect of adult social care provision in Scotland. The Scottish government also abolished tuition fees for university education. Although the more limited powers of the Welsh government meant that it had to introduce tuition fees in line with England of up to £9,000, it also introduced a cap on individual student payments of £3,810 for Welsh students studying anywhere in the UK. In Northern Ireland, fees were set considerably lower, and in 2015, at £3,805, they have been maintained at a level well below the maximum of £9,000 payable in England. All three devolved countries have continued Education Maintenance Allowances, a benefit that has been ended in England. Distinct differences in early years and childcare policy and provision emerging after devolution in terms of entitlement, models of provision and inspection have also been maintained post-2010 (Gambaro et al, 2014; Lloyd and Potter, 2014). In education, developments in England, such as the introduction of free schools, the extension of academy schools and the scrapping of modular exams for GCSE and A levels, were not adopted in other jurisdictions.

In the case of social security policy, there was initially less scope for divergence, with powers over social security in Scotland and Wales being reserved by Westminster. Northern Ireland, while theoretically having responsibility for social security policy, has, until the Welfare Reform Act 2012, largely maintained parity with legislation in Great Britain. Prior to this, examples of divergence in Northern Ireland tended to be at the margins of policy, for example, building some protection for lone parents against conditionality into the regulations of the 2010 welfare reform legislation (Wiggan, 2012; Gray and Birrell, 2012). The constraints imposed on the devolved parliaments' ability to tackle poverty resulting from Westminster control over social security, financially and legislatively, and the use of policy levers to mitigate this has been discussed (see, eg, Drakeford, 2007; Mooney and Scott, 2012). However, it was the response of the devolved administrations to the austerity measures introduced by the Westminster coalition government and the opposition to the Welfare Reform Act 2012 that was to generate greater and new divergence in social security policy.

Developing new divergence post-2010

Between 2010 and 2015, new divergences emerged in a number of policy areas. A key issue has been the response of governments to poverty, with devolved governments in Scotland and Wales demonstrating stronger institutional commitment to addressing poverty. In this area, the devolved administrations have considerable autonomy (although bearing in mind the aforementioned constraints relating to social security policy). Lodge et al (2015) argue that the strongest institutional commitment to addressing poverty can be found in Wales, pointing to the legal duty on local authorities to demonstrate how they are contributing to reducing child poverty, the number of programmes to address poverty (including the Flying Start programme focused on addressing early years disadvantage) and the existence of a cross-government action plan. While analysis shows continuing challenges to reducing poverty in Scotland (McKendrick et al, 2014; Kenway et al, 2015), Scotland has made the most consistent progress in addressing child poverty, and the range of initiatives aimed at tackling poverty indicates the prominence given to the issue by successive devolved governments. In June 2015, the Scottish First Minister announced the appointment of a First Minister's independent adviser on poverty and inequality, with responsibilities including recommending actions to tackle poverty and assessing the government's performance.

In Northern Ireland, there has been considerably less political focus on addressing poverty than in Wales or Scotland, with attention being focused on improving outcomes through economic growth but with little connection being made between economic and social policies. This is exemplified by the cross-party support for the devolution of corporation tax, which would allow the Northern Ireland executive to set a lower rate than in the rest of the UK and, it is argued, would result in greater inward investment and economic growth for Northern Ireland. Concern has been expressed about the impact of this on public spending in Northern Ireland as the Treasury offsets the reduction in tax revenue against the block grant (Horgan and Gray, 2012), and the economic argument for reducing corporation tax (Baker and Murphy, 2013; Seely, 2015). A policy document, *Lifetime opportunities* (OFMDFM, 2006), setting out broad aims and aspirations to reduce poverty, was published by the direct rule administration in 2006 during a period of suspension of the Stormont executive. When devolution resumed in 2008, the Northern Ireland executive adopted, in principle, the main aspects of the document, but there was little progress on implementation. More recently, the focus has been on a new initiative, the Delivering Social Change Framework, which the government defines as an outcomes-based approach to tackling poverty and social exclusion, although it consists of little more than a number of signature projects. In an interesting development, in June 2015, a Northern Ireland non-governmental organisation (NGO), the Committee on the Administration of Justice, won a legal challenge against the Northern Ireland executive for failing to adopt a strategy to tackle poverty, social exclusion and patterns of deprivation on the basis of objective need. Following the 2006 St Andrews Agreement, a legal duty was introduced under section 28E of the Northern Ireland Act 1998, which stated that the Executive Committee shall adopt a strategy setting out how it proposes to tackle poverty, social exclusion and patterns of deprivation based on objective need. The court ruled that there is therefore a statutory duty on the Northern Ireland executive to adopt a strategy setting out how it proposes to tackle poverty, social exclusion and patterns of deviation and to base that strategy on objective need. The judgment concluded that the executive had not presented one single, unified, final document (or collection of documents from which a single strategy is identifiable) (Northern Ireland Courts Service, 2015).

In health and social care policy, there is a mixed picture. There have been new divergences, in that none of the devolved administrations followed the major structural changes introduced in the NHS in England. The proposals in the coalition government's Care Act 2014 to impose a cap on individual social care costs and to introduce a more generous means test for residential care will create new differences in how social care will be funded between England, Wales and Northern Ireland (although the Conservative government elected in 2015 announced the postponement of these changes until 2020). The decision by the Westminster coalition government to implement the Law Commission's recommendations on a new consolidated legal framework in adult social care, and similar developments in Wales through the Social Services and Well-being (Wales) Bill 2013, and in Scotland through the Social Care (Self-directed Support) (Scotland) Act 2013 and other legislation on carers and integrated care, means that Northern Ireland is now the only part of the UK not to have modernised the legislative framework for adult social care (Duffy et al, 2015). Scotland has also set up a new system of social health and social care partnerships, with local authorities and health authorities required to provide integrated budgets.

The extent to which the devolved administrations followed Westminster's spending and policy priorities in health was brought into sharp focus in April 2014 when, during a speech to the Welsh Conservative Party, David Cameron was highly critical of the NHS in Wales, pointing to long waiting lists for acute services and a failure to meet key targets. He went on to argue that extra spending on the NHS in England had resulted in more money for the Welsh government. Referring to Offa's Dyke as a 'line between life and death', he accused Welsh politicians of making a conscious decision not to use the money for the NHS in Wales. However, the issue of whether diversity had resulted in different outcomes for users appears to be refuted in a report published later the same year looking at health care in the four nations of the UK, which indicated that there was no evidence that Wales significantly lagged behind England in terms of health outcomes (Bevan et al, 2014). While policymakers in Wales have stressed the distinct health and social care priorities being pursued by the Welsh government – to achieve a fully integrated service and a shift from acute to community care – there has been concern about the pace of progress. A number of challenges faced by the health services in Wales, such as the reducing the number of smaller acute hospitals and the difficulties presented by shifting resources from acute to social care, can also be seen in Northern Ireland, where the Transforming Your Care Agenda has largely not been implemented.

There are some examples of new divergences between Northern Ireland and the UK in relation to social issues, such as sexual orientation, same-sex marriage and abortion, with Northern Ireland becoming increasingly out of step with other UK jurisdictions. This has been linked to a more cautious and conservative approach to policymaking (Gray and Birrell, 2012), but some policy decisions have given rise to debates about the influence of personal religious beliefs on policy. Considerable controversy and legal challenge arose from a decision by a Democratic Unionist Party (DUP) Minister of Health to support a permanent ban on gay men donating blood in Northern Ireland even though this has been lifted in other parts of the UK. There has been a rather limited endorsement of equality legislation, with a sexual orientation strategy promised in the 2008 programme for government not published by 2015. Motions in support of marriage equality for gay couples supported by Sinn Fein, the Alliance Party, the Social Democratic and Labour Party and the Green Party have been defeated in the Northern Ireland Assembly. There has been some challenge to the traditional cross-party support against the reform of abortion law in Northern Ireland (the Abortion Act 1967 does not apply to Northern Ireland, and abortion is available only in very limited circumstances) as a result of individual cases involving fatal foetal abnormality attracting considerable media attention. However, the decision by the Alliance Minister for Justice to consult on amending Northern Ireland's abortion law to allow very restricted access to abortion on the grounds of fatal foetal abnormality has met with opposition from some political parties and the churches in Northern Ireland (Amnesty International, 2015).

In terms of policy innovation, it is perhaps in the response to the austerity measures and welfare reforms introduced by the Westminster coalition government that the most significant debate about, and examples of, new divergence can be found.

The responses of the devolved administrations to the Westminster coalition government's austerity measures

Each of the devolved governments introduced ameliorative measures to address cost-of-living issues, including mitigation for welfare reform. There are similarities in some of the measures introduced by the devolved administrations, including the provision of temporary financial top-ups, measures to address cost-of-living issues and enhancing entitlement to some social provisions, such as free school meals or early years provision.

In Scotland, welfare reform mitigation measures included the establishment of the Scottish Welfare Fund to address needs no longer covered as a result of the abolition of the Discretionary Social Fund, a Council Tax Reduction Scheme funded jointly by central and local government to assist people experiencing hardship as a result of the abolition of the Council Tax Benefit, and discretionary housing payments to offset the impact of the 'bedroom tax'/'spare room subsidy'. Other measures introduced to address cost-of-living issues included the extension of entitlement to free school meals to children in primaries 1 to 3 from January 2015. The Scottish government also launched a Welfare Reform Resilience Fund to support a programme of mitigation projects across some local authorities, including support for mental health issues, fuel advocacy services, housing and money advice, and increasing digital access (Scottish Government, 2014). The Scottish government has also been proactive in considering the wider impact of budget cuts; Asenova et al (2015) report that the Equality Statement published by the Scottish government in 2014 shows a clear commitment to the equality agenda and the likely impact of spending changes on protected equality characteristics. However, they also argue that there has been insufficient focus on identifying new groups with deteriorating standards of living who fall outside traditional protection – such as people at risk of in-work poverty, young unemployed people or those excluded from social protection for periods of time through various qualifying and penalty mechanisms.

The Welsh government's response to austerity and welfare reform has also been to use devolved powers to mitigate some of the impact. There has been a strong focus on addressing the impact of welfare reform on housing through capital investment to develop smaller social-rented housing, some extra funding for discretionary housing payments, funding for council tax support and financial support for research on the impact of welfare reform on housing and awareness and information campaigns. A report in January 2015 by the Auditor General for Wales (2015) on the impact of welfare reform changes on social housing tenants found that Welsh councils and housing associations were struggling to deliver effective and sustainable solutions to address the challenges resulting from the welfare reform housing changes. A report by the Public Accounts Committee in July 2015 (National Assembly for Wales, 2015) was somewhat critical of the impact of measures introduced to date by the Welsh government in relation to mitigating against welfare reform, including the decision by the Welsh government not to offset the full impact of the removal of the 'bedroom tax'/'spare room subsidy' through discretionary housing payments, as in Scotland. The committee also expressed concern about the consistency of approach to the use of discretionary housing payments across Wales.

In Northern Ireland, there is a somewhat more complex picture, with the Northern Ireland coalition government being unable to reach a consensus about the introduction of welfare reform until late 2015. Resistance to introducing the same provisions as in the Westminster legislation came from a number of parties in the executive, most forcibly, from Sinn Fein and the Social Democratic and Labour Party. The DUP has been broadly supportive of the principles underpinning welfare reform, but also stated that it would seek to ameliorate the impact on the most vulnerable. The DUP minister reached agreement with the Department for Work and Pensions (DWP) on administrative flexibilities – including that Universal Credit could be paid fortnightly rather than monthly, allowing the continuation of the payment of Housing Benefit directly to landlords rather than to the claimant and some temporary exemptions on the 'bedroom tax'/'spare room subsidy'. While social security is a devolved responsibility in Northern Ireland, there are clear financial implications of any breach in parity (Birrell and Gray, 2014). In an agreement reached in November 2015 (Northern Ireland Executive, 2015), the Northern Ireland executive agreed to a legislative consent motion which would allow the UK government to legislate for welfare reform in Northern Ireland as part of a wider process to stabilise the functioning of the political institutions in Northern Ireland. The measures included some financial support to allow the Northern Ireland executive to top up the welfare arrangements. The Northern Ireland executive has also previously acted to address some cost-of-living issues, such as discretionary payments to assist with fuel costs. The limited increases to domestic rates and the maintenance of a cap on rates and the agreement by the parties in the executive against the introduction of separate water rates have been portrayed by parties in the executive as positive measures limiting costs to families and individuals, but it has also been argued that they inhibit a more equitable distribution of resources from the better off to the more disadvantaged.

Convergence in policy, 2010–15

While the focus has inevitably been on divergence in social policies between the devolved administrations and Westminster, and the extent to which this reflects increasing ideological differences (McEwen, 2013; Mooney and Scott, 2012), a number of factors also create an environment for social policy convergence (Keating, 2012). Although, as Jeffery et al (2010) argue, there are few legislative checks on policy divergence in the UK, Westminster's control of fiscal issues, and similar economic and social conditions, can encourage convergence, for example, in the areas of public health, responses to gender violence and support for unpaid carers. Some convergence may also emerge from the need to meet the objectives set by the EU and the United Nations' treaty bodies. As the state party, the Westminster government is responsible for ensuring that the obligations are met in all parts of the UK, and devolution does not mitigate this, as pointed out by a number of United Nations committees in recent years (UN CEDAW, 2008/2013; UNCRC, 2008).

Whereas, historically, the inclination has been for other jurisdictions to follow a policy lead set by Westminster, devolved governments have been more likely to look to each other and to Europe for policy lessons (MacKinnon, 2015). As outlined earlier, this can be seen in the response of the devolved governments to the welfare reform and austerity measures introduced by the coalition government.

The legacy of the coalition government and looking to the future

Throughout the period of the coalition government, tensions surfaced in relation to reserved and devolved powers, with the Scottish and Welsh governments, in particular, suggesting that their ability to develop distinct policies was constrained by the exercise of reserved powers or the overlap in reserved and devolved powers. The different Scottish approach to immigration and the integration of refugees and migrants into the community, and the constraints presented by a Westminster immigration policy more aligned to English values, has been discussed by Hepburn (2015). It has also been argued that the restrictions placed on asylum seekers by Westminster policy have social costs that have had to be addressed by the devolved administrations (Mulvey, 2013).

As the UK Conservative government legislates for enhanced devolved powers negotiated under the coalition government, there may be increasing divergence in social policy. In the short term, the measures contained in the Conservative government's Welfare and Work Bill, published in July 2015, mean that the mitigation of welfare reform measures will be ongoing. The future ability of the devolved administrations to depart more radically from Westminster policy will be affected by decisions about the enhancement of devolved powers. In Scotland, the Smith Commission recommendations and the continuing debate about additional powers to be devolved to Scotland have implications beyond that jurisdiction, as will decisions about the future model of devolution in Wales. In Northern Ireland, there has not been the same demand for an enhancement of devolved powers, which may reflect the lack of a strong conceptual and value basis underpinning policy debates and decisions. The lack of stability in the Northern Ireland executive, the lack of progress on the Stormont House Agreement and the implications of the failure until recently of the executive to find a resolution on the implementation of welfare reform mean that the fiscal situation remains uncertain. There has been no demand for fiscal devolution other than for corporation tax.

Conclusion

Chapter One of this volume considered where the coalition government might be placed in a framework of different political approaches (see Table 1.1). It suggested that the coalition had strong similarities with the New Right. Consideration of the social policies of the devolved governments suggests that, certainly for Wales and Scotland, a different picture emerges (as summarised in Table 15.1), with the maintenance or extension of a social-democratic ethos underpinning policymaking, which was evident pre-2010. Keating (2005), for example, talks of a sense of shared responsibilities and community ethos that challenges neoliberal assumptions; Mooney and Scott (2012) have referred to continuing strong support for the welfare state and universalism in Scotland, which has manifested itself in universalist policies that are portrayed as building national and civil solidarity and even distinct forms of social citizenship (McEwen and Moreno, 2005). Whereas all of the devolved jurisdictions have adopted a mixed economy approach to the delivery of services, Scotland and Wales can be seen to be on the Left of the political dimension, favouring higher public spending, a greater emphasis on equality and inclusion, and a stronger rights-based approach to citizenship. In Northern Ireland, it is harder to discern a distinct political approach. While there is some evidence of neoliberal influences – for example, in relation to decisions about taxes and a strong focus on the economy and business in the *Programme for government* – there has also been some attempt to counter the austerity measures imposed by the UK coalition government. In the absence of any real consensus about values or principles underpinning social policy, it is easier to identify a pragmatism whereby the approach is largely what can be agreed by the different political parties in the Northern Ireland executive.

Table 15.1: Dimensions of political approaches and the devolved administrations

Dimension	Old Left	Third Way	One Nation	New Right	Coalition	Scotland	Wales	Northern Ireland
Approach	Leveller	Investor	Investor	Deregulator	Deregulator	Leveller	Leveller	Deregulator
Citizenship	Rights	Rights and responsibilities	Rights and responsibilities	Responsibilities	Responsibilities	Rights	Rights	Responsibilities/pragmatic
Outcome	Equality	Inclusion	Inclusion/some inequality	Inequality	Inequality	Inclusion	Inclusion	Some inequality
Mixed economy of welfare	State	State/private; civil society	State/private	Private	Private	State/private; civil society	State/private; civil society	State/private; civil society
Mode	Command and control	Cooperation/partnership	Command and control/cooperation	Competition	Competition	Cooperation/partnership	Cooperation/partnership	Centralised
Expenditure	High	Pragmatic	Pragmatic	Low	Low	High	High	Pragmatic
Benefits	High	Low/medium	Low/medium	Low	Low	Low/medium	Low/medium	High
Services	High	Medium	Medium	Low	Low/medium	High	High	Medium/high
Accountability	Central state/upwards	Central state/upwards and market/downwards	Central state/upwards and market/downwards	Market/downwards	Market/downwards and civil society	Devolved/localism	Devolved/localism	Devolved
Politics	Left	Left/post-ideological	Right/pragmatic	Right	Right	Left	Left	Right/pragmatic

Source: Adapted from Powell (1999, p 14, Table 1.1).

References

Amnesty International (2015) 'Northern Ireland barriers to accessing abortion services'. Available at: http://www.amnesty.org.uk/sites/default/files/eur_45_0157_2015_northern_ireland_-_barriers_to_accessing_abortion_services_pdf.pdf (accessed 12 September 2015).

Asenova, D., McKendrick, J., McCann, C. and Reynolds, R. (2015) *Redistribution of social and societal risk: the impact on individuals, their networks and communities in Scotland*, York: Joseph Rowntree Foundation.

Auditor General for Wales (2015) 'Managing the impact of welfare reform changes on social housing tenants in Wales'. Available at: http://www.audit.wales/system/files/publications/welfare_reform_change_social_housing_2015_english.pdf (accessed 12 September 2015).

Baker, A. and Murphy, R. (2013) *Corporation tax in Northern Ireland: the policy debate*, Sheffield: Sheffield Political Economy Research Institute. Available at: http://speri.dept.shef.ac.uk/2013/03/14/corporation-tax-northern-ireland-policy-debate/ (accessed 14 September 2015).

Bevan, G., Karanikdos, M., Exley, J., Nolte, E. and Mays, N. (2014) *The four health systems of the UK: how do they compare?* London: The Health Foundation and Nuffield Trust.

Birrell, D. (2009) *The impact of devolution on social policy*, Bristol: The Policy Press.

Birrell, D. (2012) *Comparing devolved governance*, Basingstoke: Palgrave MacMillan.

Birrell, D. (2015) 'Review into the operation of the Barnett Formula: comments on the Northern Ireland experience'. Available at: http://www.niassembly.gov.uk/globalassets/documents/finance/barnett-formula/written-submissions/d-birrell---review-into-the-operation-of-the-barnett-formula---march-2015.pdf (accessed 11 September 2015).

Birrell, D. and Gray, A.M. (2013) 'The structures of the NHS in Northern Ireland: divergence, policy copying and policy deficiency', *Public Policy and Administration*, 28(3): 274–89.

Birrell, D. and Gray, A.M. (2014) 'Welfare reform and devolution: issues of parity, discretion and divergence for the UK government and the devolved administrations', *Public Money and Management*, 34(3): 205–12.

Cabinet Office (2010) *The coalition: our programme for government*, London: Cabinet Office.

Cairney, P. (2011) *The Scottish political system since devolution: from new politics to the new Scottish Government*, Exeter: Imprint Academic.

Chaney, P. and Drakeford, M. (2004) 'The primacy of ideology: social policy and the first term of the National Assembly for Wales', in N. Ellison, M. Powell and L. Bauld (eds) *Social policy review 16*, Bristol: The Policy Press, pp 121–42.

Commission on Devolution in Wales (2012) *Empowerment and responsibility: financial powers to strengthen Wales*, The Silk Commission, Part 1 Report, Cardiff: Commission on Devolution in Wales.

Commission on Devolution in Wales (2014) *Empowerment and responsibility: legislative powers to strengthen Wales*, The Silk Commission, Part 2 Report, Cardiff: Commission on Devolution in Wales.

Commission on Scottish Devolution (2009) *Service Scotland better: Scotland and the United Kingdom in the 21st century*, Edinburgh: Scotland Office.

Drakeford, M. (2007) 'Progressive universalism', *Agenda*, Winter: 4–7.

Duffy, J., Basu, S., Davidson, G. and Pearson, K.C. (2015) *Review of legislation and policy guidance relating to adult social care in Northern Ireland*, Belfast: Office of the Commissioner for Older People.

Gambaro, L., Stewart, K. and Waldfogel, J. (eds) (2014) *An equal start? Providing quality early education and care for disadvantaged children*, Bristol: The Policy Press and University of Chicago Press.

Gray, A.M. and Birrell, D. (2012) 'Coalition government in Northern Ireland: social policy and the lowest common denominator thesis', *Social Policy and Society*, 11(1): 15–25.

Hepburn, E. (2015) 'Immigrant integration and policy divergence in Scotland since devolution', paper presented at the Political Studies Association Annual Conference, University of Sheffield, 30 March to 1 April.

Horgan, G. and Gray, A.M. (2012) 'Devolution in Northern Ireland: a lost opportunity?', *Critical Social Policy*, 32(3): 467–78.

Jeffery, C., Lodge, G. and Schmuecker, K. (2010) 'The devolution paradox', in G. Lodge and K. Schmuecker (eds) *Devolution in practice 2010*, London: Institute of Public Policy Research, pp 9–31.

Keating, M. (2005) 'Policy convergence and divergence in Scotland under devolution', *Regional Studies*, 39(4): 453–63.

Keating, M. (2012) 'Intergovernmental relations and innovation from cooperative to competitive welfare federalism in the UK', *British Journal of Politics and International Relations*, 14(2): 214–30.

Kenway, P., Bushe, S., Tinson, A. and Born, T. (2015) *Tackling poverty and social exclusion in Scotland*, York: Joseph Rowntree Foundation.

Lloyd, E. and Potter, S. (2014) 'Early childhood, education, care and poverty', working paper prepared for the Joseph Rowntree Foundation. Available at: http://roar.uel.ac.uk/3865/7/2014_Lloyd_Potter_JRF-report.pdf (accessed 14 September 2015).

Lodge, G., Henderson, G. and Davies, B. (2015) *Poverty and devolution: the role of devolved governments in a strong national social security system*, Manchester: IPPR.

MacKinnon, D. (2015) 'Devolution, state restructuring and policy divergence in the UK', *The Geographical Journal*, 181(1): 47–56.

McLean, I., Gallagher, J. and Lodge, G. (2013) *Scotland's choices: the referendum and what happens afterwards*, Edinburgh: Edinburgh University Press.

McEwen, N. (2005) 'Devolution and the preservation of the United Kingdom welfare state', in N. McEwen and L. Moreno (eds) *The territorial politics of welfare*, London: Routledge, pp 41–61.

McEwen, N. (2013) *Independence and the territorial politics of welfare*, The David Hume Institute Research Paper No 4/2013, Edinburgh: The David Hume Institute.

McEwen, N. and Moreno, L. (eds) (2005) *The territorial politics of welfare*, London: Routledge.

McKendrick, J., Mooney, G., Dickie, J., Scott, G. and Kelly, P. (eds) (2014) *Poverty in Scotland 2014: the independence referendum and beyond*, London: Child Poverty Action Group.

Mooney, G. and Scott, G. (2012) 'Devolution, social justice and social policy: the Scottish context', in G. Mooney and C. Scott (eds) *Social justice and social policy in Scotland*, Bristol: The Policy Press, pp 1–24.

Mooney, G., Scott, G. and Williams, C. (2006) 'Rethinking social policy through devolution', *Critical Social Policy*, 26(3): 483–97.

Mulvey, G. (2013) *In search of normality: refugee integration in Scotland*, Glasgow: Scottish Refugee Council.

National Assembly for Wales (2015) 'Public Accounts Committee responding to welfare reform in Wales'. Available at: http://www.assembly.wales/laid%20documents/cr-ld10320/cr-ld10320-e.pdf (accessed 14 September 2015).

Northern Ireland Courts Service (2015) 'Court finds executive committee failed to adopt strategy on poverty and social exclusion', Available at: https://www.courtsni.gov.uk/en-GB/Judicial%20Decisions/SummaryJudgments/Documents/Court%20finds%20executive%20committee%20failed%20to%20adopt%20strategy%20on%20poverty%20and%20social%20exclusion/j_j_Summary%20of%20judgment%20-%20In%20re%20Committee%20on%20the%20Administration%20of%20Justice%20and%20Brian%20Gormally%2030%20Jun%202015.htm

Northern Ireland Executive (2011) *Draft programme for government 2011–2015*, Belfast: Northern Ireland Executive. Available at: http://www.northernireland.gov.uk/draft-pfg-2011-2015.pdf (accessed 14 September 2015).

Northern Ireland Executive (2015) *A fresh start: the Stormont agreement and implementation plan*, Belfast: Northern Ireland Executive, http://www.northernireland.gov.uk/a-fresh-start-stormont-agreement.pdf

OFMDFM (Office of the First Minister and Deputy First Minister) (2006) *Government's anti-poverty and social inclusion strategy for Northern Ireland*, Belfast: OFMDFM.

Pollock, A. (2014) 'Submission to Health Committee enquiry: public expenditure on health and social care'. Available at: http://www.allysonpollock.com/wp-content/uploads/2014/11/AP_2014_Pollock_HealthCommitteePublicExpenditure.pdf (accessed 14 September 2015).

Powell, M. (1999) 'Introduction', in M. Powell (ed) *New Labour, new welfare state*, Bristol: The Policy Press, pp 1–27.

Powell, M. and Miller, R. (2014) 'Framing privatisation in the English National Health Service', *Journal of Social Policy*, 43(3): 575–59.

Scotland Office (2009) *Scotland's future in the UK: building on ten years of Scottish devolution*, Cm 7738, Edinburgh: Scotland Office.

Scottish Government (2014) *Welfare Reform (Further Provision) (Scotland) Act 2012: annual report 2014*. Edinburgh: Scottish Government. Available at: http://www.gov.scot/Publications/2014/06/4507/5 (accessed 14 September 2015).

Scottish Government (2015) *One Scotland – programme for government 2014–15*, Edinburgh: Scottish Government. Available at: www.gov.scot/Publications/2014/11/6336 (accessed 14 September 2015).

Seely, A. (2015) *Devolution of tax powers to the Scottish Parliament: the Scotland Act 2012*, House of Commons Library Research Paper, London: House of Commons Library. Available at: http://researchbriefings.files.parliament.uk/documents/SN05984/SN05984.pdf (accessed 14 September 2015).

Smith Commission (2014) *Report of the Smith Commission for further devolution of powers to the Scottish Parliament*, Edinburgh: Smith Commission. Available at: https://www.smith-commission.scot/wp-content/uploads/2014/11/The_Smith_Commission_Report-1.pdf (accessed 14 September 2015).

Taylor-Gooby, P. (2013) *The double crisis of the welfare state and what we can do about it*, Basingstoke: Palgrave MacMillan.

UN CEDAW (United Nations Committee on the Elimination of Discrimination Against Women) (2008/2013) *Concluding observations: United Kingdom of Great Britain and Northern Ireland 2008 and 2013*, CEDAW/C/UK/CO/6 and CEDAW/C/UK/CO/7, Geneva: Office of the High Commission on Human Rights.

UNCRC (United Nations Committee on the Rights of the Child) (2008) *Concluding observations: United Kingdom of Great Britain and Northern Ireland, 2008*, CRC/C/GBR/CO/4, Geneva: Office of the High Commission on Human Rights.

Welsh Government (2007) *One Wales: a progressive agenda for the government of Wales*, Cardiff: National Assembly for Wales.

Welsh Government (2015) 'Programme for government'. Available at: http://gov.wales/about/programmeforgov/?lang=en (accessed 14 September 2015).

West, D. (2014) 'Patient choice is not the key to improving performance', *Health Service Journal*. Available at: http://m.hsj.co.uk/5077051.article (accessed 14 September 2015).

Wiggan, J. (2012) 'Telling stories of 21st century welfare, the UK coalition government and the neo-liberal discourse of worklessness and dependency', *Critical Social Policy*, 32(3): 383–405.

Wincott, D. (2006) 'Social policy and social citizenship: Britain's welfare states', *Publius*, 36(1): 169–88.

SIXTEEN

Conclusions

Martin Powell and Hugh Bochel

Introduction

This chapter aims to place the main points identified by the contributors into the framework introduced in Chapter One. In particular, it revisits the questions of the main approaches underlying the coalition government, whether its social policies may best be seen as 'One Nation' Conservative, New Right or Third Way, and to what extent it reflected Conservative or Liberal Democrat influences. It also explores the first 100 days of the Conservative government elected in May 2015, focusing on the first Conservative Queen's Speech since 1996, the Budget of July 2015 and 100-day audits of a number of commentators.

Which way for the coalition government?

This section draws upon Powell's (1999) discussion of New Labour and the Third Way to examine changes to the provision of welfare under the coalition by setting them against the framework of alternative political approaches. It can be seen from Table 16.1 that our initial assessment set out in Table 1.1 is largely in line with the views of the contributors, suggesting that, in most respects, the coalition government can be seen as having significant similarities with the New Right.

Approach

There appears to be little use of the investor/deregulator language, but the policies of the coalition government appear to have been significantly closer to the 'deregulator' approach of the New Right than to the 'investor' approach of the Third Way. There was clearly some shared discourse with elements of the Third Way, such as in relation to transforming the welfare state from a safety net in times of trouble to a springboard for economic opportunity, the emphasis on 'welfare' offering a hand up rather than a handout, the centrality of paid work

Table 16.1: Dimensions of approaches for the coalition government

Dimension	Approach	Citizenship	Outcome	Mixed economy	Mode
Overall (Chapter One)	Deregulator	Responsibilities	Inequality	Private	Competition
Public expenditure			Inequality	Private	
Public opinion		Responsibilities			
Governance	Deregulator? (Big Society and localism?)	Responsibilities (Nudging?)		Private	Competition
Health				Private	Competition
Education					
Housing			Inequality	Private	
Social security		Responsibilities	Inequality		
Employment		Responsibilities	Inequality	Private	Competition
Adult care				Private	
Family policy				Private	
Children				Private	
Criminal justice		Responsibilities	Inequality	Private?	
Equalities			Inequality		
Devolved administrations			Inequality		

	Expenditure	Benefits	Services	Accountability	Politics
Overall	Low	Low	Medium/low	Market/downwards and civil society	Right
Public expenditure	Low	Low			Right
Public opinion	Low	Low	Low	Market?	Right?
Governance	Low	Low	Low	Market and civil society	Right
Health		NA	Protected	Market	Right
Education				Market	Right
Housing	Low	Low	Low?	Market	Right
Social security	Low	Low	NA		Right
Employment	Low	Low	NA		Right
Adult care	Low	NA	Low		Right?
Family policy	Low	Low	Low		Right

	Expenditure	Benefits	Services	Accountability	Politics
Children	Low	Low	Low		Right
Criminal justice	Low	Low	Low	Market	Right
Equalities		Low	Low		Right
Devolved administrations	Low	Low	Low		Right (UK); social-democratic (Scotland, Wales)

Note: Our interpretation of contributors' views. Italics mean some complexity or caveats (eg low benefits for people of working age, but not pensioners).

as the route out of poverty, and the emphasis on individual agency and choice. Both Labour and coalition governments remained committed to the National Minimum Wage, and also to the provision of high-quality affordable childcare. However, while both New Labour and coalition governments sought to 'make work pay', and to use a mix of carrots and sticks, for the coalition, reducing benefits and raising the income tax threshold were important tools, in contrast to the widespread use of tax credits under Labour, while the development and gradual introduction of Universal Credit was intended not only to reduce the complexity of the system, but also to increase conditionality (Chapters Eight and Nine).

The deregulatory approach was also obvious across other areas of social policy, such as: in education, with the coalition's determination to remove or reduce the powers of local authorities through a major increase in the number of academies and the creation of 'free schools'; in local government, with major spending cuts being accompanied by an emphasis on 'localism'; and in health care, with the changes introduced by the Health and Social Care Act 2012, including opening up the National Health Service (NHS) in England further to private and not-for-profit providers; and in the relaxation of controls on how individuals use their pension investments. Finally, while the language of social investment was used in some areas (see Chapters Ten and Twelve), much of this appeared to be largely rhetorical, with the degree of investment falling short of the previous government.

Citizenship

Similarly, there is significant continuity with the 'Third Way' on moving the balance between rights and responsibilities, with arguably smaller carrots and bigger sticks. There has been an increased stress on conditionality and responsibilisation in areas such as the introduction of the benefit cap and the 'bedroom tax' (Chapters Seven, Eight, Nine and Ten) and criminal justice policy (Chapter Thirteen). Bochel (Chapter Three) points to a shift from the state providing services to responsibility being shifted to individuals, families, communities and civil society. This may be in line with evidence on the hardening of public opinion on benefits claimants (Chapter Four). Conversely, some contributors point to a reduction in rights (Chapters Nine, Ten, Twelve and Thirteen). For example, Squires (Chapter Thirteen) discusses conformity to a model of neoliberal family life, education and job-seeking, with a powerful array of innovative low-intensity/low-cost measures to better regulate the poor. He points to a new hierarchy of law and discipline, with 'segments' of layering of social controls. He stresses a new tier of disciplinary welfare premised upon personal responsibility, the work ethic, behaviour modification and familial compliance linked to welfare entitlements, and at the top end, the passage of the Serious Crime Act 2015 marks a de facto convenient legal reversal, whereby an accused person finds it necessary to prove that they are *not* culpable as charged. Glasby (Chapter Ten) points to a de facto reduction in social rights due to the 'unprecedented' cuts in local government finance and austerity, citing the view of the Local Government Association that this may mean that councils in many areas 'will not have enough money to meet all their statutory responsibilities'. Daguerre and Etherington (Chapter Nine) state that, to a large extent, the coalition government's welfare reforms have strengthened a predominant work-first logic, stressing obligation and conditionality within a 'new welfare contract' of 'do the right thing and we will back you all the way. But fail to take responsibility – and the free ride is over'. More broadly, the goal of welfare reform under the coalition government was to produce self-reliant, autonomous citizens, whose dependency on the public purse could be reduced to a minimum, fostered by 'cultural change' to engineer personal responsibility and self-sufficiency through the implementation of the 'claimant commitment'.

Outcome

Following the 2010 general election, David Cameron stressed being 'all in this together', and broader shoulders bearing a greater load. In the July 2015 Budget, George Osborne claimed that inequality and child poverty had fallen, and that the rich were paying more.

The coalition government continued New Labour's concerns over social mobility, with former Labour cabinet minister Alan Milburn leading a Commission on Social Mobility. However, most contributors suggest that the coalition appears to be equally or more 'relaxed' than New Labour about the richer getting richer, with greater inequality (Chapters Eight and Fourteen).

Mixed economy

The coalition appeared to have a marked preference for provision by the private and not-for-profit sectors, including social enterprises and voluntary organisations. In particular, the 'localism' and 'Big Society' narratives clearly point towards a much smaller state. According to Bochel (Chapter Three), there was a clear preference for private and other non-state provision, with the 'Big Society' shifting away from government providing and delivering services towards an increasingly diverse range of providers, although the bulk of such provision came from the private sector. Baggott (Chapter Five) points to the failed experiment (initiated by Labour) of allowing the private operator Circle to run Hinchingbrooke Hospital. According to Somerville (Chapter Seven), there have been (somewhat contradictory) moves towards a free market in social renting. For example, social housing rents have been allowed to rise to 80% of market levels (so-called 'affordable' housing), but this makes it more attractive to develop new rented housing. Daguerre and Etherington (Chapter Nine) argue that the Work Programme was 'emblematic of the governmental strategy of opening up the public sector to the market', and extended the contracting model and delivery and the role of private providers in the delivery of previous welfare-to-work programmes. It also funded providers on a payments-by-results basis structured in relation to initial attachment to the programme, job outcomes and job sustainability, with additional payments made for higher-performing contractors.

Mode

The dominant mode appears to be competition, with the importance of choice and competition between autonomous providers stressed in health (Foundation Trusts, independent providers) and education (including free schools) (Chapters Three, Five and Six). For example, Baggott (Chapter Five) points out that the Health and Social Care Act 2012 strengthened competition from the independent sector, with a significant number of new contracts awarded to the independent sector. However, the extent to which 'real' choice exists, and its impact on improving outcomes, is far from clear. For example, Glasby (Chapter Ten) points out that Personal Budgets may result in 'zombie personalisation' (a pale and potentially sinister imitation, but with any genuine scope for innovation watered down as the old system seeks to reinvent itself).

Moreover, it seems that criticism of competition has forced 'integration' back onto the policy agenda. For example, the coalition introduced a 'Better Care Fund' to fund joint health and social care priorities, identified a series of 'integrated care pioneer' sites to fast-track local reform, and agreed to devolve combined health and social care budgets to Greater Manchester ('Devo Manc') and to Cornwall, which may forge a path for other areas to follow (Chapters Five and Ten). However, it may be difficult to join up services in a meaningful way in a system not designed with integration in mind (Chapter Ten). Finally, according to Baggott (Chapter Five), despite the coalition's proclamation of a more decentralised and autonomous NHS, there were continuities with New Labour's top-down approach. Although the Health and Social Care Act was meant to herald a non-interventionist approach, ministers nevertheless continued to intervene in the NHS.

Expenditure

Almost all of the contributors stress the importance of the 'deficit reduction programme' and the austerity agenda. However, public spending has been 'disaggregated' (Chapter Two), with differential cuts between spending departments, nations and groups (Chapters Two, Fourteen and Fifteen). Glasby (Chapter Ten), in particular, argues that the scale of the cuts faced by local government has been unprecedented. He notes that the impact of massive cuts to the local government budget 'has been truly breathtaking and has arguably dwarfed all other changes', with one prominent council leader talking of 'the end of local government as we know it'. He continues that it is hard to see the local government financial settlement as anything other than an attempt to 'roll back the boundaries of the welfare state' by significantly reducing the funding available for a wide range of local services, concluding that, in one sense, the austerity agenda may prove to be even more effective at this than previous, more explicit, attempts under the Thatcher governments of 1979–90.

Benefits

It is clear that one of the main targets for expenditure cuts under the coalition government was working-age benefits (Chapters Two, Seven, Eight and Nine), which has some resonances with public opinion on 'deserving' versus 'undeserving' groups (Chapter Four). This is related to benefit caps on overall spending and on individual families, and to uprating most working-age benefits in line with the (usually lower) Consumer Price Index (CPI) rather than the Retail Price Index (RPI).

Services

Similarly, there was a clear division of relatively protected services such as the NHS and schools, which may be linked to public opinion on universal and popular services versus 'residual' services (Chapter Four).

Accountability

The main accountability mechanism seems to be through markets: 'choice' rather than 'voice', with consumers 'voting with their feet'. Bochel (Chapter Three) states that accountability is transmitted through both market-type and informational mechanisms to individuals and civil society. The localism and Big Society agendas stressed a greater role for neighbourhoods, communities, voluntary groups and social enterprises being accountable for services (Chapter Three). However, there were nods towards 'voice' in the form of 'HealthWatch' in the NHS (Chapter Five) and elected Police and Crime Commissioners (elected on derisory turnouts) (Chapter Thirteen).

Politics

Most of the contributors point to various shades of New Right, although some stress continuity with neoliberal elements within New Labour (eg Chapters Five and Eleven), and others point to tensions within the New Right (Chapter Six). There are few mentions of 'compassionate' or 'One Nation' conservatism. Baggott (Chapter Five) points to a shift back to the Right, while Somerville (Chapter Seven) refers to echoes of the Thatcherite policies of the early 1980s. Birrell and Gray (Chapter Fifteen) compare the strong similarities with the New Right of the coalition with the maintenance or extension of a social-democratic ethos of the administrations in Scotland and Wales. According to Bailey and Ball (Chapter Six), there is a 'long shadow' of Thatcherism in social and educational policy. Over the 'longue durée', Squires (Chapter Thirteen) points to three phases of neoliberal austerity (the 1920s, the 1980s and the coalition), and argues that after just six weeks in office, Tory nastiness returned, with the 'tough' and disciplinary policies of the supposed 'nasty party' not just related to law and order, but traversing a range of social programmes. Churchill (Chapter Twelve) highlights moves from the 'Third Way social investment state' to 'the authoritarian neoliberal state', 'Conservative cultural restoration' and 'neoliberal paternalism'. According to Somerville (Chapter Seven), the 'austerity agenda' is packaged as 'localism' and 'Big Society', which can be understood, to some extent, as an example of roll-back neoliberalism in combination with 'subsidised individualism'. Edwards and Gillies (Chapter Eleven) argue that coalition government family policy was characterised by social liberalism and conservative traditionalism, and was informed by battles and uneasy alliances between the political perspectives of 'The Tory Mods and Rockers'. Churchill (Chapter Twelve) states that the Conservatives were internally divided between their 'traditional' and 'modern' family policy perspectives, and overall set out a return to neoliberal social policy goals, while incorporating their 'Broken Britain' 'social renewal' agenda. Similarly, Bailey and Ball (Chapter Six) point to a tension in policy due to the two dominant philosophical seams or rationalities of the continuing neoliberal emphasis on the minimal state and a belief in the sanctity, efficiency and effectiveness of the market, and neo-conservatism. Birrell and Gray (Chapter Fifteen) point to the differences between the UK coalition government and administrations in the devolved nations, which have introduced ameliorative measures to address cost-of-living issues, including mitigation of welfare reform.

Comparisons with previous governments

Conservative governments under Thatcher and Major

Squires (Chapter Thirteen) points to some striking parallels between the Thatcher government and the coalition, such as confronting significant popular discontent and disorder shortly after gaining office. However, he also points to significant differences, such as the relationship they had with the police ('friends no more'), and the inherited and continuing decline in the reported crime rate for the coalition. Somerville (Chapter Seven) argues that the Right to Buy for housing association tenants is a significant new Conservative policy, signalling an increased determination to reverse the decline of owner-occupation, even at the cost of undermining the coalition government's trajectory towards a free market in rented housing. It represents a departure from the Thatcherite goal of establishing what was called in the 1980s an 'independent' rented sector, in which the distinction between housing associations and private landlords would be blurred. Instead, it puts housing associations at a distinct disadvantage with respect to private landlords, whose tenants will not have this new right. McKay and Rowlingson (Chapter Eight) point to key areas of continuity between the 1979–97 Conservative governments and the coalition, such as: increases in means testing; cuts in benefits but spending rising due to recession; benefit simplification; the residualisation of social housing (though increasing costs of Housing Benefit); and poverty and inequality increasing. However, a key area of discontinuity was the treatment of pensioners, with the triple lock, maintained by the current Conservative government, compared with the dissolution of the link between pensions and earnings from 1980 onwards. Moreover, the whole array of new benefit caps for people of working age also appear to be a major difference with the Thatcher and Major governments.

New Labour under Blair and Brown

A number of contributors point to a degree of continuity with New Labour. For example, Baggott (Chapter Five) states that in health care, the coalition continued the trajectory set by New Labour, stressing competition and choice, and independent sector provision, but also the concerns over financial efficiency and cost savings that marked the latter years of New Labour's tenure. Squires (Chapter Thirteen) points to the coalition having seemingly completed the 'Blairite' mission of tuning the systems of criminal justice to the needs of the 21st century. Churchill (Chapter Twelve) points to the coalition government's use of reports commissioned by leading Labour figures. Edwards and Gillies (Chapter Eleven) state that a preoccupation with transmitted problems and highly dysfunctional families, and the targeted and harsh response in New Labour family policy, has chimed with and driven coalition approaches. The moralistic and neoliberal economic approach pursued by the New Labour administration has continued and been ramped up under the coalition to include a dismantling of the universal aspects of family service provision. McKay and Rowlingson (Chapter Eight) suggest that the coalition had important aspects of continuity, but also areas of difference when compared with New Labour. For example, the 'p' word – poverty – was still being used by the coalition – although the causes were seen as more individual and behavioural rather than structural. Both coalition and New Labour governments shared a belief that paid work was the best route out of poverty, with ever-increasing conditionality and sanctions for those not apparently trying hard enough to find a job. However, subsequently, it became clear that there is also much discontinuity: poverty was clearly not a priority for the coalition, while there were radical changes such as abandoning asset-based welfare, downgrading tax credits and introducing Universal Credit.

Glasby (Chapter Ten) argues that, at first glance, there seems to be significant continuity with the language and approaches adopted by New Labour in social care. However, behind the rhetoric, there may be less continuity than at first appears, such as less policy attention to 'integrated care' and prevention, and the unclear approach towards 'personalisation'. He concludes that it may be a question of adopting similar approaches to New Labour, but arguably of different underlying tactics and values behind the rhetoric – a question of '*it ain't what you do, it's the way that you do it*'. Bailey and Ball (Chapter Six) stress both *continuity* and *change*, that is, with coalition policy both building upon the policies of New Labour but also shifting the rhetorical and discursive problem-space of policy along some different lines. Similarly, Daguerre and Etherington (Chapter Nine) point out that there was continuity in the idea of using the benefit system to steer behavioural change and instil a work ethic among welfare recipients, but change in the balance between carrots and sticks, and in cuts to tax credits.

Coalition partners?

As discussed in Chapter One, the agreement between the two parties was set out in the *Programme for government* (Cabinet Office, 2010). While there was clearly considerable shared ground, much of the programme reflected Conservative policy as the major partner, but some influence of the Liberal Democrats could be seen both through the inclusion of some of their proposals (such as the Pupil Premium) and the blocking of some Conservative policies (such as increasing the threshold for inheritance tax).

The extent of Liberal Democrat influence varies between sectors. On the one hand, some contributors see very little influence. For example, Somerville (Chapter Seven) argues that coalition housing policy is 'indistinguishable from Conservative housing policy' as key Liberal Democrat manifesto pledges did not make it into the coalition agreement. He concludes that the influence of the Liberal Democrats on housing policy was negligible: for example, housing ministers under the coalition were all Conservative. According to Edwards and Gillies (Chapter Eleven), the mood music of coalition government family policy was shaped and dominated by the Tory Mods and Rockers. The Liberal Democrat Minister of State for Children and Families at the Department for Education, Sarah Teather, had 'little effect'. After being sacked in 2012, she revealed that she was critical of the 'immoral and divisive' policies that the coalition government was pursuing. Ellison (Chapter Two) claims that although the coalition partners disagreed fundamentally over certain areas of policy – and increasingly so as time went on – over the course of the Parliament, there was little, if any, significant disagreement about the stated approach to public spending and deficit reduction. According to Daguerre and Etherington (Chapter Nine), Conservative ministers took the lead on welfare reform, with one of the most influential intellectual influences being the work conducted by the Centre for Social Justice (CSJ), the think tank founded in 2004 by Iain Duncan Smith. However, they add that the early record of the Conservative government post-2015 indicates that the Liberal Democrats did exert a moderating influence on their senior partners in relation to workfare policies for young people and cuts to tax credits and disability benefits.

On the other hand, there was some Liberal Democrat influence in other sectors. Churchill (Chapter Twelve) states that while the Conservatives were the dominant influence, the Liberal Democrats had a significant influence in preserving some continuities with New Labour, such as progressive universalism, social liberalism and the social investment approach, pushing through incremental developments in child, youth and family policies that built on the Labour years, and probably prevented more severe retrenchment and residualisation. Baggott (Chapter Five) suggests that the Liberal Democrats exerted much influence on health policy, although with regard to the NHS reforms, they were initially compliant. Bailey and Ball (Chapter Six) point out that coalition education policy was very much dominated by the Conservatives, although the Liberal Democrats had some influence, notably, on the Pupil Premium. McKay and Rowlingson (Chapter Eight) suggest that the Liberal Democrats appear to have had a major influence on reforms in two key areas in social security: increasing the income tax allowance; and the triple lock on the state pension from 2011 and protecting other benefits for pensioners. Moreover, the Conservatives accepted both of these reforms and dropped their plan to increase the inheritance tax threshold to £1 million, alongside their proposed changes in National Insurance.

From coalition to Conservative government

Most people (and opinion polls) expected another coalition government in 2015, with the 'real election' beginning after polling day with the negotiations between the parties. However, the election resulted in a Conservative government, albeit elected on only about 37% of the vote, and with a small overall majority. The 'historical context of this achievement' was stressed by Simon Burns MP in the debate on the Queen's Speech, with David Cameron being 'the first Prime Minister who served a full term to win his second general election with more seats and a higher share of the vote since Lord Palmerston in 1857' (*Hansard*, 2015a, col 34).

The 2015 general election

As in 2010, the 2015 Conservative manifesto stressed the need to reduce the national deficit and debt. Its main message was that, once again, a Labour government had ruined the economy by overspending. This was reinforced by the rare event of a Labour politician's words featuring in a Conservative manifesto: 'As the outgoing Labour Treasury Minister put it with brutal candour, "there is no money"' (Conservative Party, 2015, p 5). However, the manifesto claimed that the coalition government had put Britain back on the right track – 'the Great Recession has given way to a Great Revival' (Conservative Party, 2015, p 7) – and that only a Conservative government could be trusted to finish the job. Much of the manifesto was based on continuity or 'more of the same', stressing that past achievements were associated with current promises.

The manifesto discussed two phases of the deficit reduction plan. The first is a continuation of the economic plan of the coalition government, continuing to reduce government spending by 1% each year in real terms for the first two full financial years of the next Parliament, the same rate as over the last five years. This involves a further £30 billion in fiscal consolidation over the next two years (compared to the £120 billion over the coalition period), which will be achieved by £13 billion of departmental savings (the same rate of reduction as the coalition), £12 billion of welfare savings (on top of the £21 billion of savings already delivered by the coalition) and at least £5 billion from continuing to tackle tax evasion, aggressive tax avoidance and tax planning (building on the £7 billion of annual savings delivered by the coalition). The second phase, from 2018/19, aims to move into surplus, with government spending growing in line with inflation:

A new fundamental principle of fiscal policy will ensure that in normal economic times, when the economy is growing, the government will always run a surplus with a state neither smaller than we need nor bigger than we can afford. (Conservative Party, 2015, p 9)

This means that total government spending as a share of national income at the end of the next Parliament is forecast to be very slightly higher than in the year 2000, 'the year before Labour lost all control of spending and the national debt started its longest rise for hundreds of years' (Conservative Party, 2015, p 9).

The manifesto produces a series of hyperbolic claims, such as 'world-class' institutions, and fairly vague slogans that are difficult to disagree with: 'Jobs for all'; 'Cutting your taxes and building a fairer welfare system'; 'Giving your child the best start in life'; 'Protecting and improving our National Health Service'; 'Helping you build the [elusive] Big Society'; 'Making government work better for you'; 'Helping you to buy a home of your own'; and 'Dignity in your retirement'. It would be difficult to differentiate many of these broad slogans in a 'spot the manifesto' game, as many were similar to those in the Labour and Liberal Democrat manifestos. However, some of the devil was in the detail, or rather the means to achieve those ends. The main policies included:

- creating 2 million jobs over the next Parliament, compared to the 1.9 million new jobs over the past five years;
- 'major reforms of tax and welfare', including: raising the income tax threshold to £12,500; reducing the household benefit cap to £23,000; continuing to roll out Universal Credit; freezing working-age benefits for two years from April 2016; and making work pay by bringing in tax-free childcare to support parents back into work and giving working parents of three and four year olds 30 hours of free childcare a week;
- ensuring a good primary school place, with zero tolerance for failure; turning every failing and coasting secondary school into an academy; delivering free schools; creating 3 million new apprenticeships; and making sure there is no cap on university places;
- spending at least an additional £8 billion by 2020 over and above inflation to fund and support the NHS's own action plan for the next five years, which will deliver seven-days-a-week hospital care by 2020; a guarantee that everyone over 75 will get a same-day appointment if they need one; integrating health and social care

through the Better Care Fund,; and leading the world in fighting cancer and finding a cure for dementia;

- building the 'Big Society', which involves the people, neighbourhoods, villages, towns and cities of Britain in the great task of improving our country; guaranteeing your child a place on the National Citizen Service; and giving those who work for a big company and the public sector a new workplace entitlement to Volunteering Leave for three days a year, on full pay;

- building more homes that people can afford, including 200,000 new Starter Homes exclusively for first-time buyers under 40; extending the Help to Buy Equity Loan scheme to 2020 to help more people onto and up the housing ladder, and introducing a new Help to Buy Individual Savings Account (ISA) to support people saving for a deposit; giving more people the chance to own their home by extending the Right to Buy to tenants of housing associations; and creating a Brownfield Fund to unlock homes on brownfield land; and

- taking the family home out of Inheritance Tax for all but the richest; continuing to increase the state pension through the triple lock, so it rises by at least 2.5%, inflation or earnings, whichever is highest; rewarding saving by introducing a new single-tier pension; giving freedom to invest and spend your pension however you like; and making sure no one is forced to sell their home to pay for care.

The manifesto concludes that the 'detailed Plan for Britain' is 'underpinned by some simple Conservative values' (Conservative Party, 2015, p 81): those who work hard and do the right thing must be rewarded; everyone should be able to rise as high as their talents and effort will take them; and that those with the broadest shoulders have contributed the most to deficit reduction – which is why inequality has fallen, and child and pensioner poverty are down – and they will continue to do so. It should be noted that some of these claims have been challenged (by opponents in the Queen's Speech debate [see later] and by some commentators).

While the government no longer contained Liberal Democrat ministers, there was significant continuity in responsibility for key areas for social policy, for example: Chancellor of the Exchequer (George Osborne); Home Secretary (Theresa May); Secretary of State for Work and Pensions (Iain Duncan Smith); Secretary of State for Health (Jeremy Hunt); and Secretary of State for Education (Nicky Morgan).

The Queen's Speech debate

Many of these manifesto pledges were unveiled as proposals for legislation in the Queen's Speech. Cameron stated that 'If the last Parliament was about a repair job, this Parliament must be about renewal' (*Hansard*, 2015a, col 42). He continued that this is a 'Queen's Speech for working people, from a one nation government' (*Hansard*, 2015a, col 43). Echoing the manifesto, he stressed 'building on a strong platform' of job creation, raising tax thresholds, free childcare and investing in the NHS (*Hansard*, 2015a, cols 45–7).

For the Labour opposition, Harriet Harman stated that 'the rhetoric at the beginning of this Queen's Speech is well honed. Indeed, the best lines look uncannily like we wrote them' (*Hansard*, 2015a, col 42). Speaking for the former coalition partners, the Liberal Democrats, former Deputy Prime Minister Nick Clegg argued that his party worked hard to ensure that the coalition government's agenda 'had a clear thread of liberalism running through it', from the priority given to mental health to the green agenda, the introduction of the Pupil Premium and the protection of our civil liberties. He stated that it was 'dispiriting ... if pretty unsurprising to see how quickly the new Conservative Government, instead of building on those achievements, are turning their back on that liberal stance' (*Hansard*, 2015a, col 71), and are weakening the coalition government's commitment to fairness. He concluded that 'it is that Budget, rather than this Queen's Speech, that will be the moment when we can judge whether the Conservative belief in "one nation" is for real' (*Hansard*, 2015a, col 71).

Not surprisingly, press comment on the Queen's Speech was divided. It was welcomed by David Skelton (2015) in the *Daily Telegraph* as combining 'economic effectiveness, strong leadership and, crucially, social justice'. He stated that 'This Queen's Speech does much to bring to life the one nation language of the first few weeks of this government' (Skelton, 2015). On the other hand, George Eaton (2015), in the *New Statesman*, wrote that it contained some measures that centrists will applaud (such as the annual report on job creation and apprenticeships; taking those working 30 hours a week on the minimum wage out of income tax; £8 billion a year for the NHS; and the doubling of free childcare from 15 hours a week to 30); however, 'too many bills will deepen the divisions that Cameron's "one nation" pitch acknowledges. The two nation conservatism of the last parliament endures'. He noted that welfare will be cut by a further £12 billion, and argued that some public services, most notably, those delivered by local government, will simply cease to exist.

The July 2015 Budget

In the Budget, Chancellor George Osborne stated that 'this will be a Budget for working people ... to keep moving us from a low wage, high tax, high welfare economy to the higher wage, lower tax, lower welfare country we intend to create' (*Hansard*, 2015b, col 322). He pointed to a 'new settlement' of a 'one nation Budget' from a 'one nation Government' (*Hansard*, 2015b, col 322). He stated that the deficit should be cut at the same pace as in the last Parliament, explaining that the coalition government inherited a 'soaring' national debt, but that this year, the debt as a share of national income is falling, 'bringing to an end the longest continued rise in our national debt since the 17th century' (*Hansard*, 2015b, cols 323–4). He announced that 'in normal economic times Governments should run an overall budget surplus, so that our country is better prepared for whatever storms lie ahead. In short, we should always fix the roof while the sun is shining' (*Hansard*, 2015b, cols 323–4). He claimed that the richest are paying a greater share of tax than they were at the start of the last Parliament, and that a greater share of state support is continuing to be devoted to the most vulnerable: 'those with the broadest shoulders are bearing the greatest burden, for we are all in this together' (*Hansard*, 2015b, cols 323–4). He also pointed to recent 'independent statistics' showing that since 2010, child poverty and inequality has been reduced (*Hansard*, 2015b, cols 323–4). He pointed to fully funding the 'Stevens plan' for the NHS, an apprenticeship levy that will create 3 million apprenticeships, replacing maintenance grants with loans for new students, new measures for home-ownership and fulfilling the 'long-standing promise' on inheritance tax that was blocked by the Liberal Democrats in coalition (*Hansard*, 2015b, cols 327–30).

Osborne argued that to live within our means as a country, to better protect spending on public services and to be fair to taxpayers it is necessary to find at least a further £12 billion of welfare savings. He set out four principles to be followed: first, the welfare system should always support the elderly, the vulnerable and disabled people; second, those who can work will be expected to look for work and take it when it is offered; third, the whole working-age benefit system has to be put on a more sustainable footing; and, fourth, the benefits system should not support lifestyles and rents that are not available to the taxpayers who pay for that system.

The measures that followed from these principles included: a tax lock to prohibit any increase in the main rates of income tax, national insurance and VAT for the next five years, and raising tax thresholds for the basic and higher rates, with no one working 30 hours a week on the national minimum wage paying tax; a rise in the minimum wage; for those aged 18 to 21, a new youth obligation that they must either earn or learn, and the abolition of the automatic entitlement to Housing Benefit; from September 2017, all working parents of three and four year olds receiving free childcare of up to 30 hours a week (*Hansard*, 2015b, cols 332–6).

Caroline Lucas (Green Party) stated that 'today's Budget will go down as a pivotal moment in the dismantling of the welfare state' (*Hansard*, 2015b, col 343). Stewart Hosie (Scottish National Party) pointed to 'a denial of the damage done in the last Parliament and a determination to repeat those mistakes, but this time with an ideological edge … a sermon from the high priest of an austerity cult' (*Hansard*, 2015b, col 351). He concluded that 'the Chancellor was right in one regard: it was a Conservative Budget, taking from the poor, giving to the rich' (*Hansard*, 2015b, col 351). For John Healey (Labour), it was 'a frontal assault on the finances of many low income families', with this welfare policy failing 'the head test as well as the heart test' and 'a Budget with no compassion and little credibility, a Budget that risks repeating many of the mistakes of the last five years' (*Hansard*, 2015b, col 353). Similarly, Khalid Mahmood (Labour) stated that:

> This Chancellor has succeeded in doing what his guru might have aspired to do. She took milk from the mouths of children. He has managed to take breakfast, lunch and dinner from the mouths of families and drive them to food banks. This is a Budget for a divided nation. (*Hansard*, 2015b, col 361)

The future Labour leader, Jeremy Corbyn, claimed that this Budget was 'exactly the same' as the last Conservative Budget:

> It is as though this is the land that time forgot.… It has exactly the same narrative of cutting taxation for the very richest, making life worse for the very poorest and selling off state assets to pay for it all along the way. (*Hansard*, 2015b, col 378)

Again, press comment was divided. In the *Daily Telegraph*, Allister Heath (2015) argued that George Osborne's world view is a 'smaller state that intervenes more'. He continued that the Budget could be seen as 'Goodbye Thatcherism; welcome One Nation Toryism,

George Osborne-style' (Heath, 2015). While, in many respects, the Budget was the Chancellor's most right-wing yet, slashing welfare and boosting defence spending, in other ways, it was his most left-wing, declaring war on landlords, raiding dividends and 'embracing a minimum wage increase so large that the Labour Party would never have dared to implement it' (Heath, 2015). He regarded this as the 'Budget's Clause Four moment', symbolically rejecting free-market thinking, with the Chancellor as a 'modern Macmillan', embracing old-school paternalistic Toryism. However, he considered that while it will help the Conservatives politically, it will cost jobs and reduce opportunities for the most vulnerable in society, and will, in time, be seen as a major step in the wrong direction.

In the *Spectator*, Fraser Nelson (2015) pointed to 'six policies that George Osborne has just stolen from Ed Miliband': massive minimum wage hike; higher taxes; more spending; whacking the non-doms; whacking hedge funds and private equity firms; and an apprentice levy. However, Paul Johnson (2015) of the Institute for Fiscal Studies pointed to a 'deeply disappointing' Budget. The 'magic moment' of a balanced budget was shifted back a year, reflecting a gentler than planned path for spending cuts, including welfare spending cuts. He noted: a higher-taxing budget; a public sector pay squeeze; benefits largely back behind 2008 levels; Universal Credit changes that make work incentives worse; and that the £4 billion of extra pay associated with the Minimum Wage would not compensate for the £12 billion of welfare cuts. He stated that the biggest single cut to welfare spending is set to come from extending the freeze in working-age benefits, tax credits and local housing allowance out to 2020, which will affect 13 million families, who will lose an average of £260 a year. He concluded that, 'unequivocally', tax credit recipients in work will be made worse off by the measures in the Budget on average, and that the changes overall are regressive.

100-day audit

David Cameron (2015) marked the first 100 days of his new government with an article for the *Daily Telegraph*. He claimed that 'our central task is to finish the job we started in turning around our economy'. He continued that, 'I am determined that we will build on this foundation. By cutting taxes, reforming welfare and increasing minimum wages we are showing we are the real party of working people'. He stressed a 'genuine one nation vision for our country', with the government delivering 'strong, centre-ground, pragmatic and progressive government', exemplified by the new 'National Living Wage' and the commitment to a real-terms increase of at least £8 billion a year by 2020 to support the NHS's own Five Year Plan. He also pointed to 'vital reforms in our public services', including the creation of a truly seven-day NHS. He announced the aim of 'every school in the country to have the opportunity to become an academy', and concluded that '100 days in, our government has the ideas to build the one nation vision – and to deliver real social mobility in our country'.

A rather different interpretation was given by Labour's shadow Home Secretary, Yvette Cooper (2015), who pointed to 'nine broken promises from the first 100 days of this Conservative Government': on Child Tax Credits; Child Benefit; rail electrification; affordable housing; decision on Heathrow; tax-free childcare; volunteering and the Big Society; the social care cap; and government transparency.

A number of commentators reviewed the government's first 100 days. For example, Andrew Sparrow (2015a), in *The Guardian*, argued that while the manifesto had provided a reliable road map in many respects, in others, the government had diverted quite strikingly from what was on offer to the electorate in May. For example, it had already had to postpone or shelve major initiatives such as a cap on social care costs (see Chapter Ten). He argued that the 100-day audit is dominated by grim austerity measures that will impact on the living standards of millions. However, he also noted that while the government had turned out to be rather more Tory than the manifesto implied in some respects, in others, it had also been rather more Labour, such as the Budget's 'national living wage', which was 'an audacious attempt to trump Labour on low pay' (Sparrow, 2015a). The 100-day audit was also revealing, he suggested, because it contained measures that would never have got past the Liberal Democrats, confounding claims that they had minimal influence in the last government.

In more detail, Sparrow (2015b) provides a list of 100 measures, divided into: 'implementing the Manifesto' (such as plans to cut welfare spending); 'surprise announcements, mostly Tory flavoured' (eg freezing working-age welfare benefits for four years); 'U turns and broken promises' (including drastically cutting tax credits); 'delays and tactical retreats' (such as extending subsidised childcare); 'excursions in Labourish territory' (including reducing tax relief for buy-to-let landlords); and 'reacting to events' (eg giving 'Kids Company' £3 million against the advice of officials).

Conclusions

There have been a number of verdicts on the social policies of the 2010–15 coalition government. According to Lupton (2015), the coalition: cut public spending, rather than raising taxes; gave relative protection to the NHS and schools, but made deep cuts to other budgets; uprated pensions while reducing other social security budgets; restructured the welfare state; and embarked on reforms to the content and design of services. This resulted in: cuts in many services and increasing pressure on others; tax and benefit changes benefited richer groups more, while contributing nothing to deficit reduction; early protection for the poor, but increasing poverty later; and pensioners were protected, children less so. They note that most data indicating changes in outcomes are only available until 2012 or 2013, making it impossible to assess the full impact of coalition policies.

Most of the social policy contributors in Seldon and Finn (2015) tend to be critical, but Seldon (2015, p 18) claims that the principal achievements of the government came on the domestic front – such as education, health and welfare – where significant, if controversial, reforms to the benefit system went some way to ensuring that welfare was targeted at the most deserving. Broadly similar views are presented by the social policy contributors to Beech and Lee (2015). Beech (2015, p 267) concludes that the coalition government's reforms were not transformative, and did not mark a paradigm shift in British politics, but were largely defined by continuities, with some notable discontinuities. However, he suggested that austerity may prove to be a transformative act.

Toynbee and Walker (2015, p 285) state that 'after five years of coalition the country feels harder and meaner'. They argue that great harm was done to the public realm because of government dogma and disarray, with ideological reforms in the NHS, free schools and Universal Credit, and an overall governing in the interests of the rich. Williams (2015, p 178) argues that Cameron's social conservatism is 'a blend of communitarianism, autonomous localism and fiscal retrenchment'. He notes that compassionate and communitarian rhetoric had been coupled with an agenda of fiscal austerity (the 'biggest cuts in public expenditure since the 1920s' (Williams, 2015, p 178), which had proved to be a major stumbling block in turning aspiration into political reality. His assessment was that the Liberal Democrats had provided an 'intermittent moderating presence' (Williams, 2015, p 189) and that there was some evidence of an apparent policy dilution, with the radicalism of Conservative social policy blunted: 'Since 2010, there has certainly been evidence of compromise and retreat from original proposals in some areas of social policy, inflicted by a combination of ideological uncertainty, public and media criticism, and Liberal Democrat scepticism' (Williams, 2015, p 210). Overall, he sees:

> an often stuttering and inconsistent social policy agenda that has at times appeared to lack practical direction, and which has failed to break away from the failed policies and initiatives connected to the orthodoxies of both the Thatcherite and New Labour eras. (Williams, 2015, p 190)

The contributors to this volume tend to follow this broadly critical line. In terms of the main issues set out in Chapter One, most of the contributors tend to echo our provisional assessments. It appears that the coalition government was closest to the 'New Right' approaches (see Table 16.1). There were significant continuities with previous Conservative (1979–97) and New Labour (1997–2010) governments, although there were also some significant discontinuities, particularly with New Labour. The Liberal Democrats did not appear to have had a significant impact in many policy areas, although perhaps this verdict may be qualified to some degree by the end of the current Conservative government. All of this suggests that the welfare state in the UK may look rather different after the coalition government, and that the direction of travel may provide a useful road map to the destination of the current Conservative government.

References

Beech, M. (2015) 'The coalition: a transformative government?', in M. Beech and S. Lee (eds) *The Conservative–Liberal coalition*, Basingstoke: Palgrave Macmillan, pp 259–69.

Beech, M. and Lee, S. (eds) (2015) *The Conservative–Liberal coalition*, Basingstoke: Palgrave Macmillan.

Cabinet Office (2010) *The coalition: our programme for government*, London: Cabinet Office.

Cameron, D. (2015) '100 days: article by David Cameron', 15 August. Available at: https://www.gov.uk/government/speeches/100-days-article-by-david-cameron (accessed 18 September 2015).

Conservative Party (2015) *The Conservative Party manifesto 2015*, London: Conservative Party.

Cooper, Y. (2015) 'Nine broken promises from the first 100 days of this Conservative government', *Huffington Post*, 6 August. Available at: http://www.huffingtonpost.co.uk/yvette-cooper/election-promises-broken_b_7949232.html (accessed 4 September 2015).

Eaton, G. (2015) 'Queen's Speech: Cameron's "one nation" gloss can't mask the divisions to come', *New Statesman*, 27 May. Available at: http://www.newstatesman.com/politics/2015/05/queens-speech-camerons-one-nation-gloss-cant-mask-divisions-come (accessed 17 September 2015).

Hansard (2015a) 'Queen's Speech debate', 27 May. Available at: http://www.publications.parliament.uk/pa/cm201516/cmhansrd/cm150527/debtext/150527-0001.htm#150527100000049 (accessed 4 September 2015).

Hansard (2015b) 'Budget debate', 8 July. Available at: http://www.publications.parliament.uk/pa/cm201516/cmhansrd/cm150708/debtext/150708-0002.htm (accessed 4 September 2015).

Heath, A. (2015) 'George Osborne's world view: a smaller state that intervenes more', *Daily Telegraph*, 9 July.

Johnson, P. (2015) 'The IFS's verdict on George Osborne's "deeply disappointing" Budget', 9 July. Available at: http://blogs.spectator.co.uk/paul-johnson/2015/07/the-ifss-verdict-on-george-osbornes-deeply-disappointing-budget/ (accessed 4 September 2015).

Lupton, R., with Burchardt, T., Fitzgerald, A., Hills, J., McKnight, A., Obolenskaya, P., Stewart, K., Thomson, S., Tunstall, R. and Vizard, P. (2015) *The coalition's social policy record: policy, spending and outcomes 2010–2015*, Social Policy in a Cold Climate Research Report, CASE, LSE.

Nelson, F. (2015) 'Six policies that George Osborne has just stolen from Ed Miliband'. Available at: http://blogs.spectator.co.uk/coffeehouse/2015/07/five-policies-that-george-osborne-has-just-stolen-from-ed-miliband/ (accessed 16 September 2015).

Powell, M. (1999) 'Introduction', in M. Powell (ed) *New Labour, new welfare state*, Bristol: The Policy Press, pp 1–27.

Seldon, A. (2015) 'David Cameron as Prime Minister, 2010–2015. The verdict of history', in A. Seldon and M. Finn (eds) *The coalition effect 2010–2015*, Cambridge: Cambridge University Press, pp 1–28.

Seldon, A. and Finn, M. (eds) (2015) *The coalition effect 2010–2015*, Cambridge: Cambridge University Press

Skelton, D. (2015) 'This was a truly "one nation" Queen's Speech', *Daily Telegraph*, 27 May. Available at: http://www.telegraph.co.uk/news/general-election-2015/politics-blog/11633158/This-was-a-truly-one-nation-Queens-Speech.html (accessed 16 September 2015).

Sparrow, A. (2015a) 'Cameron's first 100 days: what has the government actually done?', *The Guardian*, 14 August. Available at: http://www.theguardian.com/politics/2015/aug/14/david-cameron-first-100-days-what-has-conservative-government-actually-done (accessed 16 September 2015).

Sparrow, A. (2015b) '100 things the Tories did in their first 100 days', *The Guardian*, 14 August. Available at: http://www.theguardian.com/politics/ng-interactive/2015/aug/14/conservative-tory-government-first-100-days-100-things-done-david-cameron (accessed 16 September 2015).

Toynbee, P. and Walker, D. (2015) *Cameron's coup*, London: Guardian Faber.

Williams, B. (2015) *The evolution of Conservative Party social policy*, Basingstoke: Palgrave Macmillan.

Index

Note: The following abbreviations have been used – *f* = figure; *n* = note; *t* = table

Duncan, S. 58
Duncan Smith, Iain 2, 60, 357, 360
  children and young people 275
  family policy 247, 248, 249, 254, 270
  labour market 210, 211, 212, 213
  social security 181, 191
Dungavel Immigration Centre
  (Scotland) 328
Dunn, P. *see* Gilburt, H. et al
Duxbury, N. 165, 168
DWP *see* Department for Work and
  Pensions
Dwyer, P. 38

E

E-Act 140
E-Bac *see* English Baccalaureate
early intervention
  children and young people 275,
    277–8, 279, 281, 282, 311, 317, 318
  family policy 244
Early Intervention Foundation 278
Early Intervention Grant (EIG) 277
early years education *see* Sure Start
Eaton, G. 361
ECHR *see* European Convention of
  Human Rights
Economic Affairs, Institute of 3
Edmund-Davies Committee 289
education 5, 6, 10, 19, 265, 312, 353,
  357, 359, 365
  choice and competition 349, 351
  devolution 332
  family policy and 246, 247
  further education 36, 37, 136, 147n7,
    311
  governance 56, 60, 61, 64
  higher education 4, 7, 17, 60, 135,
    147n1, 311, 332
  philosophy and historical context
    130–3
  policy developments 134–7, 146–7,
    268, 270, 278–9
  'policy-ratchet' 127–30
  post-16 education 268, 271, 272, 278
  public expenditure 16, 18, 37
  school governance 137–41
  social mobility and expectations
    141–5
  Sure Start 4, 35, 37, 134, 245, 246,
    317, 318
  see also children and young people
Education Act (2011) 137, 138

Education and Adoption Bill (2015)
  136, 146
Education, Department for *see*
  Department for Education (DfE)
Education Maintenance Allowance
  (EMA) 135, 268, 272, 278, 287, 332
Education Reform Act (1988) 56, 127,
  133, 138, 144
Education Select Committee 278, 280
Educational Endowment Foundation 66
Edwards, R. 244; et al 252
efficiency savings 60–2, 102–3
Elliott, O. 55
Ellison, N. 38
Elming, W. 189
Elson, D. 274, 312, 313, 314; *see also
  under* Reed, H. et al
EMA *see* Education Maintenance
  Allowance
Emergency Budget (June 2010) 271–2
Emmerson, C. 46
Employee Ownership, All Party Group
  on (2011) 61
employment 10, 20, 266, 273, 312
Employment and Support Allowance
  (ESA) 11, 42, 187, 205, 206, 215,
  273, 297, 315, 320
Engender 319–20
English Baccalaureate (E-Bac) 136
English Housing Survey 154t, 156, 163
Environment, Transport and the
  Regions, Department of the
  (DETR) 57
Equalities Act (2010) 268, 313
Equalities Commission 267, 268
Equalities and Human Rights
  Commission 313, 314
Equality Statement (Scottish
  government) 336
Equity and excellence: liberating the NHS
  (Department of Health) 101
ESA *see* Employment and Support
  Allowance
Etherington, D. 203, 209
European Central Bank (ECB) 313
European Convention of Human
  Rights (ECHR) 57
European Court of Human Rights 288
European Social Fund 254
European Union (EU) 12, 30, 47n2,
  74, 338
Eurosceptics 12
Every Child Matters 134, 135
'evidence-based' policymaking 57, 66–7
Exchange Rate Mechanism (ERM) 2

Exley, J. *see* Bevan, G., et al
Explanatory Notes to the Mandatory
    Work Activity Regulations (2011)
    208
'Extended Troubled Families
    Programme' 254

F

Families With Multiple Problems
    initiative 254
Family Credit 194, 267
Family Intervention Projects (FiPs) 245,
    253
Family Nurse Partnership (FNP)
    251–2, 277, 278
Family and Parenting Institute (FPI)
    277
family policy 243–8, 258*n1*, 265, 269,
    355
    'family breakdown' 267, 269–70, 271
    paternity and parental leave rights 271
    stable marriage and family approach
        248–50, 255, 257–8
    targeted intervention 250–5, 270
    'Troubled Families Programme' 132,
        134–5, 221, 252
    worker-citizen unit 243, 245, 252,
        255–8
    see also children and young people;
        marriage and relationships
Farnsworth, K. 44
Farrall, S. 292–3
Farsides, T. *see* Drury, J. et al
Fawcett Society 311, 314
Fearn, H. 156, 168
Featherstone, D. et al 62, 167
Fenwick, H. 287
Fernandez, J. *see* Glendinning, C. et al
Field, F. 244, 274–5
Field, Steve 233
Financial Times 286
Finer, S.E. 54
Finn, D. 205
Finn, M. 366
FiPs *see* Family Intervention Projects
Fiscal Studies, Institute for (IFS) 33
Fitzgerald, A *see* Lupton, R. et al
'five pathways to poverty' thesis 265,
    266, 269, 274, 276, 282
Fixed Term Parliaments Act (2011) 70
Flexible New Deal 205
Flinders, M. et al 67–8
food banks 11, 312
Food Standards Agency 111

Foot, C. *see* Gilburt, H. et al
for-profit providers 15, 17, 121
Ford, M. 285–6, 295
Forrest, R. 156, 161
Foster, D. 139; *see also under* Jarrett, T.
    et al
foundation trusts 104, 105, 113, 115,
    137
'Foundation Years' services 275, 276
Fowler Review 194
FPI *see* Family and Parenting Institute
Francis Report *see* Mid Staffordshire
    Foundation Trust
Frayman, H. *see* Lewis, P. et al
free market capitalism 162–3, 170*n8*
Free School Meals 144
'free schools' 10, 17, 278, 332, 349
    policy development 133, 135, 136,
        146, 147*n7*, 148*n8*
Freedland, M. 201
Frontier Economics 163
fuel allowances 39–40, 338
Furlong, A. *see* Shildrick, T. et al
Furlong, J. 128, 130–1, 144–5
further education 36, 37, 136, 147*n7*,
    311

G

Galea, A. 101
Gallagher, J. *see* McLean, I. et al
Gambarin, A. 165
Gambaro, L. et al 332
Gamble, A. 28, 30
Gammie, M. *see* Mirrlees, J. et al
'gang culture' 288, 296, 298, 299, 300,
    301*n3*
Gannon, M. *see* Hastings, A. et al
Garnett, M. *see* Dorey, P. et al
Garside, R. 285–6, 295
Garthwaite, K. 44
General Certificate of Secondary
    Education (GCSE) 136, 146, 266,
    278, 332
General Election (2010) 5–6, 14, 20, 80
General Election (2015) 12, 17, 72, 79,
    358–60
Gibb, Nick 133, 135, 142
Gilburt, H. et al 102
Giles, C. 286–7
Gillies, V. 244, 251; *see also* Edwards,
    R., et al
Gimson, A. 161
Ginn, J. 316, 317
GLA *see* Greater London Authority

V

W